The Complete Power BI Interview Guide

A modern approach to acing the data analyst interview and landing your dream job

Sandielly Ortega Polanco

Gogula Aryalingam

Abu Bakar Nisar Alvi

The Complete Power BI Interview Guide

Group Product Manager: Kaustubh Manglurkar

Publishing Product Manager: Nitin Nainani

Book Project Manager: Aishwarya Mohan

Senior Editor: Anuradha Joglekar

Technical Editor: Reenish Kulshrestha

Copy Editor: Safis Editing

Indexer: Tejal Soni

Production Designer: Jyoti Kadam

DevRel Marketing Coordinators: Mouli Banerjee and Nivedita Singh

Publication date: April 2024

Production reference: 1070324

Published by Packt Publishing Ltd.

Grosvenor House

11 St Paul's Square

Birmingham

B3 1RB, UK

ISBN 978-1-80512-067-4

www.packtpub.com

To my mother, Cristina Polanco Garcia, and to the memory of my father, Santos Ortega, for their sacrifices and for exemplifying the power of determination. To my children, Diana and John, for being the driving force behind my everyday motivation.

– Sandielly Ortega Polanco

To my ever-patient wife, Ishwari, who endured my selective hearing during this book's creation. To our daughter, Leysha, who believed this book would turn out to be a fantasy tale.

– Gogula Aryalingam

To my loving wife, Huma, who has stood by me like a rock at every stage of our joint life journey. To my loving parents, for their sacrifices to educate me and my siblings.

– Abu Bakar Nisar Alvi

Contributors

About the authors

Sandielly Ortega Polanco is a highly experienced data analyst with over 10 years of expertise in data analytics and programming. Throughout this extensive career, he has made significant contributions to multiple companies across various sectors, including government, large-scale food sales, automotive, and the tourism industry, where he held a managerial position overseeing IT operations and data analytics processes at more than eight hotels in the Dominican Republic.

Furthermore, Sandielly has served as a consultant in diverse areas, particularly in online education, where he has played a pivotal role in shaping the skills of over 4,000 young professionals in data analysis at two of the largest digital academies in Latin America.

Fluent in multiple languages, Sandielly holds a bachelor's degree in computer engineering and has completed several diplomas in networking, security, and systems administration. Additionally, he has been a Microsoft Certified Data Analyst for over three years, demonstrating his dedication to excellence in the field.

Sandielly is a content creator on YouTube, where he shares his expertise in Power BI, Fabric, artificial intelligence, SQL, and process automation. His channel boasts an active audience of over 35,000 subscribers and growing, reflecting his influence and impact in the data analytics community.

First and foremost, I would like to express my heartfelt gratitude to my dear mother for her strong endeavor in raising us as both a mother and a father, to my beloved wife for her patience throughout the lengthy process of writing this book, to the Polanco family for their continuous support in my career, and most especially, to my lovely daughter, Diana, who has been my motivation and inspiration for writing this book.

Gogula Aryalingam is a seasoned data and AI professional working at Fortude, a technology and consulting services company committed to delivering impactful digital solutions. With a rich history of serving customers across diverse verticals in multiple technology companies, Gogula has architected, designed, and delivered data analytics and business intelligence solutions that drive business growth and innovation. A recipient of the prestigious Microsoft Most Valuable Professional award for the data platform for over 15 years, Gogula's contributions to technical communities are extensive and impactful. He is a regular speaker at both local and international technology conferences, sharing his expertise on data analytics and business intelligence topics. In addition to his speaking engagements, Gogula is actively involved in content creation for data certifications and learning for Microsoft, helping to shape the next generation of data professionals. His credentials include being 10 x Microsoft certified in data and analytics, a testament to his deep knowledge and commitment to his field. Gogula also conducts training on Power BI, Fabric, and Azure data technologies, further extending his influence and commitment to the data and AI community. His work empowers others to leverage the power of data to drive decision-making and innovation. He is based in Colombo, Sri Lanka, and he holds an MSc in information technology from the Cardiff Metropolitan University in Wales.

I would like to first and foremost thank my loving wife and daughter for their continued support, patience, and encouragement throughout the long process of writing this book. Thanks also to my boss, Gaurika, for his unwavering support.

Abu Bakar Nisar Alvi is a highly experienced product manager and certified project management professional with over 24 years of industry experience. With a demonstrated track record of leading multidisciplinary teams and successfully completing challenging projects, he has a diverse background that encompasses embedded systems development and telemetry data analytics in the defense industry. Abu Bakar has transitioned from a telemetry engineer to a full-time data analytics and business intelligence consultant and trainer. He is 4 x Microsoft certified and works with local and international clients to implement Power BI and Fabric solutions. As a Microsoft Certified Trainer, he also conducts training in this area for public and corporate clients. His contributions were recognized by the government of Pakistan in 2005 when he was awarded the prestigious Tamgha-e-Imtiaz, the fourth-highest civil award for professional excellence. He is the youngest Pakistani professional engineer to get this honor at the age of 27. He is based in Islamabad, Pakistan, and holds a master's degree in satellite communication and space systems from the University of Sussex, United Kingdom.

I would like to first and foremost thank my loving and patient wife for her continued support throughout the long process of writing this book. Special thanks to my younger brother for his encouragement in writing a book for the first time.

About the reviewers

Mohammed Adnan is a distinguished Microsoft MVP and Certified Trainer, renowned for his versatile roles as a consultant and speaker and being the creative mind behind the YouTube channel *taik18*. With a wealth of expertise in data, he excels as a data solution architect, specializing in Azure AI, Fabric, Power Platform, SQL, and Excel.

Beyond his professional endeavors, Adnan is a mentor with a personal touch, having collaborated with numerous clients, including Fortune 500 companies. His project portfolio spans diverse domains such as supply chain, manufacturing, HR, and cloud kitchen. Adnan's commitment to excellence and his comprehensive skill set make him a trusted professional in the ever-evolving landscape of technology and data management.

Ankit Kukreja has over seven years of expertise in data analytics and finance, complemented by an MBA in finance. He has excelled in driving transformative initiatives. As a senior consultant at Wipro, he leads automation with Power Automate and transitioning legacy applications to Power Apps. His tenure at Accenture and CLIX Capital involved delivering impactful solutions and orchestrating data-driven insights with Power BI. Earlier roles at Blackrock Services highlight his proficiency in risk analysis and process optimization. With certifications in Power BI, Power Platform, and Azure, Ankit is a recognized super-user in the Power BI community, poised to drive success through insights, automation, and stakeholder engagement.

Greg Deckler is an active contributor to the Power BI Community, having authored over 200 Power BI Quick Measures Gallery submissions and over 6,000 authored solutions. Seven times a Microsoft MVP for Data Platform, Greg is also vice-president of a global technology firm and has authored five books on Power BI, including the first and second editions of *Learn Power BI*, *DAX Cookbook*, *Power BI Cookbook Second Edition*, and *Mastering Power BI Second Edition*. Greg also served as a technical editor for *Extreme DAX* and *Power BI Quick Start Guide Third Edition*. Finally, Greg has authored multiple external tools for Power BI, including Microsoft Hates Greg's Quick Measures, and regularly posts Power BI videos on the YouTube channels @DAXForHumans and @MicrosoftHatesGreg.

I would like to thank my son, family, and the entire Power BI community for all their support over the years. Special thanks to Brian Julius for founding and supporting the No CALCULATE movement.

Table of Contents

Part 2: Beyond the Borders of Power BI

3

The Power BI Workflow   55

4

Data Analysis with Power BI   97

5

Preparing, Transforming, and Modeling Data   123

6

Exploring, Visualizing, and Sharing Data and Deploying Solutions   167

7

DAX Programming — 199

8

Expert Report Building — 241

9

Effective Data Storytelling   285

10

Using Dashboards and Apps and Implementing Security   339

Part 3: The Final Stretch – Preparing for the HR Round and Beyond

11

Understanding the HR Interview Process and Preparing for Success   375

12

Tips for Negotiating Salary and Benefits   407

13

Best Practices for Accepting and Rejecting Job Offers – Onboarding and Beyond   427

Preface

In the ever-evolving landscape of data analytics, Power BI has emerged as a leading tool, empowering businesses to make data-driven decisions. This book, an interview guide for Power BI, is designed not only to help you understand the intricacies of Power BI but also to prepare you for the interview process itself.

Power BI has revolutionized the way businesses interact with their data, making it more accessible and understandable. This book aims to provide you with a comprehensive understanding of Power BI's capabilities and how they can be leveraged in a business context. Beyond that, it also aims to equip you with the skills to excel in interviews by demonstrating how this comprehensive understanding of Power BI can be applied effectively in real-world scenarios.

This guide covers a wide range of topics, from the technical aspects of Power BI to the art of interviewing. It includes chapters on how to prepare for interviews, how to navigate common interview scenarios, and how to effectively articulate your knowledge and skills. The guide also walks you through the process of data analysis with Power BI, demonstrating how to build and deploy a Power BI solution in real-world scenarios. This practical focus ensures that you're not only learning Power BI but also understanding how to apply these skills in a way that resonates with interviewers. To further aid your preparation, each chapter concludes with a comprehensive list of probable interview questions on Power BI, providing you with a practical understanding of what to expect in an interview.

Remember, an interview is not only about demonstrating what you know but also about showcasing your ability to apply that knowledge. As you navigate through this guide, we encourage you to understand the concepts, ask questions, and think about how you can apply this knowledge in different scenarios.

Good luck on your journey into the exciting world of Power BI!

Who this book is for

This book is for data analysts or analytics engineers who use Power BI to build business intelligence solutions and are looking to deepen their existing knowledge for better opportunities.

The two main personas who are the target audience of this book are as follows:

- **Data analysts**: Data professionals who transform complex data into actionable insights
- **Analytics engineers**: Data professionals who build end-to-end analytics platforms where part of their role involves building Power BI content

What this book covers

Chapter 1, Exposing Your Profile, describes how to highlight your professional profile and stand out from the rest. You will learn about many of the tools and websites that recruiters use to search for human talent. Additionally, I will show you how you can create your professional portfolio, develop personal projects, and work on enhancing your resume.

Chapter 2, Support Skills for Power BI Developers, helps you discover the fundamental role of support skills in the profile of a data analyst. You will also explore the power of the SQL language for extracting data from MS SQL Server databases. Additionally, you will become acquainted with the most relevant Python libraries in the data field, such as pandas, NumPy, and scikit-learn for machine learning. Furthermore, you will be equipped with the necessary soft skills to stand out as an exceptional data analyst.

Chapter 3, The Power BI Workflow, takes you on an end-to-end journey of the workflow of activities that start with getting data into Power BI and culminate in building and publishing a solution. This chapter sets you up for the rest of the chapters, where you will dive deep into each of these activities for comprehensive understanding.

Chapter 4, Data Analysis with Power BI, explores the phases of data analysis and how they map to the workflow of activities that you learned about in the previous chapter.

Chapter 5, Preparing, Transforming, and Modeling Data, dives deep into preparing, transforming, and modeling data for your business. It explores the design aspect of your model, how you would prepare and transform data to fit your design, and finally, building the model.

Chapter 6, Exploring, Visualizing, and Sharing Data and Deploying Solutions, provides you with an understanding of how you would explore your modeled data before you visualize it and then share it for consumption. The chapter also provides you with an understanding of how you would deploy a Power BI solution once you've completed development.

Chapter 7, DAX Programming, dives into the world of the DAX language, a critical aspect of mastering Power BI. We'll cover fundamental concepts, such as scalar functions for data aggregation and distinguishing between measures and calculated columns. Additionally, we'll explore evaluation contexts using CALCULATE functions, applying filters, and understanding "context transition." Finally, we'll delve into time intelligence functions to navigate temporal data effectively.

Chapter 8, Expert Report Building, will guide you through creating a Power BI report using Power BI Desktop, focusing on popular visuals and best practices for report configuration. You'll learn how to select the most effective charts for conveying insights, utilize AI enhancements, format visuals, add tooltips, and implement drill-down or drill-through functionalities for detailed reporting.

Chapter 9, Effective Data Storytelling, provides a detailed understanding of the importance of data storytelling in report design. The chapter talks about the importance of narrative and how effective data storytelling drives decision-making for Power BI reports.

Chapter 10, Using Dashboards and Apps and Implementing Security, will learn about Power BI service functionalities, including report sharing and permissions management. We'll cover sharing content through dashboards and managing pins, tiles, and alerts. Additionally, you will discover how to use Power BI apps to consolidate reports and implement **Row-Level Security** (**RLS**), controlling data access for specific groups.

Chapter 11, Understanding the HR Interview Process and Preparing for Success, provides tips and trips to successfully negotiate the HR interview process. The chapter discusses various methodologies for test and interview preparation and how to combine your knowledge, preparation, and energy to enter the job market with confidence and success.

Chapter 12, Tips for Negotiating Salary and Benefits, discusses tips and strategies to negotiate the salary, perks, and benefits related to a job offer. The chapter discusses important tips for the negotiation process and how a balanced strategy can lead to getting the best deal for both sides.

Chapter 13, Best Practices for Accepting and Rejecting Job Offers – Onboarding and Beyond, provides an overview of the best practices for accepting and rejecting offers. These are mainly based on choosing the right set of communication skills. The chapter also provides a roadmap for onboarding and continual learning in the job role, as well as staying relevant in the data analytics job market.

To get the most out of this book

You will need to have an understanding of the basics of Power BI and a basic understanding of business intelligence concepts.

Software/hardware covered in the book	Operating system requirements
Power BI Desktop	Windows

There are many short code examples in this guide that are provided solely for demonstration purposes, and you do not need to execute these directly.

This interview guide contains many long screenshots. These have been captured to provide readers with an overview of the various features of Power BI. As a result, the text in these images may appear small at 100% zoom.

Download the example files

You can download the sample `.csv` files for *Chapter 8* from the following URL: `https://packt.link/gbz/9781805120674`.

Conventions used

There are a number of text conventions used throughout this book.

`Code in text`: Indicates code words in text, database table names, folder names, filenames, file extensions, pathnames, dummy URLs, user input, and Twitter handles. Here is an example: "Similarly, the MAX, MIN, COUNT, and AVERAGE functions are used to obtain the maximum, minimum, count, and average values, respectively."

A block of code is set as follows:

```
SUMX TEST = SUMX (
    Products,
    Products[Price] * Products[Qty]
    )
```

When we wish to draw your attention to a particular part of a code block, the relevant lines or items are set in bold:

```
Dates Between =
    CALCULATE (
        [SUM Total Sales],
        DATESBETWEEN (
            'Calendar'[Date],
            "01-01-2008", "31-03-2008"
        )
    )
```

Any command-line input or output is written as follows:

```
pip install numpy
```

Bold: Indicates a new term, an important word, or words that you see on screen. For instance, words in menus or dialog boxes appear in **bold**. Here is an example: "To do this, go to **File | Options and Settings | Options** and open the **Preview features** menu."

> **Tips or important notes**
> Appear like this.

Get in touch

Feedback from our readers is always welcome.

General feedback: If you have questions about any aspect of this book, email us at `customercare@packtpub.com` and mention the book title in the subject of your message.

Errata: Although we have taken every care to ensure the accuracy of our content, mistakes do happen. If you have found a mistake in this book, we would be grateful if you would report this to us. Please visit `www.packtpub.com/support/errata` and fill in the form.

Piracy: If you come across any illegal copies of our works in any form on the internet, we would be grateful if you would provide us with the location address or website name. Please contact us at `copyright@packt.com` with a link to the material.

If you are interested in becoming an author: If there is a topic that you have expertise in and you are interested in either writing or contributing to a book, please visit `authors.packtpub.com`.

Share Your Thoughts

Once you've read *The Complete Power BI Interview Guide*, we'd love to hear your thoughts! Scan the QR code below to go straight to the Amazon review page for this book and share your feedback.

`https://packt.link/r/1-805-12067-0`

Your review is important to us and the tech community and will help us make sure we're delivering excellent quality content.

Download a free PDF copy of this book

Thanks for purchasing this book!

Do you like to read on the go but are unable to carry your print books everywhere?

Is your eBook purchase not compatible with the device of your choice?

Don't worry, now with every Packt book you get a DRM-free PDF version of that book at no cost.

Read anywhere, any place, on any device. Search, copy, and paste code from your favorite technical books directly into your application.

The perks don't stop there, you can get exclusive access to discounts, newsletters, and great free content in your inbox daily

Follow these simple steps to get the benefits:

1. Scan the QR code or visit the link below

https://packt.link/free-ebook/9781805120674

2. Submit your proof of purchase
3. That's it! We'll send your free PDF and other benefits to your email directly

Part 1:
Getting Your First Interview

In the first part, we will delve into the professional profile of the data analyst and discover how to expose it effectively through a variety of strategic channels that will ensure visibility to even the most discerning recruiters. Additionally, we will provide you with effective techniques to enhance your resume and show you how to create an appealing portfolio. Furthermore, we will explore some key supporting skills for the data analyst, such as SQL, Python, design, and of course, those essential interpersonal skills known as soft skills, which are fundamental for success in this exciting field of work.

This part has the following chapters:

- *Chapter 1, Exposing Your Profile*
- *Chapter 2, Support Skills for Power BI Developers*

1
Exposing Your Profile

As a professional, having a standout profile plays a crucial role in the search for your first job interview. Its purpose is to communicate to the public who you are, your interests, and what you have achieved, as well as describe the set of skills you possess and what you can do with them. Think of it as the first impression that people have of you and the first thing that those who are interested in offering you a job will see as well. That is why you must know how to efficiently highlight your professional profile and stand out from the rest.

In this chapter, you will learn how connecting with people helps increase your chances of getting your first job interview. You will see the power of having an online presence on LinkedIn and the importance of creating your work portfolio.

You will also understand the importance of validating your technical skills through certifications, official courses, or conference talks. Along with that, you will see how teaching what you know is a method that can keep you constantly learning.

By the end of this chapter, you will have a set of proven techniques to properly expose your professional profile and help enhance the first good impression you will need in your first interview.

The topics we will cover in this chapter are as follows:

- The power of networking
- A quick guide to polishing your resume
- Creating a personal project portfolio
- Validating your skills
- Learning by teaching

The power of networking

The human being is the result of connections and disconnections with people throughout their lives. From a young age, we begin to create bonds with those around us, many of which last for a long time, but a large percentage do not. It is easy for us as children to greet our classmates in a friendly way or to tell them how our weekend was at the beach. However, this does not happen as easily for adults. It is as if we are slowly losing empathy or simply do not know how to start a conversation, no matter how simple it may seem.

We are social beings by nature, meaning that connecting with people is in our DNA. Even the American psychologist Abraham Maslow placed personal relationships or friendships within the famous *Maslow's hierarchy of needs*, a psychological theory that tries to explain the needs that humans try to fulfill as they satisfy those of the lower level in the pyramid. Of the five levels, belongingness and love needs are third:

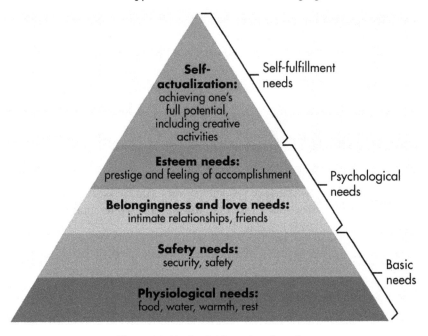

Figure 1.1: Maslow's hierarchy of needs

Connecting with people, besides being inherent to each one of us, is a method (that's right, a method that), which, at a professional level, can increase your chances of progressing in your career and, in this case, the chances of finding your first interview as a data analyst.

The six-grade theory

In his book *SAPIENS: From Animals to Gods*, Yuval Noah asserts that primitive chimpanzees could relate and coexist in troops of between 20 and 50 individuals. Any number greater than this would generate chaos among the members and would force the group to separate and form new ones again with the same number.

Another slightly more contemporary theory asserts that the maximum number of people with whom an individual can relate is 150; of course, we are talking about connections of sufficient relevance to you. You are probably calculating the exact number in terms of your circle of friends and confirming if the theory applies to you, but don't worry if you are nowhere near that number; I assure you that any person is no more than six degrees of separation from another.

The **six-grade theory** is an idea that attempts to demonstrate that an individual is connected to another with no more than six people between that connection, even across the world. That is, you and I could be connected through a chain of referrals of no more than six people.

This theory claims that, on average, each person knows about 100 people, including friends, family, colleagues, university, or gym mates. Let's say your circle of friends does not reach 100 people and is about 80 people. If each of those people knows 80 more people, you can send a message to about 6,400 people just by asking your friends to spread the word.

Networking with people enables us to tap into the collective knowledge, experiences, and resources of others. It opens doors to collaboration, mentorship, personal growth, and career opportunities. Whether it's attending conferences, joining professional organizations, or simply reaching out to acquaintances, networking helps us build a diverse and supportive community that can enrich our lives in various ways.

In summary, connecting with people is an essential aspect of human interaction and plays a vital role in expanding our social circles, fostering meaningful relationships, and accessing opportunities. By appreciating the interconnectedness of the wider world, we can effectively leverage the power of networking to enhance our professional lives.

Nowadays, reaching that number is easier than ever if we consider the number of social networks we have on our phones, but more importantly, the number of professional networks we have access to, such as LinkedIn, where connecting with people and applying the six-grade theory can have a beneficial impact on your professional profile.

Boosting your LinkedIn profile

As you saw in the previous section, creating friendly bonds is among the needs that every human being seeks to fulfill to *be happy*. We have modified this ability over time by always creating different methods to create these bonds. Just a few decades ago, our circle of friends or connections depended largely on how social the places we frequented were. However, things have changed a bit these days, thanks to the fact that we have used the internet to connect individually through the different social networks that exist today.

Social networks not only allow us to create connections but also provide a stage on which we can showcase who we are and everything we represent, such as our interests, likes, skills, achievements, the places we frequent, and the ideas we are for or against. This is the essence of any of the social networks that exist today, some with a more directed focus than others, such as TikTok and its videos, Instagram and its photos, Twitter and its 280 characters, or LinkedIn if you are looking to expose your professional profile and connect with more professionals around the world.

LinkedIn is considered the most useful professional social media network that exists today, with a well-deserved reputation, as it perfectly fulfills its mission to connect the world's professionals to make them more productive and successful. Currently, LinkedIn has around 900 million users, with the exponential growth expected to exceed 1 billion by 2025. This means more and more professionals are using it. But more importantly, more and more companies are using LinkedIn as a recruiting tool, which undoubtedly obliges you to create a profile that is optimized enough to stand out from the rest.

You probably already have a LinkedIn account, and maybe you've already changed your profile picture and clicked on recommend for the first post. However, this is a social network that gets some resistance from those who are just starting out. So, as a novice user, you may feel overwhelmed when starting to use it. However, although the network par excellence in these cases is LinkedIn, you are the professional here, and that professionalism can be taken to any social network, such as Instagram or TikTok, that you use.

Next, let's discuss the three tips that can help you make the initial process smoother.

Tip 1 – Don't let yourself feel intimidated

Many people are hesitant to use this platform because they believe it is too formal or for serious people. However, you don't need to have a university degree to create your first profile. You also don't need to be a business owner or have a job. LinkedIn is primarily used for job searching, so you can view it as an advantage to connect with the same serious people who could help you land your first job interview.

Tip 2 – Be yourself

Remember that this is a social network, a place where you can interact with people and share your ideas and the things you like. So, don't be afraid to be yourself and share your ideas. Believe me, we have all had that impostor syndrome that uses other people's opinions as a reference and makes us believe that ours is not interesting enough. At some point, that has happened to all of us, so the best thing you can do is be yourself. After all, there are people behind each profile.

Tip 3 – Connect! Connect! Connect!

One of the magical things that LinkedIn has, which other networks do not, is its high acceptance rate. Around 70% of connection requests are accepted by users, which speaks very well of the trust that users give to this network. So don't hesitate to follow anyone or, even better, send them a connection request. They will likely accept it back.

Over time, you'll adapt, and things will start to flow. The algorithm itself will suggest friendship connections and posts that are within your area of interest. However, remember that my purpose with you is to make your profile appear on the radar. To do this, you must optimize it as best you can. Some of the things that will help you optimize your profile are the following.

Make your profile public

Usually, on common social media platforms, we tend to have a certain level of privacy and secrecy so that not everyone can see our photos, comment on them, or like them; some people also limit who can send them DMs. These levels of security and privacy are great to have, and I even have some on my social media accounts, but when it comes to professional networking platforms, such as LinkedIn, where the content and audience are different, allowing others to interact with what you post and allowing others to comment on your posts is exactly what we want. Having your profile private limits the exposure you can have and, therefore, limits your chances of getting your first job interview.

To access the privacy management menu of your account, simply follow these steps:

1. Click the **Me** icon at the top of your LinkedIn home page.
2. Select **Settings & Privacy** from the dropdown.

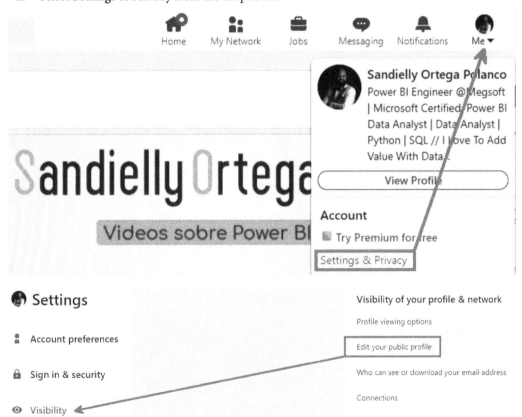

Figure 1.2: Access the Settings & Privacy menu on LinkedIn

Create a customized profile link

When you create a LinkedIn account, by default, you are assigned a unique identifier that represents your account within this network. This is usually part of the link to your profile, something like this: `https://www.linkedin.com/in/140078175`

This doesn't look very good when it comes to projecting your brand. Therefore, it's good practice to customize this link so that your profile is easier to find on search engines, such as Google, when someone searches for your name. Such a link would look something like this: `https://www.linkedin.com/in/sortega`

Besides SEO, having a customized link makes it easier to remember for those who view your resume and for you when you need to link your account with third-party pages, such as certifications.

To customize your profile URL, follow the next steps:

1. Click the **Me** icon at the top of your LinkedIn home page.
2. Click **View Profile**.
3. Click **Edit public profile & URL** on the right. You'll be redirected to the **Public profile settings** page.
4. Under **Edit your custom URL** on the right side, click the **Edit** icon next to your public profile URL.
5. Type or edit the last part of your new custom public profile URL in the text box.
6. Click **Save**.

Add a photo that represents who you are

Choosing a professional photo is a fundamental part of your profile, and when I say professional, it doesn't mean you have to run to a photography studio and spend a lot of money on a photo. Nowadays, with that screened block you carry in your pocket, you can take photos as professionally as in a studio, but just consider the following:

- Try to face the camera directly and make eye contact
- Smile even if you want to convey seriousness in your profile; smiling photos are more likable, competent, and influential
- Make the background of the photo less prominent; a solid color surface is a good idea, so if you want to show something else, it's better to save it for the banner
- Soft natural light is best for illuminating your face without excessive shine

- Avoid using the same frontal pose and expression you have in your IDs; practice in front of the mirror

- Try to wear the clothes you would wear in the job you want; sometimes, showing what you are looking for is better than showing what you currently do

- According to LinkedIn, your face should occupy 60% of the photo (you can achieve this by cropping the photo later)

- Use filters appropriately, or just don't use them; black and white is very trendy

Figure 1.3: LinkedIn header sample

Choose an attractive banner

The banner photo is the largest visual object on your profile, which means you should make a good impression with what you place there. It's a space that you can use for multiple purposes, depending on what you want to reflect in your profile. That is, it's valid to put a photo of a landscape you like, something related to what you do or would like to do, or a photo of yourself working from home. However, it's also valid if you simply put a quote from your favorite book or the address of your website. Just keep in mind that it's your professional profile, and the banner, as with your photo, should also be professional.

To change your banner, just click on the pencil icon in the top right of the banner, as can be seen in *Figure 1.3*; this will open an editor that will let you modify the image you choose by cropping, filtering, or adjusting. Here is an example of a LinkedIn banner:

Jared Thornton · 2nd
Sr. Technical Recruiter at TopTech Ventures
San Francisco, California, United States · Contact info

500+ connections

TopTech **TopTech Ventures**

The Master's University

Figure 1.4: LinkedIn banner sample

There are some third-party tools, for example, CANVA, that already have a series of templates that you can use easily. Here are two more samples of LinkedIn banners:

Figure 1.5: LinkedIn banner samples

In this section, you learned the importance of networking and how it helps you enhance your professional profile; in the next section, I will show you a brief guide on how you can make your resume stand out from the rest.

A quick guide to polishing your resume

There are several documents that we always like to keep multiple copies of. For example, I always have copies of my vehicle registration, my family's birth certificates, my identification, and my resume.

A resume is relevant and important because it's the first thing that companies ask for when you start a recruitment process. Let's say that it will be the seller of your brand. Therefore, it must show well who you are, what your skills are, how you have used them, and how you will add value to the company. A study determined that recruiters spend between 6 and 8 seconds reviewing a resume, so your responsibility is to make every second count, and this is achieved by having a resume that meets a few characteristics. Let's discuss these next.

Be sure it has the correct keywords

Before preparing your resume, you should research the industry you work in and carefully read the different job postings. This will help you realize what companies expect to find in your resume. Remember that you are creating a resume based precisely on these company requirements, and many recruiters only focus on finding those words in your resume.

For example, if you search for "senior data analyst" in the job section of LinkedIn and take five random results, you may find phrases such as strong knowledge of SQL, +5 years of experience, problem-solving, or decision-making skills in the requirements. These are words that you should include in your resume (if you have them), and you should even try to highlight them by, for example, putting them first on the list.

Focus on what you achieved rather than what you did

When preparing our resume, we always try to highlight the things that earned us pats on the back or recognition, but we must be careful about how we word it in our resume. A doer focuses on detailing the things they did within a company, while an achiever highlights the value that they brought to the company.

How do you know whether you are speaking in a language of doers or achievers? Well, there are key verbs that identify a doer's resume: completed, helped, led, or performed, while achievements are more often expressed by using the following verbs: increased, optimized, accelerated, or developed, and these are usually accompanied by precise data that demonstrate the results of the achievement. Here is an example: "I optimized the productivity of the reception department by 50% by implementing an intelligent queue ticket system based on needs, while also minimizing customer wait time".

Add relevant links

It's impossible to include all your professional information in just a few pages, but this doesn't mean you should leave out important details. Always try to include external links such as your LinkedIn profile (preferably a personalized URL), your website or blog, your professional portfolio, your GitHub repository, or any other links that support the information you're putting in your resume. This will depend on what position you're applying for. For example, even though Instagram or Twitter are not professional networking platforms, if you're applying for a content manager position, it's obvious that you should include them in your resume. Here is an example of some included information:

Sally S. Smith

123.456.7890 • Los Angeles, CA 90001 • sallysmith@gmail.com • www.linkedin.com/in/sallysmith

Figure 1.6: Resume header sample

Sometimes, putting just your LinkedIn URL should be enough if you have a well-structured LinkedIn profile, as explained in the *Boost your LinkedIn profile* section.

Choose a consistent format

Always keep in mind the 6–8 seconds that recruiters use to review your resume when strategically working on the formatting. Avoid using too many colors (resumes are usually monochromatic); if you have used italics for the years, use them consistently; if you use bold for the subtitles, use them consistently, and use easy-to-read fonts such as Calibri or Times New Roman:

CUSTOMER SUCCESS MANAGER

Client Services | Customer Relationship Management | Account Management

Reliable, energetic and resourceful customer service professional with over five years of experience resolving customer complaints and promoting conflict resolution. Ability to cultivate key client relationships for multiple campaigns in diverse industries. Expertise in client services, account management, relationship-building and communication.

WORK EXPERIENCE

Corporation XYZ - *Happy Town, CA*   09/2018 - PRESENT
Customer Service Representative
Responsible for managing 45+ accounts in manufacturing industry while ensuring quality service.
- Promptly respond to customer enquiries in person or via phone, email, mail or social media.
- Quickly and efficiently open customer accounts by accurately recording account data.
- Maintain financial accounts by processing customer adjustments timely and professionally.
- Increased customer base by 30% during the year 2019 due to the delivery of quick service.

Business LMNOP - *Springville, CA*   02/2016 - 09/2018
Telephone Sales Representative
Developed and improved the capabilities of sales representative team over the course of two years.
- Received 97% satisfaction rating from customers after completed phone or video call.
- Kept records of customer interactions, processed customer accounts and filed documents.
- Collaborated with team to quickly resolve customer complaints with appropriate action.
- Effectively managed approximately 100 incoming calls daily.

Organization QRS - *Sunny Town, CA*   03/2014 - 02/2016
Front Desk Agent
Used strong communication skills to collaborate with team members to ensure efficient service.
- Created and maintained office forms and procedures to assist with administrative tasks.
- Processed orders, determined charges, and oversaw billing and payments.
- Greeted and welcomed clients with a warm, friendly and positive attitude.
- Coordinated the repair and maintenance of office supplies and equipment bi-weekly.

Figure 1.7: Resume sample

> **Important note**
>
> Some websites, such as `Canva.com`, offer a large inventory of professional resume templates that you can use as a reference if you're not skilled in design.

Read it several times

To make errors is human, but a spelling mistake can take you out of the game in less than 6 seconds, so take your time and read your resume several times before deciding that the version you have is the final one. This will help you spot opportunities for improvement in your skills list or provide better context for a sentence in your experience section.

Layout matters

The structure of a resume hasn't changed much in recent years, but you shouldn't overlook it. Each section should go along the lines of what you want to highlight. For example, an experienced professional will place more emphasis on the work experience section, while a novice student will probably develop the education section more. According to Indeed, the standard layout is as follows:

- Contact information
- Summary or objective
- Work experience
- Education
- Skills

Figure 1.8 shows a sample resume:

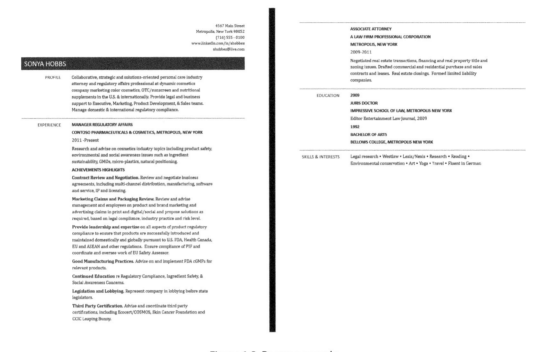

Figure 1.8: Resume sample

- As a complement, you can add some additional sections such as volunteer work, publications, conferences, languages, or hobbies.

> **Important note**
>
> According to Indeed, the size of the resume should be 1–2 pages.

Solving the picture dilemma

And what about the photo? Should you include it in your resume or not? Considering the 6–8 seconds that we have mentioned a lot, it is recommended that you simply do not include it. Ask yourself whether this photo will add any additional value to your resume, and if the answer is no, then leave it out. Photos usually take up a lot of space and can distract the attention of the reviewer without providing any value. Additionally, many large companies use **applicant tracking systems** (**ATS**) to filter potential candidates, and these systems do not prefer photos.

In many cases, I do agree that you should not include the photo, but it all depends on the country or sector you are applying to. In my country, it is still very common for resumes to include an attached photo, but this is not the case in the United States, where it doesn't matter much if you include it or not. Another example is the modeling or acting industry, where including a photo in your resume is essential.

Although resumes are still relevant in the recruitment process, many companies are looking for you to demonstrate the list of skills you possess, and this is achieved by creating a portfolio of work. In the next section, you will learn how to create one.

Creating a personal project portfolio

Today, it's not enough to just have a brilliant and extensive work experience section in your resume; when it comes to jobs in the technology field, it's good to showcase your skills and what you can do with them, and you can achieve this by creating a professional portfolio.

A work portfolio or professional portfolio is a compilation of your projects, documents, or achievements that demonstrate your skills and experience. Think of it as your personal art gallery where potential buyers can see what you're capable of. Although not all recruiters usually visit your portfolio to validate if you meet their client's expectations, this is a powerful tool that you can use to sell your brand, stand out from the rest, and showcase your professional profile.

As a data analyst and Power BI enthusiast, it's essential that you start creating your project portfolio; there are a few things you need to consider to begin with, as described in the subsections that follow.

Get sample data for your Power BI reports

Obtaining sample data to play with is one of the barriers that limits many learners from putting their knowledge into practice, but this is only because they don't know where to find the data when they need it; there are many websites with various data sources and formats that you can use in your Power BI reports. Here's a list (by type) of the most popular sites where you can find sample data sources to practice:

- **SQL databases** in `.bak` format

  - **Contoso**: This is a fictional company created by Microsoft based in Paris, France. It is a multi-national retailer with over 100,000 products, and its database is primarily used for product demonstrations. However, its fame has become more relevant in educational sectors for the same purposes but for tools such as Excel, SQL, or Power BI.

    - Download link: `https://www.microsoft.com/en-us/download/details.aspx?id=18279`
    - Requirements: SQL Server

- **AdventureWorks**: This is another fictional company created by Microsoft for the purpose of demonstrating its products. It is a company dedicated to the sale of bicycles, and its database can be found in its online transaction processing (OLTP) and online analytical processing (OLAP) transactional versions. This model can be very useful for scenarios regarding sales, purchases, manufacturing, and product management.

  - Download link: `https://learn.microsoft.com/en-us/sql/samples/adventureworks-install-configure?view=sql-server-ver16&tabs=ssms#download-backup-files`

  - Requirements: SQL Server

- **Worldwide Importers**: This is another fictional company created by Microsoft with the particularity that it is an importer and wholesale distributor of items, giving you a different perspective for all the indicators that you'll use in your analysis.

  - Download link: `https://github.com/Microsoft/sql-server-samples/releases/tag/wide-world-importers-v1.0`

  - Requirements: SQL Server

- Excel/CSV

  - **Kaggle**: This platform is one of the largest data science communities in the world, bringing together around half a million members worldwide who contribute around 2,000 publications per year. Here, you will find data sources of all kinds, which will allow you to have multiple use cases for your portfolio.

    - Download link: `https://www.kaggle.com/datasets`

    - Requirements: Registration on the website

- **PBIX**

  - **Prestructured PBIX files**: Just as Microsoft provides certain data sources in various formats, such as .csv, they also have `.pbix` files available that come preloaded with data so that you can put your knowledge into practice.

    - Download link: `https://github.com/microsoft/sql-server-samples/tree/master/samples/databases/wide-world-importers/power-bi-dashboards`

Once you've decided on the data source you'll use, it's time to play with data, and in the next section, I'll show you how.

Time to play with data

Once you have decided on the sample data to use, it is good to go to its documentation and understand the model you are working with. You need to understand certain things, such as the types of data it uses, whether there are null values, and whether there is any naming pattern with the columns that can help you determine what they contain. This will later help you correctly solve the use cases or questions you will answer with the report.

Remember that your portfolio should speak very well of your skills, so if you are a person who does not like to brag, this is not the time to hold back; you must demonstrate that you can solve complex situations in your report. Therefore, try to follow these tips:

Tip 1 – Create a story

Before creating your first measure, I recommend that you create a requirement, a situation that will help you give context and create the questions you want to answer with your report. For example, consider the next case we will be using from now onwards:

The sales management of company X requires the creation of a report that helps to monitor the monthly sales of the company's salespeople, the purpose of which is to incentivize the top three salespeople on a quarterly basis.

Tip 2 – Develop the questions to answer

After creating your requirements, it's time to ask questions based on your use case. These questions should be specific and measurable. Your list of questions should look like this:

- Who have been my top three salespeople?
- Can I see them by region?
- Can I see them by country?
- What is the monthly target that I am going to define?
- What is the average sales per salesperson?
- Do I want to highlight the salespeople who exceed the average or the target?
- What has been the sales trend of the salespeople in the last year?
- Who has decreased in terms of sales?
- Who has increased in terms of sales?
- What has been the increase in sales from the current month compared to the previous month?

Tip 3 – Start creating measures

We have our questions, so now it's time to roll up our sleeves and start creating our measures. For example, based on the previous questions, I know I will need a measure that calculates the average sales per vendor or calculates my top three vendors. Remember, put all your expertise into practice when developing the indicators. My advice is to avoid measures with simple calculations and try to play around with functions such as CALCULATE() in combination with FILTER() and ALL() or with some of the iterators, such as SUMX() or AVERAGEX(). As these are advanced combinations of functions, it is good to show that you have control over these functions.

Here are some additional functions:

- CALCULATE: This is used to modify the filter context; it evaluates an expression within a modified filter context.
- FILTER: This returns a table passed as a first argument with the rows that match the condition in the second argument.
- ALL: This returns all the rows in a table or all the values in a column, ignoring any filters that might have been applied.
- SUMX: This returns the sum of an expression, evaluated row by row.
- AVERAGEX: This returns the average of an expression, evaluated row by row.

In addition to demonstrating your DAX skills (which we will cover more deeply in *Chapter 7*), it's good to showcase your skills in choosing the best visual object or charts for each indicator. One of the roles of a data analyst is to communicate your findings through charts, and having this skill trained will improve your communication skills. This will speak volumes about your ability to tell stories with data. Some chart design references I usually use are from the datavizproject.com site, which allows you to filter visual objects by their function. For example, here are all the charts that you can use to represent parts of a whole:

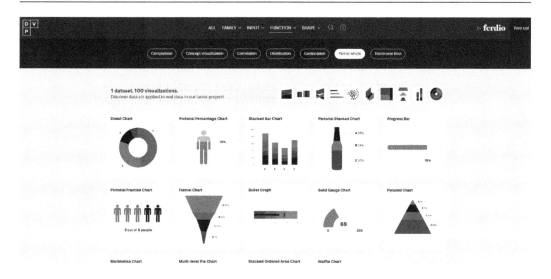

Figure 1.9: Chart designs

Although you probably won't find many of the charts that appear on this page in Power BI, these help you get an idea of how you can display your indicators.

Another inspirational resource that you should have printed and visible is the following image, in which you can see a list of possible charts, depending on the case:

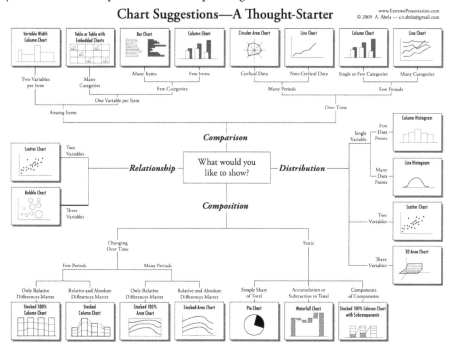

Figure 1.10: Diagram of charts grouped by usage

> **Important note**
> Here's a resource on the use of visuals: `https://datavizproject.com/`.

Tip 4 – Make your report accessible

Once you have your project ready to be published to a workspace (or at least the first version of it), it's time to make it public. For this, you must first be aware that you need a **Power BI Pro** license at a minimum. If you already have the license, you can make your report public by following these steps:

1. Log in to your Power BI Account.

2. Open a report in a workspace that you can edit and select **File** | **Embed report** | **Publish to web (public)**.

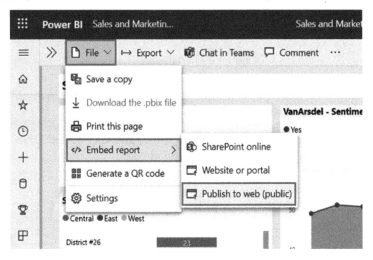

Figure 1.11: File menu after logging into app.powerbi.com

3. If you see the message shown in *Figure 1.12* on your screen, it's because you haven't enabled this feature in your tenant. To do this, you can follow these steps at the following link: `https://learn.microsoft.com/en-us/power-bi/collaborate-share/service-publish-to-web#find-your-power-bi-administrator`. Here is an example of when **Publish to web (public)** is not enabled:

Contact your admin to enable embed code creation

To publish this report on the web, ask your Power BI admin if they will allow you to create new publish to web embed codes. Once they turn that on, you will be able to publish this report to the web. Learn more

Figure 1.12: Error shown when publish to web is not enabled

4. Click on **Create embed code**.

Embed in a public website

Get a link or embed code that you can include on a public website.

You may use the publish to web functionality to share content on a publicly available website. You may not use this functionality to share content internally, including through email, your internal network, or intranet site.

Publish a live version that will remain synchronized with the source report in Power BI. Any changes you make to the report will immediately be reflected in the published public version.

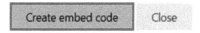

Figure 1.13: Create an Embed code option

5. Do a quick review of the warnings and click on **Publish**.

Embed in a public website

⚠ You are about to create an embed code for this report. Once published, anyone on the internet will be able to access the report and the data it contains, and Microsoft may display the report on a public website or a public gallery.

Before publishing this report, ensure you have the right to share the data and visualizations publicly. Do not publish confidential or proprietary information, or an individual's personal data. If in doubt, check your organization's policies before publishing.

Figure 1.14: Option to publish the embed report

6. If everything goes well, a dialog box, such as the one that follows (*Figure 1.15*), should appear, where you have two ways to share the report: with a URL or with HTML code if you want to embed your report on a website. In the following, we can see the ways in which we can share the report; you have the option of the size you want for the report; then, you can add a placeholder image (which you can change to a more attractive thumbnail), and finally, the default page that will be displayed.

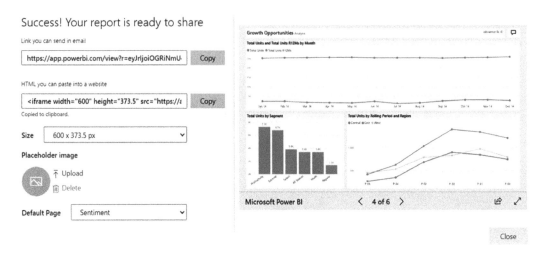

Figure 1.15: Option shown after completing the Power BI report embed process

Tip 5 – Where do I publish it?

Once we have the public link to our report at hand, we must put it in a place that is easy to access through a single URL. This is because you will not pass each of the links of your reports to those who ask for the address of your portfolio. For this, there are several options you can use. Next, we will talk about some of these options.

LinkedIn

Previously, in this chapter, we talked about the importance of LinkedIn when exposing your professional profile and that many recruiters (around 70%) use this social network to search for candidates. On top of that, you have the link to your LinkedIn profile on your resume, so why not use it to publish our projects? You can simply make a post encouraging your network to look at your project. It even works in your favor if you are a beginner since you can ask more experienced people within your network to give you their opinions on the report.

Third-party websites

If you want something a little more professional and perhaps want to spend a little bit more on a website, you can use platforms such as WordPress to create a customized website and publish your reports there. This gives you the advantage of being exposed to the entire internet and not just to your connections within a social network. It also gives you SEO positioning for your domain, it will be much easier to access for the public, and you can even add downloadable material, such as your resume, from the same page. This option is not usually the most suitable for those who are still looking for a job, considering that you must buy a Power BI Pro license to publish your report.

Figure 1.16: Sample of a portfolio website

There are also third-party websites, such as novyPro.com or **Maven Analytics**, that allow you to publish your projects for free (at least at the time of publishing this book) with a style that has nothing to envy regarding other websites. Simply click on register to gain access not only to your portfolio but also to a community of analysts who are part of this site and who share their designs and ideas with the public.

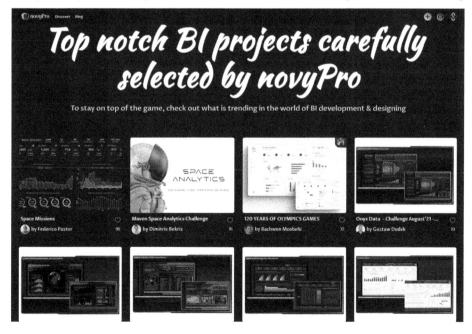

Figure 1.17: The novyPro website

In this section, you learned the importance of having a work portfolio (that proves your skills) and how you can create one in a fairly simple way. Now, it is time to know the advantages in the job market you gain by validating your skills.

Validating your skills

The success of your professional career in technology fields will largely depend on your technical skills. Even if the work experience section of your resume is loaded with achievements or you have a long list of skills, the level of expertise you possess will be left up to the judgment of whoever wants to hire you unless there is something more substantial to corroborate what you claim to know.

Validating your skills gives companies a clearer idea of your ability with those skills, but it is also an effective way to complement your resume. In technology fields, there are various methods or tools you can use to validate your knowledge, such as online courses on sites such as Coursera and IT certifications such as **PL-300**.

IT certifications are usually globally recognized accreditations that serve to demonstrate a professional's level of skill in certain areas. For example, companies such as Microsoft make you go through an evaluation process, usually in the form of exams, and upon passing them, you receive their endorsement.

The topic of certifications usually generates controversy regarding whether they are necessary or not. This is because they usually don't require previous titles, and anyone who feels capable of acquiring one can do so. This means that anyone with only a reputable certification can hold important positions and earn good salaries. Many companies even require certifications as part of their admission requirements and give them even more importance than traditional education. So, are such certifications necessary or not? Well, that's a question you must ask yourself, and it depends on your answer. If you were allowed to bring a companion to your first job interview to corroborate your experience and skills as a data analyst using Power BI, who would you bring? Your former team lead or Charles Lamanna (Corporate Vice President, Business Apps & Platform at Microsoft)?

Regardless of whether they are necessary or not, there is no doubt about the relevance and notoriety you gain by obtaining some of these certifications. Here are some of the reasons why I consider that you should obtain them.

You can become outdated

Surely, you understand the concepts of supply and demand, but if not, let me explain using apples; we are all apple sellers and the demand is the people who buy those apples. If we make an analogy with the technological job sector, there is currently a shortage of qualified professionals in various areas, including those related to data analysis. Basically, there are few apple sellers for the large number of people who want apples, and many of those people only want to buy from certified sellers (by the health department).

I make this comparison so that you have an idea of the current situation of the job market in many regions of the world, such as Latin America, where there is a deficit of around 48%, meaning this indicator refers to the percentage of positions that were not filled by the end of 2022 specifically.

As new technologies emerge, more and more companies require them and, in turn, qualified professionals in those technologies. This obliges you to stay up to date, and certifications help you not become outdated. From my perspective, it's simply a matter of increasing your chances and trying to be among the 58% qualified for positions.

One example of falling behind is Power BI. If, like me, you follow monthly updates and events where new features are announced, you will know that if you go three months without opening Power BI Desktop or the service, you will probably find new functions in DAX, additional menus, or new integrations that will make you Google these for a good while.

Confidence sentiment

The imposter syndrome is a psychological phenomenon in which competent people fail to internalize their accomplishments or feel inadequate. It's basically the inner voice that sometimes makes you question if you can do something, even when, deep down, you know you can. In other words, it's a lack of confidence in your abilities.

Validating your knowledge through certifications can be an effective method to build back that lost self-confidence. It's even part of human nature to need approval from others to feel happy, as we discussed earlier in Maslow's hierarchy of needs.

In addition to personal confidence, having a certification generates trust in others. For example, Japanese Wagyu beef has some of the most expensive beef cuts in the world. These cows undergo a rigorous feeding process, and only a limited number of them are slaughtered each year. Each cut must have a certificate of origin that indicates the breed and province in which the animal was born and slaughtered. When served, it is required that the certificate is displayed. Failure to do so may mean that the cut is not authentic. Furthermore, the restaurant must display a golden bust that is only given to restaurants that serve this type of beef. All of these elements create trust for you as a diner, both in the place and the cut you're about to taste. This whole process is what makes this cut cost up to $500 per kilogram. The same thing happens in the job market. Remember, you only have 6–8 seconds to make a good impression on your resume, so this document alone must demonstrate that you have the necessary knowledge level for the position.

Being a role model for others

One of the reasons that motivated me to study computer science and later led me to become a data analyst is that I have always had someone to look up to—a professional model—that I would like to become in several years. Many of them were my teachers in some subjects, and others were those that I'd never met, but in some way, I still followed their work, and they were a reference for me.

As a professional in any field, motivating others should be a commitment that you must assume. In addition to the credibility that you can generate for companies, you can also do it for enthusiasts who are not yet clear about where to start, and perhaps you, as someone who has already received "Microsoft's blessing", have the answers they are looking for. Undoubtedly, having an IT certification transmits an aura of knowledge around you, which can also help others to grow professionally.

Learn by teaching

In my career as a data professional, I have used different ways of acquiring knowledge, including the traditional methods of schools and universities, technical courses, workshops, diplomas, and online courses. But the one that I have liked the most and has exposed my profile as a professional to the world has been teaching others my extra 10%. Yes, you only need to know 10% more to teach others and also continue learning.

Exposing your professional profile is not just about showcasing what you have learned; it is also about giving others a portion of what you have learned over the years. Many people do not dare because they believe they do not have the gift of teaching, but that is nothing more than the "impostor syndrome" that we talked about. They also understand that they need to be people with important degrees to be a reference for others, which is not entirely true. In my experience, I have found that you simply need to know 10% more than the person you are teaching. When I talk about "teaching," I am not referring to having a classroom with desks and blackboards. I mean giving knowledge through any of the ways you prefer, whether through a blog, social media, a common talk, or any other type of physical or digital content.

Although times change and technology continues to advance, education or learning will always endure. However, the teaching method that many of the so-called digital natives require is changing to something very different from what we experienced just a few decades ago. So, to keep up with our knowledge and the exponential growth in new technologies, we must seek a method that can be effective and consistent with the educational methods that many digital natives require.

Undoubtedly, we are living in a world where traditional titles do not have as much relevance as validating your skills promptly. However, it is also no secret that in the technological field, a person who can publicly demonstrate their knowledge generates trust and credibility.

Learning by teaching not only helps you enhance your professional profile but also helps you work on your soft skills. Many elementary schools make children orally explain everything they have learned to help them work on their communication skills, self-confidence, organizing their ideas, and how to present them. As a data analyst, this is a skill that you must train well since everything revolves around how to communicate through data.

Teaching what you learn increases your interest in the topic, and you become more critical of your knowledge and work much harder to understand that knowledge since if you cannot explain what you know simply, it is because you have not fully understood it.

As I mentioned earlier, you do not need to be a genius to teach a skill that you have expertise in. Just knowing that 10% more than another person is enough. Now, how do you adopt this learning and teaching technique?

Start in your environment

Your environment is the first place you should look, that is, your close circle, such as family, friends, or simply people who have doubts about something that you have the answer to. This is a good starting point if you are shy or do not have a very extensive social circle because there is already a relationship of trust between you and your close circle.

Talks and communities

Another quite effective method, and my personal favorite, is talks and communities. Volunteering in technology communities and serving as a mentor to those new emerging minds is quite an effective method of providing knowledge and learning along the way. If you are not afraid to speak in public, this is a way that I assure you will catapult your professional profile to another level, but more than that, you will provide knowledge and strengthen your own.

Another way to collaborate in communities is by being a member of Microsoft communities. Here, you have the chance to help others solve specific problems or add your point of view to a thread related to a specific situation that someone is issuing; this makes you, as a user, relevant in the community.

Summary

In this chapter, you learned about the importance of networking and how it can help expose your professional profile. Moreover, you learned how to improve your resume and how to start creating your project portfolio. Finally, you understood the importance of validating your skills and the advantages of learning by teaching others.

In the next chapter, you will learn how to deal with the job search process.

Additional reading

- Explore Power BI pricing here: `https://powerbi.microsoft.com/en-us/pricing/`

2
Support Skills for Power BI Developers

As a basic requirement, every data analyst should handle at least one business intelligence tool. In our case, if you are interested in Power BI and decide to take that learning path, you will have to start learning each of the parts that make up the creation of a report in Power BI. This means you must know about Power Query for data extraction and transformation, have notions of data modeling to shape and create indicators for your reports using DAX, know how to choose the best chart to display the information that will be in your report, and know the best way to share your reports and manage them in the Power BI service. Knowing each of these parts and mastering them will take you to an advanced level of using the tool. However, the profile of a data analyst (interested in Power BI) goes beyond this, as it should include additional skills that will make the workflow smoother and make your profile as a data analyst more valuable.

In this chapter, you will learn about some of the skills that many companies are currently demanding as part of the data analyst or BI developer position.

By the end of this chapter, you will have a clear understanding of the importance of knowing color theories in the design of your report. You will also learn about the importance of knowing a query language such as **Structured Query Language** (**SQL**) to import the data as aggregated as possible, and how to use programming languages such as Python in conjunction with Power BI. Finally, we will see some of the soft skills that you must have to complete your profile as a data analyst.

The topics we will cover in this chapter are as follows:

- Query language – SQL
- Programming languages – Python
- Design skills
- Soft skills

Technical requirements

- Microsoft SQL Server

Importance of SQL for a data analyst

As a data analyst, having a query language in our skills inventory is essential. In large companies, analysts may have the luxury of requesting queries from the database department for use in their reports. However, not all companies have the budget to have a specific department for this, and in most cases, it is the responsibility of the data analyst to create their queries and retrieve the data they need from databases.

SQL is the most used query language for both managing and retrieving data from databases. SQL is a standard of both the **International Organization for Standardization** (**ISO**) and the **American National Standards Institute** (**ANSI**). Here is a list of the existing standards so far:

- SQL-86
- SQL-89
- SQL-92
- SQL:1999
- SQL:2003
- SQL:2006
- SQL:2008
- SQL:2011

Most of the existing databases today, such as Oracle, MySQL, PostgreSQL, and MS SQL Server, use this query language. Although you can use the SQL standard in these databases, many companies choose to create dialects or improved versions of the language based on the standard. An example of this is T-SQL, which is the language used to manage Microsoft databases such as Microsoft SQL Server.

SQL is considered a domain-specific language as it is designed to perform specific tasks. Besides that, it is also a declarative programming language, meaning that you define the result you want to obtain in a summarized and abstract way without defining how to do it. For example, suppose we have a table called Fruits with columns called Name, Quantity, and Color, and we want to get a list of green apples in the table. If we transform this requirement into a real-life proposition, it would be something like "*Bring me the green apples from the fruit basket.*" In SQL Server, we could write a declarative query that describes this process as follows:

```
SELECT Name, color
FROM Fruits
WHERE Name = 'Apple' and color = 'green';
```

Notice how this query can be almost read in natural language. In the first line, we specify the attributes we want to select from the table. Then, we specify where we will get those attributes from, and finally, the WHERE clause is where we pass a condition that each fruit must meet to be part of my list. In my case, I only want green apples.

This is a fairly simple example of what a SQL query can be and a basic explanation of what a declarative programming language is. However, if we go back to the previous proposition, *"Bring me the green apples from the fruit basket,"* and compare it with the SQL query we wrote, in both cases, we indicate the object before the place from where we want it. If you look at the query, we first write the SELECT statement and then the FROM statement, but this sequential order would not be the same if we needed to give the same instructions to a machine or a robot. We would have to modify it to something like, *"From the fruit basket, choose the apples that are green, and then bring them to me."* This is the logical order in which SQL statements are processed.

Logical process in SQL

When writing any SQL query, we must write each statement in the following order:

1. SELECT
2. FROM
3. WHERE
4. GROUP BY
5. HAVING
6. ORDER BY

However, this is not the order in which each of these clauses is executed behind the scenes, but rather the logical order is as follows:

1. FROM
2. WHERE
3. GROUP BY
4. HAVING
5. SELECT
6. ORDER BY

Here, notice that in this case we first specify where we want to retrieve our records from with the FROM clause and the SELECT statement is second to last in the list, because the last step in the logical order is the order we want to give to our records.

To give you a clearer idea of the process that occurs in each of these phases, take the query result shown in *Table 2.1* based on a `Customers` table:

ID	StateFull	Gender	First Name	Last Name	Age
1	Indiana	Male	Charlie	Palmer	29
2	Missouri	Male	Adam	Walker	31
3	South Carolina	Male	Howard	Tran	67
4	Arizona	Male	Lee	Cotten	83
5	Georgia	Male	Christopher	Platz	76
6	North Carolina	Male	Jose	Chestnut	73
7	Oregon	Male	Bruce	George	77
8	Wisconsin	Male	Joseph	Ohearn	47
9	New Jersey	Male	Robert	Zamora	20
10	Louisiana	Male	Gerald	Parkin	25
11	Wisconsin	Male	Andrew	Hicks	34
12	Kansas	Male	Mike	McCarthy	57
13	Massachusetts	Male	James	Rood	78
14	Alabama	Female	Hugo	Baylor	22
15	New Mexico	Female	Renee	Read	60
16	Massachusetts	Female	Jean	Ramsey	72
17	Colorado	Female	Laura	Patterson	55
18	North Carolina	Female	Betty	Jones	36
19	Minnesota	Female	Carol	Chapman	19
20	Georgia	Female	Lynn	Kester	41
21	Indiana	Female	Jamie	O'Connor	62
22	Connecticut	Female	Ashley	Duckworth	85
23	Missouri	Female	Amber	Oneal	40
24	Louisiana	Female	Wanda	Nelson	83
25	Oregon	Female	Natalie	Bishop	38
26	Indiana	Female	Debbie	Hill	41
27	North Carolina	Female	Theresa	Carrick	58
28	Delaware	Female	Tina	Martin	67
29	Mississippi	Female	Jeannie	Mendoza	46
30	West Virginia	Female	Karen	Valdez	43

Table 2.1: Sample Customers table

In the following query, the goal is to extract the number of customers by gender and state whose age exceeds 35 years from the `Customers` table. Likewise, we only want those records whose grouped quantity exceeds 100 customers. Finally, we will sort the results by `CustomerQuantity` in descending order:

```
SELECT StateFull as State,
    Gender,
```

```
      COUNT(*) CustomerQuantity
FROM Data.Customer
WHERE Age > 35
GROUP BY StateFull, Gender
HAVING COUNT(*) > 3
ORDER BY CustomerQuantity desc
```

If you run this query in SQL Server, in each of the phases, a table is generated that must be processed by the next phase. In the subsections that follow, I will explain in detail the process that occurs in each phase.

The FROM Phase

This is the first clause that is evaluated. In this phase, you must indicate the table or tables from where you want to obtain your result; the result of this phase is a table with all the columns that your table has. In our case, we are using the DATA.Customer table, which contains six columns. So, the result of the following phase will be the six columns of the same table:

```
SELECT * FROM DATA.Customer
```

Here is a sample of how the table looks:

ID	StateFull	Gender	First Name	Last Name	Age
1	Indiana	Male	Charlie	Palmer	29
2	Missouri	Male	Adam	Walker	31
3	South Carolina	Male	Howard	Tran	67
4	Arizona	Male	Lee	Cotten	83
5	Georgia	Male	Christopher	Platz	76
6	North Carolina	Male	Jose	Chestnut	73
7	Oregon	Male	Bruce	George	77
8	Wisconsin	Male	Joseph	Ohearn	47
9	New Jersey	Male	Robert	Zamora	20
10	Louisiana	Male	Gerald	Parkin	25
11	Wisconsin	Male	Andrew	Hicks	34
12	Kansas	Male	Mike	McCarthy	57

Table 2.2: Data.Customer result

As a result, 30 rows will be returned.

> **Note**
>
> With *, you can indicate that you want all the columns of a table.

The WHERE Phase

In this phase, we will filter the rows that we want to consider in our query. This clause will act on the table from the previous phase. In our case, it is the table of DATA.Customer with its six columns.

ID	StateFull	Gender	First Name	Last Name	Age
1	South Carolina	Male	Charlie	Palmer	29
2	Arizona	Male	Adam	Walker	31
3	Georgia	Male	Howard	Tran	67
4	North Carolina	Male	Lee	Cotten	83
5	Arizona	Male	Christopher	Platz	76
6	Massachusetts	Male	Jose	Chestnut	73
7	Kansas	Male	Bruce	George	77
8	Massachusetts	Male	Joseph	Ohearn	47
9	New Mexico	Male	Robert	Zamora	20
10	Massachusetts	Male	Gerald	Parkin	25
11	Colorado	Male	Andrew	Hicks	34
12	North Carolina	Male	Mike	McCarthy	57
13	Georgia	Male	James	Rood	78
14	Indiana	Female	Hugo	Baylor	22
15	Louisiana	Female	Renee	Read	60
16	North Carolina	Female	Jean	Ramsey	72
17	Louisiana	Female	Laura	Patterson	55
18	Oregon	Female	Betty	Jones	36
19	Indiana	Female	Carol	Chapman	19
20	North Carolina	Female	Lynn	Kester	41
21	Oregon	Female	Jamie	O'Connor	62
22	Mississippi	Female	Ashley	Duckworth	85
23	Arizona	Female	Amber	Oneal	40
24	South Carolina	Female	Wanda	Nelson	83
25	Arizona	Female	Natalie	Bishop	38
26	Georgia	Female	Debbie	Hill	41
27	North Carolina	Female	Theresa	Carrick	58
28	Arizona	Female	Tina	Martin	67
29	Massachusetts	Female	Jeannie	Mendoza	46
30	Kansas	Female	Karen	Valdez	43

Table 2.3: Query result in the where phase

This means that the rows marked in gray in *Table 2.3* will not be part of our queries since these ages are under 35.

The GROUP BY Phase

Once our table has been filtered in the previous phase, we move on to the next phase, which is data aggregation. Remember that in each phase we work with a table that comes from the previous phase. In this case, we will work with a table that does not contain records with ages under 35 years.

In the GROUP BY clause, we are indicating that we want to group our data by the StateFull column and gender, which will create a group for each of the different combinations of these two columns. The identified groups are as follows:

StateFull	Gender	ID	First Name	Last Name	Age
Arizona	Male	5	Christopher	Platz	76
	Female	23	Amber	Oneal	40
		25	Natalie	Bishop	38
		28	Tina	Martin	67
Georgia	Male	3	Howard	Tran	67
		13	James	Rood	78
	Female	26	Debbie	Hill	41
Kansas	Male	7	Bruce	George	77
	Female	30	Karen	Valdez	43
Louisiana	Female	15	Renee	Read	60
		17	Laura	Patterson	55
Massachusetts	Male	6	Jose	Chestnut	73
		8	Joseph	Ohearn	47
	Female	29	Jeannie	Mendoza	46
Mississippi	Female	22	Ashley	Duckworth	85
North Carolina	Male	4	Lee	Cotten	83
		12	Mike	McCarthy	57
	Female	16	Jean	Ramsey	72
		20	Lynn	Kester	41
		27	Theresa	Carrick	58
Oregon	Female	18	Betty	Jones	36
		21	Jamie	O'Connor	62
South Carolina	Female	24	Wanda	Nelson	83

Table 2.4: Grouped query result

As you can see, nine groups have been identified by StateFull and 14 groups by StateFull and Gender, which are the different combinations that exist between state and gender. If you look closely, the North Carolina group has the most customers, with two males and three females, for a total of five customers in North Carolina.

It's important to keep in mind that from this phase onwards, you must ensure a unique record for each of the columns that are not in the GROUP BY clause. In other words, unless you are not going to use the rest of the columns, any column that is neither StateFull nor Gender must return a unique record per group. This is done through aggregation functions such as MAX to get the maximum value from a column, SUM to add values, or AVG to get the average.

The HAVING Phase

Once the groups have been identified, we can use the HAVING clause to filter the groups based on a predicate. This predicate, like in the WHERE clause, will return true or false, but it will be evaluated for each of the groups. In our case, we only want those groups whose total count is greater than three. If you look at the groups we identified earlier, we will have to eliminate the ones marked in the following table:

StateFull	Gender	ID	First Name	Last Name	Age
Arizona	Male	5	Christopher	Platz	76
	Female	23	Amber	Oneal	40
		25	Natalie	Bishop	38
		28	Tina	Martin	67
Georgia	Male	3	Howard	Tran	67
		13	James	Rood	78
	Female	26	Debbie	Hill	41
Kansas	Male	7	Bruce	George	77
	Female	30	Karen	Valdez	43
Louisiana	Female	15	Renee	Read	60
		17	Laura	Patterson	55
Massachusetts	Male	6	Jose	Chestnut	73
		8	Joseph	Ohearn	47
	Female	29	Jeannie	Mendoza	46
Mississippi	Female	22	Ashley	Duckworth	85
North Carolina	Male	4	Lee	Cotten	83
		12	Mike	McCarthy	57
	Female	16	Jean	Ramsey	72
		20	Lynn	Kester	41
		27	Theresa	Carrick	58
Oregon	Female	18	Betty	Jones	36
		21	Jamie	O'Connor	62
South Carolina	Female	24	Wanda	Nelson	83

Table 2.5: Grouped table with clause rows selected

The final result would only be the group of Arizona with four clients and the group of North Carolina with five clients in total.

StateFull	Gender	ID	First Name	Last Name	Age
Arizona	Male	5	Christopher	Platz	76
	Female	23	Amber	Oneal	40
		25	Natalie	Bishop	38
		28	Tina	Martin	67
North Carolina	Male	4	Lee	Cotten	83
		12	Mike	McCarthy	57
	Female	16	Jean	Ramsey	72
		20	Lynn	Kester	41
		27	Theresa	Carrick	58

Table 2.6: Filtered groups with the HAVING clause

Table 2.6 shows a reference of how the resulting table would look after applying the HAVING phase; as you can see, the first and second columns group more than one record, which is not a correct behavior in SQL.

The SELECT Phase

The fifth phase is the SELECT phase, which is a bit strange considering it's usually the first clause we specify in any SQL query. In this phase, we evaluate any expressions we indicate and assign aliases to any columns. In our case, we're counting the number of customers with the COUNT(*) function and giving the resulting column the name of CustomerQuantity.

Remember that any column that isn't part of the GROUP BY clause must be contained within an aggregate function that returns a single value per group. For example, if I were to modify my query to obtain the customer's name, I would get the following error:

```
SELECT StateFull as State,
       Gender,
       COUNT(*) CustomerQuantity,
       [First Name]
FROM Data.Customer
WHERE Age > 35
GROUP BY StateFull, Gender
HAVING COUNT(*) > 3
ORDER BY CustomerQuantity desc
Msg 8120, Level 16, State 1, Line 1
Column '[Customer].[First Name]' is invalid in the select list because
it is not contained in either an aggregate function or the GROUP BY
clause.
```

> **Note**
>
> Notice that we use brackets, [], to reference columns with spaces in the name.

The final result in this phase would be a table like the following:

StateFull	Gender	CustomerQuantity
Arizona	Male	1
Arizona	Female	3
North Carolina	Male	2
North Carolina	Female	3

Table 2.7: Results after the SELECT clause

If you don't need an order for your result, the preceding table will be your end result; but in this case, we will sort this set to show you some advantages that the next phase has over all others.

The ORDER BY Phase

Finally, in this phase, we will order the result that we just obtained from the previous phase. This is basically an aesthetic phase where we will only sort the result by the number of customers in descending order, meaning from highest to lowest. This phase has the privilege of being the only one in which you can refer to an alias because it is evaluated after the SELECT phase.

In this last phase, the final result of our query would be as follows:

StateFull	Gender	CustomerQuantity
Arizona	Female	3
North Carolina	Female	3
North Carolina	Male	2
Arizona	Male	1

Table 2.8: Results after the ORDER BY clause

As a data analyst, it is important for you to have a clear understanding of the logical process in which SQL clauses are executed. This will help you mitigate many of the common errors that arise in the ETL process and make your workflow more efficient when creating your own queries to consume within Power BI.

SQL queries can be much more complex than the ones we have experienced here. However, many of these topics are beyond the scope of this book as my goal is for you to understand the fundamentals of SQL and what you need as a data analyst in your daily work.

Now that you understand the logical query process of SQL, it's time you start combining tables, more often called **joining tables**; this is crucial for a data analyst because most of the time, the useful data is spread across multiple tables. The next section is about joining tables.

Joining tables

A fundamental skill for a data analyst is the ability to know how to join different tables to produce a useful result for our calculations and analytics. It is common for much of the data we will use in our reports to be spread across various tables, and it is our responsibility to know how to join them to produce the desired result.

You may be wondering about the need to combine tables from SQL rather than doing it in Power Query, as we also have the ability to join multiple tables within the Power Query Editor. However, the recommendation is always to try to do these types of joins as close to the source as possible. This will make your report more efficient by bringing in a single table instead of multiple tables to be joined by the Power BI engine.

SQL allows us to join different tables through joins, which can be **inner joins**, **cross joins**, or **outer joins**. Here is a brief definition of each.

Inner join

An inner join allows you to join two tables based on a condition, usually the comparison of two columns, with a primary key (which is a unique identifier for each record in a table) on one side and a foreign key (which is a field that establishes a link between two tables) on the other. In the following example, we have two tables, one with items and their corresponding type id, and another table that contains all the different types. If you look at the items table, we only have the ID of each type, so to create a query where I can get the name of each item and its specific type, I need to join these two tables on the type id. In the type table, the id is the primary key and in the item table, the id is the foreign key. If we create a query like the following one, we can get the result shown on the right of the query.

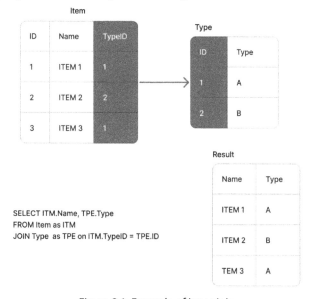

Figure 2.1: Example of inner join

> **Note**
> When using inner join, it is not necessary to write the word *inner*.

Something very important to keep in mind when using an inner join is that the result will only be the rows that match in both tables. In the previous example, we only have two types of items, and each row in the item table has a value that corresponds to the type table. This is probably because the item type is a required field when creating a new record, but what happens if the field is optional and there doesn't necessarily need to be a corresponding value in the other table? This is where the left/right joins come into play, which I will show you here.

Left/right outer join

While with an inner join, you are required to return only the rows that match the predicate you specify, with an outer join you can indicate which side you want to preserve in your final result.

In the following example, we have an Orders table and a Customers table, related by the customer ID on the customer table and the customer ID on the Orders table. Within the order table, there may not necessarily be a record that corresponds to the customer, which means you can create a query using a left join that returns all the records from the order table and also those that match the customer table.

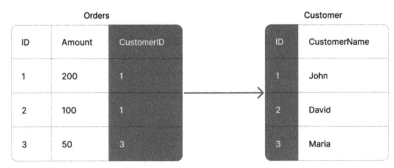

Figure 2.2: Example of left outer join

The final result is all the records from the orders table excluding the customer with the number two, which is David. If, on the other hand, we wanted to do it the other way around, that is, bring all the customers from the customers table, but also the records that match the orders table, we can use a right join as shown in *Figure 2.3*.

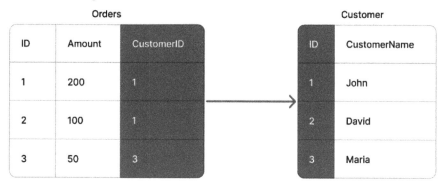

SELECT O.ID, O.Amount, C.CustomerName
FROM Orders as O
RIGHT JOIN Customers as C on O.CustomerID = C.ID

ID	Amount	CustomerName
1	200	John
2	100	John
Null	Null	David
3	50	Maria

Figure 2.3: Example of right outer join

The concept of right and left tables can confuse many data enthusiasts, but an easy way to identify them is to look at the table after the JOIN word (which in this case is the right side) and the opposite is the left side.

Cross join

Another type of join, although less commonly used, is the cross join, which essentially produces a Cartesian product of two tables. This means that it creates a result for each of the different combinations that exist between the two tables.

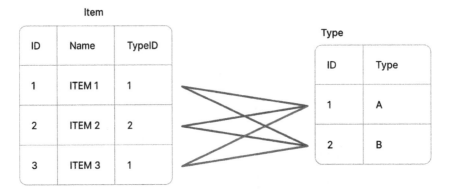

SELECT ITM.Name, TPE.Type
FROM Item as ITM
CROSS JOIN Type as TPE on ITM.TypeID = TPE.ID

ID	Name	TypeID
1	ITEM 1	1
1	ITEM 1	2
2	ITEM 2	2
2	ITEM 2	1
3	TEM 3	1
3	ITEM 3	2

Figure 2.4: Example of cross join

As you may have noticed, SQL is a language that will allow you, as a data analyst, to interact directly with the database by generating customized queries that support the analysis you will be doing within the Power BI report. There are many other elements that make up this language, which I also recommend you delve deeper into, such as stored procedures, views, subqueries, and common table expressions. However, these topics are a bit beyond the scope of this book.

Besides joining tables, a data analyst should have a programming language among their skills. The next section will explain the importance of knowing a programming language for a data analyst.

Programming languages

As a data analyst, another skill that I recommend you start including in your toolkit if you don't already have it is a programming language, and even better if this language is specifically oriented toward data analysis.

Although solutions such as Power BI offer you countless functions to create any type of indicator, there will always be gaps or improvement opportunities that many programming languages already include, such as Python.

Python is currently the most popular programming language for both data-related areas and general programming. This means that you can use Python as a backend programming language, but also use the libraries it contains to analyze data, perform complex mathematical calculations, or create predictive models.

Among the existing libraries that you can use within Python for data analysis, we have the most common ones, which are `numpy`, `pandas`, `plotly`, and `scikit-learn`. We will learn a little more about them in a bit but before that, you need to install them on your computer.

To install these libraries, follow these steps:

1. First, you need to ensure you have Python installed on your system; the following query can help with this:

    ```
    python -version
    ```

    This will return a result like the following:

    ```
    pip 21.2.4 from C:\Users\sandy\AppData\Local\Programs\Python\
    Python310\lib\site-packages\pip (python 3.10)
    ```

2. Next, to install these libraries, just run the following commands:

```
pip install numpy
pip install pandas
pip install plotly
pip install scikit-learn
```

After one of these installations succeeds, you will see a message like the following:

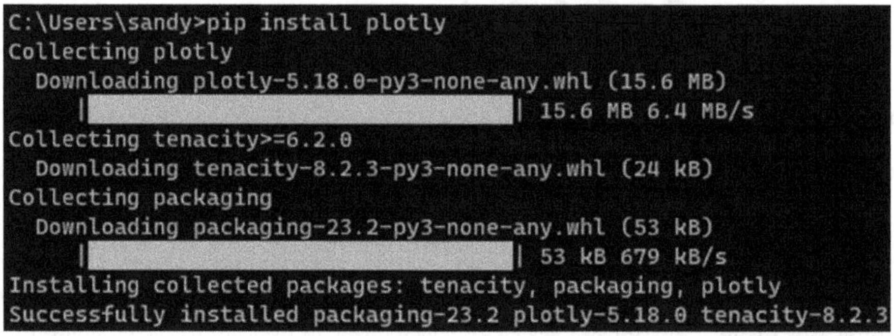

```
C:\Users\sandy>pip install plotly
Collecting plotly
  Downloading plotly-5.18.0-py3-none-any.whl (15.6 MB)
  |                                           | 15.6 MB 6.4 MB/s
Collecting tenacity>=6.2.0
  Downloading tenacity-8.2.3-py3-none-any.whl (24 kB)
Collecting packaging
  Downloading packaging-23.2-py3-none-any.whl (53 kB)
  |                                           | 53 kB 679 kB/s
Installing collected packages: tenacity, packaging, plotly
Successfully installed packaging-23.2 plotly-5.18.0 tenacity-8.2.3
```

Figure 2.5: Successful installation of plotly library

NumPy

NumPy is a Python library specialized in numerical calculation and large-scale data analysis. Its greatest advantage is its handling of arrays, which can be up to 50 times faster than Python's default lists. An example of what Python code using this library looks like is as follows:

```python
import numpy as np

# Create a 3x4 matrix
matrix = np.array([[2, 3, 4, 5],
                   [6, 7, 8, 9],
                   [10, 11, 12, 13]])

# Print the matrix
print("Original matrix:")
print(matrix)

# Add 2 to each element of the matrix
matrix_added = matrix * 2

# Print the resulting matrix
print("Matrix with 2 added to each element:")
print(matrix_added)
```

In this example, we import NumPy and create a 3x4 matrix. Then, we add two to each element of the matrix using the + operation. Finally, we print the original matrix and the resulting matrix.

Here is the result:

```
Original matrix:
[[ 2  3  4  5]
 [ 6  7  8  9]
 [ 10 11 12 13]]
Matrix with 2 added to each element:
[[ 4  6  8  10]
 [ 12  14  16 18]
 [20 22 24 26]]
```

In the preceding code, we are using NumPy to show a 3x4 array and multiplying each value by 2.

Pandas

Pandas is another commonly used Python library for data analysis and data science. It is designed specifically for data manipulation and analysis in Python. Pandas works with data frames or two-dimensional data tables. With it, you can import and export data in different formats, such as CSV or JSON, but also connect to SQL databases or Excel files. It is important to note that in Power BI, you can use Python to import data into your model and use the functionalities provided by the library.

An example of Python code using Pandas is as follows:

```python
import pandas as pd

# Read the CSV file into a Pandas dataframe
df = pd.read_csv('input_file.csv')

# Manipulate the data in the dataframe
df['new_column'] = df['existing_column'] * 2

# Write the modified data to a new CSV file
df.to_csv('output_file.csv', index=False)
```

In this example, we first import the Pandas library and use the read_csv() function to read a CSV file into a Pandas dataframe called df. We then manipulate the data in the dataframe by creating a new column called new_column, which is equal to the value of an existing column called existing_column multiplied by two. Finally, we use the to_csv() function to write the modified data to a new CSV file called output_file.csv, with the index=False parameter to avoid writing the index column.

This is just a simple example of how Pandas can be used to manipulate data in Python, but it demonstrates some of the basic functionality of the library.

Plotly

Plotly is a Python library specifically dedicated to data visualization. It helps you with the creation of complex graphs such as scatter plots, bar charts, box plots, histograms, line charts, area charts, bubble charts, and heat maps, among others. Here's an example that shows how you can use it to create a simple bar chart:

```python
import plotly.graph_objs as go

# Define data
x = ['Manzanas', 'Naranjas', 'Plátanos']
y = [3, 2, 4]

# Create the bar chart
fig = go.Figure(data=[go.Bar(x=x, y=y)])

# Define title and lables for axis
fig.update_layout(title='Frutas vendidas',
                  xaxis_title='Frutas',
                  yaxis_title='Cantidad vendida')

# Show Chart
fig.show()
```

In this example, we define the data for three types of fruits and their corresponding quantities sold. We then create a trace for the bar graph using the `go.Bar()` function, passing in the x and y data. Next, we define the layout of the graph using the `go.Layout()` function, setting the title of the graph and the labels for the x and y axes.

Figure 2.6: Bar charts created with plotly

Finally, we create the figure using the `go.Figure()` function, passing in the trace and layout objects, and use the `fig.show()` function to display the graph in a web browser window as shown in *Figure 2.6*.

Scikit-learn

Scikit-learn is a free Python library that comes with algorithms and predictive models for classification, regression, or clustering. It is commonly used with libraries such as NumPy or Pandas.

A simple code in Python using this library would be the following:

```python
from sklearn.datasets import load_iris
from sklearn.ensemble import RandomForestClassifier
from sklearn.model_selection import train_test_split

# Load the Iris dataset
iris_data = load_iris()

# Split the dataset into training and testing data
X_train, X_test, y_train, y_test = train_test_split(iris_data.data,
iris_data.target, test_size=0.2, random_state=42)

# Create the Random Forest classifier
rf_classifier = RandomForestClassifier()

# Train the classifier using the training data
rf_classifier.fit(X_train, y_train)

# Test the classifier using the testing data
accuracy = rf_classifier.score(X_test, y_test)

# Print the accuracy of the classifier
print("Accuracy:", accuracy)
```

The Random Forest classifier is trained on the Iris dataset to predict the target variable, which represents the species of iris flowers. The Iris dataset is a well-known dataset in machine learning and consists of measurements (sepal length, sepal width, petal length, and petal width) of 150 iris flowers, belonging to three different species: setosa, versicolor, and virginica.

In this example, we first import the necessary scikit-learn modules: `load_iris` to load the Iris dataset, `RandomForestClassifier` to create the decision tree classifier, and `train_test_split` to split the data into training and testing sets. We then load the Iris dataset and it splits the data into parts for training and testing. Then, it builds a model called a Random Forest that learns from the training data. The code finally checks how well the model works on the testing data and prints its accuracy.

In summary, the code predicts the species of iris flowers (setosa, versicolor, or virginica) based on their sepal and petal measurements using a Random Forest classifier and evaluates the accuracy of the predictions on a separate testing set.

Now that you understand the importance of having programming languages among your skillset, it's time you know a bit about design skills for a data analyst. The next section will cover the design methods used in the data analyst world.

Design skills for a data analyst

A skill of little interest in programming or data analysis is design, and many may even see it as unnecessary. However, remember that at the end of the day, you will communicate with visual objects, and good design will make that communication more effective. Moreover, there must be some truth to the saying, "A picture is worth a thousand words."

Don't be confused when I say you should have design skills. What I mean is that as a data analyst, you should also think like a designer and ensure that your report is affordable, accessible, and aesthetic. How? Let's find out.

Affordable design

In terms of design, when we talk about affordability, we refer to the close relationship between humans and things, but above all the actions that can be performed on them. For example, a light switch in a room is designed to be easy to find, easy to identify, and easy to operate, making it a simple task to turn on and off the lights in your home. Such devices rarely come with a manual as we intuitively know how to use a light switch. That is affordability. It does not depend on whether the person recognizes or understands how the switch works, but rather on whether the action is possible, and the object is usable. However, even if the object is usable, if it is not located in the right place or is not clearly identified, the user may have difficulty using it, which would generate a negative user experience.

You should take this same principle into account when designing a report in Power BI, for example, and ensure that each of the visual objects you use is affordable. To do this, there are some techniques that Cole Nussbaumer mentioned in her book *Storytelling with Data*, which include highlighting important things, eliminating distractions, and creating a clear hierarchy of information.

Accessible design

Usually, the topic of accessibility in the design field refers to the ability of the design to reach people with disabilities, but if we apply it to the topic of data analysis, specifically to the design of your visualizations, it refers to the ability of your report or visualizations to be used by people with different abilities. Often, we create designs from our own perspective as engineers or specialists, but in reality, those who will consume our report are people who do not have the same abilities as us and may understand what we are trying to communicate very differently.

There are some techniques you can use to make your visualizations as accessible as possible, such as having the appropriate color contrast, clear and defined labels, and not overcomplicating visuals. Always keep in mind that if something is a little difficult for you, who has knowledge of analysis and data management, to understand, it will be even more difficult for a regular user to understand what you are trying to communicate with your report.

Aesthetic design

Making things look pretty is a very subjective topic as everyone perceives beauty or what they consider to be beautiful in a very different way. However, there are general rules that we can at least try to follow within our reports to make them as aesthetically pleasing as possible for the general public. A report or dashboard that looks good obviously generates more interest from those who consume it than one that does not, and reports or dashboards that are perceived as pretty are also perceived as easier to use.

I know that design skills are not something that can be learned overnight, but when it comes to data visualizations, a technique you can use is a simple search for some existing designs on the web. In previous chapters, we mentioned that there are public pages that allow you to create your portfolios and upload your designs, and these pages can be used as a reference to see how many analysts use some visualizations. This can be a starting point for you to have your own collection of designs that you understand are attractive and that you could use in the future within your reports.

Some basic rules that you can use as a starting point are as follows:

- Don't overload your report with multiple colors and try to follow contrast standards.
- Use free tools such as Canva or PowerPoint to create backgrounds that separate visual objects from the background.
- Try to ensure that all elements are well aligned.
- Don't be afraid of white space. We often add elements to our reports simply because there is white space that needs to be filled with something.

As a data analyst and a professional in general, it's important to have soft skills that complement your profile; the next section will cover some of the most relevant to your profile.

Soft skills

In addition to the technical skills that help you solve daily tasks as a data analyst, there are subjective skills or skills tied to the person that are difficult to quantify. These are called soft skills. Every data analyst should develop at least one of the following soft skills for career complementation and professional growth.

Communication and collaboration

Knowing how to import data from an SQL database, transform it, and create measures in Power BI does not mean you are a good analyst if you don't know how to communicate what you found. Company executives expect to make decisions based on the data you found, and it is your responsibility as an analyst to transmit the information as clearly as possible.

Problem solving

To err is human, and companies and technology are not perfect. If the data between the transactional system and the report is not matching, you as a data analyst must be able to know where to start addressing this situation and how to ask the right questions, and collaborate with coworkers to find the solution to the problem. Remember that based on your analysis, executives are likely making critical business decisions.

Critical thinking

Critical thinking is a fundamental skill for data analysts. It allows you to evaluate things logically and objectively and enables you to reach informed and accurate conclusions. If you are someone who has always wondered why things are the way they are, it is essentially questioning the validity and relevance of the information you are working with.

Research

A personal phrase I have is that the analyst does not need to know everything, but often it is enough to have the number of someone who does. Knowing how to read between the lines and search for information is also one of the essential skills you should have to be successful in your career as a data analyst.

Attention to detail

As a data analyst, you must pay close attention to detail. As mentioned earlier, companies firmly believe in the information you are transmitting through reports, and being able to detect redundancy in data, a writing error, an anomaly in a time series, or anything else that should not be where it is, such as a simple punctuation mark, will prevent the distortion of the information conveyed in your reports.

You have arrived at the end of the chapter, and we have covered most of the additional skills you need to have as a data analyst. See you in the next chapter.

Summary

In this chapter, we started covering the importance of knowing SQL and how it can be helpful for you to learn this language. I also showed you some key programming languages used in the field of data analytics and continued with a few key concepts you should take care of when designing a report. In the last section, you learned about the most relevant soft skills for a data analyst professional.

In the next chapter, we will start talking about Power BI and its workflow.

Part 2: Beyond the Borders of Power BI

In this part, you will experience building a Power BI solution from end to end. You will start with understanding the workflow of activities that a data analyst performs to build Power BI content. You will then learn about the phases of data analysis and how you can take your data and content through these phases using Power BI. Next, you will learn how to design a Power BI solution according to requirements, build it using best practices, explore your solution's data, visualize it, and then deploy and share your solution. You will then start diving into specialized skills, to program with DAX to enhance your model, build reports with expert techniques, and tell effective stories using your data. Finally, you will learn how to use dashboards and apps, before implementing security.

This part has the following chapters:

- *Chapter 3, The Power BI Workflow*
- *Chapter 4, Data Analysis with Power BI*
- *Chapter 5, Preparing, Transforming, and Modeling Data*
- *Chapter 6, Exploring, Visualizing, and Sharing Data and Deploying Solutions*
- *Chapter 7, DAX Programming*
- *Chapter 8, Expert Report Building*
- *Chapter 9, Effective Data Storytelling*
- *Chapter 10, Using Dashboards and Apps and Implementing Security*

3
The Power BI Workflow

In this chapter, we delve into the process of transforming raw data into a comprehensive report through a structured workflow of activities using Power BI. As a Power BI developer, you will find yourself regularly engaging in these activities to construct various types of reports for your stakeholders. Nevertheless, the amount of time dedicated to each task may vary depending on the data's complexity and quality as well as the report's requirements.

Data for your report may originate from an array of sources, including databases, spreadsheets (Microsoft Excel), document libraries (Microsoft SharePoint), surveys (SurveyMonkey), cloud-based business applications (Microsoft Dynamics 365 Business Central), and other different types of systems. Your role as a developer will involve cleaning, shaping, converting, and sometimes combining the data into suitable structures, analyzing and visualizing the data, and, finally, building, deploying, and sharing your report solution with stakeholders. Additionally, you will need to consider the licensing options that your stakeholder's organization has so that you can choose the appropriate functionality in Power BI when you work on these activities.

With a good understanding of the workflow of activities, you can outline your development strategy with a structured approach, making it easy to estimate the time and effort required to produce a report. Further, you can also assist with designing a Power BI solution and planning its execution.

In this chapter, we're going to cover the following main topics:

- Bringing data into Power BI
- Cleansing and transforming data
- Combining data from multiple sources
- Modeling data for analysis
- Exploring and analyzing data
- Visualizing data on a report
- Publishing and sharing Power BI content

Technical requirements

- Power BI Desktop

- SharePoint Online (`https://www.microsoft.com/en-us/microsoft-365/sharepoint/collaboration`)

Bringing data into Power BI

When you are ready to create a Power BI report, the first activity is to bring data into Power BI. Despite being a rather small and seemingly insignificant step, getting data is important. You will need to determine how you get the right data and where it comes from. There are a few questions that you would need to ask before you dive in:

- What is the original source of the data?

- How close to the original source can I get?

- Is the data consistent and standardized?

- Is there a single existing repository of data and/or analytics?

Let's explore these questions.

Imagine you are tasked with creating a sales report. You will ideally want to connect to the sales system or the sales database. You would also want to go with the production database because that is where the real and latest data live. However, if organizational policy does not allow developers to connect to production databases, you would need to look for alternatives. In this case, a test database might be suggested to you, or the last few months' data may be dumped into a **comma-separated value** (**CSV**) file. You will need to determine whether the test database has the same database structure as the production database and is not an older version or has inconsistent test data, even if the structure is accurate. On the other hand, the CSV file may have accurate data with the correct structure but with only 3 months' worth of data. This will not help you later when you want to explore and analyze your dataset. For instance, if you want the sales performance trend across the last few years or create a measure to compare the current sales against the previous year, you won't have the data for it. It also does not help that it is a CSV dump. It will raise several questions: once you develop and deploy the solution, are you going to expect someone to keep providing regular CSV dumps? Where would they land the files? Would it be a sustainable approach? Is it expected that the solution will be developed using the CSV source and will be connected to the production database when you deploy it? In this case, is it going to be a seamless operation, or would you need to put effort into converting the solution to use the database?

These are all valid questions that you will have to consider before choosing your source. For the best choice, opt for the original source system, which is the production system, or one that is as close to it as possible.

Does this mean that the use of CSV or similar file types as a source is never preferred? The answer is no; there are other scenarios where these files make sense. Take an example of an organization where financial budgets are not maintained in any system other than Excel spreadsheets each year. This makes a good case for using files as your source. However, this time, there are different questions that you need to ask before you connect to the data. Where will these files be stored for Power BI to access? Surely not on your local computer. A shared folder on the network is a good idea because it can be accessed even when your local computer is off. An even better option is **SharePoint Online**, if it is an option at all. This means you will not need a gateway to access the source files when you deploy the reports. Another important question is, does each year's file have the same structure, i.e., the same number of columns, the same names for the columns, and so forth? In a lot of cases, you will find that spreadsheets maintained by business users don't have a consistent structure. You may find new columns that were not there or not in the same order in the previous year. You may find simple yet annoying problems, such as different sheet names and spelling mistakes in the column names of certain files. You may find more complicated problems such as multiple tables, ad hoc notes, multiple headers, merged headers, and more on a single sheet, which will lead to problems and complex data preparation activities that you don't want.

Hence, it is important to convey the message clearly to the stakeholders and ensure that they provide consistently structured files. One good way of doing this is by examining the source files and providing them with a template and a process to fill in the template to provide you with the data.

As much as it is ideal to have access to data that is as close as possible to the original data source, there are organizations that may have gone through a digital transformation process of bringing their data into a single repository. This can be a central staging repository, such as a data lake, or a more sophisticated one, such as a data warehouse, where data is processed and transformed into an analytical format. In such scenarios, you don't have to look for the original source. This repository will be your single source of data unless the data that you are looking for is not available on it yet. In this case, you may go back to the rule of thumb of sourcing from the closest to the original until the data are made available on the repository. The processed data, especially those of the data warehouse, will give you the added advantage of reduced data preparation since a significant portion of the data preparation would have already been done.

Regardless, it is wise to clarify the general house rules the data owners may have established for accessing the data lake and data warehouse, especially in cases where they have both. Different organizations tend to understand the concepts of data lakes and data warehouses differently. You will need to ask questions to determine their understanding of the concepts, how they have their data structured on these systems, and the intended purpose of the systems before determining how you plan to access the right one. The rule of thumb here is to tap into the most processed and transformed data possible.

To summarize, it is important that you ask the right questions from the stakeholders and determine the best source to tap into before you access data.

Depending on your requirements and the situation, how you want to connect to data from Power BI will change. This is done by choosing the right data connectivity mode.

Data connectivity modes

Data connectivity modes specify how you connect to the source when bringing data into Power BI. There are three modes that you can use to get data:

- **Import**: This is the most common and default mode, where the data that you choose are loaded into Power BI. When data are queried, for example, by a report, the loaded data are used to service the query.

- **DirectQuery**: This is an alternative mode to import, where only the metadata of the chosen data is stored in Power BI. When the data are queried, the queries that are written to get data are converted to the source's native format, and the data are returned from the source directly. There is also a live mode that works similarly to DirectQuery when you connect to an external **analysis services** model, which Power BI just represents through itself. The difference between the two is that DirectQuery holds metadata that defines the query, whereas a live connection does not.

- **Composite**: This is a mix of both the Import and DirectQuery modes, where some tables come in through the import mode and some through DirectQuery. When you combine data from multiple DirectQuery sources, it is also referred to as composite mode.

Each mode comes with its own set of pros and cons. As a developer, you will have to determine the best mode for your solution. We will explore these modes in more detail in the coming chapters. As for this chapter, let's go with the default.

In order for you to go through the Power BI workflow of activities, you will first require Power BI Desktop. This is where you start your journey of connecting to the data that you need. Power BI provides connectors to connect to the various source systems. There are more than 100 different types of sources that you can connect to from Power BI Desktop. Not all connectors work in the same way. But once you connect to the sources of your choice, most of the actions that you will perform on the data will be the same. Let us look at how we can connect to a few common data sources.

Database systems

You shouldn't have too much of a problem connecting to database systems. Organizations usually have specific documented methods of connecting to their database systems. These methods conform to the organization's standards and policies. Power BI connectors will typically allow you to connect using the documented methods. Think of Power BI as yet another way you would connect to an organizational database that is already being connected to by other tools. In case there are no documented methods, then you could refer to the documentation for connectors in Power Query (`https://learn.microsoft.com/en-us/power-query/connectors/`).

In our example, let us use a **Microsoft SQL Server** database as the source (as seen in *Figure 3.1*):

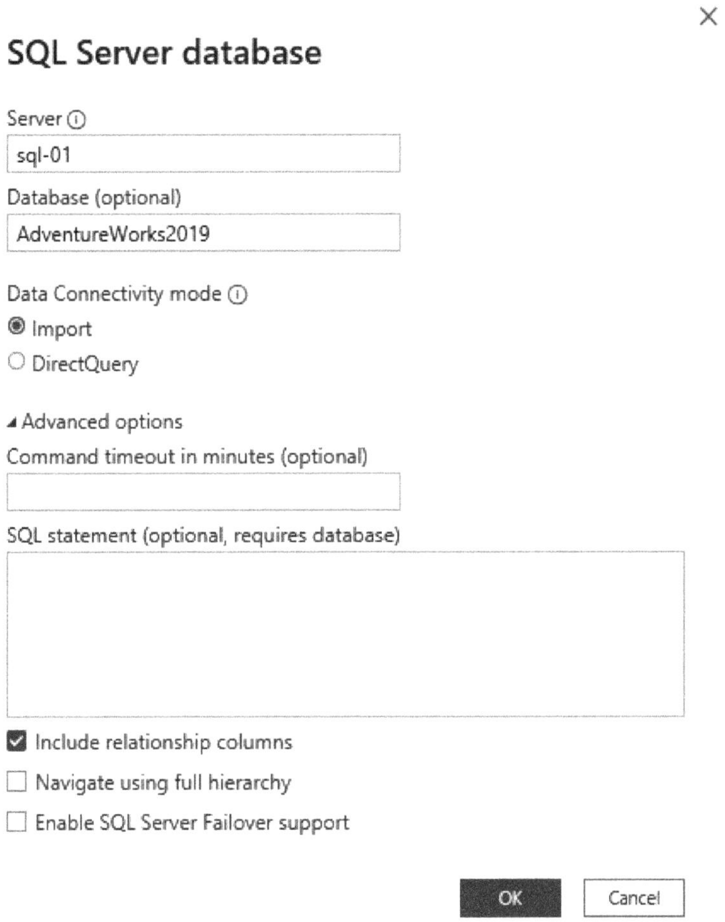

Figure 3.1: SQL Server connector dialog

We shall go with the default values for **Server** (name), **Data Connectivity Mode**, and **Include Relationship Columns**. In addition, I have selected the option of entering the database name. You can also optionally enter a SQL statement if there is a very specific dataset you want, but in almost all cases, we need the flexibility of being able to choose different tables and explore and build different types of queries to build a versatile model:

SQL Server database   ✕

🛢 sql-01;AdventureWorks2019

Windows

Database

Microsoft account

User name

| dbuser1 |

Password

| ••••••• |

Select which level to apply these settings to

| sql-01 | ▾ |

| Back | | Connect | | Cancel |

Figure 3.2: SQL Server credentials dialog

It is good to obtain read-only credentials to the source, even if Power BI will not be altering anything. Once you submit the right credentials and you get authenticated, that's all that is needed to connect to a database.

Although it is quite simple to connect to a Microsoft SQL Server database, certain other databases require additional steps before you can connect to them. For instance, **MySQL** and **SAP HANA** require additional components that you need to install before you attempt to connect. When you select the MySQL connector, for example, Power BI will prompt you with the following message with a link to learn more about what you need to do:

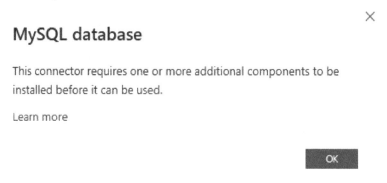

MySQL database

This connector requires one or more additional components to be installed before it can be used.

Learn more

| OK |

Figure 3.3: MySQL connector details dialog

The **Learn more** link will take you to the components that need to be installed before successfully connecting to MySQL.

Another example, **MariaDB**, requires third-party components to be installed. When you select the MariaDB connector, you will notice a slightly different message:

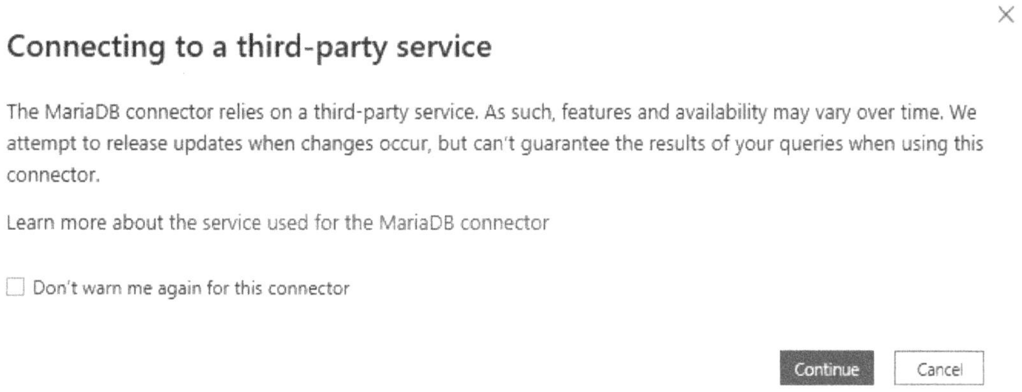

×

Connecting to a third-party service

The MariaDB connector relies on a third-party service. As such, features and availability may vary over time. We attempt to release updates when changes occur, but can't guarantee the results of your queries when using this connector.

Learn more about the service used for the MariaDB connector

☐ Don't warn me again for this connector

Continue   Cancel

Figure 3.4: Third-party service connectivity details dialog

This is Microsoft basically stating that they are not responsible for the results of the queries since the connector relies on a third-party service that may change without warning.

Next, we shall look at files and spreadsheets as sources since they are the fallback when a database system is not available as a source.

Files and spreadsheets

A couple of the most common types of files and spreadsheets are CSV files and Microsoft Excel spreadsheets. A number of organizations often use Excel spreadsheets to extend their enterprise systems that lack certain functionality, and these spreadsheets soon become an application-dashboard-reporting combination. In many cases, these combinations are provided as sources for reporting without any modifications. As explained previously in the *Bringing data into Power BI* section, this is where you need to tread with caution, look for the means to make the data structures in these files into a template, and use consistent filenames when storing them.

Spreadsheets are often used to store financial budgets and sales budgets. Since financial budgets are set annually and sales budgets are set differently per region, it is common to find yearly budget files per region. If you think about it, a group of files that is used for a single purpose is like using pieces of the same database table. Hence, a folder on SharePoint with set annual budget files can be compared to a budgets table:

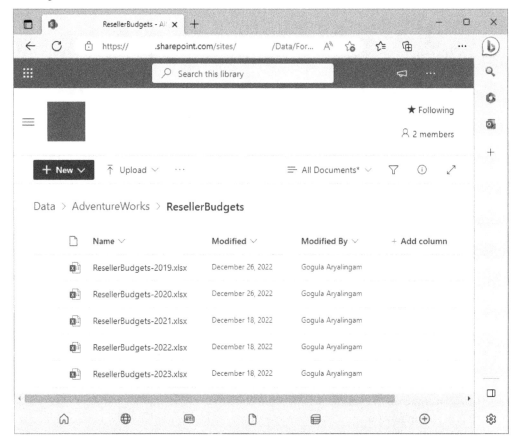

Figure 3.5: Budget files in a SharePoint Online folder

The filenames stored in the folder should have standard naming and a standard structure. The closer they are to a table, the better, as can be seen in the following image:

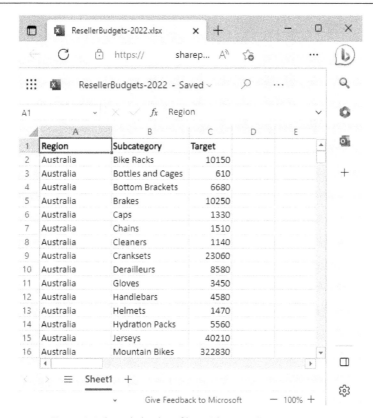

Figure 3.6: Sample budget files with a consistent structure

As a data analyst connecting with stakeholders and data owners, striving towards a standard file source is important before you start connecting to those files.

Let's take the example of connecting to a SharePoint folder with standardized annual sales budget files from Power BI.

Instead of choosing the Excel Workbook or Text/CSV connector, you would choose a SharePoint folder from the **Get Data** dialog:

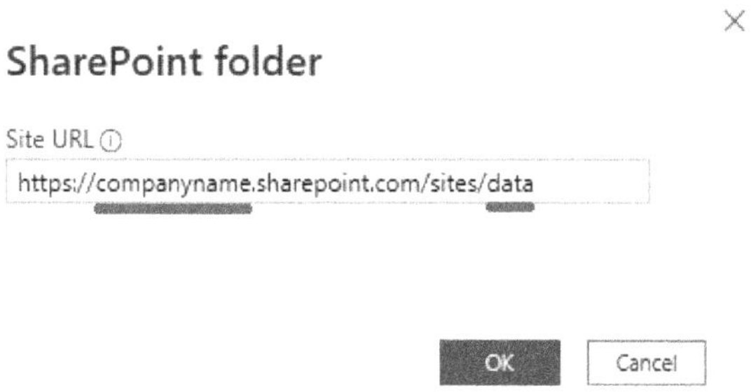

SharePoint folder

Site URL ⓘ

https://companyname.sharepoint.com/sites/data

OK   Cancel

Figure 3.7: SharePoint folder connection

The thing to remember here is that you start by connecting to the SharePoint site, which may consist of all sorts of files amongst a plethora of folders that store these files, out of which just one has the budgets files. If you compare the folder with a table that stores the same data, then the site is comparable to the database. So, in this example, by connecting to the site, you are connecting to the *database*.

The next step is to get to your table. Unfortunately, this is not very straightforward because the moment you specify the site and provide your credentials in the subsequent dialog, you get connected to the entire dataset of files, which you are left to navigate:

Content	Name	Extension	Date accessed	Date modified	Date created	Attributes
Binary	ResellerBudgets-2022.xlsx	.xlsx	null	12/18/2022 9:29:51 PM	12/18/2022 9:13:29 PM	Record
Binary	ResellerBudgets-2019.xlsx	.xlsx	null	12/26/2022 3:06:08 PM	12/18/2022 9:25:18 PM	Record
Binary	ResellerBudgets-2020.xlsx	.xlsx	null	12/26/2022 3:40:43 PM	12/18/2022 9:26:46 PM	Record
Binary	ResellerBudgets-2021.xlsx	.xlsx	null	12/18/2022 9:30:09 PM	12/18/2022 9:28:20 PM	Record
Binary	ResellerBudgets-2023.xlsx	.xlsx	null	12/18/2022 9:29:51 PM	2/4/2023 4:27:47 PM	Record
Binary	ResellerBudgetWeightage.xlsx	.xlsx	null	2/4/2023 9:00:28 PM	2/4/2023 7:11:59 PM	Record
Binary	KPITargets.xlsx	.xlsx	null	2/16/2023 11:13:39 PM	2/16/2023 10:56:50 PM	Record
Binary	KPIOwners.xlsx	.xlsx	null	2/18/2023 11:55:44 AM	2/18/2023 11:41:03 AM	Record
Binary	sales report.pdf	.pdf	null	4/9/2023 12:47:06 PM	4/9/2023 12:47:07 PM	Record
Binary	Sales Data 2022.xlsx	.xlsx	null	4/9/2023 12:47:30 PM	4/9/2023 12:47:31 PM	Record
Binary	Financial Statament-raw 23.xlsx	.xlsx	null	4/9/2023 12:47:47 PM	4/9/2023 12:47:48 PM	Record
Binary	Finance statement draft v1.23.docx	.docx	null	4/9/2023 12:48:03 PM	4/9/2023 12:48:03 PM	Record
Binary	Financial-Statement-202304.pdf	.pdf	null	4/9/2023 12:48:20 PM	4/9/2023 12:48:21 PM	Record
Binary	Mktg pres-chris-2.pptx	.pptx	null	4/9/2023 12:48:44 PM	4/9/2023 12:48:44 PM	Record

Figure 3.8: SharePoint folder preview

This is where you leave the territory of bringing data and move into the territory of cleansing and transforming data, but this is a necessary step to take if we want to get to the right folder. Just know that these steps are conceptually part of the same process of bringing data:

1. Click on the **Transform data** button, which takes you to the Power Query Editor window.

2. Filter the **Folder Path** using the **Contains…** text filter option:

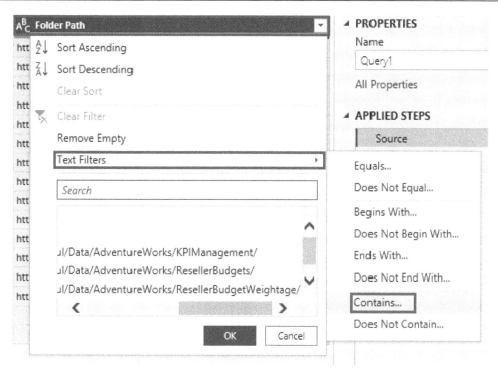

Figure 3.9: Folder path text filter option

3. Enter the relative folder path. In this example, the value is `/Data/AdventureWorks/ResellerBudgets`, which results in Power Query being filtered to only the required files.

> **Important note**
>
> Tip: Parameterize the SharePoint folder connection. Use a parameter for each of the following: the SharePoint URL, the document library portion of the folder path, and the rest of the relative folder path. This will make the file reusable against different sets of files stored across different SharePoint sites and document libraries.

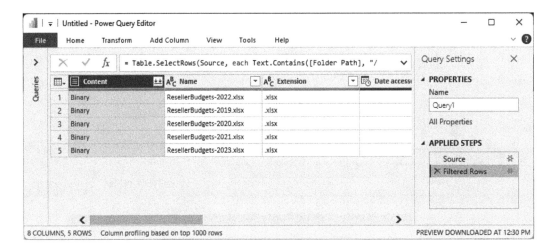

Figure 3.10: Power Query with filtered files

4.   We need to edit the query further as per the following:

   ▪   Extract the year from the filename.

   ▪   Remove other columns and leave the binary content and the year.

   The query now looks like this: the Name column was split twice, first at the hyphen ("-") and then on the period ("."), before removing the unwanted columns (*Figure 3.11*):

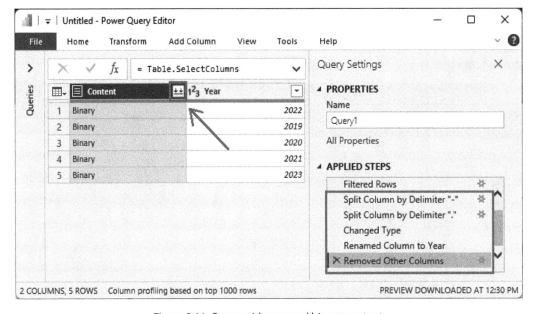

Figure 3.11: Query with year and binary content

5. The final step is to combine files. Just a click on the **Combine Files** button next to the `Content` column will set up a custom function to combine the files into a single dataset with the help of helper queries. It will also invoke the function and expand the tables of data:

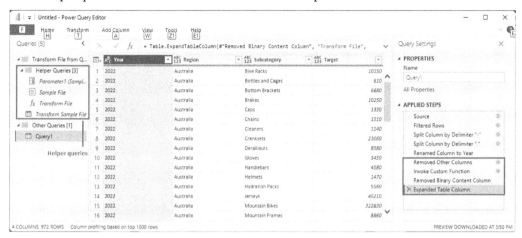

Figure 3.12: Result from Excel spreadsheets on a SharePoint folder

We now have a single result set combined from multiple similar spreadsheets across years and regions. As more files are added, the same query will combine these files into the same result set without you having to do any more work.

> **Important note**
>
> Tip: Create a connection template. Save the file as a **Power BI Template** (**PBIT**) file so that you can reuse it when you need it without having to run through the same steps each time you need to connect to a SharePoint folder.

Data lakes and data warehouses are repositories with centrally managed pre-processed data. Here, the table is turned when it comes to choosing data. Instead of looking for the original-most dataset, we need to look for the most-processed dataset from within the lake or warehouse that fits your requirements.

Data lakes and data warehouses

When connecting to data lakes, you need to keep in mind that newer implementations of data lakes use a database-like layer, such as what is offered by **Databricks**. Databricks is a data lakehouse technology that combines the best features of data lakes and data warehouses. Older implementations of data lakes may require you to tap into the file system to access files such as Parquet-formatted files. **Parquet** is an open, compressed, analytics-optimized file format that is commonly used to store data in data lakes.

With data warehouses, it becomes much easier since it is practically the same as connecting to databases. After all, many organizations still run their data warehouses on database systems such as Microsoft SQL Server.

It is also important to determine if the organization has built data marts on top of its data warehouse or data lake. Data marts are subsets of data from the data lake or data warehouse that tend to have even more processing and transformation done in them and are preferred when getting data for Power BI. However, once again, a little caution given to the wind is needed since different organizations interpret data marts in different ways. For some, a data mart can be a BI semantic model built using Azure Analysis Services or Power BI itself. For others, it can be a set of views created in the data warehouse itself as a second layer. For certain users, it may even be their first iteration of the data warehouse built only for a specific department.

Hence, use the rule of thumb to determine the best-processed system from the set of data lakes, data warehouses, and data marts the organization has.

Once you have connected to the data, the next step is to cleanse and then transform the data.

Cleansing and transforming data

Data, in their raw form, are usually not structured for analysis and may have undesired elements in them as well. Hence, it is important that the data are scrubbed of what you do not desire and are shaped into an analytics-friendly form.

Cleansing

Data stored on systems often have problems that don't make them reporting-ready. Some of these problems, which are quite common across organizations, are the following:

- **Inconsistency**: This is where data in the same table are entered in different ways by users, or different formats are used to enter the data; for example, dates are entered using the YYYYMMDD format by some and MM/DD/YYYY by others.

- **Incomplete data**: This is where data are entered only into some fields for most records or where entire important fields are left empty.

- **Incorrect data**: This is where the wrong information is entered by the users.

- **Data duplication**: This is where the same data is entered multiple times, sometimes with small, undetected variations.

Cleansing data problems ranges from simple tasks, such as replacing one value with another, to complex tasks, such as identifying outliers in a table before correcting them with the right data.

Before you start cleansing the data, you need to first visualize what your end-result tables are going to look like. This is because, along with cleansing, you will also need to transform your data.

Transforming

Data in your source systems are usually structured for transactions. In database management systems, this is usually achieved by the process of normalization. However, in BI, data needs to be structured for analytics. This means you need to use the other method of denormalization.

> **Important note**
>
> Normalization is a database design term, whereas normalizing is a data preparation term. You have encountered the former here and will encounter the latter in this chapter. You need to be vigilant about which word is being used since both terms are related.

In a transactional database, such as in a sales system, the product entity could be broken into three hierarchical tables according to normalization rules:

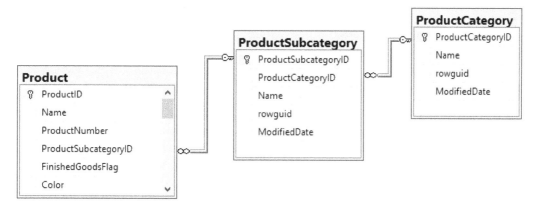

Figure 3.13: Normalized product entity on a transactional database

In a Power BI system, the product entity will be transformed into a product dimension. A dimension is designed to keep only those fields that are required for analysis and is best set as a single table:

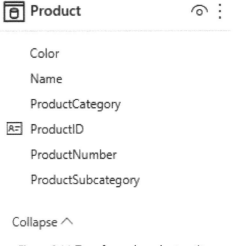

Figure 3.14: Transformed product entity

Now, before you dive into cleansing and transforming data, you will need to first visualize what your tables are going to look like. This is a much bigger exercise and involves the design aspect of data transformation and modeling. We will be exploring design in *Chapter 5*. However, for now, you need to keep in mind that transforming does not mean that you blindly convert the structure of existing tables into some obscure form. Rather, it means cleaning and fitting the source data into a pre-determined structure that you have envisioned for analysis.

Source data comes in all sorts of shapes and sizes. Even though you definitely have to consider the size aspect when building a Power BI solution, when cleansing and transforming data, you deal with the shape aspect. Cleansing and transforming data is arguably the most time-consuming activity in the Power BI workflow, where you should also keep in mind aspects of the next two activities: combining data and modeling data.

Power Query

You have already seen how Power Query comes in handy when setting up a standardized process to retrieve data. Power Query plays a much bigger part, though, in the process of cleansing and transforming data.

Let's take the example from above. Using the knowledge from earlier in this chapter, we shall connect to a SQL Server database and retrieve data from the three tables: `Product`, `ProductSubcategory`, and `ProductCategory`.

Since the option to include relationship columns was enabled by default when we connected to SQL Server (*Figure 3.1*), and since we know that the three tables are related, we only need to select the `Product` table, click on **Transform Data**, and choose the import mode:

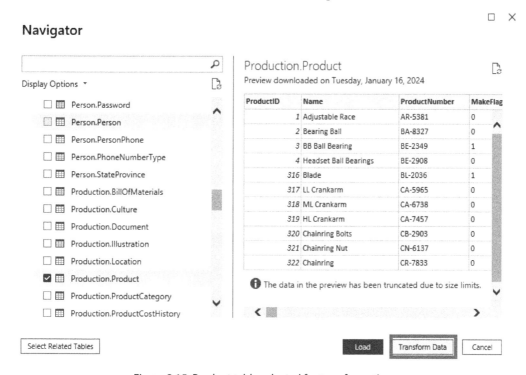

Figure 3.15: Product table selected for transformation

This will bring up the Power Query window with the Product query.

In Power Query, each table or dataset you connect to is made available in a tabular format, which we call a query. This is because we are still in the process of manipulating the data to shape them to our needs. Every action that we perform on the query provides a preview of what the result will look like. Once you are satisfied with the results and have applied the changes, the data will load into Power BI. During loading, the transformations that you defined in the query, i.e., each step, are applied to the table(s) before you get your result.

In our case, this is what we are going to do:

Choose only the columns that we need from the `Product` table, i.e., `ProductID`, `Name`, `ProductNumber`, `Color`, and `ProductLine`. In addition, `ProductModel` and `ProductSubcategory` information is also required. You will notice that the latter two columns are a representation of these tables showing up within the `Product` table since they are related to it. The **Expand column** icon next to the column header and the cell values of the column indicate this:

ProductID	Name	ProductNumber	Color	ProductLine	Production.ProductModel	Production.ProductSubcategory
200	527 Spokes	SK-9283		null	null Value	Value
201	528 Seat Lug	SL-0931		null	null Value	Value
202	529 Stem	SM-9087		null	null Value	Value
203	530 Seat Post	SP-2981		null	null Value	Value
204	531 Steerer	SR-2098		null	null Value	Value
205	532 Seat Stays	SS-2985		null	null Value	Value
206	535 Seat Tube	ST-9828		null	null Value	Value
207	534 Top Tube	TO-2301		null	null Value	Value
208	535 Tension Pulley	TP-0923		null	null Value	Value
209	679 Rear Derailleur Cage	RC-0291	Silver		null Value	Value
210	680 HL Road Frame - Black, 58	FR-R92B-58	Black	R	Value	Value
211	706 HL Road Frame - Red, 58	FR-R92R-58	Red	R	Value	Value
212	707 Sport-100 Helmet, Red	HL-U509-R	Red	S	Value	Value
213	708 Sport-100 Helmet, Black	HL-U509	Black	S	Value	Value
214	709 Mountain Bike Socks, M	SO-B909-M	White	M	Value	Value
215	710 Mountain Bike Socks, L	SO-B909-L	White	M	Value	Value
216	711 Sport-100 Helmet, Blue	HL-U509-B	Blue	S	Value	Value
217	712 AWC Logo Cap	CA-1098	Multi	S	Value	Value
218	713 Long-Sleeve Logo Jersey, S	LJ-0192-S	Multi	S	Value	Value
219	714 Long-Sleeve Logo Jersey, M	LJ-0192-M	Multi	S	Value	Value
220	715 Long-Sleeve Logo Jersey, L	LJ-0192-L	Multi	S	Value	Value

Figure 3.16: Product expanded with columns from other tables

Clicking on the icon will list the columns from the table, where we expand the table with only the columns we need. In the case of `ProductModel`, we only need **Name**:

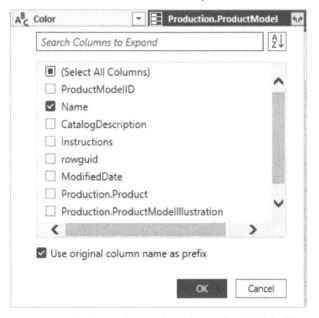

Figure 3.17: Column selection from the ProductModel table

In the case of `ProductSubcategory`, we need the `Name` and `ProductCategory` fields. You will notice that `ProductCategory` itself is a table that needs to be further expanded to retrieve the `Name`.

Once we have the names of all three tables and have renamed them accordingly, the result will look like the following:

	ProductID	Name	ProductNumber	Color	Model	Subcategory	Category
	● Valid 100% ● Error 0% ● Empty 0%	● Valid 100% ● Error 0% ● Empty 0%	● Valid 100% ● Error 0% ● Empty 0%	● Valid 51% ● Error 0% ● Empty 49%	● Valid 59% ● Error 0% ● Empty 41%	● Valid 59% ● Error 0% ● Empty 41%	● Valid 59% ● Error 0% ● Empty 41%
1	1	Adjustable Race	AR-5381	null	null	null	null
2	2	Bearing Ball	BA-8327	null	null	null	null
3	3	BB Ball Bearing	BE-2349	null	null	null	null
4	4	Headset Ball Bearings	BE-2908	null	null	null	null
5	316	Blade	BL-2036	null	null	Pedals	Components
6	317	LL Crankarm	CA-5965	Black	null	null	null
7	318	ML Crankarm	CA-6738	Black	null	null	null
8	319	HL Crankarm	CA-7457	Black	null	null	null
9	320	Chainring Bolts	CB-2903	Silver	null	null	null
10	321	Chainring Nut	CN-6137	Silver	null	null	null
11	322	Chainring	CR-7833	Black	null	null	null
12	323	Crown Race	CR-9981	null	null	null	null
13	324	Chain Stays	CS-2812	null	null	null	null
14	325	Decal 1	DC-8732	null	null	null	null
15	326	Decal 2	DC-9824	null	null	null	null
16	327	Down Tube	DT-2377	null	null	null	null

Figure 3.18: Expanded product data

Next, let's clean up a little. You may notice a lot of empty or null values across several of the fields. Null values are frowned upon when analyzing data. A good way to get rid of them is to replace them with a placeholder value, such as `Unknown`, `Unspecified`, or `N/A`. This will provide a more streamlined experience when reporting and analyzing information. It will also give the business the extent of the missing information on their systems and lead to corrective action:

	ProductID	Name	ProductNumber	Color	Product Line	Model	Subcategory	Category
200	527	Spokes	SK-9283	<Unspecified>	<Unspecified>	<Unspecified>	<Unspecified>	<Unspecified>
201	528	Seat Lug	SL-0931	<Unspecified>	<Unspecified>	<Unspecified>	<Unspecified>	<Unspecified>
202	529	Stem	SM-9087	<Unspecified>	<Unspecified>	<Unspecified>	<Unspecified>	<Unspecified>
203	530	Seat Post	SP-2981	<Unspecified>	<Unspecified>	<Unspecified>	<Unspecified>	<Unspecified>
204	531	Steerer	SR-2098	<Unspecified>	<Unspecified>	<Unspecified>	<Unspecified>	<Unspecified>
205	532	Seat Stays	SS-2985	<Unspecified>	<Unspecified>	<Unspecified>	<Unspecified>	<Unspecified>
206	533	Seat Tube	ST-9828	<Unspecified>	<Unspecified>	<Unspecified>	<Unspecified>	<Unspecified>
207	534	Top Tube	TO-2301	<Unspecified>	<Unspecified>	<Unspecified>	<Unspecified>	<Unspecified>
208	535	Tension Pulley	TP-0923	<Unspecified>	<Unspecified>	<Unspecified>	<Unspecified>	<Unspecified>
209	679	Rear Derailleur Cage	RC-0291	Silver	<Unspecified>	<Unspecified>	<Unspecified>	<Unspecified>
210	680	HL Road Frame - Black, 58	FR-R92B-58	Black	R	HL Road Frame	Road Frames	Components
211	706	HL Road Frame - Red, 58	FR-R92R-58	Red	R	HL Road Frame	Road Frames	Components
212	707	Sport-100 Helmet, Red	HL-U509-R	Red	S	Sport-100	Helmets	Accessories
213	708	Sport-100 Helmet, Black	HL-U509	Black	S	Sport-100	Helmets	Accessories
214	709	Mountain Bike Socks, M	SO-B909-M	White	M	Mountain Bike Socks	Socks	Clothing
215	710	Mountain Bike Socks, L	SO-B909-L	White	M	Mountain Bike Socks	Socks	Clothing
216	711	Sport-100 Helmet, Blue	HL-U509-B	Blue	S	Sport-100	Helmets	Accessories
217	712	AWC Logo Cap	CA-1098	Multi	S	Cycling Cap	Caps	Clothing
218	713	Long-Sleeve Logo Jersey, S	LJ-0192-S	Multi	S	Long-Sleeve Logo Jersey	Jerseys	Clothing
219	714	Long-Sleeve Logo Jersey, M	LJ-0192-M	Multi	S	Long-Sleeve Logo Jersey	Jerseys	Clothing
220	715	Long-Sleeve Logo Jersey, L	LJ-0192-L	Multi	S	Long-Sleeve Logo Jersey	Jerseys	Clothing

Figure 3.19: Cleansed and transformed product data

Now that we have cleansed and transformed the product data into a shape that is optimized for analysis, let's get into the next section: combining data.

Combining data from multiple sources

Combining data from multiple tables from within a single system and across systems is a common data preparation activity. It is advisable and is a general rule of thumb to first have the data from each table cleansed as much as possible before you attempt to combine it with another. Of course, there can always be exceptions to this rule, such as when you want to combine multiple similar files, in which case you must first combine and then apply the same cleansing rules across all these files in one go.

In the *Cleansing and transforming data* section, while cleansing and transforming, we inadvertently combined data from multiple tables: `Product`, `ProductSubcategory`, and `ProductCategory`. Having related tables from a transactional database, such as SQL Server, provides the option of automatically combining the tables based on foreign keys (*Figure 3.1*). Hence, we did this without having to think too much by selecting columns from the related tables through the `Product` table itself.

However, this may not always be the case, especially if the data are coming from two separate systems. Consider this example: The product line of each product is marked only as **M, R, S,** and **T** in the `Product` table (*Figure 3.19*). When analyzing sales and putting up information on reports, an end user would prefer to see the proper name of the product line against the sales numbers instead of an abbreviation. The product line names are stored in a Microsoft Excel spreadsheet since the database does not have a table that holds this data. Let's host this spreadsheet on the same SharePoint document library that we used earlier and bring it into Power BI using the same method (*Figure 3.7*):

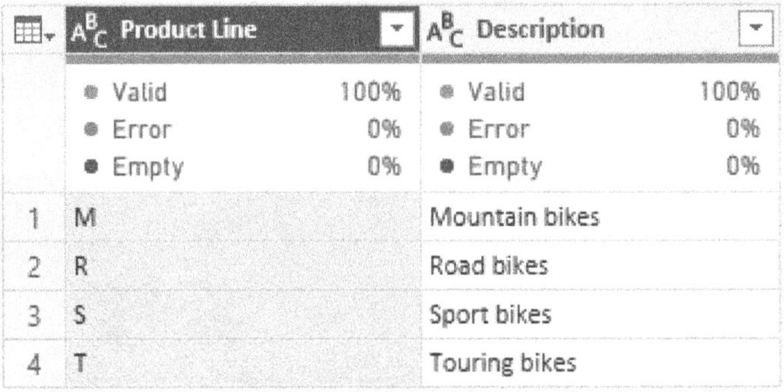

⊞▾	A^B_C Product Line	▾	A^B_C Description	▾
	● Valid	100%	● Valid	100%
	● Error	0%	● Error	0%
	● Empty	0%	● Empty	0%
1	M		Mountain bikes	
2	R		Road bikes	
3	S		Sport bikes	
4	T		Touring bikes	

Figure 3.20: Product line data

Now that we have the two queries ready (*Figure 3.19* and *Figure 3.20*), we can now combine them. `Product`, as we have already determined, represents the primary table here. When selecting the **Product** query, click on the **Merge Queries** button on the **Home** tab of Power Query. This will open the **Merge** window with the `Product` table selected. In the drop-down below it, select the `Product Line` table, which is the table you want to join **Product** with. You then select the `ProductLine` column from `Product` and the `Product Line` column from the `Product Line` table to indicate that these are the columns you want to join. From the **Join Kind** dropdown, we shall choose **Left Outer** to indicate that we want all the records from the primary table, `Product`, and the matching rows from the `Product Line` table:

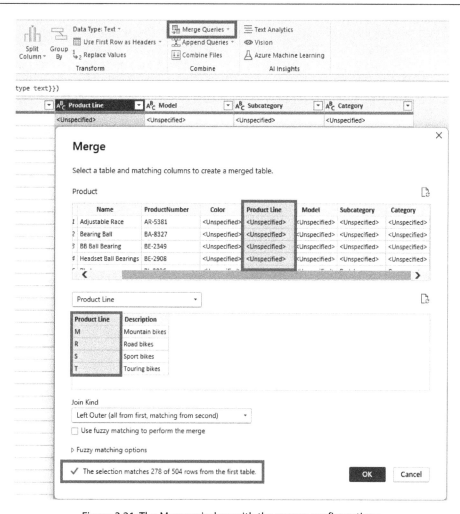

Figure 3.21: The Merge window with the merge configurations

This would now result in our **Product** query looking like the following:

ProductLine		Model		Subcategory		Category		Product Line	
● Valid	100%	● Valid	100%	● Valid	100%	● Valid	100%	● Valid	100%
● Error	0%	● Error	0%	● Error	0%	● Error	0%	● Error	0%
● Empty	0%	● Empty	0%	● Empty	0%	● Empty	0%	● Empty	0%
<Unspecified>		<Unspecified>		<Unspecified>		<Unspecified>		Table	
<Unspecified>		<Unspecified>		<Unspecified>		<Unspecified>		Table	
<Unspecified>		<Unspecified>		<Unspecified>		<Unspecified>		Table	
<Unspecified>		<Unspecified>		<Unspecified>		<Unspecified>		Table	
<Unspecified>		<Unspecified>		Pedals		Components		Table	
<Unspecified>		<Unspecified>		<Unspecified>		<Unspecified>		Table	

Figure 3.22: Product Line merged within Product

This is a familiar screen from when we included the columns from `ProductModel` and `ProductSubcategory` into `Product` (previously, see *Figure 3.18*), except that instead of `Values`, it shows `Table`. When you expand the table, Power Query will list the columns, where we just choose **Description** since we already have the product line. The result is the **Product** query with the product line descriptions. Since not all products have product lines, and since we used a **Left Outer** join, you will notice many descriptions showing up with null values, which is expected. When you scroll down, you will notice the records with product lines showing up with the correct descriptions. By applying a bit of the cleansing technique we learned earlier, we will now have a **Product** query holding the perfect product line description:

A^B_C Model		A^B_C Subcategory		A^B_C Category		A^B_C Product Line.Description	
● Valid	100%	● Valid	100%	● Valid	100%	● Valid	100%
● Error	0%	● Error	0%	● Error	0%	● Error	0%
● Empty	0%	● Empty	0%	● Empty	0%	● Empty	0%
<Unspecified>		<Unspecified>		<Unspecified>		<Unspecified>	
<Unspecified>		<Unspecified>		<Unspecified>		<Unspecified>	
HL Road Frame		Road Frames		Components		Road bikes	
HL Road Frame		Road Frames		Components		Road bikes	
Sport-100		Helmets		Accessories		Sport bikes	
Sport-100		Helmets		Accessories		Sport bikes	
Mountain Bike Socks		Socks		Clothing		Mountain bikes	
Mountain Bike Socks		Socks		Clothing		Mountain bikes	
Sport-100		Helmets		Accessories		Sport bikes	
Cycling Cap		Caps		Clothing		Sport bikes	

Figure 3.23: Product with product line information combined

Merging two tables is a way of combining (joining) related tables side by side to include more columns. Sometimes, there is also the need to combine similar but entirely different datasets to create a larger dataset. For example, you may have regular channel-based sales data coming from your database, while the lesser channel of direct sales is tracked through spreadsheets at the factory outlet. These datasets, however, must be combined vertically (appended) so that direct sales and distributor sales are in one single table. To append data, you will use the **Append Queries** option in Power Query.

Once you have cleansed, transformed, and combined data, you are done with the data preparation phase. The next phase is where you model the data.

Modeling data for analysis

Modeling is where you structure your Power BI semantic model to represent the business processes from an analytical standpoint. In essence, modeling actually starts before development. It is part of designing your Power BI solution.

We shall dive deeper into the details of modeling in *Chapter 5*. Here, let us look at what you, as a developer, would do. But remember, at every point of modeling data, you are, or should be, following a design that has been thought out. Even the data that you cleanse, transform, and combine are driven by what your model design dictates.

To model data effectively, you will need to use the right modeling technique. Let us look at the **star schema**, a popular analytics modeling technique.

Star schema

The recommended design technique for Power BI models is the star schema modeling approach. Regardless of your requirements, building your model according to this technique gives users a versatile, performant, and intuitive analysis experience. When you use the star schema to model data on Power BI, you categorize your tables into either dimension tables or fact tables. You then connect the fact tables to the applicable dimension tables to create the star.

> **Important note**
> The concept of the star schema is covered in depth in *Chapter 5*, where we learn how to design a semantic model. For now, let's just ride the wave to obtain a simple star.

Throughout the examples we've covered thus far, we now have sales data and product data already in place in Power Query. Hence, we can start modeling these data by applying the star schema principle to them.

We click on the **Close & Apply** button on Power Query to load data into Power BI. We can quickly determine that **Sales** is the fact table because it holds the facts we want to analyze. Facts are almost always numerical in nature and are aggregated for analysis.

In this case, our facts are **Quantity** and **Amount**. Along with these, the sales table also comes with a few ID columns that represent the customer, salesperson, and product, as well as the order date. This tells you that these are the dimensions that you can analyze your facts with.

You will also notice that we did not bring many other probable dimension IDs and other columns when we queried sales. One reason is to keep things simple. In the real world, you will look at all applicable dimensions and bring them in. However, columns that don't fit into the fact or dimension criteria can be left behind, for example, row GUIDs, comments, and last updated time.

Next, you need to relate the two tables. To relate two tables in Power BI, you will need to have at least one column that is the same on both. In this example, we've already worked our way there by ensuring the `ProductID` is present on both tables. You also will need to ensure that the relationship between the two tables is one-to-one or one-to-many. Power BI supports many-to-many relationships between two tables. However, since this needs to be used with caution, we shall cover that in a later chapter.

The `Product` table naturally has one record per product. The `Sales` table, on the other hand, has multiple transactions that are made against the same product. This makes it a one-to-many relationship and will work well for us.

Now that we have determined that `ProductID` is the relationship column, to create the relationship, we need to navigate to the **Model view** in Power BI.

You will notice that the relationship is already automatically created. Power BI considers the names, data types, and the data of the related columns to determine if a relationship is possible and creates it for you. In certain cases, this does not happen, in which case, you just need to click and drag one column onto the other to establish the relationship:

Figure 3.24: Sales–Product relationship

Apart from ensuring that the tables support the right type of relationship, you also need to ensure that the data types of each column on either table are compatible. This means that having a whole number on one side and text on the other side would not work, whereas having a whole number on one side and a decimal number on the other would work. Yet, the rule of thumb should be to keep both sides using the same data type.

We have two more dimensions for **Sales** support, customers, and salespersons. By going through the same process of getting, cleansing, transforming, and combining data, we can bring in the **Customer** and **Salesperson** tables for the schema, as per the following:

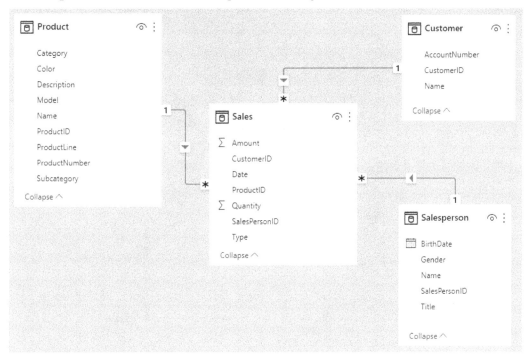

Figure 3.25: Sales with product, customer, and salesperson relationships

Just as we think we are done with relating tables, the Date column catches our eye. In business intelligence, a date and its variations (such as month, quarter, and year) represent a flexible analysis playground. Hence, a date or calendar table is something that you would see in almost every business intelligence solution. We shall, however, leave the Date table out for now since we will be looking at it in depth later. Nevertheless, we can use Power BI auto-generated date hierarchy in place of the Date table for now.

When we focus on the table relationships, we clearly see the `Sales` fact table at the center and the three dimension tables around it, resulting in a star structure, albeit one with just three points (*Figure 3.26*):

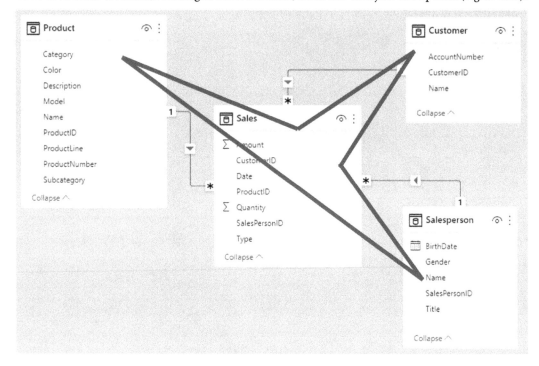

Figure 3.26: Basic star schema with three dimension tables

We now have a basic model. Next, we need to enhance it so that end users and analysts have a better analysis experience.

Model enhancement

Business users often don't only analyze the bare metal facts in the tables. There are calculations that they do on top of these to get specific business insights. They call these calculations business measures, and these are part of an organization's standard method of measuring success and performance.

Another closely related term is **key performance indicator** (**KPI**), which is basically a business measure that is aligned with targets or goals and is usually stringently monitored for trends and conformity. Part of your data modeling should cater to providing business measures and KPIs, which can be done by creating Power BI measures using DAX. **Data analysis expressions** (**DAX**) is a formula language used in Power BI for creating different types of calculations.

The sales table in our example contains two main types of sales: reseller sales and internet sales. There is also a lesser type, direct sales, that happens on a small scale. When compared to the main types, direct sales numbers are almost negligible. However, certain analyses will require looking only at direct sales. Hence, you can create a measure called **Direct Sales** using the aggregated `Amount` fact column and set the filter to take only direct sales from the `Type` column. Measures can be created using the **New Measure** option from the **Home** ribbon using the following DAX expression:

```
Direct Sales = CALCULATE ( SUM ( Sales[Amount] ), Sales[Type]="Direct"
)
```

The measure will appear among the columns of the table you have selected at the time of creation. You can easily move the measure to a suitable table if required. In our case, we'll keep the measure in the sales table. Users now have a ready-to-use measure for direct sales and do not have to filter it each time they want to use it.

When a dimension has many columns, sometimes the order in which a certain set of columns should be used may not be very clear to users. Creating a hierarchy of related columns to reflect their natural hierarchy in the business provides yet another intuitive way for business users to analyze data.

The product dimension's `Category`, `Subcategory`, and `Name` form a natural hierarchy in the business. With a few easy clicks, you can create a hierarchy as per the following steps:

1. Right-click on the top-level column, `Category`, and select **Category Hierarchy**, which immediately creates a hierarchy named **Category Hierarchy**.

2. To add the next-level columns `Subcategory` and `Name` to the hierarchy, right-click on each column, select **Add to hierarchy**, and then select **Category Hierarchy**.

3. Rename the hierarchy to something meaningful, such as `Categorization`. You can create as many hierarchies as possible that make sense.

> **Important note**
>
> Tip: Housekeeping a clean look. Columns that are not used for analysis can be hidden from the model. Instances of such columns are the ID columns that are used to relate tables, the columns that are frequently used as part of a hierarchy and rarely as an individual column, and the columns only used to sort other columns, such as fiscal month number. Remember that these columns are important and are very much required in a model; it is just that their primary function is not to be used for analysis.

Figure 3.27 shows the spruced-up model from the model and report views. Note that the report view (on the right) will give most business users an intuitive feel, with only the elements needed for analysis present. Further housekeeping tasks on your model may include the following:

* Appropriately configuring the column data types and formatting options, such as with currency and percentages.

- Renaming columns into space-separated words; for example, `Account  Number` instead of `AccountNumber`.

Figure 3.27: Model with a clean look (model and report views)

Your model is now golden for sharing amongst business users and for you to do your own analysis. Remember, apart from being the source for reports and dashboards, your model is the epitome of versatile analysis, meaning it is a first-class object that business users can interact with to obtain insights and do their own analysis; it should not be considered just a back-end database.

Once you've built your model, it's time to take it out for a spin.

Exploring and analyzing data

This is where you start exploring the data that you have modeled, try to make sense of it, and look for insights.

We have two measures that we can play around with in a model: `Amount` and `Quantity`. Let's start out our analysis by putting up `Amount` broken down by `Type`, just to check how big the `Direct` sales are compared to the main channels, and then also break it down further by `Year` to double-ensure that it is indeed the case every year:

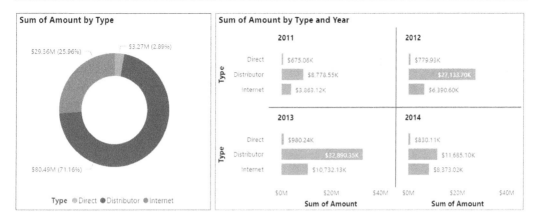

Figure 3.28: Verifying direct sales' makeup for total sales

The hypothesis that we tested is true. Hence, we can safely disregard direct sales and analyze them separately later if required. Let's turn our attention back to the main sales channels by filtering out direct sales.

Let's continue by looking at the sales amount by year (*Figure 3.29*); they show an increase each year and a dip in the last year. What if we break it down by product category to see if there's anything indicative? What's prominent, though, is that the `Bikes` category makes up for a very large portion of the sales each year:

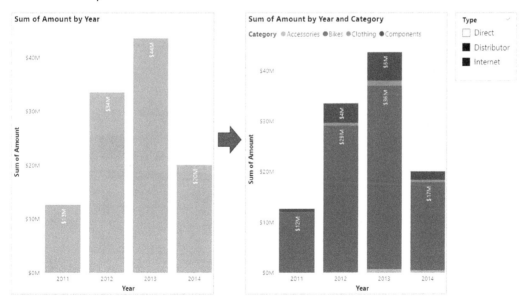

Figure 3.29: Sales by year and further broken down by category

This tells us maybe we should analyze bikes separately from the rest. Grouping up the rest of the categories and providing it as a single collective categorization seems like a good idea.

Since the Category field is hidden (due to model housekeeping) and grouping cannot be done on hierarchy elements, we shall set the view to show the hidden fields and right-click on the Category column to choose the **New group** option. Let's name the group Category Group, and move Bikes into its own group, and set the option to include the rest under **Other** (*Figure 3.30*):

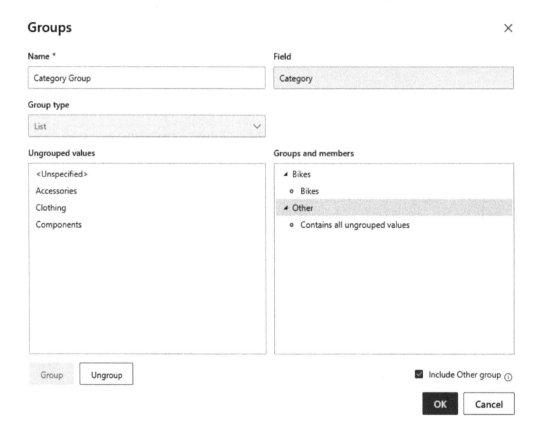

Figure 3.30: Grouping product categories

By using this, users now have the option to analyze sales by categories that have much smaller numbers than Bikes as a single grouping:

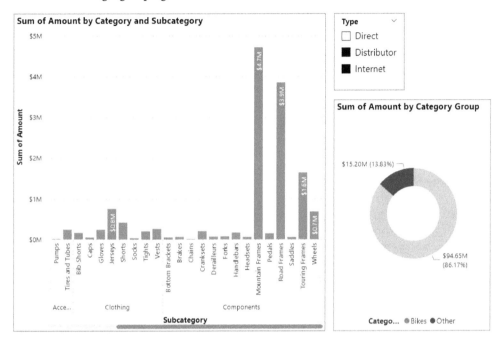

Figure 3.31: Analysis of sales using categorizations other than Bikes

The analysis of the amount of sales using the new category group provides a clear picture of Bikes vs. the other categories (*Figure 3.31*).

By exploring and analyzing the model, we were able to understand more about the data, test hypotheses, and build further enhancements to the model. We shall dive deeper into analyzing data in the next chapter.

Now that we have explored the data model and know our way around it, the next step is to visualize the data on a report in an organized way to tell a story.

Visualizing data on a report

Power BI reports are not the conventional type of report that most businesses are used to. Conventional, pixel-perfect, print-ready reports are called paginated reports and are indeed part of the Power BI offerings.

Let's get back to the default analytical reports in Power BI. Due to its functionality that allows for different types of visuals to be put together and paint an analytical picture, the word dashboard is quite commonly used by business users to refer to Power BI reports. Dashboards in Power BI are, however, a somewhat similar yet different artifact.

I will not disagree with users who want to call Power BI reports dashboards every time. Very often, we build Power BI reports to the effect of dashboards to fulfill the requirements of users wanting to see their KPIs and business measures at a high level. Keeping this in mind, we shall use the correct technical terminology in this book unless explicitly noted.

Reports are created for different purposes for different users. Users asking for reports with all the possible filters and pages upon pages of different analyses is not uncommon. It is up to the developer to understand the requirement and suggest the best design for the requirement. For instance, you can break down the requirement in a way that can be fulfilled by multiple reports focusing on different subject areas, business processes, and meetings.

A good way to start a report is to identify the purpose of the report, how often it is reviewed, and who the audience is. In our case, let's pick up a requirement to monitor the performance of sales measures monthly:

Figure 3.32: Monthly sales overview report

The **Monthly Sales Overview** report (*Figure 3.32*) provides two slicers. The category group slicer allows for the analysis of each group separately due to the inevitably huge difference in numbers between bike sales and the other category sales.

In this way, separate reports do not have to be created for those who are responsible for bike sales and those who are responsible for other category sales; they only need to use the slicer to flip between each view. The year and month slicer allows users to go to their desired month for analysis.

The first two cards show the sales amount and quantity for the selected context, while the **Product Analysis** visual breaks down the same using the categorization hierarchy of the **Product** dimension, allowing users to drill down all the way to the individual product. The line chart on the right shows the trend of how sales (amount and quantity) have performed across the years. The year and month slicer is set to not filter this visual for this effect to work.

The bar chart below showcases the top seven salespersons based on distributor sales. For this, the sales amount measure is filtered on the Type column. The colors of the bars are set to a dark shade for the highest numbers of sales made, with a light shade to indicate the lowest number of sales that were made. In this way, we can visually indicate two measure values. The card next to it shows the overall distributor sales, which is also filtered by the Type column.

The final pieces showcase direct sales through a card visual that uses the measure we created previously and a doughnut chart to show the breakdown of direct sales by product subcategory.

Since the report is interactive, users can take advantage of the cross-filtering feature in Power BI to understand various aspects of the analysis. For example, Lynn Tsoflias, who is not very impressive compared to the rest of the top 7 salespersons, is the top salesperson for selling touring bikes!

The report is now done. The job of a Power BI developer does not end with creating the report. You need to now put it up for others to see and use. This is where publishing and sharing the content comes into the picture.

Publishing and sharing Power BI content

The content you create on Power BI Desktop cannot be shared while it is on Power BI Desktop. You can forward files around, but that will not be practical at all, especially with the data size and potential for multiple versions of the truth. Power BI Desktop is the only authoring tool for Power BI and needs to be treated as such. The Power BI service is where all Power BI content goes live, is shared, and is used.

Publishing Power BI content

All Power BI content published to the service is housed within workspaces, and so is content that is created on the service. Workspaces are where you would collaborate with your peers on the content before making it available to a wider audience.

Workspaces are usually created for different types of requirements. Think of the various types of analytical requirements that you would need to cater to. Then, think of how you can organize the content that you create for the requirements into workspaces. For example, a set of semantic models that contain sales and marketing KPIs and business measures can go into the **sales & marketing** core workspace. A set of reports, dashboards, and related semantic models for monthly financial analysis will have its own workspace. The daily sales report and weekly sales review scorecard can have their own workspace. The management dashboards for the company board can have another. The list goes on.

Let's proceed to create a workspace on the Power BI service and publish the report we created:

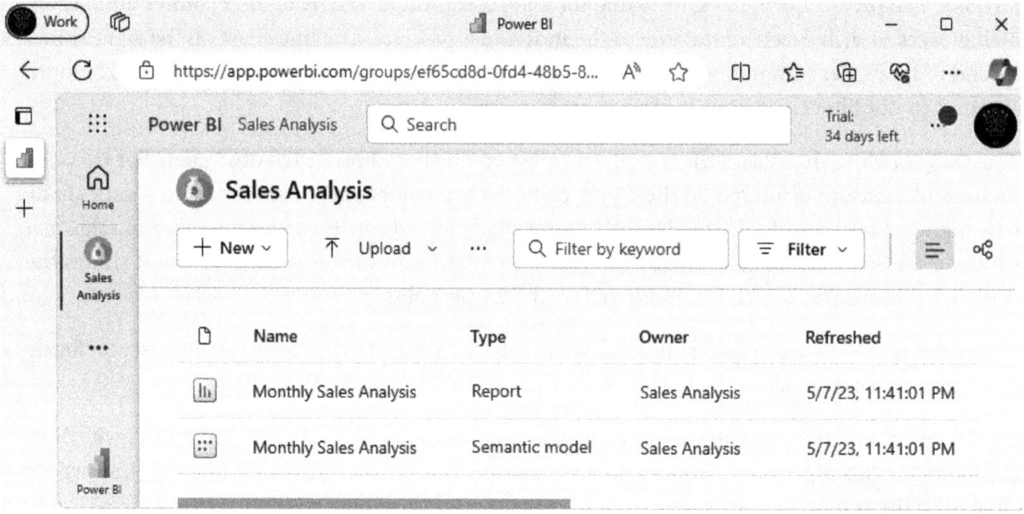

Figure 3.33: Report published to the Power BI service

You will notice that the semantic model and the report are split up into two distinct objects. This allows us to create more reports directly from the semantic model, edit the report in place on the service without affecting the model, and even copy out the report to other workspaces.

Changing the workspace view to the **Lineage view** shows the lineage of the data from the semantic model's source all the way to the report (as well as the dashboards and metrics, if present). Our semantic model, you will notice, has two connections, as was expected: one to the SQL Server database and the other to the SharePoint site. It is important to remember that the connections to the sources, which were established with your local Power BI Desktop when you are creating reports, are broken when you publish your report to the service; this means you need to ensure that the connection is re-established when you publish the report the first time.

Figure 3.34: Workspace lineage view

Power BI supports more than 100 different connectors, including cloud and on-premises sources. While you can connect to cloud sources directly from the Power BI service, on-premises sources require a secure line through which Power BI can connect to get into the network and access the system. This is because Power BI sits outside of the organization's infrastructure, and each organization has its own security standards.

Connectivity to on-premises systems is implemented by using a Microsoft on-premises data gateway. The data gateway software needs to be set up on a designated server on the network that hosts the source. The simplest way is to install and configure the data gateway software on the source system itself. However, this is not recommended because the data gateway may induce resource contention on the server, thereby affecting the source system's usage of critical resources, such as CPU and memory. Hence, a dedicated server as the data gateway makes more sense. It will also help if Power BI needs to connect to more source systems on the network.

The on-premises data gateway can be configured in personal or standard mode. Unless it is used for connecting to your personal on-premises computers, the standard mode is what is recommended. Once you install and configure the gateway on the designated server, you should see it in the Power BI service (from **Settings**).

Once the gateway is set up, we can go to the semantic model's settings and connect the sources from under the **Gateway connection** and **Data source credentials** options.

Once connectivity is set up with its sources, the semantic model needs to be refreshed with data automatically at designated time intervals so that users can see the latest data.

Setting up data refreshes

Data refreshes can be set up from within a semantic model's settings. Hence, while you are already in the semantic model settings from the previous section's last step, you can use the **Refresh** option to do the necessary configurations. All we need to do is specify if it's a daily or weekly frequency and select the time zone and the times you want to refresh the semantic model. Depending on the workspace's license mode, the time intervals allowed between data refreshes will change:

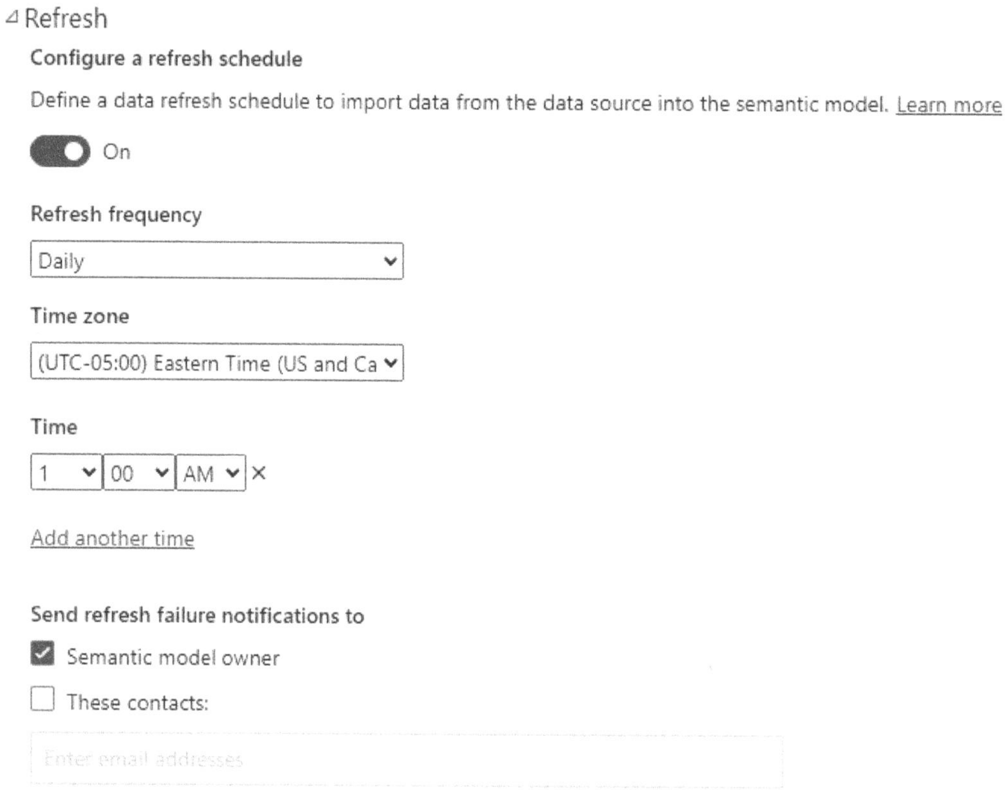

◁ Refresh

Configure a refresh schedule

Define a data refresh schedule to import data from the data source into the semantic model. Learn more

⬤◯ On

Refresh frequency

| Daily ⌄ |

Time zone

| (UTC-05:00) Eastern Time (US and Ca ⌄ |

Time

| 1 ⌄ | 00 ⌄ | AM ⌄ | ×

Add another time

Send refresh failure notifications to

☑ Semantic model owner

☐ These contacts:

| Enter email addresses |

Figure 3.35: Semantic model scheduled refresh settings

You have the option to send failure notifications to the semantic model owner and other designated folk if required. If the option has been set, error notifications will be sent to the appropriate administrators.

The **Refresh history** of the semantic model will provide the history of how your scheduled refreshes have performed, with the error messages (if any):

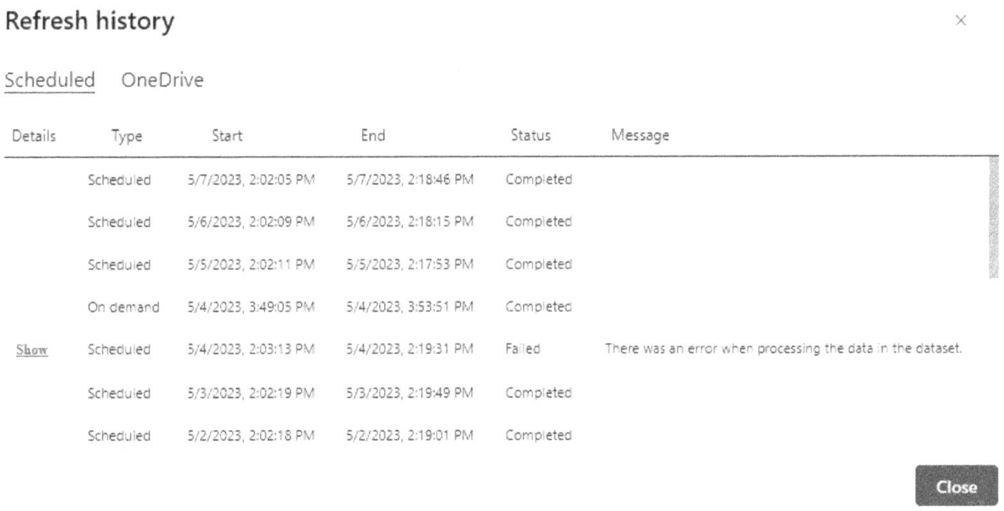

Refresh history   ×

Scheduled   OneDrive

Details	Type	Start	End	Status	Message
	Scheduled	5/7/2023, 2:02:05 PM	5/7/2023, 2:18:46 PM	Completed	
	Scheduled	5/6/2023, 2:02:09 PM	5/6/2023, 2:18:15 PM	Completed	
	Scheduled	5/5/2023, 2:02:11 PM	5/5/2023, 2:17:53 PM	Completed	
	On demand	5/4/2023, 3:49:05 PM	5/4/2023, 3:53:51 PM	Completed	
Show	Scheduled	5/4/2023, 2:03:13 PM	5/4/2023, 2:19:31 PM	Failed	There was an error when processing the data in the dataset.
	Scheduled	5/3/2023, 2:02:19 PM	5/3/2023, 2:19:49 PM	Completed	
	Scheduled	5/2/2023, 2:02:18 PM	5/2/2023, 2:19:01 PM	Completed	

Close

Figure 3.36: Semantic model refresh history

Figure 3.36 shows a sample semantic model refresh history. You can see that all except one refresh has succeeded. The failed refresh will display an error message with an option to show details.

Once your content is published and the schedules have been set up for continued data refreshes of the content, users can now let others consume this content. This is where sharing comes in.

Sharing the published reports

Published reports can be easily shared using the **Share** button found on the report viewer. Semantic models can be shared, too, by using the **Share semantic model** button, which can be found when you open the semantic model. These options, however, are ad hoc options and are not recommended when you have a lot of Power BI artifacts across many workspaces.

Collaboration

Collaboration usually occurs among a small group of folks with a vested interest in the content you've created. This could be a small finance team, a sales leadership team, or a few operations managers, for example. This group will be provided with specific access to the content's workspaces that allow them to review, test, and vet the published semantic models and reports. For example, **read only** will only allow the user testing the semantic model to read from it, and they will not be able to update it in any way. Collaborators can also chat on Teams using the report as context:

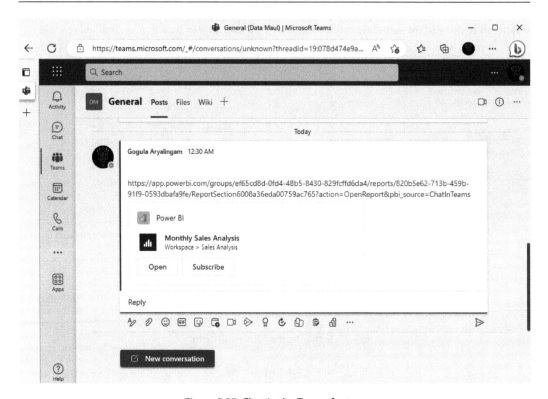

Figure 3.37: Chat in the Teams feature

Creating and publishing apps

Once the report is finalized, which may take a few rounds of testing, reviews, feedback and edits, you can send it out to a wider audience. This could be a large group of business users who will take data-driven actions by regularly viewing and examining the report. You can package your workspace content into an app and distribute it amongst selected groups or the entire organization.

Creating an app is easy. You just click on the **Create App** button on the workspace, and you are then taken through an intuitive three-step wizard to set up your app, include and sequence the content you want to share, and specify the audience. Once you click on the **Publish App** button, the app is published, and you're given a link to distribute it to users. The setup has an option for the app to be automatically installed in the **Apps** section of the Power BI home page (*Figure 3.38*):

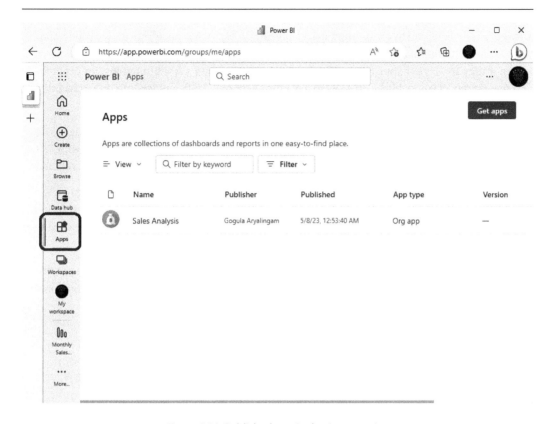

Figure 3.38: Published app in the Apps section

The option to allow people to use the semantic model to build content will let users of the app create their own reports against the semantic model powering the app.

When providing access to different users, it is important that licensing be taken into consideration. Without the organization procuring the required licenses, users will not be able to publish, share, and consume content on Power BI. Hence, let us take a look at the licensing options that Power BI provides.

Licensing options

Power BI Desktop is a free piece of software provided by Microsoft with which to author reports and semantic models. The moment the report (and semantic model) is published to the service, Power BI's licensing modes come into play.

The **free** license allows you to publish only to the **My Workspace** workspace for a personal experience. This means no one else can view your content, nor will you be able to share the content.

The **Pro** license allows you to create workspaces outside of **My Workspace** and allows you to start collaborating with other users using that workspace. However, these users will need a Pro license, too, even if they are to view your report. The Pro license comes with a few limitations; for example, each semantic model you publish can grow to a maximum of only 1GB, and you can only schedule a maximum of 8 refreshes per day on a semantic model.

The **premium per-user** (**PPU**) license allows you to have 100 GB semantic models and up to 48 refreshes a day on semantic models. It also provides several more features that are not found with Pro, for example, creating data marts. To use content on a PPU workspace, each user accessing it requires PPU, even to read the content.

The **premium per-capacity** license allows you to have 400 GB semantic models, while users will not require a per-person license to read the content. They will only need a Pro or PPU license to author content.

Choosing the right licensing option can be a little overwhelming. However, it is recommended that an organization start small with only the minimum required Pro licenses. As usage, adoption, and content size grow, decisions to invest in licensing can be taken.

Q&A

Here are a few questions related to the Power BI workflow that may arise during the interview.

Question 1: What are the steps you would take from end to end when developing a Power BI report?

Answer: Here are the steps that I follow:

1. I start with choosing the data sources and connecting to them.
2. I then cleanse and transform the data to match a model that I have in mind for the report.
3. Next, I model the transformed data, ensuring that fact tables and dimension are designed right, and then I create the required measures and make the necessary enhancements to the dimensions.
4. Finally, I visualize the data on a report and publish it to Power BI.
5. Once published I would configure connectivity to the data, share the report, and allow users to collaborate on it.

Question 2: What do you usually consider when choosing a data source for your Power BI projects?

Answer: The first thing I usually consider is how much is the data already processed. If the data provided is preprocessed, it can mean that someone's logic is already applied, and that can corrupt my final output. Hence, it is important that I get data that is as close to the source as possible. The best for me would be the application's database tables. However, certain preprocessing, such as what happens in a data lake or data warehouse, is acceptable, since this would be standardized and generic pre-processing. It is important that documentation is available for these sources so that I can understand the preprocessing that is done. Other considerations would be the consistency and completeness of data at the source.

Question 3: What are the typical transformation activities you perform when building a model in Power BI?

Answer: A common type of data source I receive is pivoted Excel files. Since pivots are already processed data, I first unpivot the files so that I have columns of dimension and facts. Combining data from multiple tables to generate a dimension is a favorite of mine. I enjoy reducing the number of source tables to fewer, more meaningful tables. I also often combine similarly structured files. My usual practice is to ensure that each file that has the same type of information is structured to a specific standard before combining them.

Summary

In this chapter, you learned about the workflow of the steps that need to be carried out to implement a Power BI report. During its course, you will wear multiple hats: that of a developer and that of a data analyst.

You start by determining where to obtain your data from and look at the right methodology for connecting to and extracting data. You may not have the experience of connecting to every source supported by Power BI. It is not a realistic expectation. However, as a developer, some due diligence is encouraged to conduct research on the probable source systems that the organization uses and be prepared with overall knowledge about connecting to those systems.

You then embark on a journey of cleansing, transforming, and combining the data into an analytical shape. Power Query has many functionalities for this purpose, meaning that you rarely must clean data at the source before bringing them into Power BI. You learned that this is not done ad hoc but that there is a design that you will adhere to and shape the model against. The star schema modeling technique is the golden standard recommended for modeling data on Power BI.

Once you've modeled your data, you switch to being a data analyst so that you can explore the data and look for insights. Your exploration can often provide ideas for improving your model further and making it business-friendly. Such a model allows for the intuitive analysis of business data. Reporting the insights that you've uncovered, or reporting to set requirements, is the next as an analyst. An analytical report that provides high-level information before getting into the details provides structure and intuitive reading to users. Interactivity, such as drill-downs and cross-filtering, gives an additional layer of understanding to users.

You finally publish the report before collaborating with peers to finalize it. Once finalized, the report is packaged as an app and distributed amongst the organizational audience.

By understanding and familiarizing yourself with the Power BI workflow, you will be able to prepare and plan your reporting solution efficiently. In the next chapter, we will dive deeper into data analytics using Power BI. We will look at the different data analysis phases and how Power BI comes in as a data analysis solution.

4

Data Analysis with Power BI

In this chapter, we will explore the six phases of data analysis that a data analyst would take, from taking raw data to acting upon the insights generated by that data. Even though an analyst can take different approaches to analyzing data, such as starting from a phase in the middle or using a different order, knowing the phases will help them understand the bigger picture, appreciate the state the data is in, and help put together the best possible data analysis solution for the scenario.

We will also learn how Power BI can be used as a data analysis solution by mapping and exploring the steps in the Power BI workflow that we learned in *Chapter 3* against the six phases.

It only makes sense that we complete this chapter by looking at how organizations have succeeded with Power BI by taking the right approach to data analysis and how its components were put together for a complete solution.

In this chapter, we're going to cover the following main topics:

- The six data analysis phases
- Power BI as a data analysis solution
- A success story – Analyzing data using Power BI

Technical requirements

- Power BI Desktop
- Power BI Pro license
- Teams
- PowerPoint

The six data analysis phases

The six data analysis phases were defined by Google as part of their **Google Data Analytics Professional certificate** (`https://www.coursera.org/google-certificates/data-analytics-certificate`). Why should we even look at Google's definition in relation to Power BI, a tool that's definitely not from Google? Well, let me clarify: Google's definition essentially represents a standardized version of the typical phases employed in data analysis; it's a component of Google's educational framework, and what's noteworthy is that it is not fixated on any specific product. This means you can seamlessly harness the capabilities of a particular product, such as Power BI, while staying aligned with a widely recognized industry standard endorsed by popular data analyst certifications. In essence, even though Power BI isn't a Google product, you can still apply these phases effectively when using data analysis with Power BI.

Let's now get started with each phase.

The first phase of data analysis involves initiating the process by asking the right questions about your requirements and the data necessary to fulfill those requirements.

Phase 1 – Asking questions for data-driven decision-making

Asking the right questions will help you understand the requirements of the stakeholders and the organization. It will also give you a good background of where any data are stored and how they are used in the organization. In addition, the information that different people in the organization want to see, the type of analysis they would do, what tools and techniques the users are used to, and whether the users are likely to be open to and embrace the change once you build a solution using Power BI are factors that you need to consider.

Let us start with understanding the organization.

Organization overview

Start at the top of the organization. Understand the business, what it does, the industry it is in, and how it operates within the industry. Then, outline the business units and the business functions and/or departments of the organization, along with finding out who runs each unit. These organizational components may vary based on factors such as size, industry, and the overall structure of the organization.

Based on the size and structure of the organization, your Power BI solution might cover the needs of the entire organization or the needs of just a unit. It will also determine if your Power BI solution will be the only BI solution or if it will be part of a larger analytics solution. Since organizations come in a variety of formations, it is important to understand what this aspect is and get a feel for the different organizations that you will have to deal with.

Let us start with a small organization and put a face to the example.

Assume the existence of a private medical consulting practice operating in Sydney, Australia. It is headed by two founding medical consultants and includes a finance department with three personnel, an administrative department with two personnel, and a consulting department that employs 25 consultants. An organization such as this may not be focused on exponential growth in terms of size and may not have a big budget for analytics. They may, however, need to report very accurate numbers with metrics that have complex calculations. They may also not be able to offer a dedicated businessperson to provide you with input, and priorities may often change.

At the other end of the spectrum, you may find a multinational organization with distinct business units in different countries or multiple business units federated across multiple countries. If we were to put a face to this example, think of an apparel manufacturer in Asia with multiple business units in multiple countries, each focusing on producing specialized garments that all of the other units do not. Each unit has its own manufacturing process, but the business functions, such as finance, supply chain, and marketing, are centrally operated from the corporate headquarters with satellite offices at each business unit and in each country. Certain business functions, such as human resources, however, are country-specific and operate on their own. People-wise, too, there's a big difference, with 30–40-personnel-sized finance and marketing teams, a board with corporate leadership, 2000 professional workers, and 50,000 factory workers. Most metrics the organization uses are standard business measures and KPIs that are used across the industry, but the complex organization structure is sure to exert its own set of challenges in terms of implementation. Despite this, such organizations will be able to afford a dedicated person or team to provide you with input for the solution, as well as allocate a good budget for the project.

Of course, numerous organizational structures exist on this spectrum, each operating distinctly from each other, even within the same industry. Hence, getting a good understanding of the organization will help you with designing a solution that best suits them.

When understanding the organizations, start at the top and then wind your way down by understanding the business and what it does, including the industry the organization is in. Then, outline the business units, business functions, and/or departments of the organization and who runs each unit. This will depend on the size and structure of the organization.

Hence, first, you need to understand the organizational structure and who owns what in the organization. These folk will likely be the main stakeholders for data-driven decision-making. This makes it easier to know who to talk to start gathering your requirements. The stakeholders are also the most likely to tell you what metrics they look at to understand the performance of the unit, function, or department they own. They will also be able to tell you which metrics they send up to the corporate leadership or the board for organization-wide performance reviews.

An organizational diagram depicting the units, functions, and departments is a good way to start documenting your requirements:

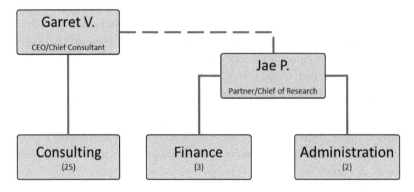

Figure 4.1: Organization chart of a small private medical consulting practice

Figure 4.1 depicts the organization chart of a small private medical consulting practice, while *Figure 4.2* depicts the organization chart of a large multinational apparel manufacturer. These were two examples we used earlier in this section to understand the diversity among the organizations you can come across:

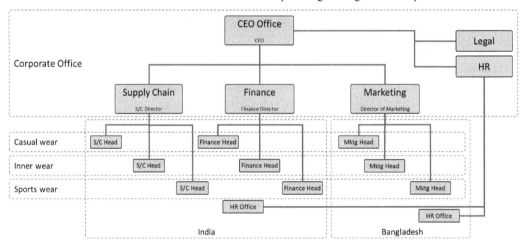

Figure 4.2: Organization chart of a large multinational apparel manufacturer

It is also helpful to depict the stakeholders of each unit, along with their priority or importance. In most cases, it is obviously finance that comes first in importance, but there are many instances where operations and sales are given top priority.

To better understand the metrics that are looked at, it is wise to first get an understanding of the business units, business functions, and/or the departments in terms of how they operate.

An entity operates by following a collective of business processes. Such a process has a start and an end and tries to achieve an objective. How often a process succeeds or fails to achieve this objective is an indication of the process's performance; the collective performance of the processes will determine the performance of the department or business function and, eventually, the business units and the organization. This is exactly what the stakeholders at the different levels want to know.

Understanding what each business process does and understanding how it is measured is the next step that you would want to take. A good way to understand a business process is to document the process flow, at which points it is measured, and how this is measured. Mark the metrics on a diagram, including what the metrics are measured against, and note down the calculations used to compute those measurements.

You now have the following requirements for data-driven decision-making:

- The divisions that possess the business processes and their stakeholders

- The business processes

- The metrics (and metric calculations) that measure the business processes

Comprehensive documentation of the above, along with additional information about how the metrics will be used and by whom, will provide a roundup of the gathering of the requirements.

Once you are at the calculation level, you will need data to apply those calculations. This is when you transition into asking the data questions.

Data questions

Data questions attempt to understand how and where the data is stored, how you would access it, and how reliable the data is. You will then attempt to understand the right logic and queries to retrieve the data for the metric calculations.

A good idea would be to document any understandings under these topics:

- **Storage**: Identify where the data are stored in their most original form, e.g., internally, within organizational systems, or externally, obtained from a third party (usually at a premium). Internal data can include SaaS-based offerings tied to the organization. You will also need to understand how the data are stored, such as in a database or as files. You will also have to determine which sources can be used for master data and which can be used as sources for transactional data.

- **Access**: You will then need to understand how you can access the data, e.g., if you will have direct access to the source, if someone will download and stage the data for you, or, alternatively, if an API will be provided for access. You will also need to know who the owner of each system or data source is, what type of access they are willing to provide you with, and up to what level of sensitivity you are allowed.

- **Reliability**: Next, you will need to determine how reliable the data are. This means that the data are accurate when pulling them off the source and require no alterations to ensure the correct information is present. It also means that your data are quality data so that you don't have to perform unnecessary cleansing before using them.

- **Logic**: Finally, you will have to discover the logic to write the queries to retrieve the data needed for the calculations and then the logic for the calculations themselves. You will need to look for scenarios where the logic may differ at times, such as seasonality, or if variants of a calculation are needed, such as a previous value, a year-to-date value, and a month-to-date value.

A comprehensive document of the above data that needs to be discovered will effectively complement the requirements gathering. You must also consider the best practices you will follow when preparing data for analysis. For instance, when modeling data, one of the preferred methods is the dimensional modeling (also known as the star schema) technique. We touched upon this briefly in *Chapter 3*, under the section *Modeling data for analysis*. Here, tables are identified as either fact or dimension tables; although the metrics are identified in fact tables, we will also need to identify and structure what the dimension tables will look like when slicing and dicing the facts. The logic to craft the dimension data should also be determined and co-located with the fact logic.

Phase 2 – Preparing data for processing

Once you have asked all the relevant questions and are ready to dive into the data, you need to first prepare the data. It is good practice to first profile the data that you bring in for analysis.

Data profiling

As we saw earlier in the *Data questions* section above, we need to obtain data in their most original form and understand what they look like. This usually involves the database of the application. Profiling the data will include identifying and recording the exact field or fields the data are going to come from, their types, and other metadata, such as the nullability of columns, the frequency of nulls, the number of unique values, and the number of occurrences of each unique value. The relationship amongst the tables also plays a part in identifying how data relate to each other so that you know the following:

- How you can combine multiple tables for the dimensions
- The granularity of the facts

Knowing this information will help you design optimized methods for extracting the information for processing. It is also important to identify the type and version of the database so you can get ready with the appropriate querying methods.

Spreadsheet and flat file data are frequently found fragmented by period, business unit, or other facets. When we prep such data, we need to ensure that it is packaged in a way that is akin to databases. One way of doing this is organizing the same type of data into folders that will play the role of tables, and a collection of these folders will play the role of a database. Using SharePoint document libraries is a good way of doing this (*Figure 4.3*):

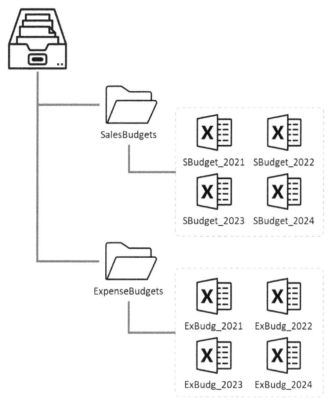

Figure 4.3: Files organized in a folder collection in a document library

An **application programming interface** (**API**) exposed by an application can also be likened to a database, with each dataset it returns likened to tables.

Another paradigm that you might come across is where the data are already available in a data lake or data warehouse. This means someone before you had done a lot of the hard work of preparing and extracting the data from the various sources into one single repository. It is just as important to prepare for your part of the data analysis when considering this repository as the source for your reporting. Often, the data lake or data warehouse will have data way beyond what is necessary for your context; hence, which tables will suffice and what to filter out of those tables is what you need to determine.

Once you've understood the data sources and profiled their structure, you need to figure out how you will extract the data. To extract and sample the data from a database, you will need to know a querying language, such as SQL, and the appropriate variant of SQL, depending on the database system, whereas extracting data from spreadsheets will require Excel skills. Of course, with Power BI, you may not need to have these skills since Power BI allows you to query and extract data from within it. However, as a data analyst, you must often dive deep into the systems to figure out the data, which is where these skills will come in handy.

Bad data

Even if you have profiled the data, there are many instances where you will notice bad data. This can range from the data entered using a different case in a column to metadata pollution. **Metadata pollution** is when metadata is tagged along with the data in a column with the intention of giving it more meaning. For example, think of an ERP system's product table with close to 100 columns. This table has a column to store the subcategory and category of the product. However, during a period of a year, users have been using the category column to store both subcategory and category data while ignoring the subcategory column (*Figure 4.4*):

Product ID	Name	Color	Category	Subcategory ID	Subcategory	Category ID
833	ML Road Frame-W - Yellow, 40	Yellow	Components, Subcat: Road Frames			214
834	ML Road Frame-W - Yellow, 42	Yellow	Components, Subcat: Road Frames			214
835	ML Road Frame-W - Yellow, 44	Yellow	Components, Subcat: Road Frames			214
836	ML Road Frame-W - Yellow, 48	Yellow	Components, Subcat: Road Frames			214
904	ML Mountain Frame-W - Silver,	Silver	Components. Subcat-Mountain Frames			212
905	ML Mountain Frame-W - Silver,	Silver	Components. Subcat-Mountain Frames			212
906	ML Mountain Frame-W - Silver,	Silver	Components. Subcat-Mountain Frames			212
917	LL Mountain Frame - Silver, 42	Silver	Components. Subcat-Mountain Frames			212
918	LL Mountain Frame - Silver, 44	Silver	Components. Subcat-Mountain Frames			212
919	LL Mountain Frame - Silver, 48	Silver	Components. Subcat-Mountain Frames			212
920	LL Mountain Frame - Silver, 52	Silver	Components. Subcat-Mountain Frames			212
942	ML Mountain Frame-W - Silver,	Silver	Components. Subcat-Mountain Frames			212
944	LL Mountain Frame - Silver, 40	Silver	Components. Subcat-Mountain Frames			212
707	Sport-100 Helmet, Red	Red	Helmets	31	Helmets	4
709	Mountain Bike Socks, M	White	Socks	23	Socks	3
710	Mountain Bike Socks, L	White	Socks	23	Socks	3
711	Sport-100 Helmet, Blue	Blue	Helmets	31	Helmets	4
712	AWC Logo Cap	Multi	Caps	19	Caps	3
713	Long-Sleeve Logo Jersey, S	Multi	Jerseys	21	Jerseys	3
714	Long-Sleeve Logo Jersey, M	Multi	Jerseys	21	Jerseys	3
715	Long-Sleeve Logo Jersey, L	Multi	Jerseys	21	Jerseys	3
716	Long-Sleeve Logo Jersey, XL	Multi	Jerseys	21	Jerseys	3
842	Touring-Panniers, Large	Grey	Panniers	35	Panniers	4
843	Cable Lock	<No color	Locks	34	Locks	4
844	Minipump	<No color	Pumps	36	Pumps	4
845	Mountain Pump	<No color	Pumps	36	Pumps	4
846	Taillights - Battery-Powered	<No color	Lights	33	Lights	4
847	Headlights - Dual-Beam	<No color	Lights	33	Lights	4

Figure 4.4: Metadata pollution in the category field in some columns of the product table

Stakeholders usually expect bad data to be handled by a data analyst under the notion that it is part of data cleansing. While there are certain scenarios where bad data can be handled by you while cleansing, there are other scenarios where you should not. Generally, if the bad data scenario can be resolved with a simple cleansing activity, such as a single catch-all conversion to title case if there is mixed case data, it should not be a problem. However, if it is a case of complex logic that must be written, and there is room for further addition to that logic in the future, it is wise to mark it as bad data and recommend the business take appropriate action on the data.

Profiling bad data and recommending appropriate action to the business will help you prevent unpredictable situations when working with the data.

Sensitive data and data privacy

You will often have to work with data that are deemed sensitive. This could be salary information, **personally identifiable information** (**PII**), or organizational finances. The level of sensitivity can vary from the type of data, the organizational unit it comes from, or something else. Regardless of this, it is important that you have the necessary permissions from the appropriate authority to see this information and undergo the necessary processes of nondisclosure.

You will also be expected to ensure that sensitive information is processed and presented in an appropriate manner where it cannot be tracked back to identify a specific entity. Anonymizing source data will help in this case, such as masking credit card data or generalizing people's ages by bucketing them into age ranges.

In conclusion, it's crucial to approach data with a level of respect akin to how you would treat a person. This entails ensuring that the data you select for analysis are relevant only to the specific context.

Phase 3 – Processing data for analysis

The outcome of your data processing is the correct and successful conversion of the source data into the model that you have designed based on the requirements you elicited. We will dive deep into modeling in *Chapter 5*; however, you will need to have a good understanding of the target model that you are going to process the data.

Processing data can be thought of in terms of two unique yet intertwined steps: data cleansing and data transformation.

Data transformation

You can expect your source data to be within a much different structure to that of your model. The data can also come from different tables or even different databases. You start by connecting to the data source and selecting the appropriate tables and columns that you need. You would typically use a querying mechanism, such as a query language, or a visual query editor, such as Power BI's Power Query editor.

Subsequent activities may include joining multiple tables, creating custom columns based on logic, appending multiple tables, aggregating columns with other columns, and more. You may choose to do some or all of this at the source by writing an SQL query or by using Power BI, whichever works best. However, it is recommended that you outline the standard querying process that you will use for different sources. For example, you may choose to shape the query at the source if it were a database and choose to shape the query within Power BI if it were a collection of flat files on SharePoint. Here, the database system provides performant query processing in the case of the former, and Power BI provides the flexibility of treating SharePoint-based data as a table.

The final output of transformation is to have the data shaped in the structure of your model.

Data cleansing

Prior to and while transforming data, you will regularly come across the need to cleanse the data. This includes activities such as removing unwanted rows and columns, handling null values (e.g., replacing them with a standard identifier), standardizing the case of the values, converting data types into the most appropriate ones, and more.

Depending on the situation, you may decide to apply certain cleansing actions along with the transformation itself; for example, writing an SQL query at the source where you shape the dataset for the destination along with cleansing logic for the case.

When you have your final output of data transformation, data cleansing is the fine-tuning that you apply to those data.

Issue handling

Part and parcel of data processing is encountering errors and data issues. Even if bad data have been identified during preparation and prevention or handling measures have been put into place, there is no guarantee that bad data will not pop up in some form or another. Errors, too, can happen when least expected, such as losing database connectivity or mistakenly joining tables. Hence, suitable remedies must be put into place so that the integrity of the data is not compromised when issues or errors occur.

Phase 4 – Analyzing data

Data analysis is when you start making sense of the data that you have. All the answers you got from asking questions in Phase 1 get realized in this phase. Analyzing data requires that you put your data in order, which means that you essentially start sowing the seeds much before you come to this phase.

Model design

Designing your model begins when you start asking questions about the metrics that the users measure and review. The moment you start documenting the measures and their calculations and logic, you need to start thinking about what the model will look like. The model should adhere to a standard methodology, be intuitive, and be expandable. You then start sketching in reverse, starting with the metrics, what they are made of, where the data for them comes from, and what queries you need to write to extract the information. You then start thinking about how the data will be stored in the model in the most effective way possible. The final sketch you make will be your model design.

Model building

When you start bringing in the data through your data processing mechanisms, you start building the model. You map out your design to actual tables, choose the right data types, and perform necessary aggregations before storing the data. You will also go about enhancing your data by formatting the data in the right way, creating hierarchies wherever possible, writing calculations to create the measures, and organizing all of these for intuitive reading.

Data analysis

This is when you hand over the data to users so that they can do their analysis, or based on your organizational role, you dive into the data to look for insights that tell you a thing or two about the organization's performance.

Once you have pre-established the calculations for the metrics required by users, the process involves examining them from various contexts or perspectives. For instance, if net sales is a metric monitored by the sales department, it's simply a matter of displaying it on a dashboard. Since the calculation of gross sales minus discounts and taxes is already applied, users need not perform additional steps. They can then refine the context by filtering the value for the current year and possibly breaking down the net sales figure by region. Similarly, diverse analyses can be conducted throughout the organization, leading to the generation of ideas for new metrics and insights.

Phase 5 – Sharing analytical findings and insights

Crafting an analysis of the organization's performance data or insights is just the beginning. To derive value from this information, it is crucial to share it with relevant stakeholders and communicate the necessary course of action that will be taken. Without this dissemination and implementation, the data remains meaningless.

Numerous methods exist for disseminating your findings, with the most prevalent being through a dashboard. This involves selecting a specific scenario for reporting, choosing relevant metrics, and dissecting them with the appropriate context and perspectives. A well-designed dashboard offers users the ability to conduct further analysis interactively. Scorecards provide another avenue for hierarchically monitoring KPI performance over a fixed period. Enabling users to ask the model directly questions by using natural language is yet another approach for addressing queries that may not be predetermined.

Stakeholders often seek additional clarification when presented with an analysis, appreciating the value provided and a desire to get to the bottom of your analysis. Therefore, it should come as no surprise if multiple iterations of one or more phases are required to effectively conclude a compelling data narrative.

In conclusion, by leveraging the various methods and tools at their disposal, analysts should be adept at crafting an effective data narrative. This ensures that stakeholders gain a clear understanding of the organization's dynamics, enabling informed decisions and the implementation of the most appropriate course of action.

Phase 6 – Acting on your findings and insights

The significance of acting upon analytical results cannot be overstated. Once you generate and share your analysis and insights, the true value lies in translating the findings into tangible actions. Leaving analytical conclusions unattended risks rendering them mere artifacts, and organizations must bridge the gap between information and impact. By establishing clear objectives, fostering collaboration between analysts and decision-makers, prioritizing actionable insights, and creating a culture of accountability, businesses can ensure that analytical results drive meaningful change. The iterative nature of the process encourages continuous improvement, enabling organizations to adapt to evolving challenges and opportunities.

In simple terms, analytics becomes powerful when it inspires action in a business. Recognizing the importance of using insights and taking a strategic approach allows organizations to fully benefit from data-driven decision-making. This turns analytics into a catalyst for innovation, improvement, and lasting success.

Now that we have an understanding of the six phases of data analysis, let's now take a look at how these phases can be applied to Power BI. You may remember the Power BI workflow that we learned in *Chapter 3*. In the next section, we shall relate the steps from the workflow to the six phases.

Power BI as a data analysis solution

Power BI is a versatile tool capable of constructing a comprehensive data analysis solution, contrary to the misconception that it is solely for creating reports and dashboards. It can be effectively taken through the six phases of data analysis, excelling notably in certain phases where its performance is particularly strong. Let's now look at how we can map the usage and functionality of Power BI with that of the six data analysis phases.

Phase 1 – Asking questions for your Power BI solution

During the first of the six data analysis phases, a documentation tool and Microsoft Excel are typically employed to record organizational requirements and profile essential metrics. This combination allows for a straightforward listing of the necessary measures and KPIs, including their calculations, making the use of Power BI unnecessary in this context. However, for smaller, agile organizations, a prototype-based approach might be suitable, where comprehensive documentation is not a strict requirement.

A **prototype-based approach** is where you utilize Power BI to outline the semantic model up-front without bringing in any data. You can utilize Power BI functionality to define the measures, the tables, the relationships, and anything else you would need to include in your model. You can also document the model by using the description property that is available across most objects in Power BI.

You start on your prototype by adding the tables you envision your model to contain by using the **Enter data** option, while adding some sample data. You can also create a table to specifically hold your organization's business measures. You do this using the following DAX query:

```
Business Measures = CALCULATETABLE({0})
```

Then, you just hide the default column that is created and start adding the measures. We use the name `Business Measures` since `Measures` is a reserved word in Power BI. However, any meaningful name that fits the business will work. After that, all you must do is create your measures in this table, and then you have your prototype.

As you move through the rest of the phases, you will start connecting to the data sources, replacing the tables in the model with the tables transformed from the sources, and improving your model until you arrive at the completed product. What you will realize is that through implementing this agile process, you have already been asking different questions with which to understand the organizational requirements, and you fulfill these in the model.

Figure 4.5 depicts a prototype of a semantic model with just a single table using a single measure:

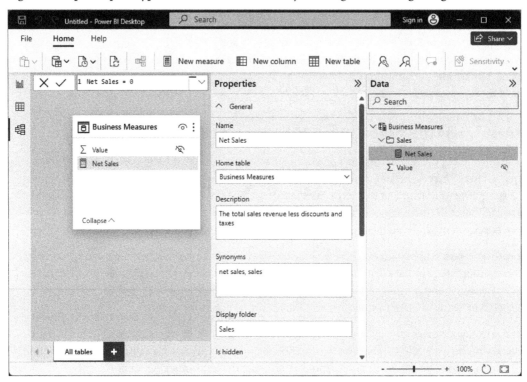

Figure 4.5: The measures table with a single measure and its description

When revisiting the approach you would take for larger implementations, a good place to start would be a requirements specification that focuses on the high-level analytical and reporting requirements of an organization and then follows this down into the deeper layers. For instance, one way of doing this will be to document the following:

- **Organization-level goals and the probable solution(s) to achieve these goals**: This can be the organization wanting a single source of truth for analytics. The goal they want to achieve is that every report that is created for decision-making is sourced from here and that all organizational KPIs are generated and monitored with a single tool.

- **Division-level (i.e., Business function/domain/department-level) requirements**: This can be the business processes each division wants to measure and monitor to make effective decisions and how the targets for the measures are managed.

- **Business process-level requirements**: These can be the specific business measures that are used to gauge success or failure or to quantify how well these business processes are functioning.

The requirements specification can be supplemented by profiling the measures in a spreadsheet, where you will describe the measure, their calculations, their relationships with other measures, and perhaps the queries used to retrieve the data from the source systems. Similarly, profiling the dimensions necessary to analyze the measures is a good idea as well.

Now that we have asked the right questions and documented the requirements of what needs to go into your semantic model, let's get started with preparing the data.

Phase 2 – Preparing data with Power BI

Once you are all set with the source systems for your data, you will need to ensure you can connect to them. We covered quite a good detail about connecting to the common types of data sources in the *Getting data to Power BI* section of *Chapter 3*. Once you've established connectivity to your sources, you need to profile the data.

Data profiling

Power BI offers robust tools for **data profiling**. Profiling your data using these tools allows you to gain insights into the realities of the data, such as data quality, the specifics of bad data, the distribution of column values, and a thorough understanding of your data, including detailed statistics. There are three features that Power BI offers to profile your data. You can find them in the Power Query editor on the **View** tab (*Figure 4.6*) when you connect to your data:

- Column quality
- Column distribution
- Column profile

Figure 4.6 shows how to enable the data preview features in the Power Query editor:

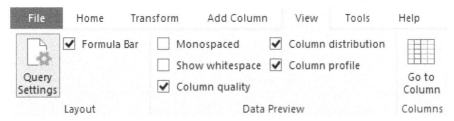

Figure 4.6: Data preview (profiling) features in the Power Query editor

Let us now take a look at each of these features in detail.

Column quality

Column quality serves as a means to assess the quality of data within your source datasets. You can use this to determine whether values are valid, contain errors, or are empty, enabling you to take necessary actions. These actions may include removing records with errors or empty values or devising action plans to address and mitigate any issues associated with poor data quality.

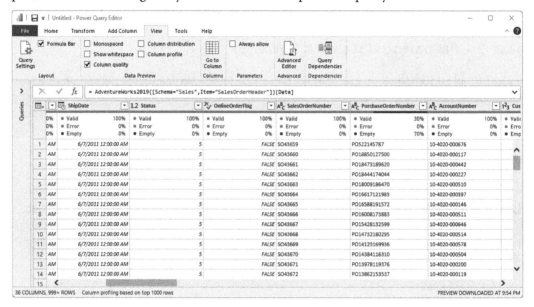

Figure 4.7: A sales order table with Column quality enabled

Figure 4.7 shows the sales order table that has the **Column quality** feature enabled. The quality statistics of each column are shown just below the respective column names.

Column distribution

Column distribution enables you to grasp the frequency and distribution of values within a column. This helps you figure out the number of unique values in a column and identify whether these values are unique across the entire set of records. Understanding column distribution allows you to determine the keys and attributes of the dimensions. In addition, it aids in identifying anomalies within the data, such as instances where the same order number is applied to multiple orders.

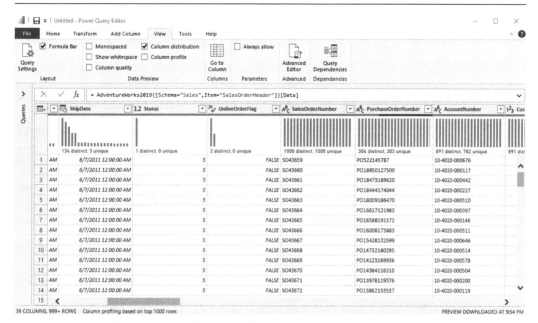

Figure 4.8: The sales order table with column distribution enabled

Figure 4.8 shows the sales order table that has the column distribution feature enabled. The distribution of column values is shown just below each column name.

Column profile

Column profiling offers a detailed understanding of the values within a column, which is particularly useful when identifying anomalies or focusing on a column for specific purposes, such as establishing a business key. In addition to providing records, errors, and empty value counts, it includes essential statistics, such as minimum, maximum, and average values, among others.

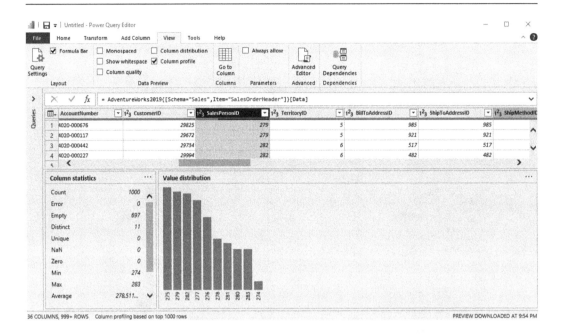

Figure 4.9: The SalesPersonID column of the sales order table with Column profile enabled

Figure 4.9 shows the sales order table that has the **Column profile** feature enabled. The detailed statistics of the selected column are shown along with the distribution of values in a separate pane.

Selecting essential data

When selecting the data for analysis, the simplest best practice is to choose only the essential data at the beginning. This can be easily done using filters in Power Query at the beginning of the query to limit the number of records. In addition, you can use the **Choose Columns** option to select only the columns that are needed for the context. Data sensitivity/privacy measures can be taken by simply restricting the data you choose by following these two approaches. Further, this also contributes to query performance as well.

Performance

Query performance is another important consideration when preparing your data. When combined with further query performance measures that you take downstream, you can set yourself up for quick refreshes of your Power BI models once you build them.

Choosing the right connector for your data source is key for performance. However, this is only if the source, for example, SQL Server, has multiple connectors or methods to connect to. Using an SQL Server connector instead of an ODBC connector provides multiple performance advantages, including query folding, where Power BI will generate code to convert your Power Query to a single SQL query that runs on SQL Server efficiently. This way, there is less strain on Power Query to process large datasets.

We have now prepared the required data. Next, we will go ahead and process it with Power BI.

Phase 3 – Processing data with Power BI

Processing your data involves transforming and cleansing your data using Power Query. In the process, you may also handle errors that are thrown your way.

Power Query provides numerous functionalities for you to shape and clean your data for analytics. While we will dive deep into all those functionalities in *Chapter 5*, let us explore some best practices that should be considered when transforming your data.

Modular processing

In many cases, especially when you connect to a single source but have multiple queries that you need to connect (one for each destination table), it is best that each query is not connected to the source. While contributing to performance implications, this approach becomes cumbersome the moment you need to switch to a different source, where you will have to edit the connections on each query.

This becomes quite handy if you have a complex query with a large number of steps, where you can split the query into multiple queries based on functionality, and each query refers to the previous one. For example, if you were combining the sales order header and detail tables, you may have the following queries linked up, as depicted in *Figure 4.10*:

- Query A: Database connection
- Query B_1: Connection to sales order header table
- Query C: Connection to sales order detail table
- Query B_2: Sales orders with headers combined and their details

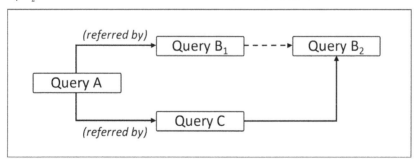

Figure 4.10: Schematic of queries using references

Dataset orientation

A common structure that you may come across when processing budget data is when they are (often) stored in a pivoted structure. For instance, if we take sales budgets, this may be structured with product categories in a column and the budgeted values per category in 12 columns, each representing the month of the year. In cases such as this one, you may want to change the orientation of the 12 values so that instead of the 12 values, you have the product category and the month as columns, with a third column to hold the budget values. Transformations such as this can be easily accomplished by using the **Unpivot Columns** option.

Using functions

As you further process your data, you may notice that you might want to perform a set of standard operations against multiple queries. Say, for instance, you need to cleanse all text columns by replacing null values with Unknown and rename all columns by splitting them into multiple words by breaking them at an underscore character or at each upper-case character; these cleansing activities, too, will come under similar treatment as your transformations. Here, since you must apply the same set of steps to multiple queries, a good idea is to create parameterized functions:

- Query D: Connection to the products table
- Function A: Replace empty text-based cells with the value Unknown
- Function B: Rename columns by separating existing column names at the upper-case characters

The resulting query structure example would look like *Figure 4.11* when applied to the previous example:

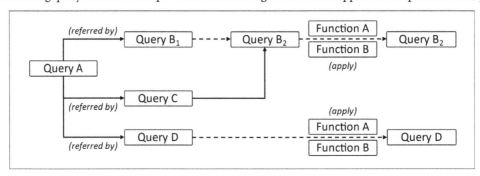

Figure 4.11: Schematic of queries using references and with functions applied

Once we are done with data processing, we then move into using the processed data for modeling.

Phase 4 – Data analysis with Power BI

If you remember, we already laid the foundation of the model in *Phase 1* itself. And in *Phase 3*, we processed the data to match this model. The next step is to structure the model for intuitive analysis.

Designing the model

While we are dedicating the whole of *Chapter 5* to modeling, it is good to briefly look at it at this point. The typical modeling technique recommended by Microsoft is the **star schema** (dimensional modeling) technique. When data is processed into Power BI, it is important that the resultant tables match the tables in the design and that the relationships among the tables are also established. This can be done by referring to the model view in Power BI. You will see that all the queries that you've created are represented as tables, and wherever Power BI can determine a relationship, it will show as a line between the related tables.

It is typical that not all the tables that appear in the model are part of your design. For instance, Query B_2 and Query D from *Figure 4.11* represent the end results. Whereas Queries A, B_1, and C, which are helper queries, will need to be hidden since the end users who use the model do not need to see them:

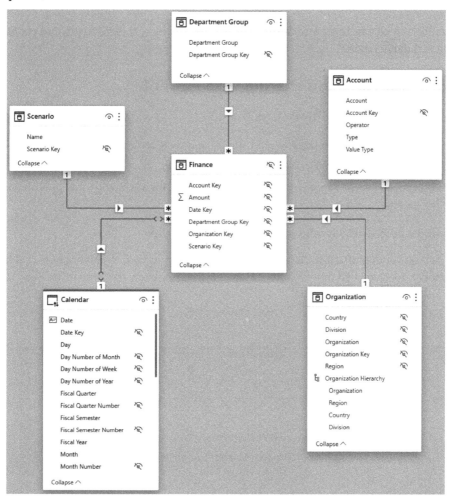

Figure 4.12: A semantic model using the star schema methodology

Building the model

Building the model involves all the actions you would take to ensure that the model is developed according to the design that you have put down. Typically, this involves the following:

- Establishing relationships between tables (if Power BI hasn't done so already)

- Hiding the columns and tables that are not required by the end users

- The creation of measures that were drafted in *Phase 1*

- The creation of hierarchies for the dimension tables

- Organizing the measures, dimension attributes, and hierarchies

All these actions can be performed from within the model view in Power BI.

Once the model is built, you then start on (or allow it to be used for) gaining insights and publishing those insights through reports.

Phase 5 – Reporting and sharing with Power BI

You can build reports in Power BI in two ways:

- First, publish the model to the Power BI service and then connect to it either to the service itself or to Power BI Desktop

- Build the report on the same Power BI Desktop file you are working on and publish both to the service later

In both these methods, you build your report using the **Report** view.

Once you publish your report, regardless of the method, your report will always be connected to the semantic model. You can build more reports for various needs by using the same model:

Figure 4.13: Lineage view of a workspace indicating the lineage
from source to model with multiple reports

Power BI apps

Once built, reports can be shared in multiple ways. A best practice is to group reports into workspaces based on agreed-upon criteria. For example, you may think the marketing division within the sales and marketing department may have a requirement for a set of assorted marketing reports, while the finance department may have a need for standard financial reports. These workspaces will have a set of collaborators who oversee building, reviewing, and governing the report and (once complete) can generate an app, which is a collection of artifacts—in this case, a set of reports—to share across the organization:

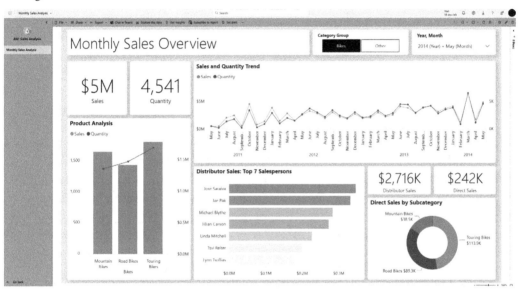

Figure 4.14: A published app containing a report

Dashboards in Power BI

Reports can also be shared directly but are not usually recommended. Users can also include important parts of multiple reports onto a dashboard, which will act as the point of entry for review.

Metrics in Power BI

Another means for sharing and reviewing measures is to create metrics, where measures from a report are selected within a context, are set a target, and are reviewed across a period:

Figure 4.15: Metrics depicted as a hierarchy on a scorecard in Power BI

Collaboration with Power BI

Users can also collaborate on reports and dashboards by selecting a visual and then tagging another user. Reports and dashboards can also be reviewed and collaborated on from within Microsoft Teams. In addition, live reports can be embedded within PowerPoint presentations for interactive, data-driven meetings:

Figure 4.16: A snippet of a report showcasing the collaboration functionality in Power BI

Phase 6 – Acting on your data with Power BI

Once data are shared with other users and are reviewed, there comes a point where action may have to be taken. Power BI, however, is not the ideal tool for actioning decisions. However, there are a few things that can be done with Power BI. You set alerts on reports and dashboards, for instance, to indicate to stakeholders any anomalies in the expected values. For metrics, automated check-ins can review the changes in metrics against their targets and update the status.

The ideal means of acting on the data would be to use Power BI's complementary solutions from **Microsoft's Power Platform: Power Apps and Power Automate**. The former can be used to build no-code applications that will perform a wide variety of tasks, while the latter can be used to listen to changes in Power BI data before kicking off a workflow that calls Power Apps applications.

A success story – Analyzing data using Power BI

Power BI is a versatile tool that can be used to build an end-to-end business intelligence solution. For certain organizations, especially small organizations or the business units of a large organization, it can be used to build a complete BI solution. In contrast, for larger organizations, it is usually used in conjunction with a data warehouse or data lake solution for a comprehensive analytics solution. In this section, let us explore the success story of the latter scenario.

The organization is a multinational apparel manufacturer headquartered in Asia. There are more than 10 business functions, which include procurement, manufacturing, and marketing, taking part in operations. Meanwhile, the other business functions help run operations, including finance, legal, human resources, and engineering. The organization has more than 1000 white-collar staff and more than 20,000 blue-collar workers using numerous systems, including enterprise resource planning, customer relationship management, human resources management, logistics, and other enterprise applications. The organization's reporting and analytics were a mess, with most of the reporting being done in Microsoft Excel and with the data extracted from these systems. Each business function—and even the divisions within the business functions—had its own processes for reporting. In most cases, reporting was delayed by weeks, was error-prone, and included multiple versions of the truth for the same measures reported by different business functions.

The data from the various systems, amounting to multiple terabytes in volume, were ingested into a data lakehouse, where they were standardized and preprocessed into dimensional structures for the entire organization, with a context of 10 years. Power BI then came into use, with this single data source used to build semantic models for each business function. Each of these semantic models included business measures specific to the business function. Analysts and businesses from the respective business functions were then trained to use the models to build their own reports, dashboards, and metrics, and to share and collaborate.

As a result, the time taken for reports to be generated was greatly reduced, with users being able to create reports within a few hours without having to worry about up-to-date data and calculation errors. Further, everyone across the organization only saw one exact value for any chosen measure provided they had the same context applied instead of different business functions reporting different numbers.

The same kind of success can be repeated regardless of the size of the organization and regardless of using a data warehouse or data lake.

Q&A

Here are a few questions related to data analysis in Power BI that may arise during the interview.

Question 1: How do you usually start the process of building a Power BI solution?

Answer: A Power BI solution is basically a way to provide answers to an organization's business problems. I start by asking questions in a structured way. This involves first understanding the organization structure, business functions or domains, and business processes. Then I question the metrics that drive the business processes, functions, and organization. I then find out how these metrics are calculated, where the data for these are sourced, and how they are queried. Finally, I start designing my solution based on this information.

Question 2: How do you handle repetitive processes that you have to handle when processing data?

Answer: I use functions to encapsulate commonly used logic. For instance, I have a function that I use to split column names into multiple words to make it user friendly. I also have common connectivity and processing steps saved as a Power BI Template (PBIT) file. This is helpful when I need to connect to a SharePoint library and traverse multiple levels of folder to get to the data. Since I've made it parameterized, this saves a lot of time. I also have a Power Query script for my date dimension, which I reuse in almost all my projects.

Question 3: Can you relate a Power BI success story that you've been part of?

For your answer: Refer to the *A success story – Analyzing data using Power BI* section and formulate a story along the same lines of a project you were part of.

Summary

In this chapter, you learned about the six phases of data analysis for data-driven decision-making in an organization and how these phases map to Power BI, making it a complete data analysis solution. We then looked at a success story of how Power BI enabled an organization to become data-driven by going through these phases.

In the next chapter, we shall breathe life into some of the phases we looked at in this chapter. We will get into the meat of designing and developing a semantic model in Power BI.

5

Preparing, Transforming, and Modeling Data

In this chapter, we'll deep dive into the meat of preparing, transforming, and modeling data in Power BI. We will pick up on areas that we discussed at a high level in *Chapters 3* and *4*, where we first encountered preparing, transforming, and modeling data as part of the Power BI workflow, and then as part of the six phases of data analysis. Developing a semantic model that mirrors the business numbers that an organization relies on, and providing business users (sometimes referred to as just *users*) with an intuitive and performant means to review and interact with these numbers, is ultimately what the model needs to achieve.

In a data-driven organization, semantic models should be the go-to source for anything related to decision-making. Every report, dashboard, and scorecard should come from a standardized set of semantic models. Hence, the models must deliver the ability to address this need and have the right context set around each of them. This means that a good deal of thought needs to be put into their design, while also having the model open for continuous improvement. From a technical standpoint, to ensure this, the semantic models you build should be performant and modular.

In this chapter, we're going to cover the following main topics:

- Designing a model
- Preparing data
- Building the model
- Exploring advanced modeling considerations

Technical requirements

- Power BI Desktop (to develop the model and report)
- SharePoint Online (as an optional data source)
- SQL Server or Azure SQL Database (as an optional data source)
- Power BI (to publish online and share with other users)

Designing a model

In *Chapter 4*, we talked about how the design of your semantic model starts in phase 1, which is when you start asking questions and recording the requirements. We call this design thinking. But before we explore this further, let's try to understand what a semantic model is, and what it should ideally look like.

Multiple design methods can be used to design a semantic model in Power BI. However, the recommended approach by Microsoft, and what Power BI is best used with, is the **star schema**. We have already touched upon this in previous chapters, but we shall dive deep here.

What is dimensional modeling?

Dimensional modeling, also known as the star schema methodology, was made popular by Ralph Kimball and has been used for a very long time to design data warehouses. If you look at a semantic model very closely, it carries a lot of characteristics of a data warehouse. You can also think of a semantic model as an enhanced, specialized piece of a data warehouse. If you have no experience with data warehouses, don't worry – once we are done with this chapter, you will have enough knowledge to understand what a data warehouse is, which is a bonus. Let's take a look at the concepts a star schema revolves around.

Understanding facts and dimensions

The star schema is fundamentally built on two main concepts – facts and dimensions:

- **Fact**: This is what is measured by the business
- **Dimension**: This is what you measure a fact with

This may seem oversimplified but is important to understand these concepts at this level – that is, from a business's perspective, since that is all they want to do with their data. Let's explore this further. A fact is a piece of information that's usually stored in a column in a data source that is measured by the business to understand how they have performed. For different departments or business functions, a fact can be something different, yet in some cases, the entire organization may review the same fact.

In some cases, a fact can be enhanced to mean something unique to each department. Let's look at a few examples of facts:

- Quantity of items sold (sales)
- Sales value (sales)
- Number of calls taken (customer service)
- Number of gadgets serviced (customer service)
- Target number of gadgets to service (customer service)

Each of these facts tells the users something about their business. The *number of gadgets serviced* tells them how many gadgets the business serviced for their customers, while the *target number of gadgets to service* tells them how many gadgets the business should service for their customers.

Despite providing these facts, these numbers are not enough to give business users a clear picture of what is going on. The moment they see that the *number of gadgets serviced* is 14,135, they will have more questions: Which month of which year is this for? Which division is this for? This is because the users need context before understanding the picture. This context is provided by dimensions. Dimensions are collections of one or more related pieces of information that describe an entity that provides context. A few examples of this are as follows:

- Calendar
- Division
- Employee
- Region

We can now start applying context to the business user questions:

- Which month of which year is this for? Answer: June 2023
- Which division is this for? Answer: Mobile devices

This provides the users with a better understanding of the business. They can now ask for further details. For example, how many gadgets were serviced for each division during June 2023? You will be able to answer this question with ease because you have the related dimensions with you; you can draw a bar chart sorted by the number of gadgets serviced, with the `division` dimension's name on the *Y* axis and the chart filtered for June 2023 using the `calendar` dimension (*Figure 5.1*):

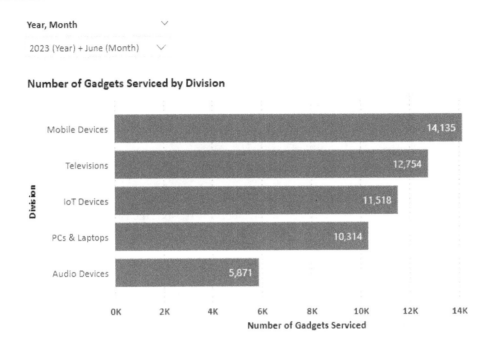

Figure 5.1: A fact value filtered by one dimension and split into another dimension

Now, let's pick this scenario apart and categorize what we have in terms of facts and dimensions using *Table 5.1*:

Fact(s)	Dimension(s)	Dimension attribute(s)
Number of gadgets serviced	Calendar	Month
		Year
	Division	Name

Table 5.1: Facts, dimensions, and dimension attributes from the scenario

You will notice that a dimension may have multiple attributes that typically allow for the hierarchy to be rolled up or a fact to be filtered in different ways. The more attributes you have the better because you can answer different types of questions.

The data for the facts and dimensions come from the various source systems. For instance, the number of gadgets serviced would just be a count of the records stored in the service records table. The calendar dimension would be a table that you would generate of your own based on a set of continuous dates, while the division dimension would come from the division table. However, it is important that the table that the fact comes from, and the tables that the dimensions are based on, have some sort of relationship that can be established.

When understanding the requirements of business users, you must drive the conversations in a way that they boil down to the facts and the dimensions. Often, users will also talk about requirements that go beyond just the basic facts. These requirements are shaped into **measures**.

Exploring measures

To understand what measures are, let's explore the preceding example further. While the *number of gadgets serviced* is a great fact, a user may sometimes want to see the *average number of gadgets serviced per day* or something a little more complex, such as the *rate of gadgets serviced*. The latter two are not facts. If you look closely, these two are variations of the fact *number of gadgets serviced*. An additional bit of logic is applied to the *number of gadgets serviced* to calculate each of these. This is essentially what measures are; the calculations that you apply to facts. An interesting detail to note is that while you attempt to flesh out the calculation logic, you may identify more facts. Let's take the two examples and dissect them. First, we have the *average number of gadgets serviced per day*. You can define this with the following calculation:

$$Average\ number\ of\ gadgets\ serviced\ per\ day\ = \frac{Number\ of\ gadgets\ serviced}{Number\ of\ days\ worked}$$

We can immediately spot that the *number of working days* is another fact that we must include. Let's try the next measure, the *rate of gadgets serviced*, which is calculated by dividing the number of gadgets that have been serviced against the number of gadgets that are targeted to be serviced:

$$Rate\ of\ gadgets\ serviced\ = \frac{Number\ of\ gadgets\ serviced}{Number\ of\ gadgets\ targeted\ for\ service}$$

Once again, this involves the use of a new fact, the *number of gadgets targeted for service*. You now have three facts and two measures that you have derived out of this scenario. *Figure 5.2* maps out the three facts and the measures they contribute to that were identified in the scenario:

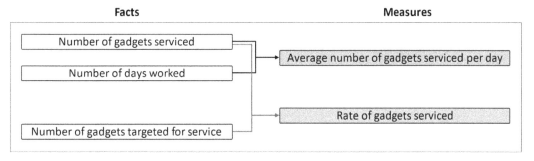

Figure 5.2: Facts and measures derived from the facts

As you dive deeper into your requirements conversation, you will find your list of measures and facts naturally increasing. You need to be aware that you must separate the facts from the measures properly. If measures are incorrectly listed as facts, you will end up creating measures within tables, which can make your queries quite complex. For every requirement that you come across, make sure you ask further questions so that you can break it down to the lowest element, which is your facts. You can then work backward to define the calculations that will make up the measure.

You may have noticed that we have not expanded *Table 5.1* to include the new facts that we identified. This is because doing that will make the list of dimensions repeat, leading to confusion. There is a better way of depicting this, which we shall look at shortly. First, let's delve into what business processes are.

What are business processes?

When you group related facts and measures, you will notice that these metrics are what business users use to understand the performance of what they call a **business process**. A business process is an activity that an organization performs to achieve a goal. For instance, the facts and measures we used in the prior examples are all part of the *service operations* business process, which involves repairing and maintaining the gadgets that customers send to them to ensure good quality.

One of the exercises you must do when identifying facts and measures is to group them by business processes. It is always best to start by outlining the business processes and then proceed with your questioning of facts and measures per business process. When you go down this method of requirements elicitation, you will also notice that often, a business process has a set of dimensions that are common to its facts (and measures). Once you are done with the business process, the next thing you must do is draw up a bus matrix.

Understanding the bus matrix

The **enterprise bus matrix** (referred to in short as the *bus matrix*), is a standard design pattern that's used when building a data warehouse for an organization. It captures the business requirements at a high level and is used as a guide for the data warehouse's design. Hence, it is a good tool to use, even when you're designing your semantic models. It primarily gives you a good understanding of the dimensionality of your models, and which dimensions can be reused across multiple business processes.

The service operations business process, once depicted in the bus matrix, will look like what's shown in *Table 5.2*:

Business Process	Dimension		
	Calendar	Division	Employee
Service operations	X	X	X

Table 5.2: Bus matrix with the service operations business process

You will notice that the Employee dimension has also been included since it makes sense that you can review the service operations facts and measures from an employee angle as well – for example, the *average number of gadgets serviced* per day by each employee.

Let's consider another business process example to see what the bus matrix will look like. The service excellence business process deals with how well the organization has rendered its services (*Table 5.3*):

Business Process	Dimension			
	Calendar	Division	Employee	Season
Service operations	X	X	X	
Service excellence	X	X	X	X

Table 5.3: Bus matrix with two business processes mapped

Granularity refers to the level of detail at which the facts are stored. In the example of service operations, this means that the related facts must be stored for each calendar date, division, and employee combination. At the same time, service excellence facts must be stored for each calendar date, division, employee, and season combination.

Now that we can identify a business process, its facts and measures, the dimensions associated with it, and its granularity, we need to see how this can be depicted using a star schema.

Putting together a star schema

To depict the dimensional model so that it can be easily understood, we must put together a drawing called the star schema. We start by mapping the business processes as fact tables in the schema. Each business process will become one or more fact tables. Whether the business process becomes a single table, or many, depends on granularity. The dimensions each become a dimension table.

Figure 5.3 depicts the star schema for service operations:

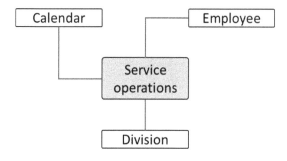

Figure 5.3: Star schema for the service operations business process

In this case, the fact table will look like what's shown in *Table 5.4*:

Column	Notes
Date	The date of the service.
Division Code (or ID)	The column that uniquely identifies the division of the service.
Employee Code (or ID)	The column that uniquely identifies the employee who provided the servicing.
Number of gadgets serviced	The number of gadgets serviced for a particular date, for the division, by the employee.
Number of days worked	The number of days worked by the employee, for the division, on a particular date. Note that this does not make sense in this table since this field will always have a value of 1 if the employee had worked on that date. A simple count operation on the Date column will suffice once the model is done. Hence, this column can be removed. However, it is not wrong to keep it.
Number of gadgets targeted for service	The number of gadgets that have been set as the target to service on a particular date, for the division, by the employee. In many cases, targets are not set at a detailed level. For example, to be fair to the employees, targets are set for the month so that there is a chance to achieve this if performance is low on some days. In such cases, the granularity will slightly change, and the fact will split into another fact table with the calendar month, division, and employee granularity.

Table 5.4: Fact table structure for service operations

Now, let's look at what the dimension tables will look like. *Table 5.5* depicts what the calendar dimension table looks like. The calendar dimension is made up of a range of dates that spans the history of data the business wants to review:

Column	Notes
Date	Each date in the range of applicable dates.
Day Number	The day number starts with either 0 or 1, indicating the start of the week.
Day	The corresponding day starts with Sunday, Monday. or another day. depending on the business case.
Week Number	The week number the date belongs to – for example, 1.
Week	The corresponding name of the week. Week 1 will be the first week of the year.
Month Number	The month number the date belongs to – for example, 1 for January.
Month	The month name of the corresponding month.
Quarter Number	The quarter number the date belongs to – for example, 1 for the first quarter.
Quarter	The quarter name of the corresponding quarter – for example, Q1 for the first quarter.
Year	The year the date belongs to – for example, 2024.
Year Label	The year label of the corresponding year – for example, CY2024 for calendar year 2024.

Table 5.5: The calendar dimension table structure

What's provided in the calendar table here (*Table 5.5*) are only a few fields that you can expect. Usually, you will find many more fields, each describing a certain aspect of a date, including the financial calendar such as fiscal month, fiscal year, and so on.

In this scenario, the division dimension table (*Table 5.6*) is small. It only contains the identifier and the name of each division. If the source table contains fields that can be added as attributes to this dimension, by all means, they should be included:

Column	Notes
Division Key	Unique identifier for each division
Name	Name of the division

Table 5.6: Division dimension table structure

The employee dimension table (*Table 5.7*) is also similar to the division dimension:

Column	Notes
Employee Key	The unique identifier for each employee
Name	The name of the employee
Department	The department the employee belongs to
Region	The region the employee is based in

Table 5.7: Employee dimension table structure

What you can expect once you have built the tables and set the relationships is the star schema in its simplest form (*Figure 5.4*):

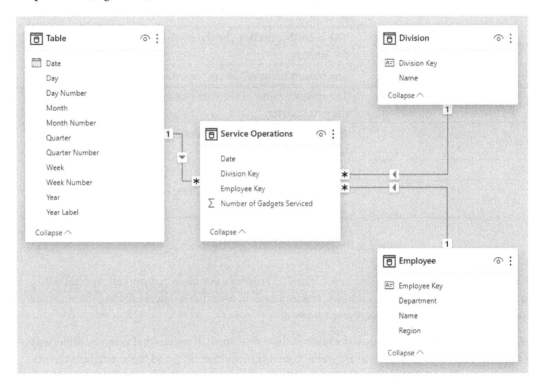

Figure 5.4: Post-development star schema

Further reference

The star schema is a very important concept when building a semantic model. Refer to this article for a deeper understanding of its role in Power BI: https://learn.microsoft.com/en-us/power-bi/guidance/star-schema.

Now that we've learned how to design a semantic model using the dimensional modeling technique, let's dive into preparing data. This is something we must do before developing the model.

Preparing data

Once you have a design for your semantic model, you must prepare the data required to build your semantic model.

In *Chapter 4*, we explored the six phases of data analysis, with a focus on preparing data for processing and processing data for analysis. In that chapter, preparing data involved readying it for analysis through connecting and profiling. On the other hand, processing data encompassed cleaning and transforming the prepared data. It's important to note that in the broader context, the term "data preparation" or "data prep" includes activities from both the aforementioned phases – connecting, profiling, cleansing, and transforming the data. In this section, when I mention preparing data, you'll see that I am referring to the latter set of activities. However, before we get started with data preparation and the rest of the activities, we need to review the requirements.

Reviewing the requirements

For our data preparation exercise in this chapter, we'll use a new design that's quite different from the one we utilized earlier in this chapter. This will provide you with an opportunity to explore a different scenario to help simulate the varied experiences you might encounter while working on diverse Power BI projects in the real world.

In this section, our example is going to be that of sales orders from the famous fictional organization AdventureWorks Cycles. Sales is a business function that quite a lot of people are familiar with. *Figure 5.5* shows the design that we shall use in this section – tracking orders:

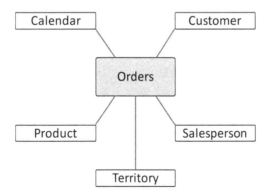

Figure 5.5: Star schema design for the sales semantic model

The design has also come through with a bus matrix for sales (*Table 5.8*):

Business Process	Dimension				
	Calendar	Customer	Salesperson	Territory	Product
Orders	X	X	X	X	X
Order budgets	X			X	X

Table 5.8: Bus matrix for partial sales business processes

The facts and measures that have been identified from these processes are depicted in *Table 5.9*:

Fact/Measure	Calculation	Source
Order Quantity	SUM(OrderQty)	SalesOrderDetail
Order Value	SUM(LineTotal)	SalesOrderDetail
Order Count	DISTINCTCOUNT(SalesOrderNumber)	SalesOrderHeader
Ave. Basket Count	Order Quantity / Order Count	
Ave. Order Value	Order Value / Order Count	
% Order Growth	[(Order Value - PY Order Value) / PY Order Value] * 100	

Table 5.9: Facts and measures profile

Now that we have a good understanding of what the requirements and a high-level design for a semantic model look like, we can connect to the data sources.

Connecting to the data sources

Our example will connect to the AdventureWorks database on a SQL Server instance for most of our data requirements.

> **The AdventureWorks database**
>
> The AdventureWorks database is available as a backup file to download for free from the Microsoft Learn website. To use it, you will need to restore the backup on a SQL Server. Here's the download link: https://learn.microsoft.com/en-us/sql/samples/adventureworks-install-configure.

We'll start with the *orders* business process, where the data is stored on two tables on the AdventureWorks database:

- `SalesOrderHeader`
- `SalesOrderDetail`

These tables are at two levels, sourcing the required facts for orders. As a data analyst, when I profile the tables, I notice that the header table has a single record per order, including the order number, the order date, and the total amounts before and after tax and shipping, among others. The detail table has the breakdown of the line items in the order, including the product, price, quantity, and line discounts, among others. To keep things simple, and to cater to the exact requirement, let's just select the required columns and proceed to profile them further.

Data profiling

Using the methods that we learned about in *Chapter 4* to connect to a SQL Server database, let's connect to the AdventureWorks database, select the `SalesOrderHeader` table, and select the fields listed in *Table 5.10*:

Field	Purpose
`OrderDate`	Key to the Calendar dimension.
`OnlineOrderFlag`	Provides the ability to analyze online or in-store orders. This is a dimension that does not have its own dimension table since it is the only column. These types of dimensions are called degenerate dimensions.
`SalesOrderNumber`	Another degenerate dimension is mainly used to get a count of orders. Apart from this, using it as a dimension would not make much sense except for users to drill down to see a list of orders that contributed to a particular analysis result; for example, what orders are less than 50 USD? As an alternative, we could turn this into a fact named Order Count by using the `DISTINCTCOUNT` function over SalesOrderNumber.
`CustomerID`	Key to the customer dimension.
`SalesPersonID`	Key to the salesperson dimension.
`TerritoryID`	Key to the territory dimension.
`Sales.` `SalesOrderDetail`	Link to the SalesOrderDetail table. This has been automatically linked due to the relationship between the two tables on the database. The facts that we need are to be taken from here.

Table 5.10: Columns selected from the SalesOrderHeader source table

One of the things that immediately caught my attention regarding the selected columns in *Figure 5.6* is that 15% of the values of `SalesPersonID` are empty. I confirmed this when I switched on the **Column profile** option. For analysis to be effective, it is important that some meaning is given to the missing data. When I investigated this further by filtering **SalespersonID** to null, I noticed that all the rows show `OnlineOrderFlag` as **Online**, indicating that online sales do not have a salesperson:

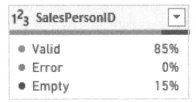

Figure 5.6: Column profile on the SalesPersonID column

Now that we're armed with these statistics and profile information, let's transform the data.

Transforming data

One thing that you may have realized is that no fact columns have been selected. Though there was a `SubTotal` field in the source table, we did not select it as part of the query because it would have only given me the subtotal of the entire order and not at the line level. We need the line-level value so that we can analyze sales from elements at the line level – for instance, product. Hence, the idea here is to pick up the line totals from the sales order detail table. *Figure 5.7* shows the `SalesOrderDetail` table showing up as a column, along with the columns selected on the `SalesOrderHeader` table:

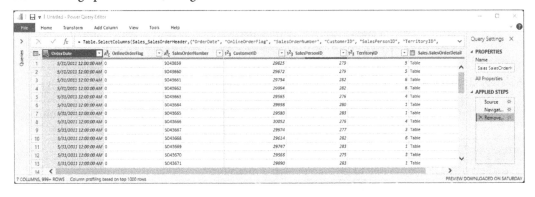

Figure 5.7: The SalesOrderHeader table queried with the required columns in Power BI

Next, we need to choose the required columns from the related `SalesOrderDetail` table. Using the `Power` functionality, this can easily be done by expanding on the `Sales.SalesOrderDetail` column:

Field	Purpose
OrderQty	The fact that aggregates the order quantity
LineTotal	The fact that aggregates the order value at the line level

Table 5.11: Columns selected from the SalesOrderDetail source table

The resulting table will resemble *Figure 5.8*:

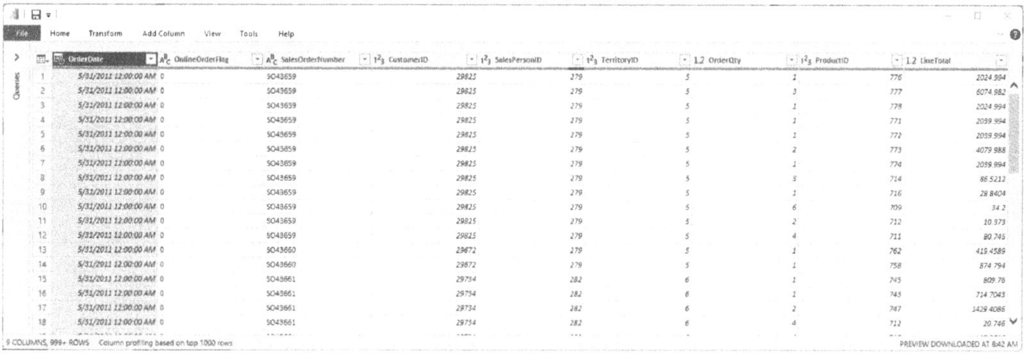

Figure 5.8: Columns selected from SalesOrderHeader and SalesOrderDetail

The structure of the query that we have derived so far reflects the fact table that we require. We now need to ensure that the fact table is aggregated across dimensions using the **Group By** option:

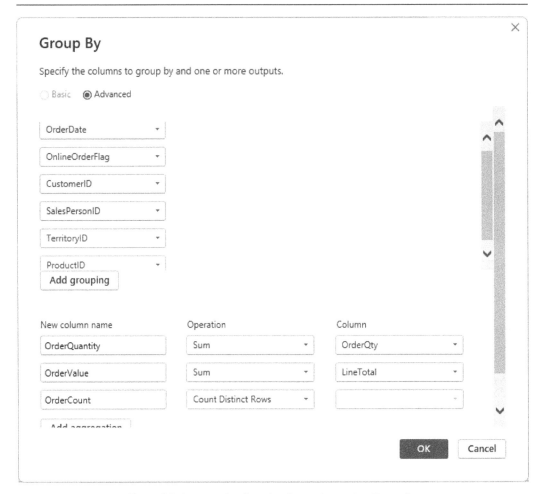

Figure 5.9: Aggregating facts by dimensions using Group By

If you look at the **Group By** dialogue box in *Figure 5.9*, you'll see that we have grouped by the dimension columns that we have identified, save one – SalesOrderNumber. This is because we intend to use it to create the OrderCount fact, which will specify the number of unique orders across the rest of the dimensions. You will also notice that OrderQty and LineTotal are being summed up as part of the aggregation. Similarly, the idea was to perform a distinct count of the SalesOrderNumber column. However, the **Group By** function is limited in that it can only count the number of rows.

Luckily, we have a workaround for this. When you observe the formula for the action in the **Formula Bar** area, you will notice a portion of the code that counts the distinct records in the table (*Figure 5.10*):

```
= Table.Group (#"Expanded Sales.SalesOrderDetail", {"OrderDate", "OnlineOrderFlag", "CustomerID", "SalesPersonID", "TerritoryID"},
                    {
                        {"OrderQuantity", each List.Sum([OrderQty]), type nullable number},
                        {"OrderValue", each List.Sum([LineTotal]), type nullable number},
                        {"OrderCount", each Table.RowCount(Table.Distinct(_)), Int64.Type}})
```

Figure 5.10: The Group By formula from the Formula Bar area

All we need to do is replace the portion with a reference to the `SalesOrderNumber` column (*Figure 5.11*):

```
= Table.Group (#"Expanded Sales.SalesOrderDetail", {"OrderDate", "OnlineOrderFlag", "CustomerID", "SalesPersonID", "TerritoryID"},
                    {
                        {"OrderQuantity", each List.Sum([OrderQty]), type nullable number},
                        {"OrderValue", each List.Sum([LineTotal]), type nullable number},
                        {"OrderCount", each Table.RowCount(List.Distinct(_[SalesOrderNumber])), Int64.Type}})
```

Figure 5.11: The Group By formula updated to include a distinct count of SalesOrderNumber

With that, the fact query has been structured with five dimensions and three facts that are aggregated across these dimensions. A little more touch-up and the query should be good to go:

Req. No.	Requirement
1	Change the data type of `OrderDate` to `Date` from `DateTime`
2	Separate the words in the column names to make the column names user-friendly
3	Change the values of the OnlineOrderFlag to either `Online` or `In-store` instead of 1 or 0
4	Rename `OrderDate` and `OnlineOrderFlag` to `Date` and `Channel`, respectively
5	Rename the query to `Orders`

Table 5.12: Data preparation requirements

Let's look at how we can fulfill these data preparation requirements:

- *Requirement number 1:* It can be easily performed by right-clicking on the column and changing the data type.

- *Requirement number 2:* It will require more of a workaround since there is no straightforward, visual way it can be done. However, the solution is not very complicated. The logic we need to follow is to cycle through each column, retrieve the column name, and split the text of the name at each lowercase-to-uppercase transition by inserting a space in between. This logic can be carried out by adding a new step to the query, and entering the code that does that:

```
= Table.TransformColumnNames(#"<Name of previous step>", each
Text.Combine(Splitter.SplitTextByCharacterTransition({"a" ..
"z"}, {"A" .. "Z"})(_), " "))
```

- *Requirement number 3:* It can be fulfilled in multiple ways. The simplest would be to right-click and choose **Replace Values** twice – once for 1 and again for 0.

- *Requirement number 4:* It is even simpler to fulfill; you just have to double-click on the column name and provide a new name for the columns.

- *Requirement number 5:* Like *number 4*, it just needs you to click on the Name property of the query on the right (or double-click its name on the left) to change the query's name.

The Orders fact query with the requirements fulfilled will resemble *Figure 5.12*; it has a granularity of Date, Channel, Customer, Salesperson, and Territory:

	Date	Channel	Customer ID	Salesperson ID	Territory ID	Product ID	Order Quantity	Order Value	Order Count
1	5/31/2011	In-store	29825	279	5	776	1	2024.994	1
2	5/31/2011	In-store	29825	279	5	777	3	6074.982	1
3	5/31/2011	In-store	29825	279	5	778	1	2024.994	1
4	5/31/2011	In-store	29825	279	5	771	1	2039.994	1
5	5/31/2011	In-store	29825	279	5	772	1	2039.994	1
6	5/31/2011	In-store	29825	279	5	773	2	4079.988	1
7	5/31/2011	In-store	29825	279	5	774	1	2039.994	1
8	5/31/2011	In-store	29825	279	5	714	3	86.5212	1
9	5/31/2011	In-store	29825	279	5	716	1	28.8404	1
10	5/31/2011	In-store	29825	279	1	709	6	54.2	1
11	5/31/2011	In-store	29825	279	5	712	2	10.373	1
12	5/31/2011	In-store	29825	279	5	711	4	80.746	1
13	5/31/2011	In-store	29672	279	5	762	1	419.4589	1
14	5/31/2011	In-store	29672	279	5	758	1	874.794	1
15	5/31/2011	In-store	29734	282	6	745	1	809.76	1
16	5/31/2011	In-store	29734	282	6	743	1	714.7048	1
17	5/31/2011	In-store	29734	282	6	747	2	1429.4086	1
18	5/31/2011	In-store	29734	282	6	712	4	20.746	1
19	5/31/2011	In-store	29734	282	6	715	4	115.8616	1
20	5/31/2011	In-store	29734	282	6	742	2	1445.1896	1
21	5/31/2011	In-store	29734	282	6	775	3	6074.982	1
22	5/31/2011	In-store	29734	282	6	778	2	4049.988	1
23	5/31/2011	In-store	29734	282	6	711	2	40.375	1
24	5/31/2011	In-store	29734	282	6	741	2	1687.4	1
25	5/31/2011	In-store	29734	282	6	778	4	8099.976	1
26	5/31/2011	In-store	29734	282	6	773	2	4079.988	1
27	5/31/2011	In-store	29734	282	6	716	2	57.6808	1

Figure 5.12: The Orders fact query prepared with data

In addition, it is a good idea to rename the steps of the query with meaningful phrases so that it can double up as documentation (*Figure 5.13*). To do this, you can just right-click and **Rename** each step of the query:

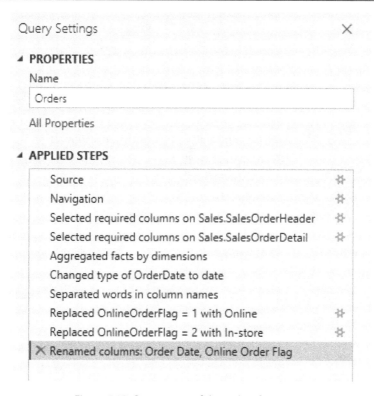

Figure 5.13: Query steps of the orders fact query

Now that we have the fact query for the business process done, we need to start preparing the queries for the dimensions. The data preparation requirements for the dimension queries are specified here:

Req. No.	Query	Requirement
6	Product	Combine the `Product`, `ProductSubcategory`, and `Category` source tables
7	Product	Select columns for the `ProductID`, `Name`, `Color`, `SubcategoryID`, `Subcategory`, `CategoryID`, and `Category` dimension attributes
8	Product	Replace null values on the `SubcategoryID` and `CategoryID` columns with a value of `-1`, and the columns with the subcategory and category names with `<Uncategorized>` to indicate that there is no categorization.
9	Product	Replace null values on Color with a value of `<No color>` to indicate that the particular products do not have a color.
10	Product	Separate the words in the column names to make the column names user-friendly.

Req. No.	Query	Requirement
11	Territory	Combine the `Sales.SalesTerritory` and `Person.CountryRegion` source tables. This is because the `SalesTerritory` table only has country codes, and not the country name, which will provide an intuitive analysis.
12	Territory	Select columns for the `TerritoryID`, `Name`, `CountryCode`, `Group`, and `Country` dimension attributes.
13	Territory	Separate the words in the column names to make the column names user-friendly.
14	Customer	Combine the `Sales.Customer`, `Person.Person`, and `Sales.Store` source tables.
15	Customer	Select columns for the `CustomerID`, `Person Type`, `FirstName`, `LastName`, and `Name` (of the customer store) dimension attributes.
16	Customer	Merge `FirstName` and `LastName` as `Name`.
17	Customer	Separate the words in the column names to make the column names user-friendly.
18	Salesperson	Combine `Sales.Salesperson`, `HumanResources.Employee`, and `Person.Person` source tables.
19	Salesperson	Select columns for the `Salesperson ID`, `Organization Level`, `Job Title`, `Birth Date`, `Gender`, `FirstName`, and `LastName` dimension attributes. (Note: `Salesperson ID` originates as `BusinessEntityID` in the source.)
20	Salesperson	Rename `BusinessEntityID` as `SalespersonID`.
21	Salesperson	Merge `FirstName` and `LastName` as `Name`.
22	Salesperson	Separate the words in the column names to make the column names user-friendly.

Table 5.13: Data preparation requirements for the dimension queries

Let's dive into fulfilling these data preparation requirements:

- *Requirement numbers 6-7*: The `Product` dimension query will require connecting to the database and selecting the `Production.Product` table from the source. After selecting the required fields, you just need to select the field that represents `Production.ProductSubcategory`, and then from within that, the field that represents `Production.ProductCategory`. The only fields that are required from the latter two tables will be their ID and name fields:

1²₃ ProductID	Aᴮ_C Name	Aᴮ_C Color	1²₃ ProductSubcategoryID	1²₃ ProductCategoryID	Aᴮ_C Name.1	Aᴮ_C Name.2	
1	Adjustable Race	null	null	null	null	null	null
2	Bearing Ball	null	null	null	null	null	null
3	BB Ball Bearing	null	null	null	null	null	null
4	Headset Ball Bearings	null	null	null	null	null	null
316	Blade	null	13	2	Pedals	Components	
317	LL Crankarm	Black	null	null	null	null	null
318	ML Crankarm	Black	null	null	null	null	null
319	HL Crankarm	Black	null	null	null	null	null
320	Chainring Bolts	Silver	null	null	null	null	null
321	Chainring Nut	Silver	null	null	null	null	null
322	Chainring	Black	null	null	null	null	null
323	Crown Race		null	null	null	null	null
324	Chain Stays		null	null	null	null	null
325	Decal 1		null	null	null	null	null

Figure 5.14: Required columns selected from the source tables for the Product dimension query

- *Requirement numbers 8-9*: The **Replace Values** function will easily take care of these requirements, similar to what we did with the `Orders` fact query (refer to *requirement number 3*).

- *Requirement number 10*: The same code used for *requirement number 2* on orders should work perfectly here as well, and you've got the `Product` dimension query all set:

	1²₃ Product ID	Aᴮ_C Name	Aᴮ_C Color	1.2 Subcategory ID	Aᴮ_C Subcategory	1.2 Category ID	Aᴮ_C Category	
1	1	Adjustable Race	<No color>	-1	<Uncategorized>	-1	<Uncategorized>	
2	2	Bearing Ball	<No color>	-1	<Uncategorized>	-1	<Uncategorized>	
3	3	BB Ball Bearing	<No color>	-1	<Uncategorized>	-1	<Uncategorized>	
4	4	Headset Ball Bearings	<No color>	-1	<Uncategorized>	-1	<Uncategorized>	
5	316	Blade	<No color>	13	Pedals	2	Components	
6	317	LL Crankarm	Black	-1	<Uncategorized>	-1	<Uncategorized>	
7	318	ML Crankarm	Black	-1	<Uncategorized>	-1	<Uncategorized>	
8	319	HL Crankarm	Black	-1	<Uncategorized>	-1	<Uncategorized>	
9	320	Chainring Bolts	Silver	-1	<Uncategorized>	-1	<Uncategorized>	
10	321	Chainring Nut	Silver	-1	<Uncategorized>	-1	<Uncategorized>	
11	322	Chainring	Black	-1	<Uncategorized>	-1	<Uncategorized>	
12	323	Crown Race	<No color>	-1	<Uncategorized>	-1	<Uncategorized>	
13	324	Chain Stays	<No color>	-1	<Uncategorized>	-1	<Uncategorized>	
14	325	Decal 1	<No color>	-1	<Uncategorized>	-1	<Uncategorized>	
15	326	Decal 2	<No color>	-1	<Uncategorized>	-1	<Uncategorized>	
16	327	Down Tube	<No color>	-1	<Uncategorized>	-1	<Uncategorized>	
17	328	Mountain End Caps	<No color>	-1	<Uncategorized>	-1	<Uncategorized>	
18	329	Road End Caps	<No color>	-1	<Uncategorized>	-1	<Uncategorized>	
19	330	Touring End Caps	<No color>	-1	<Uncategorized>	-1	<Uncategorized>	
20	331	Fork End	<No color>	-1	<Uncategorized>	-1	<Uncategorized>	

Figure 5.15: Sample results of the completed Product dimension query

- *Requirement numbers 11-13*: Similar steps to that of the `Product` query will get you where you want with the `Territory` dimension query:

Territory ID	Name	Country Code	Group	Country
1	1 Northwest	US	North America	United States
2	2 Northeast	US	North America	United States
3	3 Central	US	North America	United States
4	4 Southwest	US	North America	United States
5	5 Southeast	US	North America	United States
6	6 Canada	CA	North America	Canada
7	7 France	FR	Europe	France
8	8 Germany	DE	Europe	Germany
9	9 Australia	AU	Pacific	Australia
10	10 United Kingdom	GB	Europe	United Kingdom

Figure 5.16: Sample results of the completed Territory dimension query

- *Requirement numbers 14-22*: The `Customer` dimension and `Salesperson` dimension queries also follow closely in the footsteps of the former dimension queries. Here's the results of the completed `Customer` dimension query:

Customer ID	Person Type	Person Name	Name
1	29484 SC	Gustavo Achong	Next-Door Bike Store
2	29485 SC	Catherine Abel	Professional Sales and Service
3	29486 SC	Kim Abercrombie	Riders Company
4	29487 SC	Humberto Acevedo	The Bike Mechanics
5	29488 SC	Pilar Ackerman	Nationwide Supply
6	29489 SC	Frances Adams	Area Bike Accessories
7	29490 SC	Margaret Smith	Bicycle Accessories and Kits
8	29491 SC	Carla Adams	Clamps & Brackets Co.
9	29492 SC	Jay Adams	Valley Bicycle Specialists
10	29493 SC	Ronald Adina	New Bikes Company

Figure 5.17: Sample results of the completed Customer dimension query

And here's the result of the completed `Sales` dimension query:

1²₃ Salesperson ID	1.2 Organization Level	A⁼C Job Title	Birth Date	A⁼C Gender	A⁼C Name
1	285	2 Pacific Sales Manager	1/11/1975	M	Syed Abbas
2	283	3 Sales Representative	2/11/1974	M	David Campbell
3	278	3 Sales Representative	2/4/1975	M	Garrett Vargas
4	279	3 Sales Representative	1/18/1974	M	Tsvi Reiter
5	277	3 Sales Representative	8/29/1962	F	Jillian Carson
6	275	3 Sales Representative	12/25/1968	M	Michael Blythe
7	288	3 Sales Representative	7/9/1975	F	Rachel Valdez
8	287	2 European Sales Manager	9/20/1957	F	Amy Alberts
9	276	3 Sales Representative	2/27/1980	F	Linda Mitchell
10	282	3 Sales Representative	12/11/1963	M	José Saraiva
11	289	3 Sales Representative	3/17/1968	F	Jae Pak
12	290	3 Sales Representative	9/30/1975	M	Ranjit Varkey Chudukatil
13	274	2 North American Sales Manager	10/17/1951	M	Stephen Jiang
14	286	3 Sales Representative	2/14/1977	F	Lynn Tsoflias
15	280	3 Sales Representative	12/6/1974	F	Pamela Ansman-Wolfe
16	284	3 Sales Representative	1/5/1978	M	Tete Mensa-Annan
17	281	3 Sales Representative	3/9/1968	M	Shu Ito

Figure 5.18: Sample results of the completed Sales dimension query

Now that we have connected, profiled, cleansed, and transformed the data needed for the semantic model, we need to start building the model.

Building the model

In this section, we will look at building the semantic model that we've designed and prepared data for in the previous sections. Building a semantic model involves using the queries that were prepared using Power Query, loading them into Power BI Desktop, and then performing the following tasks:

1. Reviewing and enabling relationships among the tables.

2. Ensuring the correct data types of the columns.

3. Structuring the tables according to the requirements and standards.

4. Creating and organizing measures.

5. Creating and organizing hierarchies.

When you load the data that you prepared for the model by clicking on the **Close & Apply** option in the Power Query window, the queries will connect to the source and start applying the set of steps defined on each query, thereby extracting, transforming, and loading the data into Power BI Desktop. Depending on the size of the source tables, it may be a quick action that takes a few seconds, though it may be longer, such as several minutes.

Once the data has been loaded, you can go to either the **Table view** tab or the **Model view** tab to check this. While the **Table view** tab allows you to check the data on each table that is now loaded via the queries, the **Model view** tab will show you the metadata of the tables that were loaded. After quickly checking on the data on the **Table view** tab, we can switch to the **Model view** tab because it is a more versatile view to build our semantic model with.

If our data preparation has been done correctly, according to the requirements, you will see a model that looks like what's shown in *Figure 5.19* (with a little bit of rearranging). You will notice that the relationships are already created automatically by Power BI. If one or more of the relationships are not there, they can be easily created by clicking and dragging the column from one table to the related column of the other table – for example, `TerritoryID` on `Territory` to `TerritoryID` on `Orders`:

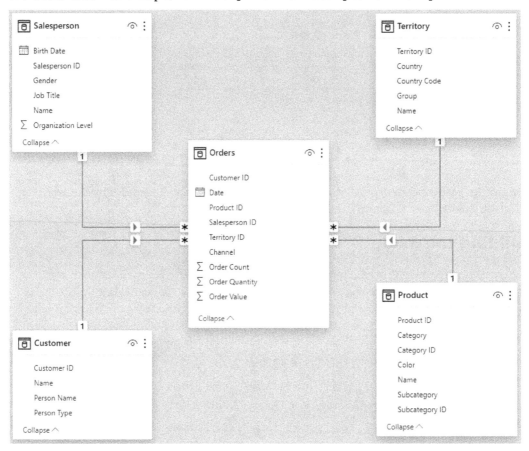

Figure 5.19: First iteration of the sales semantic model

We now have the fact table and dimension tables generated from the source system. Next, we'll fulfill the rest of the requirements by ensuring we have all the required dimension tables.

Looking at the calendar (or date) dimension table

When we compare the model at hand with that of the star schema design in the *Designing a model* section, you will have noticed that we don't have a calendar (that is, a date) dimension table. The fact and dimension tables that we currently have were sourced from designated tables on the AdventureWorks database. However, a calendar table usually does not have a source table on an application database. Proceeding to use the dates from a column such as `OrderDate` from `SalesOrderHeader` as an alternative will not work. This is because a calendar dimension table requires an unbroken list of dates, whereas the list of dates in `OrderDate` may not be complete since there can be days on which orders were not submitted. A calendar dimension is also used for time intelligence, which requires the list of dates to include dates from prior years as well. Due to these reasons, a calendar dimension table is generated from scratch. In Power BI, all you will need are two dates: the starting date and the ending date for your list. In our example, since the only transactions come from the `SalesOrderHeader` table, which has been converted into the `Orders` table, we can pick the start and end dates to be the oldest and latest dates from this table. In other scenarios, where you might have multiple fact tables, since you would want the calendar dimension to cater to each of these, you may want to look across these tables to feed the start and end dates for the calendar.

> **Note**
>
> Choosing the start and end dates from the fact tables is only one approach. You may wish to choose an approach that makes the most sense when you design different solutions.

We'll proceed to create the `Calendar` table by clicking on the **New table** option on the home ribbon and using the following DAX code:

```
Calendar =
VAR StartDate = MIN ( Orders[Date] )
VAR EndDate = MAX ( Orders[Date] )
RETURN
ADDCOLUMNS (
    CALENDAR(StartDate, EndDate),
    "Weekday Number", WEEKDAY( [Date] ),
    "Weekday", FORMAT ( [Date], "dddd" ),
    "Month Number", MONTH ( [Date] ),
    "Month Name", FORMAT ( [Date], "mmmm" ),
    "Quarter Number", ROUNDUP( DIVIDE ( MONTH ( [Date] ), 3), 0),
    "Quarter Name", "Q" & ROUNDUP( DIVIDE ( MONTH ( [Date] ), 3), 0),
    "Calendar Year", "CY " & YEAR ( [Date] )
)
```

The preceding code creates two variables for the start and end dates and populates them with the oldest and newest dates, respectively. Then, it uses the ADDCOLUMNS function to generate a table. The first column it adds is the Date column, which is, in turn, generated by the CALENDAR function. You will notice that the CALENDAR function uses the variables to provide a start date and an end date. The column will also be populated with values between the two dates. Next, a column is added for the weekday number using the WEEKDAY function, which makes use of the Date column to generate the number of the weekday. Similarly, the weekday name, month number, month name, quarter number, quarter name, and calendar columns are added:

Date	Calendar Year	Month Name	Month Number	Weekday	Weekday Number	Quarter Number	Quarter Name
1 July, 2012	CY 2012	July		7 Sunday	1	3	Q3
2 July, 2012	CY 2012	July		7 Monday	2	3	Q3
3 July, 2012	CY 2012	July		7 Tuesday	3	3	Q3
4 July, 2012	CY 2012	July		7 Wednesday	4	3	Q3
5 July, 2012	CY 2012	July		7 Thursday	5	3	Q3
6 July, 2012	CY 2012	July		7 Friday	6	3	Q3
7 July, 2012	CY 2012	July		7 Saturday	7	3	Q3
8 July, 2012	CY 2012	July		7 Sunday	1	3	Q3
9 July, 2012	CY 2012	July		7 Monday	2	3	Q3
10 July, 2012	CY 2012	July		7 Tuesday	3	3	Q3
11 July, 2012	CY 2012	July		7 Wednesday	4	3	Q3
12 July, 2012	CY 2012	July		7 Thursday	5	3	Q3
13 July, 2012	CY 2012	July		7 Friday	6	3	Q3
14 July, 2012	CY 2012	July		7 Saturday	7	3	Q3
15 July, 2012	CY 2012	July		7 Sunday	1	3	Q3
16 July, 2012	CY 2012	July		7 Monday	2	3	Q3
17 July, 2012	CY 2012	July		7 Tuesday	3	3	Q3
18 July, 2012	CY 2012	July		7 Wednesday	4	3	Q3
19 July, 2012	CY 2012	July		7 Thursday	5	3	Q3
20 July, 2012	CY 2012	July		7 Friday	6	3	Q3

Figure 5.20: The generated calendar table

The calendar table that we've created should be considered the bare minimum. In an ideal scenario, the calendar table will be much more comprehensive than this and include the financial calendar, holidays, and organization-specific columns as well. The following link provides a reference calendar table template that you can take advantage of for various Power BI solutions: https://www.sqlbi.com/articles/reference-date-table-in-dax-and-power-bi/.

There's one more thing that you need to do on the `Calendar` table: mark it as a `Date` table. By marking a table as a date table, you are allowing time intelligence functionality to work – for instance, if you need to get the value of a fact from the same month of the previous year. Marking your calendar table as a date table is a simple configuration. The **Mark as date table** option appears when you select the table and go to the **Table tools** ribbon. All you need to do is select the column that has an unbroken list of dates – in our case, `Date`:

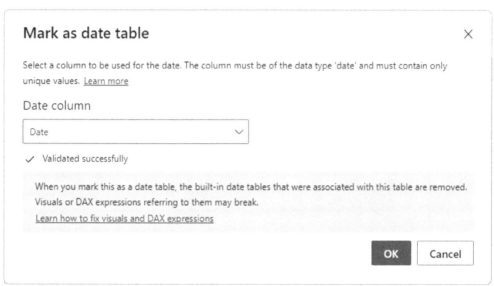

Figure 5.21: Marking the calendar table as a date table

Once connected to the `Orders` table, the star schema will match our design (*Figure 5.22*). One easy way to connect tables is by dragging the `Date` column from the `Calendar` table over the `Data` column on `Orders`. If all the necessary settings are in place, the relationship will be established. If not, the **Edit relationship** window will open, where you can configure the relationship:

Figure 5.22: Star schema aligned with the design

With that, we have built the foundation of the semantic model; the star schema is in place and is in line with the design. However, we are not done yet. We still need to shape the model into something intuitive for business users.

Shaping the model

When you look at the model from an end user's perspective, you will want to see the data elements that you are familiar with, and not additional pieces of data that can throw you off or confuse you. The structure of the model should also be easy to navigate and use. Let's look at ways in which we can touch up the model.

The ID fields on the fact table and the dimension tables are not usually something that can be used for analysis. Users would rather use the names or categories and such. Hence, one of the first things we must do is hide these fields. This can be done by selecting the fields and switching on the **Is hidden** option. Alternatively, we can click on the eye icon next to the field to hide it. You will do this for all the ID fields. I will also hide the `Date` column on `Orders` since `Date` on `Calendar` can be used instead.

Next, when you look around at each table, you will notice that some of the fields have the sigma (Σ) symbol next to them. This indicates that Power BI is applying an aggregation to them. While Power BI gets it right sometimes, other times, it does not. In our example, `Order Count`, `Order Quantity`, and `Order Value` are the right candidates for aggregation, while `Month Number`, `Quarter Number`, and `Weekday Number` on `Calendar`, and `Organization Level` on `Salesperson`, are not. For instance, you will want to analyze the total `Order Value`, whereas the total of the month numbers does not make much sense. Hence, to save some confusion that users might have, we can disable aggregation on these columns by changing the value in the **Summarize by** property to **None**. While we are at it, it makes sense to check if the **Summarize by** setting is set to **Sum** for the three facts on the `Orders` table.

You can set summarization by clicking on the relevant column in the **Model view** tab, and then setting the **Advanced | Summarize by** property on the **Properties** pane.

Organizing dimension hierarchies

Now, let's focus on the dimensions to figure out the hierarchies that we could create. **Hierarchies** help users easily set up visuals with drill-down. It also provides the users with a pre-defined hierarchy instead of letting them figure it out for themselves. *Table 5.14* provides a list of hierarchies that are required for the dimensions:

Table	Hierarchies
Product	Category > Subcategory > Name
Calendar	Calendar Year > Quarter Name > Month Name > Date
Territory	Group > Country > Name

Table 5.14: Hierarchy requirements on dimension tables

There are a couple of ways to create hierarchies on tables. I shall use the method available in the **Model view** tab. I will start by right-clicking on the `Category` column (the top-level element I want in my hierarchy) in the `Product` table on the **Data** pane and selecting **Create hierarchy**. The hierarchy gets created, as well as some properties that I can use to add the rest of the columns. I will select `Subcategory` and `Name` and then apply the changes:

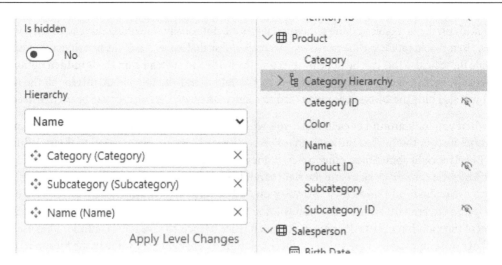

Figure 5.23: Creating a hierarchy on a dimension

Furthermore, I will also rename Name in the hierarchy to Product to give it a more intuitive feel and rename the hierarchy as well, to Categorization. This gives the hierarchy a complete and intuitive feel.

However, the Category, Subcategory, and Name columns are still there, right next to the hierarchy. There are a couple of things you can do about this. To reduce the confusion that users may have as to which category field, or which subcategory field, should they choose, we can either hide these fields or put them away in a folder so that if they are needed individually, users can open the folder to pick them. Let's try the latter option. All we need to do is select the three fields, and then type the name of the folder in the **Display folder** property; let's use **Additional Attributes**. Finally, when you go into the **Report view** tab, which is the view that business users will be using, you will see a tidy, intuitive dimension table under Product (*Figure 5.24*):

Figure 5.24: The Product dimension is intuitive to use

The steps to create the hierarchies for `Calendar` and `Territory` will be very similar:

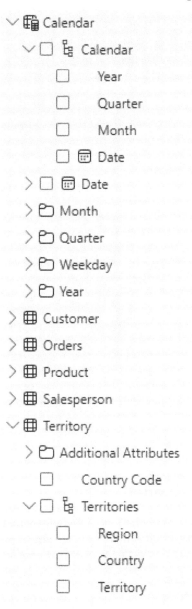

Figure 5.25: The Calendar and Territory dimensions with a clean look

The dimensions' hierarchies are now organized since are the columns of the dimensions. Next, let's look at how we can categorize some of the data elements to make analysis more intuitive.

Categorizing data

We have one final configuration we must perform on the dimensions – setting the `Country` attribute of the `Territory` dimension to be recognized as a country, especially on map visuals. This way, the visuals will know where exactly to place data points if they are related to a country. All we need to do is select the `Country` column and set the `Data` category property under **Advanced** to `Country/ Region`:

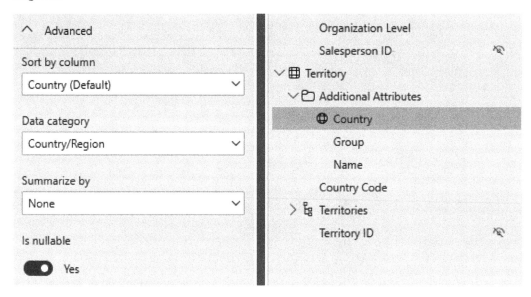

Figure 5.26: The Country attribute set with a data category

With that, we have finished setting up the dimensions. The next job is to complete the measure requirements on the fact table.

Adding measures to the model

The requirements for measures in our example (*Table 5.9*) list three measures that need to be created. Measures in Power BI are calculations that you define using one or more columns from the tables. When you create a measure, it's housed in the table that is selected at that time. However, unlike a column, measures are not bound to a table. This means that the context of a measure is global within the semantic model. You can, however, narrow down its context by slicing and dicing a measure using attributes of a dimension. Examples of slicing and dicing are filtering and drilling down. A measures' home table can also be changed if you need it to. You will also not see a measure as a column of the table when you go into the **Table view** tab.

Since the fact columns that we are going to create the measures with are in the Orders fact table, let's also create the measure in the Orders table. We can create a measure using the **New measure** option after selecting the table we want it housed in. Measures are created using DAX; hence, you will see the prompt to write the DAX code in the **Formula Bar** area. The first measure can easily be created using the following code. You will notice Power BI's IntelliSense kicking in to help you while you do that:

```
Ave. Basket Count = SUM ( Orders[Order Quantity] ) / SUM (
Orders[Order Count] )
```

Since measures are aggregated values, we can use the SUM function to sum up the order quantity and the order count facts before performing the divide operation. We can also use the DIVIDE function, which has the added advantage of allowing you to handle division by zero errors by specifying an alternate result. Let's try that on the next measure:

```
Ave. Order Value = DIVIDE ( SUM ( Orders[Order Value] ), SUM (
Orders[Order Count] ), 0 )
```

For the third measure, the denominator requires a previous year's value to determine the growth. We can do this by first creating a measure just for the previous year's order value, and then using it in the calculation, or injecting the formula within the main calculation itself. Let's use the former method; this way, we'll have yet another measure that users can take advantage of if needed:

```
PY Order Value = CALCULATE ( SUM ( Orders[Order Value] ),
SAMEPERIODLASTYEAR ( 'Calendar'[Date] ) )
```

Here, we use the CALCULATE function to get the sum of the order value, and then filter it by the list of dates from the previous year. The SAMEPERIODLASTYEAR function determines the current period based on the context that is selected (for example, CY 2014 or CY 2014 > January) and then gets the corresponding period from the previous year. This measure will only make sense if it is being used within the context of the calendar; for example, a filter set to the current year.

Next, let's create the final measure:

```
% Order Growth = DIVIDE ( SUM ( Orders[Order Value] ) - [PY Order
Value], [PY Order Value], 0 )
```

You may have noticed that I have not multiplied the result by 100 to get the percentage. That's because I am going to leave that to the measure formatting that I am going to apply using the **Measure tools** ribbon.

I have applied the Percentage format to % Order Growth, the Currency format to Ave. Order Value and PY Order Value, and the Decimal format to Ave. Basket Count in addition to setting it with a *thousands separator*. I also took the opportunity to set the formatting of our three fact columns – Order Value, Order Quantity, and Order Count – with the appropriate formatting.

To test these all out, let's go to the **Report view** tab and select all the facts and the measure on a table visual, alongside the `Year` attribute from the Calendar dimension (*Figure 5.27*):

Year	Sum of Order Value	PY Order Value	% Order Growth	Sum of Order Quantity	Sum of Order Count	Ave. Basket Count	Ave. Order Value
CY 2011	$12,641,672.21		0.00%	12,888	5,716	2.25	$2,211.63
CY 2012	$33,524,301.32	$12,641,672.21	165.19%	68,579	21,689	3.16	$1,545.68
CY 2013	$43,622,479.05	$33,524,301.32	30.12%	131,788	56,573	2.33	$771.08
CY 2014	$20,058,118.78	$43,622,479.05	-54.02%	61,662	37,343	1.65	$537.13
Total	**$109,846,571.37**	**$89,788,452.59**	**22.34%**	**274,917**	**121,321**	**2.27**	**$905.42**

Figure 5.27: Facts and measures displayed against the calendar year

Let's perform one last task to organize the elements in the Orders table into a folder (*Figure 5.28*):

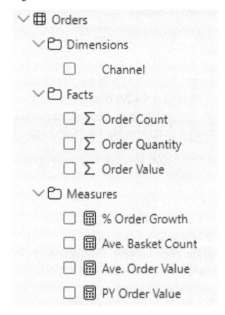

Figure 5.28: Elements of the Orders table organized into folders

The construction of the semantic model is now complete. In this section, we loaded the data from the queries into tables in Power BI and created a Calendar table. We ensured the correct relationships among the tables for a star schema and structured, formatted, and organized the tables. Finally, we built the measures in the model that users will use for their analysis and reporting.

Now, we'll look at some advanced modeling options.

Exploring advanced modeling considerations

Once you have a basic semantic model – one with a simple star schema – there can always be further requirements that would need you to perform more advanced modeling to cater to those requirements. Let's take a look at what happens when you have multiple business processes to handle.

Catering to multiple business processes

The original requirements of this example consisted of a second business process that we have still not addressed (*Table 5.8*): Order budgets. The order budgets are stored across multiple annual Excel workbooks in a SharePoint folder. A sample of one of these files is depicted in *Figure 5.29*:

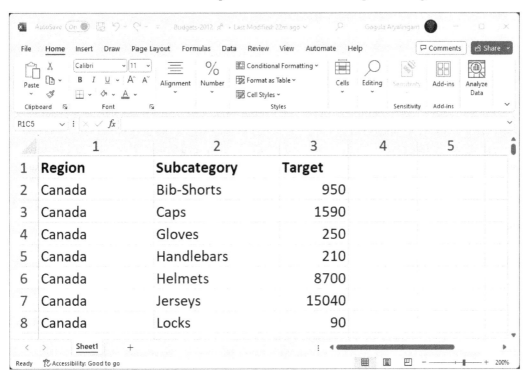

Figure 5.29: Sample of the Order budgets file for 2012

Using the method that we learned about in *Chapter 3*, in the *Files and spreadsheets* section, and lessons from this chapter, we must process these set of files into a fact table (*Figure 5.32*):

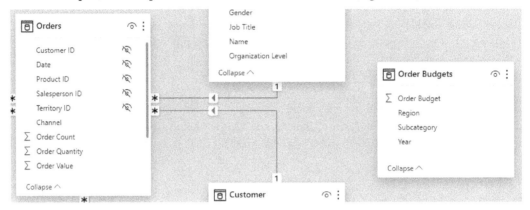

Figure 5.30: The Order Budgets fact table among the rest of the tables

One of the things that a user would like to see is the order value against the budget value so that they can analyze it across years and other dimensions. If you look closely at the budget fact table, you will notice that the granularity is at a higher level than what it is on the orders fact table. Also, the channel, customer, and salesperson dimensions are not considered for budgets. However, if you want to measure the order value against the budgets, you will need to create a relationship with the dimensions.

To do this, according to standard dimensional modeling techniques, you will need to break the dimensions into a snowflake structure. For example, if you take product, you will have to create one table with the product level, and another with the subcategory level upwards, while maintaining a relationship between them. You can then link the `Subcategory` dimension table with `Order Budgets`.

However, with Power BI, you have the option of using a many-to-many relationship, which takes away the need for snowflaking your dimensions. All you need to do, in this case, is drag the `Subcategory` field from the `Product` table to the corresponding field on `Order Budgets`. Then, you need to set the **Cross filter direction** property to **Single (Product filters Order Budgets)** (*Figure 5.31*). Doing a similar kind of configuration using `Region` and `Year` will complete the setup:

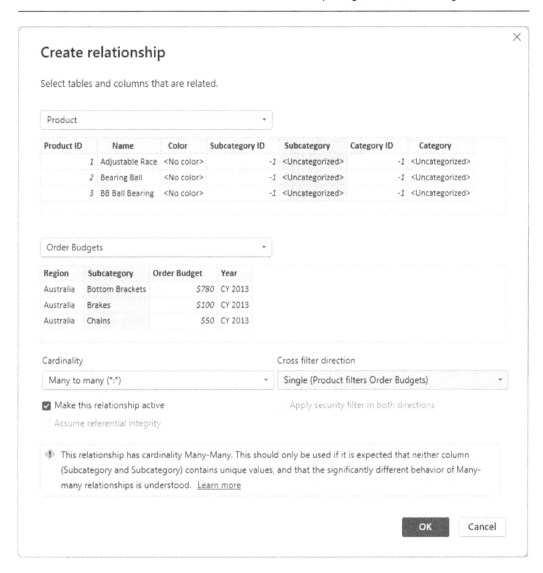

Figure 5.31: A many-to-many relationship between Product and Order Budgets

Once you've arranged the tables in the **Model view** tab, you may notice a complex diagram due to the increased number of tables (*Figure 5.32*):

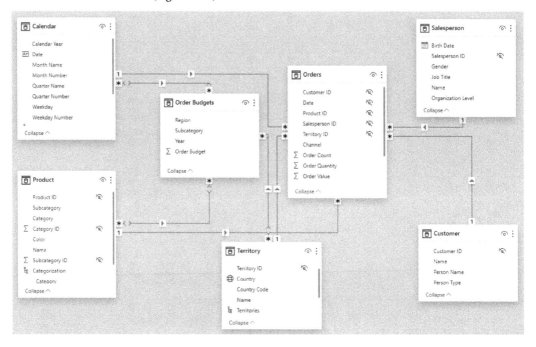

Figure 5.32: The complete star schema with two fact tables

However, if we add a new diagram with only the Order region and the related dimensions, you will see a perfect star (*Figure 5.33*):

Figure 5.33: A star schema with only Order Budgets and its related dimensions

To test out the values from each fact table against the year, I selected the appropriate columns for the canvas. I also created a measure using facts from both tables:

```
% Order Value vs Budget = DIVIDE ( SUM ( Orders[Order Value] ), SUM (
'Order Budgets'[Order Budget] ), 0 )
```

Here's the output:

Year	Sum of Order Value	Sum of Order Budget	% Order Value vs Budget
CY 2011	$12,641,672.21	$832,460	1518.59%
CY 2012	$33,524,301.32	$23,835,580	140.65%
CY 2013	$43,622,479.05	$32,212,860	135.42%
CY 2014	$20,058,118.78	$46,132,830	43.48%
Total	**$109,846,571.37**	**$103,013,730**	**106.63%**

Figure 5.34: Measures from two fact tables viewed against a dimension

Now that we know how to cater to multiple business processes in a single semantic model, let's move on to another paradigm where dimensional modeling is mostly done for you.

Modeling on a data warehouse

A data warehouse is a database that aggregates data for analysis. One of the most popular methods to build one is to use the dimensional modeling technique itself. In fact (pun intended), dimensional modeling was first used to build databases before the concept was used to base tools such as Power BI on. This means more in-depth concepts related to dimensional modeling are used in data warehouses. One of the concepts that is regularly used is the concept of surrogate keys on dimension tables. A surrogate key is a numeric column (usually auto-incrementing) that's introduced to each dimension to uniquely identify each record. Though most dimensions come with their own ID from the source, such as the customer ID or the product ID, different sources use different formats and data types. Also, in some scenarios, a particular system, such as a **customer relationship management** (**CRM**) system, is used for a few years, before being replaced by a brand-new one. If all the customers in the old systems are not migrated and the organization wishes for you to use the new system going forward for new customer information, you will essentially end up having a dimension with data from two systems, where the key can be of different data types or the same data type with overlapping IDs. The solution to handle this is using a surrogate key. You will still keep the original key so that you can match it against the source when integrating data.

A data warehouse also has the design and functionality to store the historical information of a dimension. However, in Power BI, this is very limited because we tap into the source at its current state for our data. Whenever we need to connect to a data warehouse, we will need to know that most of the star schemas are done for us. We just need to choose a subset that will fit our requirements. Once we've imported that data, we may only have to create the measures and touch up the dimensions by creating hierarchies and hiding unwanted columns.

> **Tip**
>
> A good idea when playing around with data from a data warehouse in Power BI is to use the sample AdventureWorksDW database, which contains the same data that we are working with converted into a data warehouse. Here's the download link: `https://learn.microsoft.com/en-us/sql/samples/adventureworks-install-configure`.

Next, let's look at an advanced modeling scenario that you may encounter, regardless of whether you're using a regular operational source or a data warehouse.

Derived dimension attributes

As a data analyst, you tend to continuously improve the analysis that you are trying to do. When you look at our example, you notice that the Customer dimension's `Birth Date` attribute doesn't help much. Analyzing sales by the salesperson's year of birth might make sense sometimes, but what would be much better would be if the analysis could be done by the salesperson's age group. Let's try deriving an attribute from the birth date:

```
Age Range =
VAR Age = INT ( YEARFRAC ( [Birth Date], TODAY(), 3 ) )
RETURN
SWITCH ( TRUE(),
                 Age >= 20 && Age < 30, "20-29",
                 Age >= 30 && Age < 40, "30-39",
                 Age >= 40 && Age < 50, "40-49",
                 Age >= 50, ">= 50"
)
```

In the first portion of the code, the `YEARFRAC` function calculates the difference between the birth date and the current date in a fraction of years and then casts it to an integer to remove the fraction portion, resulting in the age. The age is then matched against predetermined ranges to obtain the correct one.

One thing you need to remember is that, on each day, the age range that a salesperson belongs to can potentially change. If you are analyzing sales by the salesperson's age, range this may not be ideal. What you are looking for is the salesperson's age range at the time of sale. For this, you will need to create the column in the `Orders` table itself, where you will use the order date of the row instead of the current date. However, the column will not be part of the `Salesperson` dimension, but rather a degenerate dimension, much like `Channel`.

In this section, we explored catering to multiple business processes in your semantic model, and how to build a model if most of the modeling was done for you in a data warehouse. We also explored how to design and build derived dimension attributes.

Q&A

Bringing your data into Power BI and developing the perfect semantic model is what we have worked toward since *Chapter 3*. Hence, it makes sense that we look at a few probable questions that you can be asked in an interview. You need to understand that these questions can be potentially asked in different ways, so you must prepare for them accordingly.

Question 1: Why is it important to design a semantic model before you build one?

Answer: The design provides a way for you to envision what the result of the model will look like. It also ensures that all the business requirements are considered and mapped to the output of the model. The model author now has a guideline against which they can develop the model without any unnecessary deviations.

Question 2: What methodology have you used to design a semantic model?

For your answer: Refer to the *Designing a model* section in this chapter and prepare a summary of dimensional modeling that you can talk about with your interviewer. Here are some important points to consider in your answer:

- Facts
- Dimensions
- Measures
- Business processes
- Fact tables
- Dimension tables

Ensure that you provide your answer with examples. Generating simple examples using the `AdventureWorks` database, as we did in this chapter, works well.

Question 3: How would you design a semantic model that has two fact tables with different granularities, while sharing some of the dimensions with each other?

For your answer: Refer to the *Understanding the bus matrix* and *Catering to multiple business processes* section in this chapter, and prepare a summary that talks about how a bus matrix documents the business processes, which are then mapped as fact tables in your design, and how you handle granularity in Power BI using a many-to-many relationship.

Question 4: What is a snowflake schema and how is it different from a star schema? (This question is related to question 3.)

Answer: A snowflake schema is typically used to support multiple fact tables that are of different granularities. For example, you can split a `product` dimension into two – `product` and `product category` – if one fact table (for example, `sales orders`) tracks orders at the product level, and another fact table (for example, `sales targets`) tracks orders at the product category level. However, with Power BI's many-to-many relationship capability, you can avoid this. Snowflake schemas can also be used when one dimension (for example, `product`) is related to another dimension (for example, `manufacturer`), and product and manufacturer are used to analyze one fact table (for example, `sales`), and manufacturer is used to analyze another fact table that's unrelated to the sales business process (for example, `manufacturer performance`).

Question 5: What's the importance of a date or calendar dimension?

Answer: Refer to the *Looking at the calendar (or date) dimension table* section and prepare a summary to explain why a date dimension is needed, including mentions of an unbroken list of dates, and time intelligence. It will also be a bonus if you explain how you would generate a date or calendar table. The section only covers building the calendar dimension on Power BI using **DAX**. However, you should also talk about how this can be achieved using **Power Query**. The following article will give you a good understanding of this topic: `https://radacad.com/all-in-one-script-to-create-date-dimension-in-power-bi-using-power-query`.

Question 6: How would you recommend bringing in data from multiple files of the same structure into Power BI?

For your answer: In *Chapter 3*, in the *Exporting data into Power BI* section, in the *Files and spreadsheets* subsection, I talked about importing multiple files of the same structure into Power BI from **SharePoint Online**. Refer to this subsection and prepare a summary where you talk about how you can do this. Also, it is good to mention that this is a better way than hosting the files in a folder on an on-premises computer, where you will have to ensure that the computer is always on and requires an on-premises data gateway.

Question 7: Can you combine data from multiple sources to create a single dataset?

Answer: Respond to the affirmative. This was covered in *Chapter 3*, in the *Combining data from multiple sources* section. Prepare a summary to describe how you would combine data from a database and a file. Ensure you talk about having a key to relate the two datasets on.

Summary

In this chapter, we learned how to develop a semantic model using Powe BI. We started by putting down the design for the model using a concept called dimensional modeling, also known as a star schema. You learned how you would start by identifying the business processes, the dimensions associated with the business processes, and how you would map them out in an enterprise bus matrix. This allows you to easily sketch the star schema, which would act as the outline for your model. Then, you learned how to identify the facts and the measures that users want to measure, and how to map them to your business process.

Once the design was laid out, you learned how you would prepare the data – that is, by connecting, extracting, transforming, and loading the data into Power BI by mapping the star schema from the design. You learned how to establish relationships among the tables, create the measures, structure the dimensions, and organize all of the elements into an intuitive model.

Finally, you looked at a few advanced modeling considerations that you may be faced with when building a semantic mode The model is now set up for analysis.

In the next chapter let's explore how business users can use it to build reports, perform their ad hoc analysis, connect to it from Excel, and even build scorecards.

The model is now set up for analysis. In the next chapter let's explore how business users can use it to build reports, perform their ad hoc analysis, connect to it from Excel, and even build scorecards.

6

Exploring, Visualizing, and Sharing Data and Deploying Solutions

In this chapter, you will journey through the key skills needed for data analysis and sharing the results with your audience. We'll start by exploring semantic models and using various techniques to reveal valuable insights. Then, we'll learn how to visualize these insights with various functionality provided by Power BI, along with packaging these outputs for your audience. Next, we'll focus on the various methods we can use to publish and share Power BI content so that it reaches end users effectively. Finally, we'll conclude by covering deployment strategies, refreshing schedules, and configurations so that you can seamlessly integrate data for your solutions.

This chapter deals with the second part of data analysis. The first part, *Chapter 5*, focused on bringing data from various places, putting it together, and making it available for consumption through semantic models. This chapter will deal with using that data to disseminate intelligence to the relevant folks so that informed decisions can be made.

In this chapter, we're going to cover the following main topics:

- Exploring data
- Visualizing data
- Publishing and sharing data
- Deploying your solution

Technical requirements

For this chapter, you will require the following:

- Power BI Desktop

- Power BI Service

- A Power BI Pro license

- A Power BI **Premium Per User** (**PPU**) license or Premium capacity

- Power BI gateway standard mode

- SharePoint Online

- SQL Server or Azure SQL Database

Exploring data

To make decisions on the direction of your business, you need to know where you stand. To do that, you will need answers to the questions you have. Sometimes, the answers that you receive prompt you to ask even further questions – questions that you didn't have before but are suddenly important. That's why exploring data is very effective when it comes to decision-making: you get to dynamically take your path to the insights. However, to make it an effective process, you need to have the data ready and shaped in the way you want. Having the data shaped in the way you want is what we looked at in *Chapter 5*, where we designed and built a semantic model. It provides multiple ways of looking at a certain piece of data. We will look at getting the data ready in the last section of this chapter. First, we'll learn how to explore data using Power BI.

Exploring data with Power BI

Let's start by exploring data ad hoc. This is because we do not have a dashboard or report yet that would tell us what we need to know. This type of analysis is called self-service because we choose the data elements that we want to see, rather than be provided with a standard picture with a set of pre-determined data elements arranged in a specific way. Let's look at a couple of methods of exploring data.

Understanding management by exception

The best way to start exploring data is with a question that you already know; using the same scenario from *Chapter 5*, "*I want to see the order value compared to last year for this month.*" This is a question that you have been asking on a monthly because you want to see how well you have done since you took over sales for the North American region at the beginning of the year. That's an easy question to answer since we are using the same example from *Chapter 5*, and also since the semantic model already has the % Order Growth measure. Let's jump into exploring the data.

To explore the data with Power BI, I will use the same file that we used in *Chapter 5* and switch to the Report view to perform the following actions:

- Select the `% Order Growth` measure from the `Orders` table and switch the visual to the `Card` type.

- Set the context to the current year and month (May 2014), and choose the North America region. For this, I will use two slicer visuals: one for the year and month from the `Calendar` dimension, and the other for the region from the `Territory` dimension:

Figure 6.1: Order growth depicted for a month and territory

Satisfied that my main question had a positive answer (*Figure 6.1*), I want to know more to make sure that growth has been positive for the entire year so far and has also been consistent each month.

To verify the first question, I must select the completed months of the current year in the **Year, Month** slicer; I immediately notice the value drop. However, it is still positive (*Figure 6.2*):

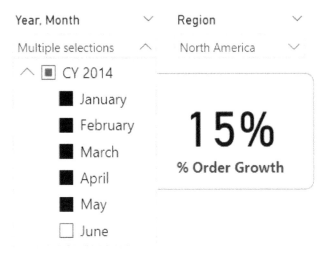

Figure 6.2: Order growth for the territory and completed months

The drop in the number is concerning, meaning that May 2014 was a very good month, but what would that say about the rest of the months? Using a line chart to plot % Order Growth across the completed months for the year (2014) reveals something bleaker (*Figure 6.3*):

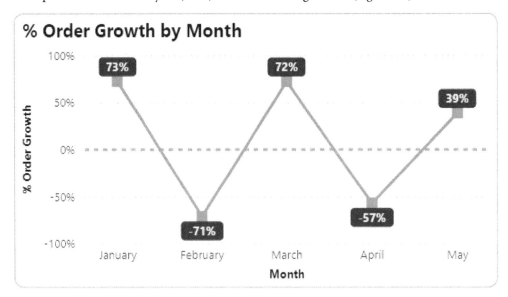

Figure 6.3: Order growth across the months

The pattern of how the order growth alternates each month between positive and negative with a grand difference between each makes it very curious for me. This leads to me wanting to know more since there is no consistency at all in my growth. Hence, the next step is to get to the element that contributes to this growth – that is, the *order value* itself. Let's use a line and clustered column chart to plot this. We'll go with both the *order value fact* and the *PY order value* measures so that we can compare them. We'll also map this down to the *date* level:

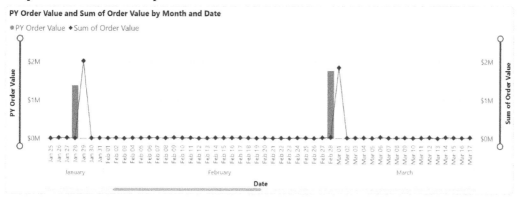

Figure 6.4: Order value and PY order value against dates (January to March)

Figure 6.4 shows the order value and PY order value at the beginning of the year from January to March, while *Figure 6.5* continues from March to May:

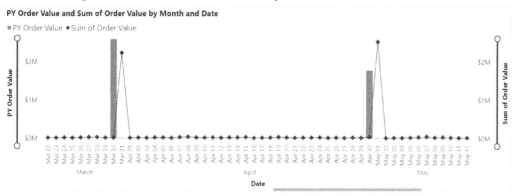

Figure 6.5: Order value and PY order value against dates (March to May)

As we scroll to the right, along the *X*-axis (Date), there are spikes at the end of each month for the past year's order value indicating a very large number of orders on one of the last few days of the month. However, for the current year, the spike is on the first day of the next month for the shorter months (February and April). It makes sense why these months show significant negative growth and the following months show significantly higher growth.

On a hunch, I decided to relook at the charts from the `Channel` dimension. Let's add the **Channel** attribute from the **Orders** table as a slicer and select **Online**. It shows a very significant and consistent growth across the months for online sales (*Figure 6.6*):

Figure 6.6: Order growth further sliced by the online channel

To confirm my hunch, I switched to the **In-store** channel. The analysis confirms my hunch (*Figure 6.7*). February and April have a -100% growth, which is proven by the date-wise breakdown where no sales have been recorded for the end of each month save January.

I now have insights into North American sales growth. While my focus had been on boosting online sales, the in-store sales, which amount to more than 70% of sales, had been seemingly neglected since they sit at -12%. Furthermore, the actionable insights I derived prompted me with two action items:

- **Short-term**: On-site sales, which are provided manually, are not being updated on time – that is, at month-end – leading to skewed numbers at a monthly level. This is an indication of an internal issue rather than an external one; once fixed, this should allow me to look for any external ones.

- **Medium-term**: Upgrade on-site systems so that site-level information can be updated in the system daily rather than at the month-end:

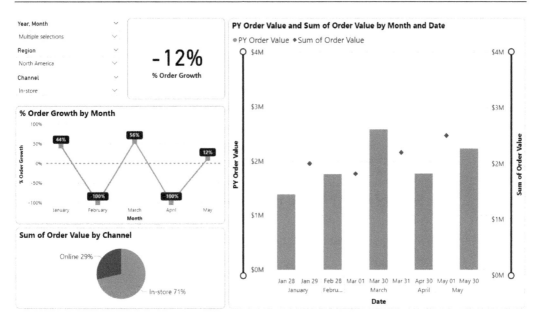

Figure 6.7: Order growth sliced by the in-store channel

The method of analysis that we just concluded contributes to a management strategy called **management by exception**. This is where managers focus their attention on scenarios that do not go according to their expectations or plans. This helps them be more efficient in addressing the issues that may sometimes go unnoticed. In our example, we did not stop short when the analysis showed a positive picture at a high level. We dove deeper, noticed a problem, and then went down that path to see what caused the problem. From the insights we gained by analyzing it, we came up with action items to solve it. Now, let's look at another type of data analysis.

What is Pareto analysis?

Another type of analysis that is popular is **Pareto analysis**. This concept follows the 80/20 rule, which states that 20% of the factors contribute to 80% of the results. Using this rule in our example, we can try to determine which 20% of the products contribute to 80% of the order value, if they even do, and then take necessary action.

Let's start with the same filters that we had in the previous section – Year, Month, Region, and Channel set to May 2014 for North America by **In-store** sales. Let's also add a doughnut chart with the sales value sliced by category and subcategory from the Product dimension. We will immediately see that a little over 80% of the sales are contributed to by one of four categories (25%) – bikes (*Figure 6.8*):

> **Note**
> It is important to know that the 80/20 distribution is not always exact.

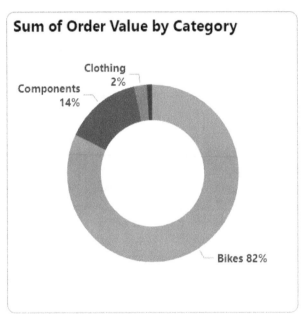

Figure 6.8: Order value by product categories

When I turn on the drill-down toggle and drill down on bikes, the subcategories show that the order value was distributed almost evenly among the three (*Figure 6.9*). Hence, I decided to skip subcategories and hypothesize that 20% of the products under bikes make up 80% of the order value:

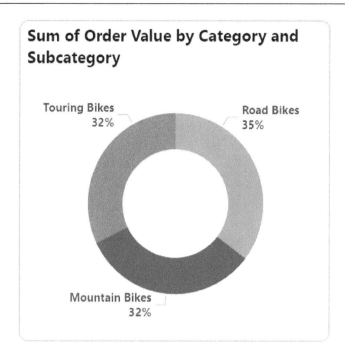

Figure 6.9: Order value by bike subcategories

The next step is to list the products sorted by the order value in descending order. My idea is to select the products one by one from the top while referring to a running *count of products* and *sum order value* as percentages of their total. For these, I will create two measures and drop them onto the canvas (*Figure 6.10*):

- % of Product Count:

```
% of Product Count = DIVIDE (
        DISTINCTCOUNT ('Product'[Product ID] ),
        CALCULATE ( DISTINCTCOUNT ('Product'[Product
ID] ), ALL ( 'Product'[Name] ) ),
        0
)
```

- % of Order Value:

```
% of Order Value = DIVIDE (
        SUM ( Orders[Order Value] ),
        CALCULATE ( SUM ( Orders[Order Value] ), ALL (
'Product'[Name] ) ),
        0
)
```

The canvas now looks like what's shown in *Figure 6.10*, where the two measures provide insights at a glance:

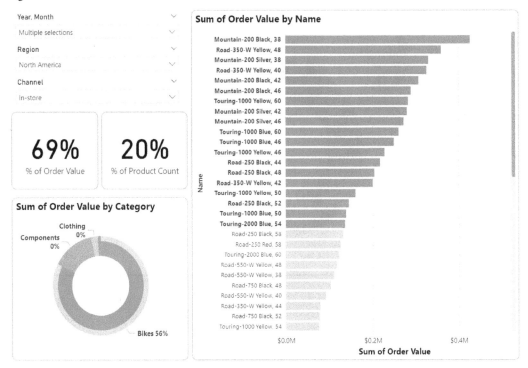

Figure 6.10: Products selected to make up 20% of the top bikes

Once I reach 20% product count, I stop selecting the items to see that these products contribute to 69% of the orders. Hence, I can conclude that according to the Pareto rule, these products have the potential to perform better in terms of sales and will act to better market these products.

This is an example of how, as a business user, with some hands-on experience or the help of a data analyst, can perform exploratory analysis to arrive at actionable insights using the built-in visualizations in Power BI. Power BI also supports third-party visuals that you can use on your canvas. For instance, Pareto analysis can be done using the third-party Pareto visual, which you can import from Microsoft's AppSource (*Figure 6.11*):

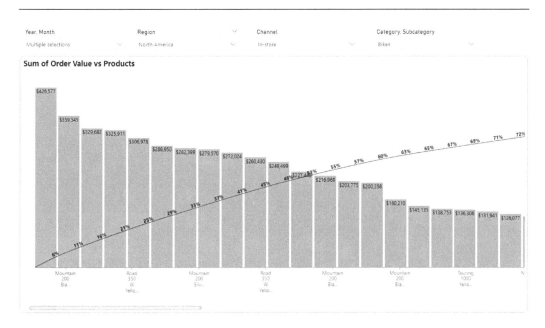

Figure 6.11: Pareto visual on order value and products

With that, we have looked at a couple of ways of exploring data in Power BI. To perform both these analyses, we used the same Power BI Desktop (PBIX) file that we built our semantic model on. Next, we'll cover some best practices on how analysis can be done more efficiently.

Exploring published semantic models

While exploring your data directly via the PBIX file is a great way to test out your model, a best practice would be to first publish the model to Power BI. You can then connect to it from Power BI using the browser or from Power BI Desktop to perform your analysis. Creating separate reports used for different purposes and connected to a single model demonstrates the flexibility of a well-designed star schema. Furthermore separate report files provide a fine grained mechanism to manage and maintain your report code, such as in a code repository. Keeping the model separate allows the different groups of content creators to work independently and not let specific analyses "contaminate" the generic rules a model is designed to have.

We'll dive deeper into publishing models later in this chapter. First, let's look at how we can explore Power BI data with Microsoft Excel.

Exploring data using Microsoft Excel

In addition to employing Power BI for data analysis, Microsoft Excel serves as a valuable tool. This feature proves particularly beneficial when it comes to dealing with users who are more accustomed to Excel and are in the process of transitioning to Power BI, which may take some time for full adoption.

To analyze your semantic model with Excel, the model must be published to Power BI, and the user should have the right type of access. Once you've located and selected the semantic model in its Power BI workspace, you just need to click on the **Analyze in Excel** option, and then the **Open in Excel for the web** button (*Figure 6.12*):

> **Note**
>
> Your administrator will need to turn on the feature that allows users to connect to a live connection from Excel if anyone is to use Excel to explore a semantic model. This can be done through the **Tenant settings** area of Power BI's **Admin portal**.

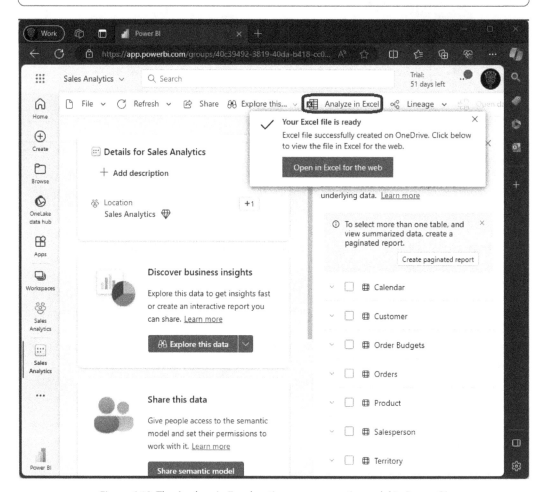

Figure 6.12: The Analyze in Excel option on a semantic model in Power BI

The Excel sheet that opens up contains a PivotTable into which you can select the measures and columns from the semantic model, and also filter the data. You can also write formulas on the sheet using the data from the model.

Figure 6.13 shows the order value and order budget facts depicted against the completed months of CY 2014, while the *% Orders vs Budget* calculation is written in Excel to calculate the ratio between the orders and the budget:

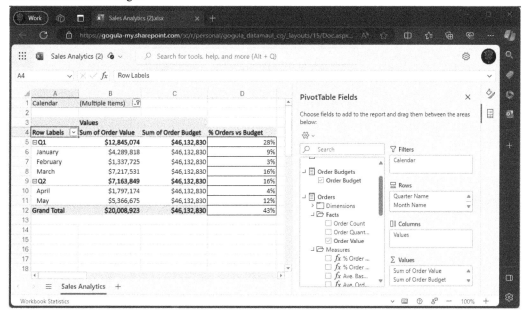

Figure 6.13: The semantic model accessed and analyzed in Microsoft Excel

You can also connect to Power BI semantic models from third-party applications, such as Tableau, using XMLA endpoints. There are also third-party tools that you can use to enhance your model.

In this section, we explored data using Power BI for insights. We used standard, built-in visuals for this purpose, and we also tried out a third-party visual. Power BI also provides AI-powered visuals for advanced analysis. You will learn more about the different types of visuals, including the AI-powered ones and how to use them, in *Chapter 8*.

In the next section, we'll focus on how you can visualize your insights so that others can consume them.

Visualizing data with Power BI

In the previous section, we explored data using Power BI. Our exploration ended with the discovery of insights. These insights are helpful for decision-making. Hence, it is always a good idea to structure your analysis and its results for later use. For instance, if you were looking for some specific insights, or if you found some interesting insights after ad hoc analysis of a hunch you were following, there's a good chance that you would want this information to be updated with the latest data each month.

Creating Power BI reports

When we explored data in the previous section, we inadvertently used the Report view. This is the same canvas that we would use to turn the analysis that we have into a report. As we discussed in the previous section, it is a good idea to have reports independent of their models.

Creating a report against a published model can be done by using Power BI Desktop or directly from Power BI. However, the Desktop experience provides you with a slight edge in terms of flexibility.

To create a report from Power BI Desktop, you can use the **Get data** menu from the **Home** ribbon and select the **Power BI semantic models** menu item. You need to make sure you are signed into your organization on Power BI to be able to get a list of models you have access to (*Figure 6.14*). Once this list has been exposed, you just need to select the model of your choice and you'll be connected. You will notice that if you are connected live to a semantic model, you will only see the **Report view** and **Model view** tabs:

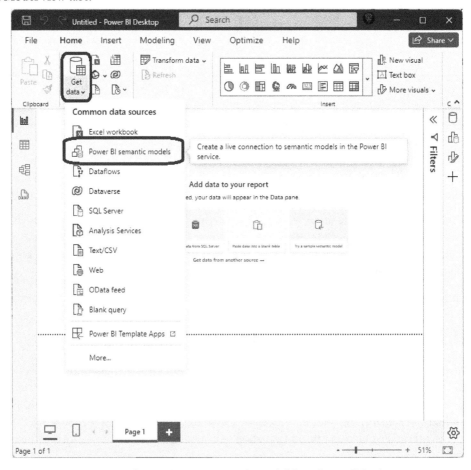

Figure 6.14: Connecting to a semantic model from Power BI Desktop

To create a report from Power BI, you will need to sign into Power BI on your browser. Then, you must navigate to the workspace that holds the model, or search for the model on your Power BI home page. Once you've found your model, you must select it and choose the **Create report** option; Power BI will load your canvas within your browser. You will notice that this browser-based experience is quite like the desktop experience (*Figure 6.15*):

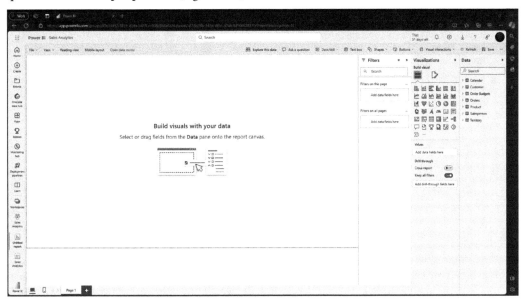

Figure 6.15: Power BI report canvas connected to a semantic model on Power BI

Once you are connected to the semantic model, either from Power BI Desktop or from Power BI itself, you can start crafting the data story for your report. It is a good idea to reflect on the insights you gained from the data exploration and analysis that you performed before deciding on what should go in your report. You can start with a high-level picture of the topic you want to talk about, and then dive into the details.

The **In-store sales** report example (*Figure 6.16*) has the insights drawn up at a summarized level so that users can see how the order value has performed against the same period of the previous year. It contains the % Order Growth measure, along with its make-up, as well as Order Value and PY Order Value, with the breakdown across the completed months below it so that anomalies can be seen at once. The order value is also presented across three visuals, where each is broken down by a dimension so that further dicing can be done if required. The original analysis was done for the North American region. However, by adding a region slicer, this report can be used by personnel across each region:

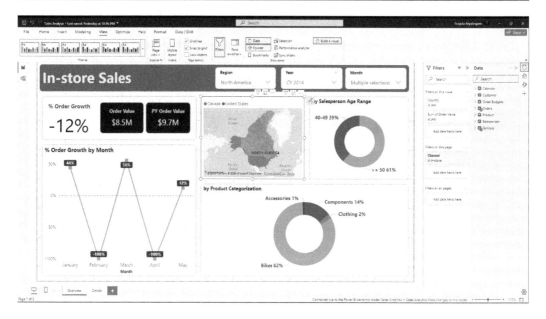

Figure 6.16: Overview page of the report

The second page of the report is designed as a detailed page so that users can drill through from the main page based on a selected element. For instance, the user can select a section of a visual, such as **Bikes**, and drill through to the detailed page where the context will then filter for all bikes (*Figure 6.17*):

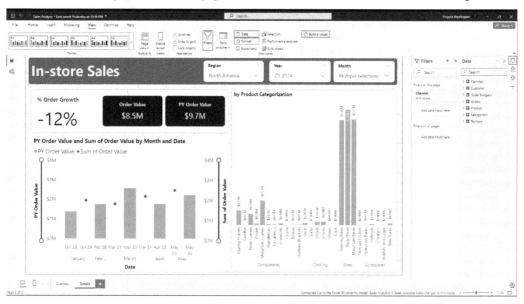

Figure 6.17: The detail page of the report

Using the right type of visuals and organizing your report to relate a story is very important when providing insights to users. You will learn more about these aspects in *Chapters 9* and *10*.

Not all users carry notebook computers with them, and even if they do there are moments when a notebook computer is too cumbersome to use. Mobile reports allow your Power BI reports to be viewed in a mobile-friendly, responsive format.

Once you've built your Power BI report, all you need to do is switch to the *mobile view* (*Figure 6.18*), where you can arrange the same elements that you have on the main report on a mobile canvas. Since it is a mobile rendition, you can choose to skip certain visuals and use the more important ones. Once you've published your report to the service, depending on the device you're using and the orientation of the device, Power BI will choose the appropriate view. For instance, if you're using a mobile phone and holding it upright (portrait mode), Power BI will show you the mobile view. If you switch the orientation to landscape, the report will change to the standard format.

You must consider incorporating both the web and mobile views when you create reports so that users have a more enriching experience when looking at their data:

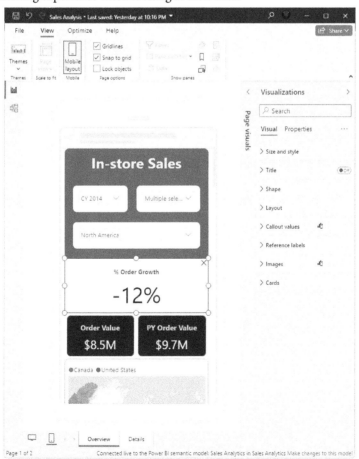

Figure 6.18: Mobile view of the report

Other visualizations in Power BI

In this section, we'll look at some other types of visualizations in Power BI:

- **Dashboards**: Power BI dashboards allow you to pin the elements of various reports on a single canvas. A practical scenario involves choosing key visuals from a collection of sales reports, each focused on a unique business process, and displaying them on a consolidated dashboard.

  One thing that you need to be mindful of when talking to business users is that the concept of dashboards in Power BI is usually confused with Power BI reports. This is because reports are also visual and dashboard-like solutions can be built with them. Many users and organizations regularly build reports that are completely visual and often fulfill their dashboard requirements. Hence, the distinction between the two must be made clear to end users.

- **Scorecards**: The **Metrics** feature in Power BI allows users to organize selected measures from your reports and track them against specific objectives. You can set up the metrics on a scorecard to keep track of this by using manual or automated methods. A scorecard helps provide visibility on important metrics and helps make decisions based on progress.

- **Paginated reports**: As opposed to the analytical nature of Power BI reports, paginated reports are used to create printable reports, often in a tabular structure. These types of reports are preferred if a detailed representation of data is needed, and there is a tendency for these reports to be printed.

In this section, we looked at the different ways in which you could visualize the data and insights you have. Once visualized, the next step is to publish their content so that it can be shared with others.

Publishing and sharing data in Power BI

The Power BI content that you create must be published before it can be consumed by others. This content, such as the semantic model and the reports that you create on Power BI Desktop, need to be published to Power BI before they can be shared with others. Content that you create on Power BI, such as reports, dashboards, and scorecards, are published when you save them by default.

> **Note**
> Sharing Power BI Desktop (PBIX) files through regular file-sharing methods is not the intended way of sharing Power BI content.

Next, we'll look at what needs to be in place before you can publish your report.

Understanding workspaces

Power BI workspaces are the first step toward publishing your content. All published content goes to live in a workspace. You can think of a workspace as a collection of content that shares a common theme, such as a specific requirement, a business process, or a team of individuals that share a common interest. A workspace usually grants access to a small team that contributes to the workspace's content, such as building the content or reviewing the content.

Let's consider an example. The organization wants all its standard business measures to be organized in one place for the entire organization to use. To solve this, a group consisting of data analysts, functional consultants, and business function heads is put together. With help from the consultants on business logic, the analysts build semantic models that have the core business measures of the organization. They build three models – one each for finance, sales, and operations – that the respective function heads review and approve once the consultants test them. All these actions occur within the context of a workspace, where only these roles are provided access to collaborate.

Once these models are live, everyone in the organization is given read-only access to them. The marketing division of the sales department creates a workspace for its three-member marketing team and builds reports and dashboards using the sales model, while the data analyst working for the executive committee of the organization brings in selected measures from all three models to their model and builds executive reports for management. *Figure 6.19* shows how workspaces can be used to contain different types of content in Power BI so that different personas have specific types of access to each:

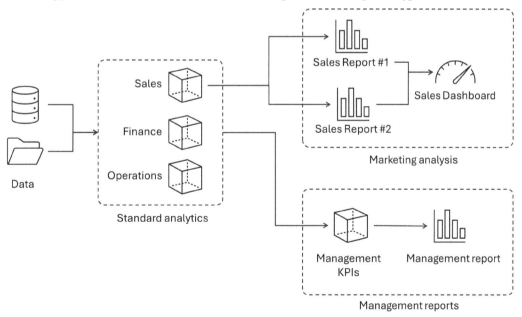

Figure 6.19: Usage of workspaces to organize Power BI content

Now that you've set up your workspace with your content, let's look at how it can be packaged.

Leveraging apps in Power BI

Apps in Power BI are packaged content that you distribute to a broader audience, unlike in workspaces, where you only use them to share content among collaborators. An app is created out of your workspace. You can think of your workspace as the backend and the app as the frontend where you choose only the content you want to share and bundle it up before sharing it with a wide audience. *Figure 6.20* depicts how workspace content gets packaged as an app in Power BI:

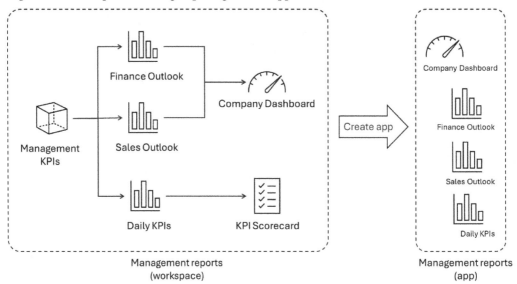

Figure 6.20: Depiction of an app created from selected workspace content

You will learn more about using apps in Power BI in *Chapter 11*.

Other ways of sharing Power BI content

Using workspaces and apps contributes to a structured way of sharing content. However, there are several other ways in which you can share Power BI content. Some of these options allow you to interact with colleagues regarding the content. A few of these are as follows:

- **Direct sharing**: One of the popular methods is ad hoc sharing of content, such as semantic models, reports, dashboards, and scorecards using the **Share** option. Ad hoc sharing can get difficult to manage as more and more objects are shared this way.

- **Embedding in PowerPoint**: You can also present reports by embedding a report directly into your PowerPoint presentation and presenting it live while interacting with the report from within your presentation.

- **Embedding in SharePoint Online**: An alternative way to exhibit the insights on your report is to embed them within a report web part in SharePoint Online. This is a great way, for example, for your organization or your team to see the state organizational metrics when they navigate to their intranet web hosted on SharePoint.

- **Chat in Teams**: This option allows you to share your Power BI report with a person, group, or channel on Microsoft Teams. They can then open the report from within Teams to view and chat with you about it.

- **Comment**: Users can also interact with each other directly on the report using the **Comment** option, where you can mention a colleague and collaborate with them on the entire report or a single visual.

> Important note
>
> Reports can also be embedded within public websites. To do this, you will have to generate a public link using the **Publish to web (public)** option. This option needs to be used with caution or avoided since users will not be authenticated and sensitive information on your dashboard will become publicly available.

Licensing authors and consumers

To author content (write) and to consume (read) published Power BI content, users will require a *Power BI Pro* license. If the workspace is on a *Power BI Premium* capacity, consumers can read for free, while each content author will need a Power BI Pro license. If the content was created using a *Power BI PPU* license, you will need the same license to consume the content.

In this section, we explored how to publish and share Power BI content with an audience. However, publishing your content is not the only action that ensures your solution is ready for use. In the next section, we'll explore how to deploy content as a complete solution.

Deploying your solution

A Power BI solution, once built and published, should be able to continually refresh the latest data from its sources to its elements, such as reports and dashboards. The solution also should go through a standard development life cycle where the solution is tested and then deployed to a production environment that works without breaking. In this section, we'll look into deploying a Power BI solution to various environments and ensure data connectivity.

Exploring semantic model settings

When you build your semantic model using Power BI Desktop, the connections that you create to the data sources are local to the computer that you do this on. The moment that you publish your semantic model to Power BI, that connection is no longer there. This is because the service, unlike your development computer, has not been provided with connectivity information. You will notice this when you try to refresh the dataset for new information.

Hence, once you publish your model, the first thing you would need to do is go to the model's settings and navigate to the **Gateway and cloud connections** section. There are two types of connections that you can have from your semantic model:

- **Cloud connections**: The easiest to configure are connections to cloud sources such as SaaS-based services and databases. Azure SQL database, SharePoint Online, and Salesforce are some examples.

- **Gateway connections**: These are connections to on-premises sources such as SQL Server databases on an organization's data center and even databases on Azure VMs.

First, let's look at how you would configure a cloud connection.

Establishing a cloud connection from Power BI

Let's use our example from earlier in this chapter to connect to a cloud data source. In our example, the order budgets came from Excel files stored on SharePoint Online. When you go to the semantic model's settings on Power BI, you'll notice that one of the connections listed is to the *SharePoint Online document library*. From the **Maps to** dropdown, select **Create a connection** (*Figure 6.21*):

Cloud connections

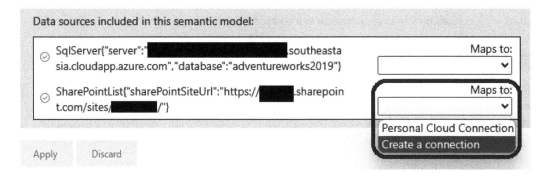

Figure 6.21: The Cloud connections section of the semantic model settings

Then, we must establish the connection to the SharePoint library (*Figure 6.22*):

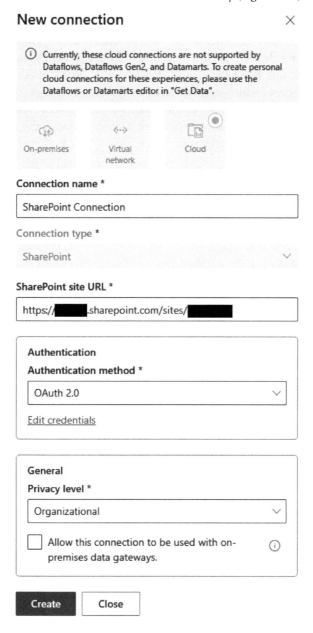

Figure 6.22: A new connection to SharePoint Online

Now, let's learn how to configure a gateway connection.

Establishing a gateway connection from Power BI

While cloud services are meant to be accessed off the internet, secure connectivity is built-in, and connectivity is made easy. However, systems that are on-premises are largely meant to be accessed within boundaries and have elaborate security mechanisms implemented. Hence, having Power BI access different types of security mechanisms, most of which are unique to the organization, is difficult. To counter this, Power BI comes with **Power BI Gateway**. The gateway is a piece of software that you install on a computer in the organization's domain – either on the data source host computer or on a computer that has access to the database host computer. Once configured, the gateway will provide exclusive connectivity from Power BI to the data source.

The links to download Power BI Gateway can be found on the Power BI home page, where you'll be pointed to the two gateway types: **standard mode** and **personal mode**. *Standard mode* should be used when multiple users need access to different sources, and they use a single gateway to do this. As its name suggests, *personal mode* is for individual use and cannot be used in scenarios where other users need to access data sources.

As part of the gateway installation process, you can sign in with your Power BI account and register your gateway on your Power BI tenant. You can also create a gateway cluster when doing this if you plan on connecting to several data sources, and thereby want to share the load among multiple gateways. *Figure 6.23* shows a Power BI gateway configured and running:

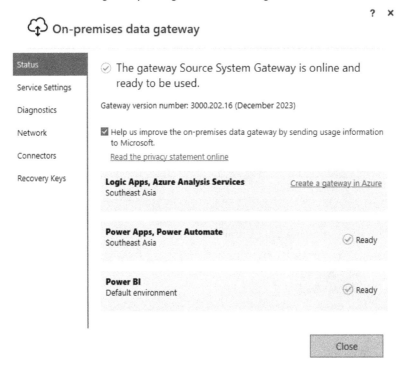

Figure 6.23: A Power BI gateway configured and connected to Power BI

When you go to Power BI and access the **Manage connections and gateways** link under **Settings**, you'll see that your gateway is ready:

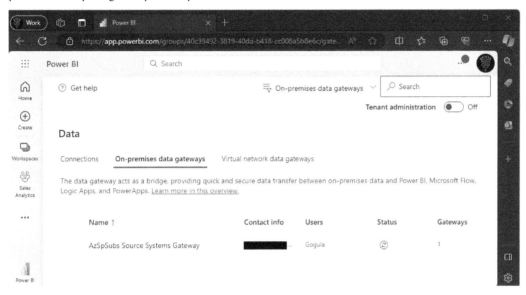

Figure 6.24: The gateway cluster listed on Power BI

Now, when you go to the semantic model settings to configure the on-premises data source, you will see the gateway, through which you can create a connection to the source:

Figure 6.25: The on-premises connections section of the semantic model settings

Once the connections have been established on the semantic model, we can try manually refreshing it. Each refresh will reflect the data updates in the model and subsequently all elements, such as other models, reports, dashboards, and scorecards, that are linked downstream.

> **Virtual network (VNet) data gateways**
>
> Using VNet gateways is an alternative option to connect to data sources without having to install a data gateway. You use an Azure VNet that securely connects to the different data sources. To create an Azure VNet, you must have an Azure subscription.

Scheduling refreshes

Power BI allows your semantic models to be refreshed on a schedule. If you are on the Pro license, you can schedule data refreshes up to eight times a day, while Premium licenses allow up to 48 times a day. *Figure 6.26* shows a daily refresh schedule that runs once at 2:00 A.M. and again at 1:00 P.M:

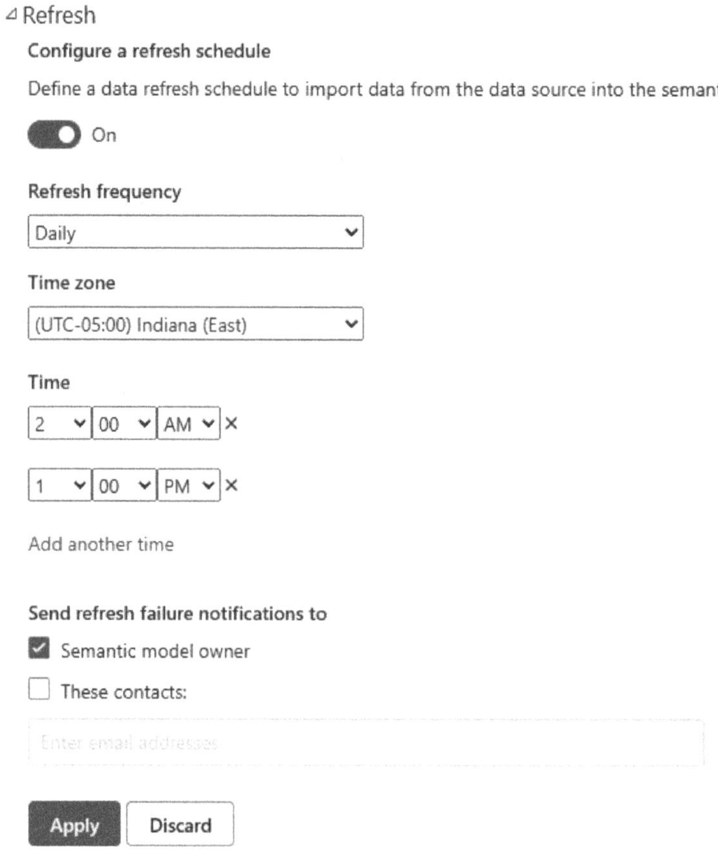

⊿ Refresh

Configure a refresh schedule

Define a data refresh schedule to import data from the data source into the semantic model.

🔘 On

Refresh frequency

Daily ⌄

Time zone

(UTC-05:00) Indiana (East) ⌄

Time

| 2 ⌄ | 00 ⌄ | AM ⌄ | × |

| 1 ⌄ | 00 ⌄ | PM ⌄ | × |

Add another time

Send refresh failure notifications to

☑ Semantic model owner

☐ These contacts:

Enter email addresses

Apply   Discard

Figure 6.26: Refresh settings with a schedule

Once you've set up your refreshes, your model will be populated with the latest data each time the schedule runs. Next, you'll learn how to deploy your solution to other environments where users will test and eventually use it live.

Understanding deployment pipelines

When you build an analytics solution, it is not just a model or a report that you create. Rather, you create a set of connected objects. For instance, you are part of the marketing team; you create a set of four reports for various purposes, and then pin important elements from each report to a dashboard that acts as a summary. Before you publish this package as an app, it is good practice for it to be quality tested, and then published for general usage.

To follow such a methodology, we usually use a three-environment approach. Of course, more environments can be used based on complexity and organizational standards if required:

- **Development**: The environment where all the created content will be published. Content creators will perform their testing (called developer testing) on this environment.

- **Test**: Once done, all the content will be published in the test environment with a clean slate. Data will once again be refreshed, and designated test users will test the solution without the intervention of the content creators. Usually, content creators are not allowed write access to this environment.

- **Production**: This is the consumer environment where the live solution lives. Content creation is not allowed in this environment. Any changes to the solution will have to come through the process of **development-test-production** (**dev-test-prod**).

When creating content using the dev-test-prod approach, you will need to create three separate workspaces to represent each environment. In the case of our example, the workspace was called *Sales Analytics*. This will be the *production workspace*, and ideally, no content creation should happen here. The development and test workspaces can be named *Sales Analytics-Dev* and *Sales Analytics-Test*. All the content creation exercises that we went through in our examples will be published to *Sales Analytics-Dev*. Then, we can initiate a deployment pipeline by using the **Create deployment pipeline** option (*Figure 6.27*):

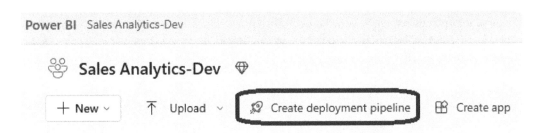

Figure 6.27: The Create deployment pipeline option on the workspace

The deployment pipeline creation wizard will require you to provide the pipeline with a name, add additional stages (or environments) apart from the standard three, and ask you to assign workspaces to each stage. *Figure 6.28* shows the deployment pipeline with the appropriate workspaces assigned at each stage:

Figure 6.28: The sales analytics deployment pipeline with workspaces in each stage

As you assign the workspaces, the content from the previous stage gets deployed to each stage. You can then provide deployment rules on your models. For instance, you might be asked to develop using a test database as the source, but for testing and production, you might be asked to use the live database. You can set up *deployment rules* that map the connections to the appropriate database. *Figure 6.29* shows how you can easily parameterize using a different source database when you deploy the solution to production:

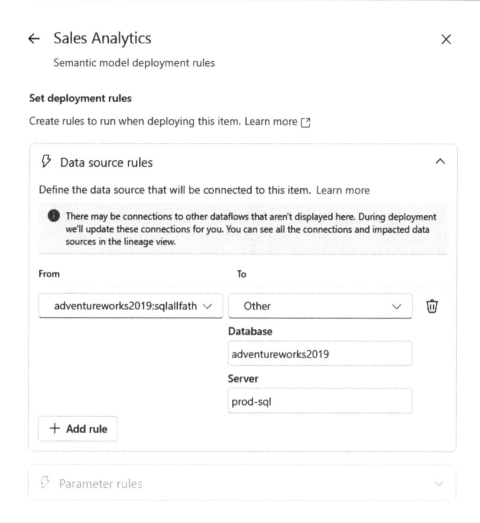

Figure 6.29: The deployment rule for using the production database
instead of the test database in the production stage

With the deployment pipeline set up, every time you add or update content in the development stage, all you need to do is click on the **Deploy** button. The deployment pipeline will check for differences between the stages, apply the deployment rules, and publish the content to the next stage.

> **Note**
> Deployment pipelines are only available with Premium workspaces.

In this section, we explored how you can deploy your Power BI solution for use once development is complete. Now, let's summarize this chapter.

Q&A

The second part of developing a Power BI solution is to explore and visualize data, after which you will share and deploy your data. Hence, it is good to look at some questions that you may potentially be asked during your interview.

Question 1: How is data consumed once you build a semantic model in Power BI?

Answer: Data can be consumed in many ways. The natural and most intuitive step would be to explore it using Power BI itself, though if users are not too familiar with it, they can analyze data with Excel using pivots. One method I usually use is to look at measures at a high level, such as for the current year and for the region I operate in. I use the Power BI canvas and use the appropriate visuals to draw the picture. I look for whether the measures have met their targets or are on their way to meeting them. If I notice that this is not the case, I dive deeper to see where things may have gone wrong by adding further dimensions, or attribute levels of dimensions that I am using. I may use visuals to drill down or cross-filter for this purpose. Finally, when I arrive at my conclusion and my insights, I take action. I also save my analysis and make it into a report that I can reuse.

Question 2: How do you make use of other types of visualizations other than by reporting in Power BI?

Answer: I usually create my standard reports with my measures of interest at a high level and then have more additional pages with detailed analyses by different dimensions. These reports are usually created for a single or related set of business processes. I create a dashboard with the high-level visuals from each report. The business users I report to are given the dashboard so that they have a bird's-eye view of their business processes. When they see a measure not performing well, they just need to click on it, and it will take them to the relevant report. I also link the high-level measure visuals from these reports to metrics that I create on a scorecard. These are used by the function heads weekly to review how the measures have progressed.

Question 3: I have a semantic model on a Power BI Desktop file that is connected to my on-premises SQL Server. How do I ensure that the model refreshes data automatically when I publish it to Power BI?

Answer: The moment you publish a semantic model to the service, you are disconnected from the source. This means you will have to re-establish connectivity to your sources from Power BI for your model. You can do this in the model's settings. Connections to cloud sources can be directly established from Power BI, while you will have to use a data gateway if you need to connect to on-premises sources, such as SQL Server in this case. Once you've established your connection, you can schedule automated refreshes of your model.

Refer to the *Exploring semantic model settings* section of this chapter to prepare for this question.

Question 4: Can you explain a scenario where you've packaged a Power BI solution effectively?

Answer: I built a solution containing a semantic model and 10 reports that use the model. I also created a dashboard that acts as the linking page of the solution with key measures from the 10 reports. Then, I created a report that tracks the usage of the reports. All these were contained in a single workspace. Only two other people were given access to the workspace; they would review and approve my work. The workspace was then packaged into an app, with the dashboard as the landing page. The semantic model and the usage tracking reports were not included in the app since we wanted to control how the model was used, and the usage tracking report was internal to us, the workspace contributors. Finally, I published the app to about 30+ sales users.

Refer to the *Leveraging apps in Power BI* section to prepare further.

Question 5: If I need to deploy a Power BI solution from my development workspace to another workspace for users to test, how would I go about this with the least effort?

Answer: You can use deployment pipelines to easily set up a dev-test-prod scenario, and easily deploy at the click of a button. You can also have additional environments such as a UAT environment between test and production. However, deployment pipelines are a premium feature that will require you to have the necessary licensing and/or capacity.

Refer to the *Understanding deployment pipelines* section of this chapter to prepare for this question.

Summary

In this chapter, you learned how to consume the content that you created in the previous chapter. This involved exploring the content in different ways to arrive at insights using methods such as management by exception and Pareto analysis. We learned that different users can use different methods and even different tools, such as Microsoft Excel, to explore the data on your semantic model. Exploration gives way to visualizing when you start crafting a story using the insights and analysis you came up with. To visualize data, you must create Power BI reports to visually represent the analysis compellingly. We also learned of other means of visualizing data, including using dashboards, paginated reports, and scorecards. Next, we learned how the content that we've created can be packaged, published, and shared with other users. We learned how users can interact with these solutions to gain deeper insights. Finally, we learned about the importance of deploying a Power BI solution and setting up connectivity and data refreshes from the Power BI service for data continuity. We also learned about deployment pipelines and how we can use them to create a streamlined deployment strategy.

In the next chapter, let's dive into DAX programming and how it can enhance your semantic models and reports.

7

DAX Programming

On many occasions, it is commonly thought that a data analyst only deals with Excel formulas or charts and that programming languages are rarely touched upon. This notion is fueled by the emergence of many business intelligence solutions that allow you to perform comprehensive analysis straightforwardly on any dataset, without delving too deep into complex calculations. However, in tools such as Power BI, mastering the programming aspect, specifically the **Data Analysis Expressions** (**DAX**) language, is crucial for achieving the professional success you are seeking.

While I consider DAX a simple language to learn, it is considered one of the most challenging topics for those learning or delving into data analysis, particularly with Power BI.

In this chapter, you will learn the basics of DAX, explore the primary aggregation functions, create some measures and calculated columns using this language, and delve into slightly more complex measures while addressing topics such as time intelligence, filters, and evaluation contexts.

By the end of this chapter, you will have a clearer understanding of the topics you need to master within this language to increase your chances of landing your first data analyst job interview.

The topics we will cover in this chapter are as follows:

- What is DAX?
- Basic aggregation functions
- Measures versus calculated columns
- Let's filter some data
- Evaluation contexts
- Time intelligence functions
- Complex DAX measures

Technical requirements

- Power BI Desktop

What is DAX?

According to Google, the data analysis process consists of six phases. In the first phase, we identify the problem, generating a series of questions that will likely be answered through our analysis. In the second phase, we prepare the data we will analyze, determining what we will measure, what factors we need to consider, and where the data is located. The third phase involves data processing, where we make the data useful. This is essentially the transformation phase in the ETL process. The fourth phase is the analysis phase, where we start creating all the measures and indicators that will help us answer the questions we posed in the first phase. The fifth phase is the sharing phase, where we create our reports by choosing the best visual object for each of the indicators we will present. Lastly, there is the acting phase. In this sixth phase, we provide recommendations based on the analysis we have conducted on our model.

DAX is used in the analysis phase. Its execution environment is within the data model as a formula language that defines calculations and indicators. This means that the complexity of the model will impact the code you generate using DAX, and your skills with DAX will also determine the design and performance of your model.

DAX is a language developed by Microsoft that interacts with data in various platforms or tools that support it, such as Power Pivot in Excel, SSAS, and Power BI.

Considerations about the DAX language

Before delving deeper into this language, there are a few things you should consider to make your learning experience as smooth as possible.

DAX is not Excel

You should remember that, although the main goal of DAX developers was to include it within Excel, specifically with Power Pivot, it has notable differences from Excel. Being aware of these differences will even help you better understand the behavior of many DAX formulas. Here are some examples:

- The row and column coordinates concept does not exist in DAX since we work with context
- Excel has a limited number of rows and columns while DAX in Power BI lets you manage a large amount of data
- DAX code is more complex and SQL-like; this is because you have to deal with tables, relationships, contexts, and filters rather than only creating nested `if` statements like we usually do in Excel

In many learning processes, you don't always follow a straight line; sometimes, you must take a step back and unlearn a small piece of what you already know. With DAX and Excel, this is exactly what happens.

It requires some analysis

Perhaps this is why I mentioned earlier that many people fear DAX when learning about Power BI. DAX requires a certain level of analysis to understand how it works. If you come from the programming world, you will know there are many websites and forums where you can consult about a pattern or logic you don't understand well. If you're lucky, someone may have already posted the solution, and you can simply copy that portion of code, paste it into your project, and maybe change some variables – in most cases, this works. The same goes for not knowing how to formulate a formula in Excel – you can simply copy a formula you found on the internet and paste it into your spreadsheet after modifying the cell references and other elements. However, this doesn't happen with DAX in most cases because each model is different, and you need to understand the concept of evaluation contexts. We will cover this in subsequent sections of this chapter.

It is a functional language

When I say *functional*, I mean that it is a language based on functions. This means that each expression is a request for a function, and the parameters of that function can also be requests or calls to other functions.

Syntax of DAX

The syntax of DAX is a crucial part of your learning as you need to know how to write this language. This will allow you to express your logic in a measure, but above all, you should be able to recognize any DAX formula at a glance.

A measure that uses DAX looks like this:

```
Total Sales = SUM ( Sales[SalesAmount] )
```

The first thing is that we need to give the measure a name. This name must be unique within our entire model; it doesn't matter if there are spaces between the words. A recommendation is to always try to find a name that defines what the measure does in the shortest possible way.

Then, the equals sign indicates the beginning of the formula that will return our results. In this simple example, we are using the SUM function to sum the values of the SalesAmount column from the Sales table.

As you may have noticed, we are passing the column in parentheses since most DAX functions require at least one value. Also, note that in this case, we are specifying the table and the specific column we are using in the function. It doesn't matter if you don't specify the table and only put the column in brackets, but this can lead to ambiguities if there is another column with the same name in your model. Therefore, it is a good practice to always use the full name of the column – that is, include the table prefix. There are even functions that require you to pass the column in this way.

In some cases, you may see that the table name is enclosed in single quotation marks. This happens when the table name contains white spaces, as in this case.

> **Note**
>
> Keep the use of single quotation marks and double quotation marks in mind since double quotation marks are only used for text strings.

Operators in DAX

In most cases, our measures have mathematical expressions:

Operator Type	Symbol	Use	Example
Parenthesis	( )	Precedence order and grouping of arguments	(5 + 2) * 3
Arithmetic	+	Addition	4 + 2
	-	Subtraction/negation	5 3
	*	Multiplication	4 * 2
	/	Division	4-feb
Comparison	=	Equal to	[CountryRegion] = "USA"
	<>	Not equal to	[CountryRegion] <> "USA"
	>	Greater than	[Quantity] > 0
	>=	Greater than or equal to	[Quantity] >= 100
	<	Less than	[Quantity] <0
	<=	Less than or equal to	[Quantity] <=100
Text concatenation	&	Concatenation of strings	"Value is" & [Amount]
Logical	&&	AND condition between two Boolean expressions	[CountryRegion] = "USA" && [Quantity]>0
	||	OR condition between two Boolean expressions	[CountryRegion] = "USA" || [Quantity] > 0

Table 7.1: Common operators

Here are the operators we can use within mathematical expressions:

- Although I mentioned earlier that functions use parentheses for their parameters, we can also use them to prioritize any mathematical calculation.

- We also have the common arithmetic operators of addition, subtraction, multiplication, and division. However, it is not recommended to use the forward slash for division; there is another function for that, which you will see later.

- We will use comparison operators for our conditions. They include the equals sign, not equals, greater than, greater than or equal to, less than, and less than or equal to.

- If we want to concatenate text strings, we can use the ampersand symbol or "&".

- For logical operators, we can use the double ampersand for the AND operator and double backslashes for the OR operator.

Although operators will be very useful when creating mathematical or conditional expressions, there are functions such as DIVIDE that are much more efficient when performing division, no matter how simple it may seem.

Data types available in DAX

It is important that you are familiar with the different data types that DAX can handle and that Power BI specifically recognizes. This will determine how the data is stored in your model and how efficient your measures will be:

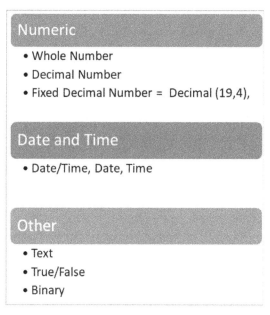

Figure 7.1: DAX data types groups

Let's look at the data types that we can handle in DAX.

To handle numbers, we have the integer data type. As its name suggests, this type is used for handling whole numbers. It is one of the most commonly used data types because Power BI uses it by default when numbers do not have decimals.

Next, we have the decimal data type. This data type is used for storing numbers, and in this case, you can also store fractional or decimal values with up to 15 digits.

Following that is the fixed decimal number type. It has the characteristic that, in addition to storing decimal values, the decimal portion it stores is fixed to only four digits. In other words, you can have up to four decimal places. This can be useful in cases where rounding decimal values can introduce errors or inconsistencies, and this data type can help mitigate those situations.

Within the types that are used for dates and times, we have date/time, date, and time. As in other tools, the information stored in these data types is stored as a decimal value, where the integer part represents the date and the decimal part represents the time.

The text data type is one of the most generic types, so to speak, as it is the default data type in Power BI when it is unable to recognize the data type of a column.

Next is the true/false data type, which is essentially a Boolean data type that stores a true or false state, or 1 or 0.

Finally, there is the binary data type, which is more commonly used when we want to store data that cannot be represented as text, such as images or documents. So, it can be very useful if you want to present any type of image in your report.

Basic aggregation functions

Although one of the goals of data warehousing is to bring the data in the most aggregated and organized form possible, it is necessary to have functions within the BI tool that allow you to aggregate the data in various ways. DAX has several aggregate functions, such as the SUM function that you saw a few sections ago. This function sums all the values in a column.

Similarly, the MAX, MIN, COUNT, and AVERAGE functions are used to obtain the maximum, minimum, count, and average values, respectively. Each of these functions has a different tolerance for certain types of data, and it is important to know their particularities because you will have to use at least one of them in your day-to-day work as a data analyst.

Using MAX and MIN

In the following measure, you can see one of the ways you can use the MAX or MIN function. In this case, two values are passed to the function to obtain the greater of the two, and in this example, the result would be 15:

```
Max number = MAX(3, 15)
```

However, if you modify this function and change one of the two parameters to a text data type, you will get an error similar to the following:

```
Max number = MAX(3, "ABC")
```

MAX does not support comparing integer values with type text values. Consider using the VALUE or FORMAT function to convert one of the values.

This happens because when searching for the maximum or minimum, it is obvious that both values should be numeric, except for blanks, as shown here:

```
Max number = MAX(3, BLANK())
```

When we use blank values with the MAX or MIN function, they are treated as 0s; the result of the previous example would be 3.

> **Note**
> The BLANK() function returns a blank value.

In addition to using the MAX or MIN function with two parameters, you can also use it by passing only the column from which you want to obtain the minimum or maximum value, as shown here:

Item	Price
A	200
B	500
C	100
D	50
E	
F	
G	150

Figure 7.2: Sample table

Now, let's say you write the following code line:

```
min value = MIN( TABLE[Price] )
```

You will get Result = 50.

Using AVERAGE

Another aggregate function that you will frequently use and therefore should be familiar with is the AVERAGE function. This function calculates the arithmetic mean of a column, excluding null or blank values and including zero values. In the following example, you can see that if we try to calculate the average of the Price column from *Figure 7.2*, the mathematical expression would be 1,000/5, returning Result = 200.

```
average price = AVERAGE(Products[Price])
```

This result would not be the same if, for example, the prices of items E and F were 0 as they would be part of the divisor in the mathematical expression:

Item	Price
A	200
B	500
C	100
D	50
E	0
F	0
G	150

Figure 7.3: Sample table with zero added in a few records

So, in simpler terms, let's say we write the following instruction:

```
average price = AVERAGE(Products[Price])
```

The expression would be 1,000/7, returning Result = 142.86.

Using COUNT

When we want to get the count of rows in a column, one of the functions we can use is the COUNT function. It returns a single value representing the count of non-blank rows. Let's say we use the sample table in *Figure 7.2* and apply the COUNT function to the Price column, like so:

```
count price = COUNT(Products[Price])
```

We would get Result = 5 because only five rows have a value, while two rows are blank.

Iterators

Each of these functions returns a single value. In the examples you've seen, we worked with a specific column. But what if I need to aggregate the data from the result of an expression? In other words, instead of using a specific column, I want to aggregate the data from the multiplication of two columns. This can be achieved using the enhanced versions of these functions, which are called iterators. You can easily identify them because they all have an "X" at the end (SUMX, MAXX, MINX, COUNTX, AVERAGEX, and so on). I refer to them as the X functions.

Let's suppose we add an extra column to the previous example table, representing the quantity sold for each of these items. If I wanted to create a measure to calculate the total sales, I would need to multiply the price by the quantity and then aggregate that result to obtain a single value. This can be achieved using the SUMX function in the following way:

Item	Price	Qty
A	200	2
B	500	3
C	100	1
D	50	2
E		
F		
G	150	5

Figure 7.4: Sample table with the Qty column added

Let's look at the following code:

```
SUMX TEST = SUMX (
    Products,
    Products[Price] * Products[Qty]
    )
```

Here, we would get `Result` = `2,850`.

Notice that in this case, when using the SUMX function, we need to provide two parameters. The first parameter is the table on which we will perform the operation, iterating row by row. The second parameter is the expression we want to aggregate. In our case, we are multiplying the `Price` column by the `Quantity` column, and aggregating the result. As you can see, the result is `2,850`:

```
The same behavior applies when using the MAXX function.
TEST = MAXX (
    Products,
    Products[Price] * Products[Qty]
    )
```

The preceding code will return `Result` = `1,500`.

This time, the result would be 1,500 as that is the maximum value obtained from multiplying the `Price` and `Quantity` of item B `(500 X 3)` row by row.

> **Note**
>
> The first parameter of these functions can be a table existing in your model or a function that returns a table. We will cover some of these table functions later.

Another interesting fact about aggregation functions is that the basic functions (those without the X prefix) are considered a shorthand version of the X functions.

Measures versus calculated columns

After showing you the basic aggregation functions in DAX, it's important to know that this language is used for creating measures and calculated columns. Unlike Excel, where adding a column to a table is simply done by right-clicking and adding the column to the left or right, in Power BI, it's a bit different. Here, we have to specify the expression that will define the column, and this expression must be written in DAX.

A calculated column is essentially an additional column that's added to a table that you can use in the same way as other columns in your model. You can use aggregation functions on them and even use them to create relationships with other tables. The DAX expression you define for this column will be executed on the current row, row by row. This means you can't directly access values from other rows like in Excel, unless you modify the filter context. The topic of filter contexts is something we'll cover later.

You can create a new calculated column in two ways:

- The first way is in the **Data** view. Select the table you want the column from the right section, right-click on any of the columns, and select **Add new column**:

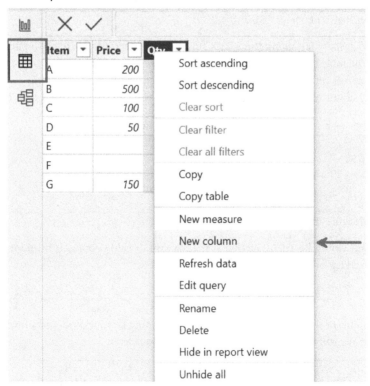

Figure 7.5: A menu option to create a new column

- The other way is to go to the **Home** menu. In the **Calculations** section, you'll find a button that says **New Column**:

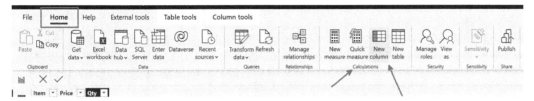

Figure 7.6: Another menu option to create a new column

Let's suppose we want to create an additional column in our Product table that contains the same expression you saw previously (calculating the `Price` column multiplied by the quantity). We can do this in the following way:

```
1 Total = Products[Price] * Products[Qty]
```

Item	Price	Qty	Total
A	200	2	400
B	500	3	1500
C	100	1	100
D	50	2	100
E			
F			
G	150	5	750

Figure 7.7: DAX code in a calculated column

Notice that this time, it is enough to simply specify the two columns we want to multiply with their respective multiplication operator. Unlike the measures we created with the SUMX function, where we had to specify the table on which to execute that function row by row, since we are creating the column directly in the products table, we don't need a function for this, and therefore we can create the expression as shown in the preceding screenshot.

By now, you're probably asking yourself the same question that most people ask: What is the difference between creating a measure and creating a calculated column? Next, we will cover two main points that will help you understand the difference between these two terms.

Execution process

The first difference we can notice is the environment in which calculated columns and measures are executed. When you create a calculated column, the expression it contains is processed when you define it or when the data is loaded into the model. In simpler terms, it is executed when you refresh your report or create the columns, as we did in the previous example. This means that calculated columns consume RAM to be processed and also take up physical storage in your model. The more calculated columns you have, the larger your model will be.

Taking our small products table as an example, the values in that new column will not change because they were already calculated when I created them. However, if any of the values they depend on change, such as the price or quantity of those particular products, the values in the calculated column will also change, but not during user interaction with any visual objects in the report.

This is not the case with measures as their calculation is performed when we add them to a visual object or when we interact with the report. Measures also do not occupy much storage as they are saved as a formula that defines the desired result, rather than the result itself.

Execution context

Another notable difference between measures and calculated columns is the execution context of expressions. When creating a calculated column, you strictly depend on the context of the current row. This means the calculation has access to all the values in the columns, but only in the row where the expression is being executed – unless you modify the execution context, as you will learn later in this chapter. This notion of the current row allows calculated columns to automatically know which row to execute the expression on.

On the other hand, measures do not have this built-in feature as they aggregate data and return a value. Instead, you must explicitly specify the context in which you want the expression executed. This is similar to what we did earlier when using the SUMX function. The calculated column already knows it is in the products table because that's where we define it. Still, with a measure, we need to pass the products table as the first parameter within the SUMX function so that it knows to execute the calculation of price multiplied by quantity row by row in that table.

To give you a clearer idea, imagine that we create another column that classifies each product's total sales as high or low, as shown in the following figure. We could use this column later to filter the data using a slicer since it won't change. However, if we wanted to obtain the minimum or maximum value of sales classified as low but only consider the products from a specific category or brand, we would have to resort to a measure for this:

Item	Price	Qty	Total	Price Class
A	200	2	400	Low
B	500	3	1500	High
C	100	1	100	Low
D	50	2	100	Low
E				Low
F				Low
G	150	5	750	Low

Figure 7.8: Table with a column that has classified products as High or Low

Always remember that calculated columns are evaluated once and this happens when you refresh the dataset; if your goal is to have complicated dynamic calculations and you need to consider complex filters in your result, then *measures* are your best fit.

When to use measures or calculated columns

Now that you understand the difference, you probably have the following question: When do I use a calculated column or a measure? The answer will depend on the purpose of the calculation. Whenever you need to categorize values, as in the previous example, or perform a row-by-row calculation, such as in the price x quantity example, use calculated columns. On the other hand, if your calculation is more complex and requires playing around with filters and contexts, measures are the solution.

Understanding evaluation contexts

In the previous section, we used the SUMX function to sum the result of multiplying price by quantity. Similarly, we achieved the same result by creating a calculated column without the need to use the SUMX function.

Measures

The following code refers to a measure:

```
SUMX TEST = SUMX (
    Products,
    Products[Price] * Products[Qty]
    )
```

Calculated column

The following code refers to a calculated column:

```
Total = Products[Price] * Products[Qty]
```

The fact that both calculations return the same result is related to the execution environment, specifically the evaluation context in which they are executed.

A simple example to understand this concept is by adding the measure to a card in your report. As you can see, the result is the total sum of each multiplication of price by quantity. This is essentially the total sales as we have renamed the measure:

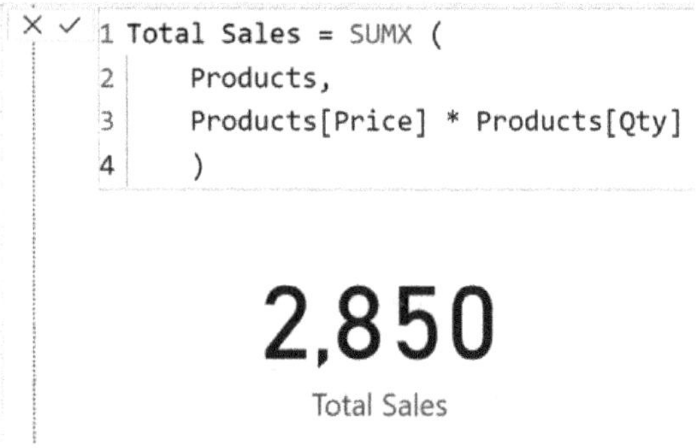

```
1 Total Sales = SUMX (
2        Products,
3        Products[Price] * Products[Qty]
4     )
```

2,850

Total Sales

Figure 7.9: A card visual with a measure added

However, if instead of using a card, we use a table and add the calculated column of Price Class, which classifies the sales as high or low, we'll get the following output:

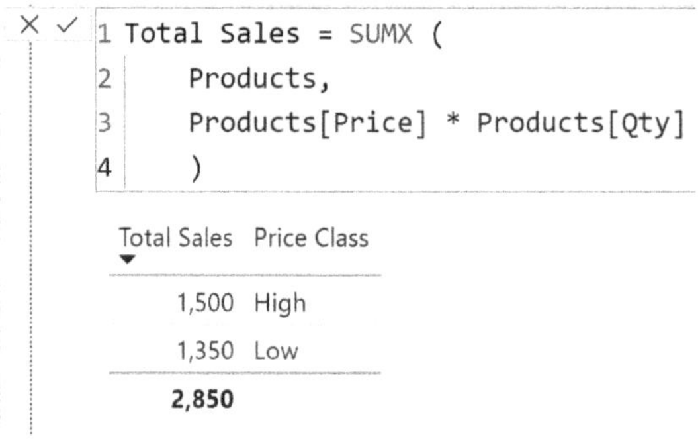

```
1 Total Sales = SUMX (
2        Products,
3        Products[Price] * Products[Qty]
4     )
```

Total Sales	Price Class
1,500	High
1,350	Low
2,850	

Figure 7.10: Table with a measure and a calculated column added

Although the measure remains the same and the total remains the same, notice that the measure has a different value in each of the rows. So, why does this happen? At no point have we specified that our formula should operate on a specific set of data. The answer lies in the context in which the measure is being executed. In each of the rows, the measure is constrained by the price class, but in the total, since there is no price class at that level, I am obtaining the global total.

Row context

To explain the row context, let's go back to the calculated column we created earlier:

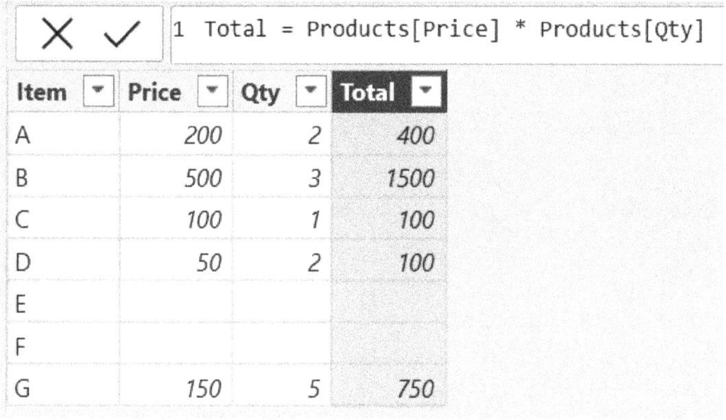

Figure 7.11: Calculated column of Total

When creating a calculated column, we don't need to specify the table on which we want to perform the calculation – rather, we don't need a row context because it is already implicit in the calculated column. However, when we want to achieve the same result with a measure, we need to use a function that can introduce that context; that's what we saw with the SUMX function.

The row context is "The Current Row", and it essentially tells DAX which row to use for executing the calculation row by row. In the Total Sales measure, we had to pass the Products table to the measure so that it knows the row context to use when executing the expression.

> **Note**
>
> All the X functions have the particularity of introducing a row context to the expression and allow you to access columns as if you were creating a calculated column.

This may be a bit surprising if you come from creating formulas in Excel, where each formula must specify the cell from which it will retrieve the values for the calculation. However, in Power BI, this is one of the core concepts, so it's important to have a clear understanding of it since most incorrect calculations in measures are related to contexts.

Filter context

In simple terms, the filter context refers to all the filters that affect the result of a measure. Let's consider a matrix like the one shown in the following figure, which displays total sales by category. At the top of the matrix, we have two slicers: one filtering by Country with "United Kingdom" selected, and another filtering by Year with "2009" selected. If you observe closely, each result is different because the matrix creates a filter context that conditions the result to a specific category. Additionally, we have the two filters applied from Year and Country, which also directly impact the result of this measure:

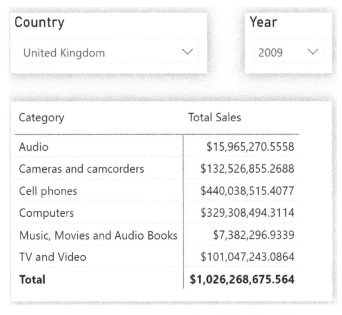

Category	Total Sales
Audio	$15,965,270.5558
Cameras and camcorders	$132,526,855.2688
Cell phones	$440,038,515.4077
Computers	$329,308,494.3114
Music, Movies and Audio Books	$7,382,296.9339
TV and Video	$101,047,243.0864
Total	**$1,026,268,675.564**

Figure 7.12: A Power BI report with a table and two slicers

Do not confuse the use of matrices with tables, even though they may have some visual similarities (in some cases). Calculations in matrices are not performed row by row; instead, they create a filter context that modifies the result of the measure. For example, if we add the product class to the columns, the result would be as follows:

Country: United Kingdom   Year: 2009

Category	Cheap	Premium	Regular	**Total**
Audio	$8,474,777.4366	$1,843,234.5365	$5,647,258.5827	**$15,965,270.5558**
Cameras and camcorders	$46,169,337.2118	$20,823,592.28	$65,533,925.777	**$132,526,855.2688**
Cell phones	$355,693,235.9996	$62,903,631.0065	$21,441,648.4016	**$440,038,515.4077**
Computers	$105,124,943.8474	$56,948,481.118	$167,235,069.346	**$329,308,494.3114**
Music, Movies and Audio Books	$1,989,926.0222	$3,116,856.3412	$2,275,514.5705	**$7,382,296.9339**
TV and Video	$35,529,197.034	$11,878,863.59	$53,639,182.4624	**$101,047,243.0864**
Total	**$552,981,417.5516**	**$157,514,658.8722**	**$315,772,599.1402**	**$1,026,268,675.564**

Figure 7.13: A Power BI report with a matrix and two slicers

These products are classified as cheap, regular, and premium. This means that by adding this additional column to the matrix, we will have a result for each combination of category and class. Similarly, we have data aggregated in the column totals and row totals. Each of these totals responds to a different filter context. For example, the total result of the first row only responds to the filter for the audio category, the country being the United Kingdom, and the year being 2009. On the contrary, the total of the first column is affected by the "cheap" class, all product categories, the country being the United Kingdom, and the year being 2009. Another tricky form of filtering that's happening in this table is the top left cell with the value of $8,474,777.4366. In this case, this is affected by the interception of class and category, the country, and the year.

Each of these filters can be enabled either from the visual object itself by interacting with them, from the filter pane, or by creating cross-filter relationships between visual objects. The combination of each of these filters creates the famous filter context.

Both the row context and the filter context are topics that may not be fully understood at first. So, don't hesitate to read this section several times whenever you have doubts about the difference between them. There is another concept called context transition, but we will be more practical with this topic and I will show you examples in the following sections.

> **Notes**
> A cross-filter relationship lets the filter pass across tables through relationships and affects the way visuals behave. Its use is not recommended due to performance issues.

Filtering data and modifying contexts

Not all calculations will be as simple as a sum or an average. In many cases, you may need to perform calculations under specific conditions – for example, averaging the sales of products in a particular category or determining which customer had the most orders above a certain amount. To achieve this, we need to use a fundamental function that allows us to modify the execution context of our measures: the CALCULATE function.

CALCULATE

In the previous section, I showed you what the filter context and row context are. We mentioned that the context conditions the result of a measure. However, sometimes, it is necessary to bypass the rules or modify the context to obtain the desired result. There is a privileged function within DAX that allows us to modify the filter context of an expression, and that function is CALCULATE.

The CALCULATE function is the only function allowed in DAX for modifying the filter context or adding a new one. to This function takes a scalar expression as its first parameter, and the following parameters are the filter arguments. As an example, let's go back to our small example table and try to obtain the maximum price of products classified as "low:"

Item ▾	Price ▾	Qty ▾	Total ▾	Price Class ▾
A	200	2	400	Low
B	500	3	1500	High
C	100	1	100	Low
D	50	2	100	Low
E				Low
F				Low
G	150	5	750	Low

200

MAX LOW Price

Figure 7.14: Example of using the CALCULATE function

A measure for this would be as follows:

```
MAX LOW Price =
    CALCULATE (
        MAX ( Products[Price] ),
        Products[Price Class] = «Low»
    )
```

As you can see, the maximum price of the product classified as "low" is item A with a value of 200. As you may have noticed, what we did was add a condition in the second parameter of the CALCULATE function, indicating that the price class should be equal to "low." Now, observe what happens when we place this measure in a table compared to the same measure without the CALCULATE function:

Price Class ▾	MAX LOW Price	MAX Price
Low	200	200
High	200	500
Total	**200**	**500**

Figure 7.15: A measure with the CALCULATE function in a table

In the function we just created, each row ignores the filter context that comes from Price Class and replaces it with the one I just specified (Products[Price Class] = "LOW"). On the other hand, the other measure that simply brings the maximum value respects the filter context that comes from the Price Class column and gives me the maximum of each class.

FILTER

In addition to creating simple conditions for the filter argument, we can create more complex filters using functions such as FILTER. Essentially, this function takes a table and returns a similar one but filtered according to the condition we specify. FILTER is considered an iterator function as it scans the condition in the second parameter row by row, checking if each row meets the condition and including or excluding it from the result.

The syntax is as follows:

```
FILTER ( <table>, <condition> )
```

It is important to note that all filter arguments you pass to the CALCULATE function are expressions that return a table, also known as "table expressions." For example, the measure we saw earlier where we filtered products classified as "low" is transformed by DAX in the following way:

```
MAX LOW Price =
    CALCULATE (
        MAX ( Products[Price] ),
        FILTER (
            Products,
            Products[Price Class] = «LOW»
        )
    )
```

One way to verify the result of this function is by creating a calculated table using only the portion of code from the FILTER function, as shown here: 

```
1  TEST FILTER Table =
2      FILTER (
3          Products,
4          Products[Price Class] = "LOW"
5      )
```

Item	Price	Qty	Total	Price Class
A	200	2	400	Low
C	100	1	100	Low
D	50	2	100	Low
E				Low
F				Low
G	150	5	750	Low

Figure 7.16: Calculated table to verify the FILTER function

The result is only the rows that meet the condition we passed as the second parameter. This table is the one that CALCULATE uses as the context when calculating the maximum price in the previous measure.

To create a calculated column, follow these steps:

1. If you are in the **Report** view, navigate to the **Modeling** menu and select **New table**:

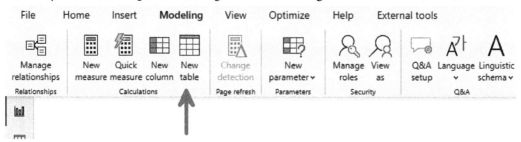

Figure 7.17: Creating a table from the Modeling menu

2. If you are in the **Data** view, navigate to the **Home** menu and select **New table**:

Figure 7.18: Creating a table from the Home menu

3. Finally, you can select **New table** from the **Table Tools** menu:

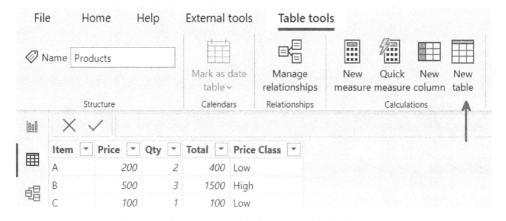

Figure 7.19: Creating a table from the Table Tools menu

The conditions we pass to the FILTER function can be as complex as we want. For example, if we modify our calculated table as follows, in addition to getting the products with the "low" class, we are also restricting the products whose price is greater than 100:

```
TEST FILTER Table =
    FILTER (
        Products,
        Products[Price Class] = «LOW»
            && Products[Price] > 100
    )
```

The result would be only two records:

Item	Price	Qty	Total	Price Class
A	200	2	400	Low
G	150	5	750	Low

Figure 7.20: A small table using the FILTER function

> **Note**
>
> Since the FILTER function returns a table, you can pass it as a parameter to any function that allows it, such as the X functions we saw earlier.

ALL

In addition to the FILTER function, there are other functions we can use to modify the filter context alongside the CALCULATE function. One of them is the ALL function, which returns all the contents of a table while ignoring the filter context.

This function can take one or multiple columns as parameters or a table, though it can also be used without any parameters if you want to remove the entire filter context:

```
ALL ( <column> )             - Remove Filter from column
ALL ( <column>, <column> )   - Remove Filter from Columns
ALL ( Table )                - Remove filter from Table
ALL ()                       - Remove Filter from All Tables
```

Let's rewrite the measure that I showed you previously, which calculated the maximum value of products classified as "low," in the following way:

```
MAX LOW Price =
    CALCULATE (
        MAX ( Products[Price] ),
        FILTER (
            ALL ( Products ),
            Products[Price Class] = «LOW»
        )
    )
```

The result would be as follows:

Item	Price Class ▼	Price	MAX LOW Price
A	Low	200	200
C	Low	100	200
D	Low	50	200
E	Low		200
F	Low		200
G	Low	150	200
B	High	500	200
Total		**1000**	**200**

Figure 7.21: A table with a measure showing the use of CALCULATE with the ALL function

In each row, we are getting the same result because we are ignoring all the context that can be applied from the Products table.

> **Note**
> There is another function called REMOVEFILTERS that does the same as the ALL function, but its name is a bit more intuitive. However, you can only use it to modify the context while using the CALCULATE function and not as a table expression like you can with the ALL function.

Time intelligence functions

Time intelligence functions are a crucial topic on the path to becoming an experienced data analyst. These functions allow you to perform calculations based on time dimensions such as dates, hours, months, or years. They enable you to make comparisons, identify trends, and conduct historical analysis more effectively.

In this section, I will show you some of DAX's most commonly used time intelligence functions. Before introducing the first function, it's important to know that time intelligence functions have a few minimum requirements to function correctly. These requirements are as follows:

- There must be a calendar table in your model
- All dates must be present for the period you are looking for
- The calendar table should always start on January 1 and end on December 31, including each day within this period
- The calendar table must contain a column of type DateTime or Date
- The calendar table must be marked as the date table
- Two functions in DAX can help you create a calendar table easily: CALENDAR and CALENDARAUTO

A calendar table is crucial for time intelligence functions, and there are many ways you can create one in your model – you can use DAX, you can create one in Power Query, or you can import one from a database in case you already have one.

Let's take a look at some of these functions in detail.

CALENDAR versus CALENDARAUTO

The CALENDAR function takes two parameters: a start date and an end date. The result is a table that contains all the dates within this range. The resulting table has a column called Date of the DateTime type, as shown here:

```
Calendar = CALENDAR ( "01-01-2023", "01-30-2023" )
```

Here's the output:

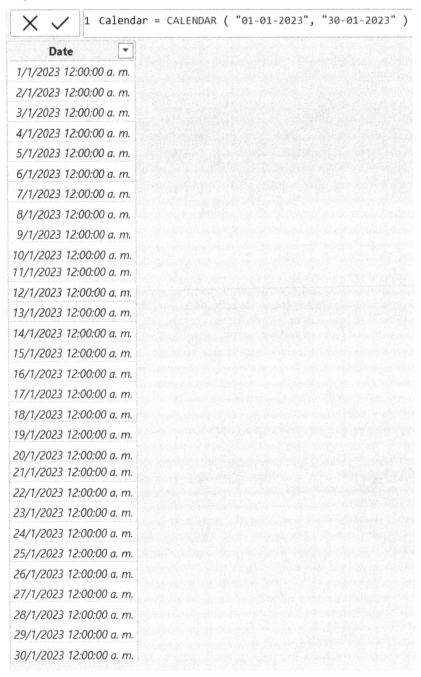

Figure 7.22: A table with dates created with the CALENDAR function

On the other hand, the CALENDARAUTO function in DAX takes a single optional parameter, which is the month in which the fiscal year ends (in case you want to consider fiscal years in your model). This function, like the CALENDAR function, returns a table with a single column of the DateTime type called "date," with the only difference being that this function takes the minimum and maximum dates found in all columns across all tables in your model as its start and end dates, except for calculated columns.

If our model had a sales table with records from January 1, 2008, to December 31, 2022, those would be the dates that the function would use as a reference to create the date table. However, if I pass the number 3 as a parameter, it would bring the missing dates from the initial fiscal period, which are the months from April to December in 2007, and likewise, the missing months from January to March in 2023.

DATEADD

The DATEADD function returns a table that contains a column of dates shifted forward or backward in time. This function takes parameters for the dates, the number of intervals, and the interval by which it will shift forward (a positive number) or backward (a negative number).

The syntax is as follows:

```
DATEADD(<dates>,<number_of_intervals>,<interval>)
```

In the following example, we're creating a measure that returns the total sales 7 days backward from the selected day:

```
Sales Last 7 Days =
    CALCULATE (
        [SUM Total Sales],
        DATEADD ( 'Calendar'[Date], -7, DAY )
    )
```

The preceding code will give us the following result:

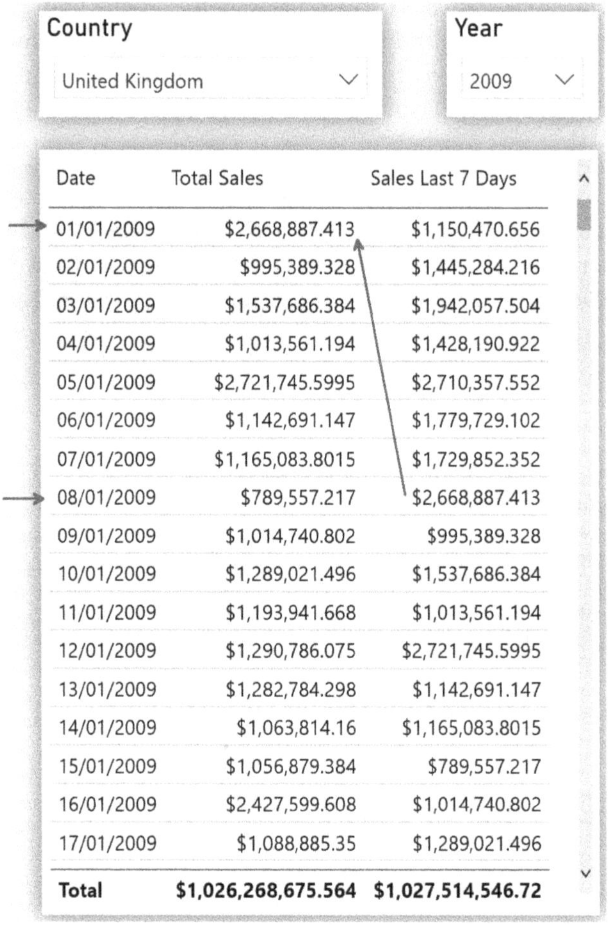

Date	Total Sales	Sales Last 7 Days
01/01/2009	$2,668,887.413	$1,150,470.656
02/01/2009	$995,389.328	$1,445,284.216
03/01/2009	$1,537,686.384	$1,942,057.504
04/01/2009	$1,013,561.194	$1,428,190.922
05/01/2009	$2,721,745.5995	$2,710,357.552
06/01/2009	$1,142,691.147	$1,779,729.102
07/01/2009	$1,165,083.8015	$1,729,852.352
08/01/2009	$789,557.217	$2,668,887.413
09/01/2009	$1,014,740.802	$995,389.328
10/01/2009	$1,289,021.496	$1,537,686.384
11/01/2009	$1,193,941.668	$1,013,561.194
12/01/2009	$1,290,786.075	$2,721,745.5995
13/01/2009	$1,282,784.298	$1,142,691.147
14/01/2009	$1,063,814.16	$1,165,083.8015
15/01/2009	$1,056,879.384	$789,557.217
16/01/2009	$2,427,599.608	$1,014,740.802
17/01/2009	$1,088,885.35	$1,289,021.496
Total	**$1,026,268,675.564**	**$1,027,514,546.72**

Country: United Kingdom   Year: 2009

Figure 7.23: Example of using DATEADD

In this measure, we are using the CALCULATE function to modify the filter context in which the measure called [SUM Total Sales] will be executed. The measure calculates the total sales. As a filter argument, I pass the DATEADD function while specifying that I want the last 7 days. However, since this function only has one visible date within its context, it returns the date from 7 days backward from the selected day. That's why I'm obtaining the value of the sales for that date.

SAMEPERIODLASTYEAR

Another function that allows us to travel in time and is widely used is the SAMEPERIODLASTYEAR function. This function returns a table that contains a set of dates shifted 1 year back, based on the current context.

The syntax is as follows:

```
SAMEPERIODLASTYEAR(<dates>)
```

As you can see, this function only takes one column that should contain the dates to be shifted 1 year back. This parameter can be a column containing dates, an expression that returns a table with a single column of dates, or a Boolean expression that defines a table with a single column of dates:

```
Sales Same Period Last Year =
    CALCULATE (
        [SUM Total Sales],
        SAMEPERIODLASTYEAR ('Calendar'[Date])
    )
```

In the following matrix, we have sales by year and month, along with the measure we just created. In the January row of 2008, we are getting the total sales for the same month but in the previous period, which is 2007. Since this model only has records starting from 2007, this measure returns blank for the months where there is no data for the previous year:

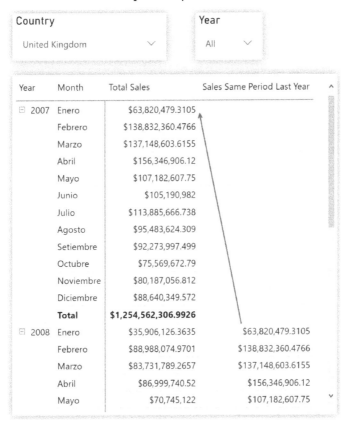

Figure 7.24: Example of using SAMEPERIODLASTYEAR

> **Note**
>
> The dates that are returned by this function are equivalent to using the DATEADD function as follows: DATEADD (dates, -1, year).

DATESBETWEEN

This function also allows us to perform time intelligence calculations. Similar to the previous function, it returns a table that contains a column of dates starting from an initial date specified as a parameter and continuing until an end date, which is also specified in the third parameter.

The syntax is as follows:

```
DATESBETWEEN(<Dates>, <StartDate>, <EndDate>)
```

In the following code, we have created a measure using the DATESBETWEEN function. I only want the date range between January 1 and March 31, 2008:

```
Dates Between =
    CALCULATE (
        [SUM Total Sales],
        DATESBETWEEN (
            'Calendar'[Date],
            "01-01-2008", "31-03-2008"
        )
    )
```

The result is the sum of sales for these three months, as shown here:

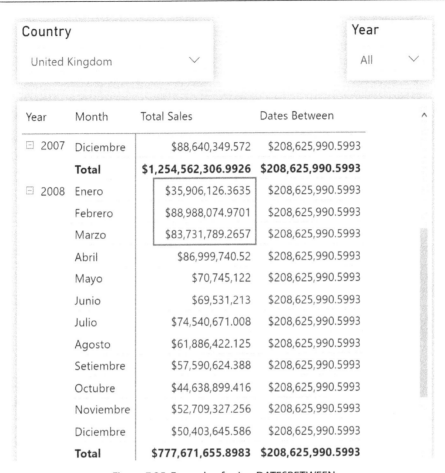

Figure 7.25: Example of using DATESBETWEEN

Remember, the DATESBETWEEN function returns a table, which means you can use it as a context modifier, like we did in the preceding example, or you can use it in any function that accepts a table in one of its parameters.

DATESINPERIOD

Another slightly more flexible option you have for obtaining a date range is the DATESINPERIOD function. This function returns a table that contains a date column starting from an initial date we provide as a parameter and continuing for a specified time interval and interval type.

The syntax is as follows:

```
DATESINPERIOD(<dates>, <start_date>, <number_of_intervals>,
<interval>)
```

In the following example, we have created a measure to always obtain the sales for the last two months. Notice that as the second parameter, I have passed the MAX function to obtain the last day of the month. For example, in March 2008, the MAX function will return (03-31-2008), and that is the date I will use as the initial date within the date range I want. The subsequent parameters indicate the interval and the quantity I desire within that interval. Remember that a positive number will move you forward in time, while a negative number will take you backward:

```
Dates In Period =
    CALCULATE (
        [SUM Total Sales],
        DATESINPERIOD (
            <Calendar> [Date],
            MAX ( <Calendar> [Date] ),
            -2,
            MONTH
        )
    )
```

The preceding code will return the following result:

Year	Month	Total Sales	Dates In Period
⊟ 2007	Diciembre	$88,640,349.572	$168,827,406.384
	Total	**$1,254,562,306.9926**	**$168,827,406.384**
⊟ 2008	Enero	$35,906,126.3635	$124,546,475.9355
	Febrero	$88,988,074.9701	$124,894,201.3336
	Marzo	$83,731,789.2657	$172,719,864.2358
	Abril	$86,999,740.52	$170,731,529.7857
	Mayo	$70,745,122	$157,744,862.52
	Junio	$69,531,213	$140,276,335
	Julio	$74,540,671.008	$144,071,884.008
	Agosto	$61,886,422.125	$136,427,093.133
	Setiembre	$57,590,624.388	$119,477,046.513
	Octubre	$44,638,899.416	$102,229,523.804
	Noviembre	$52,709,327.256	$97,348,226.672
	Diciembre	$50,403,645.586	$103,112,972.842
	Total	**$777,671,655.8983**	**$103,112,972.842**

Figure 7.26: Examples of using DATESINPERIOD

> **Note**
>
> Due to the flexibility of this function, it is recommended to use `DATESINPERIOD` instead of `DATESBETWEEN` when working with intervals of days, months, quarters, or years.

Complex DAX measures

Creating measures in DAX can sometimes be complex if you don't have a good understanding of certain functions or concepts. It can also be frustrating when you're unsure how to implement a specific requirement within your report. However, some tricks can be very helpful in finding a solution for the measure you're working on.

Complex model = complex measures

In previous sections, I mentioned that your data model will influence the complexity of your measures and, consequently, their results. For example, the following data model includes a calendar table and a table with sales records, specifically internet service sales. As you can see, three relationships are established between these tables, although Power BI only allows one of them to be active at a time. On the calendar table side, we always have the `DateKey` column, which is involved in the relationships, while on the sales table side, we have the `DueDateKey`, `OrderDateKey`, and `ShipDateKey` columns.

Figure 7.27 highlights the first disabled relationship:

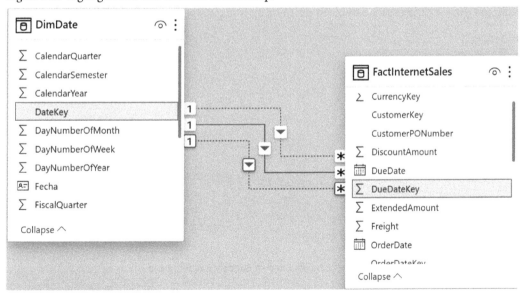

Figure 7.27: Disabled relationship highlighted

In Figure 7.28, the active relationship is highlighted:

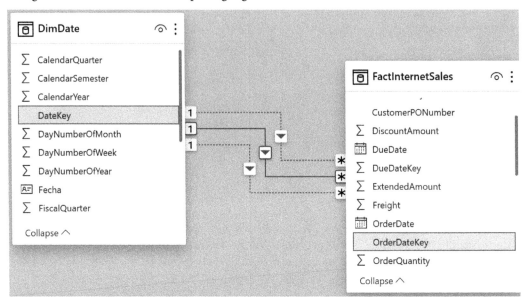

Figure 7.28: Active relationship highlighted

Finally, in *Figure 7.29*, the second disabled relationship is highlighted:

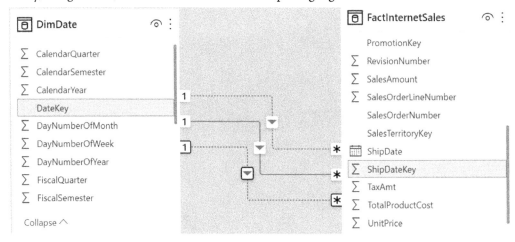

Figure 7.29: Second disabled relationship highlighted

If we create a measure as follows, the result would be the sales whose order date is in the previous year to the one selected in the current context:

```
Sales LY =
    CALCULATE (
        [Sum Sales],
        SAMEPERIODLASTYEAR ( DimDate[DateKey] )
    )
```

However, if we activate the relationship between the `DateKey` column and the `ShipDateKey` column, the result would be the sales whose shipment date is 1 year before the selected period. So, which relationship is correct? The answer depends on the business logic. If most of your calculations require working with the order date, then that should be the active relationship:

```
Sales Shipped LY =
    CALCULATE (
        [Sum Sales],
        USERELATIONSHIP (
            DimDate[DateKey],
            FactInternetSales[ShipDateKey]
), SAMEPERIODLASTYEAR ( DimDate[DateKey] )
    )
```

In any case, you can activate other relationships at runtime using the `USERELATIONSHIP` function, as shown in the preceding code.

Context-define the results

Creating a measure that returns the desired result can become a trial-and-error process. Even if you search well on Google, it can still be challenging. However, understanding the concept of contexts within DAX is a skill of Power BI ninjas.

The following measure is a bit more complex than what we have seen so far, but don't worry – I'll explain it briefly.

As you may have noticed, we are introducing a new concept, which is variables. You can create variables with the VAR prefix and give them any name that is not the name of any DAX function. In this case, I am storing the result of the SUM Total Sales measure in a variable. This measure essentially calculates the sum of the `Total Sales` column in my sales table.

Then, in another variable named `Result`, I am using the `DIVIDE` function to divide the "sales" variable by the result of the expression in the `CALCULATE` function, which I have set as the denominator.

This expression in the denominator modifies the filter context by removing all filters from the calendar table. This way, I can divide the sales by the global total, regardless of the date.

Finally, we use the `Return` keyword to return the variable that contains our result:

```
Percent Of Total =
VAR Sales = [SUM Total Sales]

VAR Result =
    DIVIDE (
        Sales,
        CALCULATE (
            [SUM Total Sales],
            ALLSELECTED ( 'Calendar' )
        )
    )

Return
    Result
```

If we use this measure in the following way, notice that I am obtaining the percentage that the sales represent for each level in the date hierarchy (years, quarters, months). For example, 12.06 is the percentage that the sales of the second quarter of 2007 represent. As you can see, this 12% is divided among April, May, and June:

Year	Quarter	Month	Total Sales	Dates In Period	Percent Of Total
⊟ 2007	⊟ Q1	Enero	$63,820,479.3105	$63,820,479.3105	2.09 %
		Febrero	$138,832,360.4766	$202,652,839.7871	4.54 %
		Marzo	$137,148,603.6155	$275,980,964.0921	4.48 %
		Total	**$339,801,443.4026**	**$275,980,964.0921**	**11.11 %**
	⊟ Q2	Abril	$156,346,906.12	$293,495,509.7355	5.11 %
		Mayo	$107,182,607.75	$263,529,513.87	3.50 %
		Junio	$105,190,982	$212,373,589.75	3.44 %
		Total	**$368,720,495.87**	**$212,373,589.75**	**12.06 %**
	⊟ Q3	Julio	$113,885,666.738	$219,076,648.738	3.72 %
		Agosto	$95,483,624.309	$209,369,291.047	3.12 %
		Setiembre	$92,273,997.499	$187,757,621.808	3.02 %

Figure 7.30: Power BI matrix visual object

First of all, notice how we are using the CALCULATE function as a parameter of another function – in this case, the DIVIDE function. This is because the divisor is the value for which we want to modify the filter context and obtain the desired percentage. Similarly, this divisor can be as complex as you want it to be. However, the purpose of this example was to simply demonstrate that contexts are a fundamental part of any DAX measure, no matter how basic it may seem.

> **Note**
>
> As an experienced data analyst, you should always use the DIVIDE function instead of the / operator when performing division since it handles division by zero.

Filters are tables

Filter arguments are also a fundamental part of achieving the correct result in any expression you perform in your measure using DAX, and they can be the cause of many headaches when your measure is not returning the desired result.

As you saw previously with the CALCULATE function, we need filter arguments based on the measure's complexity. These arguments can be Boolean expressions or literal tables that contain the subset of data on which the desired expression will be executed.

With the following measure, our goal is to only obtain sales for products from Fabrikam:

```
Sales Fabrikam =
    CALCULATE (
        [SUM Total Sales],
        Product [Brand] = "Fabrikam"
    )
```

And here's the result:

Year	Quarter	Month	Total Sales	Sales Fabrikam
⊟ 2007	⊟ Q1	Enero	$63,820,479.3105	$6,968,462.13
		Febrero	$138,832,360.4766	$17,724,800.438
		Marzo	$137,148,603.6155	$21,217,862.84
		Total	**$339,801,443.4026**	**$45,911,125.408**
	⊟ Q2	Abril	$156,346,906.12	$29,081,678.6
		Mayo	$107,182,607.75	$21,529,540
		Junio	$105,190,982	$22,129,875

Figure 7.31: A matrix showing a measure with sales from the Fabrikam brand

Previously, you learned that when we pass a Boolean filter argument in this way, the CALCULATE function transforms this expression into a table expression using the FILTER function, as follows:

```
Sales Fabrikam =
    CALCULATE (
        [SUM Total Sales],
        FILTER (
            ALL ( Producto[Brand] ),
            Producto[Brand] = "Fabrikam"
        )
    )
```

But what happens if, in addition to the products of the manufacturer brand, I also want those in the Computers category and I add the condition using the && operator, as follows?

```
Sales Fabrikam & Computers =
    CALCULATE (
        [SUM Total Sales],
        FILTER (
            ALL ( Product[Brand] ),
            Product[Brand] = «Fabrikam»
                && Product[Category] = "Computers"
        )
    )
```

The answer is that this measure would throw an error because the first parameter we are passing to the FILTER function is the ALL function with only the Brand column, while the condition we added includes the Category column. This can be resolved by removing the Brand column from the ALL function and keeping only the Product table. However, by doing this, we would be including all the other columns from the Product table that are not needed for our calculation. Therefore, the correct approach would be to include only the columns we need, which in this case are the Brand and Category columns, as shown here:

```
Sales Fabrikam & Computers =
    CALCULATE (
        [SUM Total Sales],
        FILTER (
            ALL ( Producto[Brand], Producto[Categoria] ),
            Product[Brand] = «Fabrikam»
                && Product[Category] = «Computers»
        )
    )
```

Remember that when we use the ALL function with multiple columns, it creates a table with all possible combinations between them – in our case, the brands and categories. The FILTER function iterates over this table, bringing only the records that match the conditions we specify. This context is then used by the CALCULATE function to execute the initial expression.

> **Note**
>
> Always restrict your filters to the minimum number of columns possible.

What happens if the filter we want to use comes from a table in your model, such as a calculated table? In the following figure, notice that I have created a table with only two records, Q1 and Q2. I have related this table to my calendar table using the Quarter column, and I have passed the table as an argument directly to the CALCULATE function as a filter:

1. First, I created a calculated table with the following code:

```
Filtered Months = {"Q1","Q2"}
```

> Here's the result:

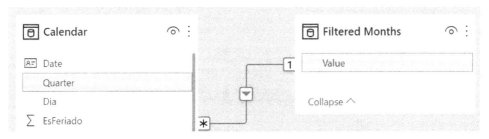

Figure 7.32: Sample table with quarters

2. Once the table was created, I added a relationship between the table and the Calendar table:

Figure 7.33: Relationship between the Calendar table and the Sample Quarters table

3. After that, I created a measure, as follows:

```
Sales Quarter 1 & 2 =
    CALCULATE (
        [SUM Total Sales],
        <Filtered Months>
    )
```

As you can see, the result is only the sales in the first and second quarters of the year:

Year	Quarter	Month	Total Sales	Sales Quarter 1 & 2
⊟ 2007	⊟ Q1	Enero	$63,820,479.3105	$63,820,479.3105
		Febrero	$138,832,360.4766	$138,832,360.4766
		Marzo	$137,148,603.6155	$137,148,603.6155
		Total	**$339,801,443.4026**	**$339,801,443.4026**
	⊟ Q2	Abril	$156,346,906.12	$156,346,906.12
		Mayo	$107,182,607.75	$107,182,607.75
		Junio	$105,190,982	$105,190,982
		Total	**$368,720,495.87**	**$368,720,495.87**
	⊟ Q3	Julio	$113,885,666.738	
		Agosto	$95,483,624.309	
		Setiembre	$92,273,997.499	
		Total	**$301,643,288.546**	
	⊟ Q4	Octubre	$75,569,672.79	
		Noviembre	$80,187,056.812	
		Diciembre	$88,640,349.572	
		Total	**$244,397,079.174**	

Figure 7.34: The result of passing a sample table as an argument to the CALCULATE function

Note

Several table functions can be very useful for managing filter arguments alongside the CALCULATE function. You can more information about these functions in Microsoft's documentation on table manipulation functions in DAX: (https://learn.microsoft.com/en-us/dax/table-manipulation-functions-dax.

Identifying the context of the requirement

Each of the measures in our models responds to a requirement that will help us achieve reporting objectives. As data analysts, we often find ourselves in meetings where the main ideas of the analysis are presented, and our role is to transform those ideas into specific requirements and then into measures.

The trick is to know how to identify those keywords that allow us to map the word to the available functions. For example, suppose we have the following requirement:

The warehouse department has requested a report that allows them to measure the average time elapsed from when an order is placed until it is delivered to the customer. This report aims to identify stores with the longest and shortest delivery times on a weekly and monthly basis. It would also be interesting to know if product properties such as weight, category, or class are related to an increase or decrease in delivery time.

Based on this statement, we should have answers to the following questions:

- Do we have a column that stores the order creation date and the date it is shipped?

- How are the stores related to the orders?

- Does our calendar table have a column for weeks?

As we have seen in previous examples, when we talk about sales orders, the sale and the date of shipment are usually recorded. Similarly, each record in the sales table probably has a column that identifies the customer who placed the order. If that is the case, our two questions will be answered.

After that, we proceed to identify the measures needed for the analysis and the functions that can help us. A list of these measures could be the ones here from M1 to M6:M1:

- The difference between `OrderDate` and `ShipDate`:

    - SUMX

    - Simple subtraction

- M2 – Average of `OrderDate` – `ShipDate`:

    - AVERAGEX

    - Reference to M1

- M3 – Average of `OrderDate` – `ShipDate` for the previous month:

    - DATESINPERIOD

    - DATEADD

    - DATESBETWEEN

    - Reference to M2

- M4 – Average of `OrderDate` – `ShipDate` for the previous week:

  - `DATESINPERIOD`

  - `DATEADD`

  - `DATESBETWEEN`

  - Reference to M2

- M5 – Difference between the current month and the previous month:

  - Reference to M3 and M2

- M6 – Difference between the current week and the previous week:

  - Reference to M4 and M2

Then, we make a list of the visual objects that can help explain our analysis. In our case, the following can be very useful:

- Show the average over time, a comparison to the previous period, and identify stores with higher or lower average time:

  - Line chart

  - Bar chart

- Explain the relationship between product properties and time:

  - Influence diagram

Finally, we must delve into topics of design and conditional formatting based on the measures we have defined here. This mental roadmap will help you transform business requirements into measures.

Q&A

During the interview process for the position of data analyst or Power BI Engineer, as many companies often refer to it, the topic of DAX is often touched upon in practical scenarios and problem-solving. However, you may encounter some technical questions that tend to be somewhat complex, so you should be prepared for that moment.

Below, I present some of the questions that may arise during the interview, some of which I have personally asked while interviewing candidates, while others have been asked to me in some interview processes.

Question 1: What is the advantage of the DIVIDE function compared to the regular expression Expression A / Expression B?

Answer: Using the DIVIDE function has several advantages. One of them is preventing the display of invalid values in the report. Additionally, it avoids division by zero in cases where the denominator is an expression that could return zero.

Question 2: What is the difference between a measure and a calculated column?

Answer: The difference between both calculations depends on the use you will give them. If you need to categorize values, create values derived from existing columns, or perform row-by-row calculations, then calculated columns are ideal. On the other hand, if you need your calculation to be dynamic, respond to applied filters, or modify the execution context, measures are the best option.

Question 3: If I ask you to create a measure that calculates the sales generated last year, what functions would you use to achieve this result?

Answer: To solve this request, we must first identify the base measure of sales and modify the filter context with the CALCULATE function. Then, as a filter argument, we would use the SAMEPERIODLASTYEAR function with the date column of the calendar table as a parameter so that this calculation runs under the context of the previous year.

Question 4: A user reports that the date filter used to filter sales allows selecting dates up to the year 1998, which is quite strange because there are no sales recorded on those dates. What do you think might be happening?

Answer: This is a common case when using the CALENDARAUTO function to create calendar tables in models. This is because this function takes the minimum date of all existing date-type columns in the model and does the same for the maximum date. That is, that date is probably the birthdate of an employee or another column unrelated to sales.

Question 5: So far, users in a department have been using a sales report that they can filter by the date of each sale. However, there is a need to perform analyses related to goods shipments within the same report. The sales table is related to the calendar table by the order date, but not by the shipment date. What method would you use to perform measures using the shipment date in calculations?

Answer: The first thing to consider is that two tables cannot have more than one active relationship. However, this does not prevent additional relationships from being created, even if they are disabled. Therefore, the first step would be to create the relationship between the calendar table and the sales table using the shipment date. Then, the USERELATIONSHIP function can be used in each measure where you want to consider the shipment date as context.

Summary

In this chapter, you learned about DAX concepts that are essential for mastering any job interview. First, I started by mentioning some points to take into account so that the learning process of this language is as fluid as possible. Then, we saw some of the basic aggregation functions such as MAX, MIN, and SUM, as well as some very practical examples of these functions. In the next section, we started by discussing the differences between measure and calculated columns and when you should use them.

Next, you saw a brief definition of what evaluation contexts are and the role played by the filter context and the row context inside measures. You also understood the importance of these to master the creation of complex measures using DAX. In the final stretch, you also saw some time intelligence functions, as well as some very useful examples that taught you how to go back and forth in time with these functions.

Finally, I showed you some advanced concepts about DAX and how to abort some common situations for data analysts.

With all this knowledge, you will surely be eager to move on to the next chapter, where you will learn about report creation and put much of what you learned in this chapter into practice.

8

Expert Report Building

Now that you have the fundamentals of **data analysis expressions** (**DAX**), it's time for you to start translating the language of data into actionable information through **charts** or **visual objects**, as they are commonly referred to in Power BI. Mastering the creation of reports and their interaction with users is a fundamental skill for today's data analyst. Remember that among all the phases of data analysis, this is the only one the end user interacts with. Moreover, many job postings commonly include requirements such as *designing Power BI dashboards/reports* or *data analysis and reporting skills*, so having this skill on your list only adds value and increases your chances of acing the job interview.

This chapter will teach you the fundamental aspects to consider when creating a Power BI report or dashboard. These are the topics that we will cover in this chapter:

- Best practices before adding your first visual
- Choosing the appropriate visual
- AI-powered visuals
- Conditional formatting
- Slicing and filtering
- Configuring visual tooltips
- Adding bookmarks
- Using drill-through
- Page navigation

Technical requirements

- Download the sample .csv files from the following URL: `https://packt.link/gbz/9781805120674`

- Install Power BI Desktop from the web: `https://www.microsoft.com/en-us/download/details.aspx?id=58494`

- Install Power BI Desktop from Microsoft Store: `https://aka.ms/pbidesktopstore`

Best practices before adding your first visual

Just as painters prepare their tools before making their first brushstroke, you must also prepare your report before adding your first visual object. In this section, I will show you some things to consider before creating your report in Power BI.

In Power BI, when we talk about visuals, we are referring to any graphical component inside the report that helps us visualize the data. These can be bar charts, cards, or simple text with information. These visuals try to translate our findings and analytics into useful information for the user; however, before adding your first visual, it's good to consider some essential settings for your report.

> **Note**
> Remember that visual objects in Power BI refer to the charts in which we will display the information.

Once you have downloaded the sample `.pbix` file and installed Power BI Desktop on your computer, it should appear as follows when you open the document:

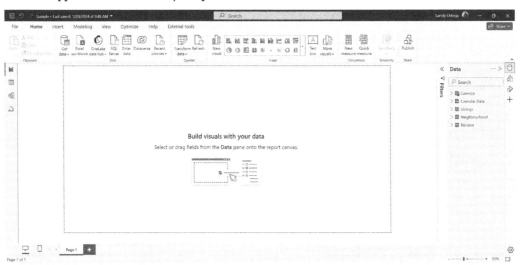

Figure 8.1: Power BI Desktop version May 2023

The report has a blank report with a total of five tables that make up your model. This report contains the occupancy information of Airbnb accommodations in New York City until March 2023. The tables are as follows:

- **Calendar Data**: Detailed listings calendar data

- **Calendar**: Calendar table

- **Listings**: Summary information and metrics for listings in New York City

- **Neighborhood**: Neighborhood list

- **Reviews**: Summary review data and listing ID

Let's take a look at some best practices to set up your report one by one.

Enabling preview features

One of the first steps you will take is to navigate to the menu where new preview features are located. To do this, go to **File** | **Options and Settings** | **Options** and open the **Preview features** menu.

Here, you will see a list of features that Microsoft has released that are still in the testing phase. Many of these features have been in this state for a long time, so they will likely be selected by default. As you can see in *Figure 8.2*, I have two options that are not enabled: **On-object interaction** and **Save to OneDrive and SharePoint**. The former option lets you edit each element of a visual within the same object, and the latter extends the capabilities to open/save reports in OneDrive. I will leave them as they are for now since we won't need them.

Remember that if you have any of these options selected and enable them, you will often need to restart Power BI Desktop. This means you will have to close and reopen the report.

Options

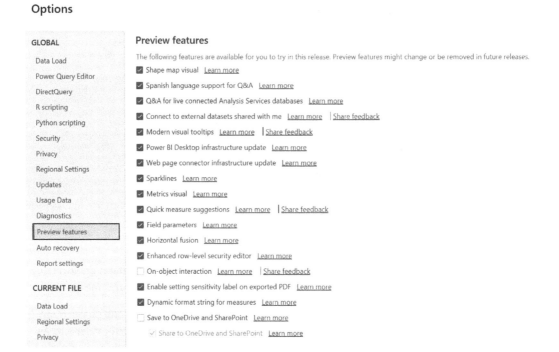

Figure 8.2: Power BI Desktop Preview features menu

> **Note**
>
> The settings in this menu are grouped into two sections: **GLOBAL** and **CURRENT FILE**, as you can see on the left side of *Figure 8.2*. Please note that these preview options can affect the current development of your report, so be careful when enabling any function.

Disabling Auto date/time

Once you enable preview features, you will navigate to the **Data Load** menu. As you can see in *Figure 8.3*, this menu has several options, such as type detection in columns or allowing imported relationships from the data sources. However, the option we will focus on is **Time intelligence**. I recommend disabling this option, as keeping it enabled can increase the size of your model depending on the number of datetime columns you have. For each of these columns, Power BI will create a calendar table based on the minimum and maximum dates in that column.

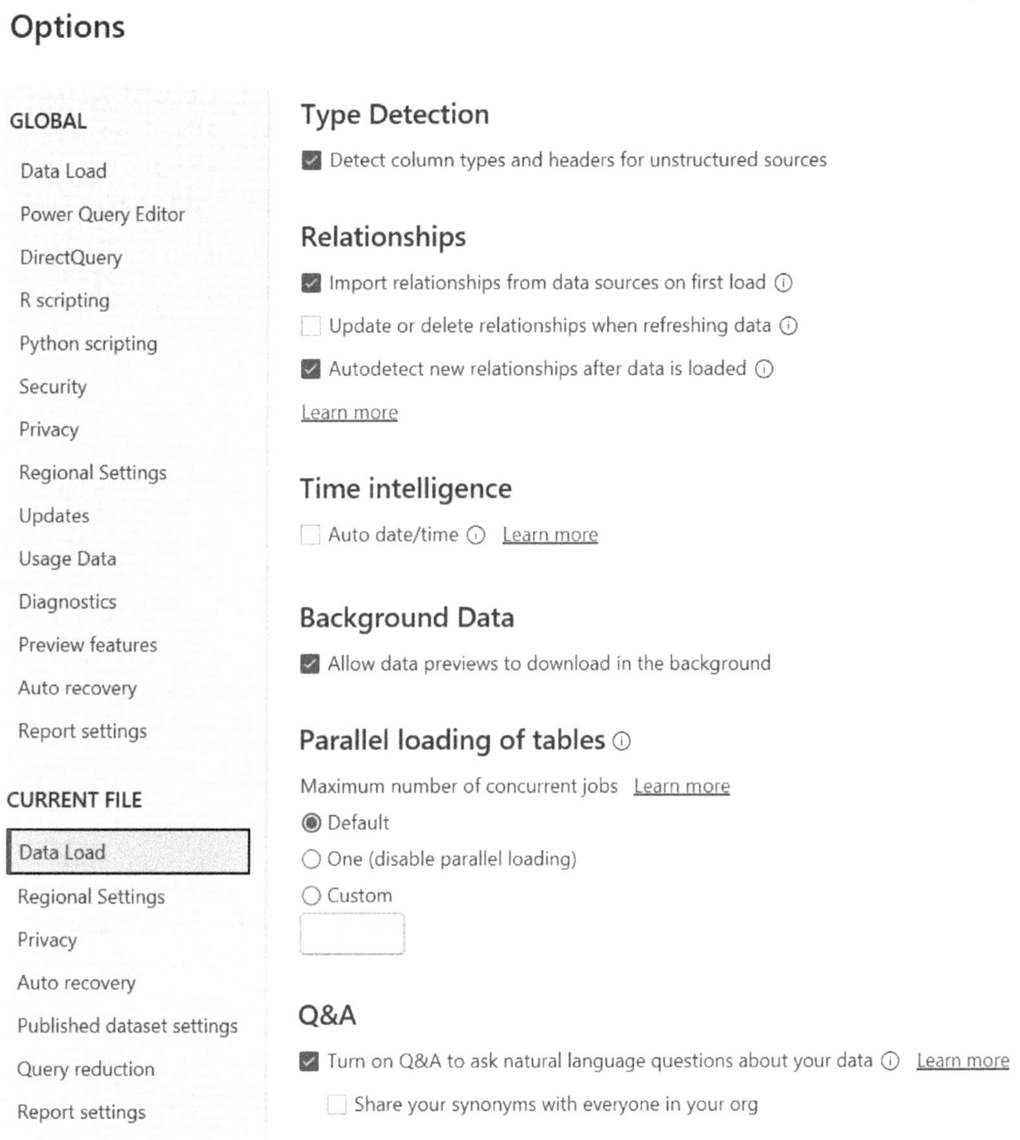

Options

GLOBAL

Data Load

Power Query Editor

DirectQuery

R scripting

Python scripting

Security

Privacy

Regional Settings

Updates

Usage Data

Diagnostics

Preview features

Auto recovery

Report settings

CURRENT FILE

Data Load

Regional Settings

Privacy

Auto recovery

Published dataset settings

Query reduction

Report settings

Type Detection

☑ Detect column types and headers for unstructured sources

Relationships

☑ Import relationships from data sources on first load ⓘ

☐ Update or delete relationships when refreshing data ⓘ

☑ Autodetect new relationships after data is loaded ⓘ

Learn more

Time intelligence

☐ Auto date/time ⓘ   Learn more

Background Data

☑ Allow data previews to download in the background

Parallel loading of tables ⓘ

Maximum number of concurrent jobs   Learn more

◉ Default

○ One (disable parallel loading)

○ Custom

Q&A

☑ Turn on Q&A to ask natural language questions about your data ⓘ   Learn more

☐ Share your synonyms with everyone in your org

Figure 8.3: Power BI Desktop Data Load menu

Editing application languages

- In the same **Options** menu, navigate to the **Regional Settings** within the **GLOBAL** settings group. Make sure that **Application language** is set to your desired language and that the separator option is set according to the recommended setting for your region. In my case, I will leave the recommended option to use commas as list separators and a period as the decimal separator.

Figure 8.4: Power BI Desktop regional settings (GLOBAL)

Changing report settings

- Finally, go to the **Report settings** menu in the group of settings for the current file. By default, there are some options that are disabled, such as the **Cross-report drillthrough** or **Personalize visuals** options. It's up to you to decide whether you will use any of these functions. In *Figure 8.5*, the option for **Modern visual tooltips** is enabled:

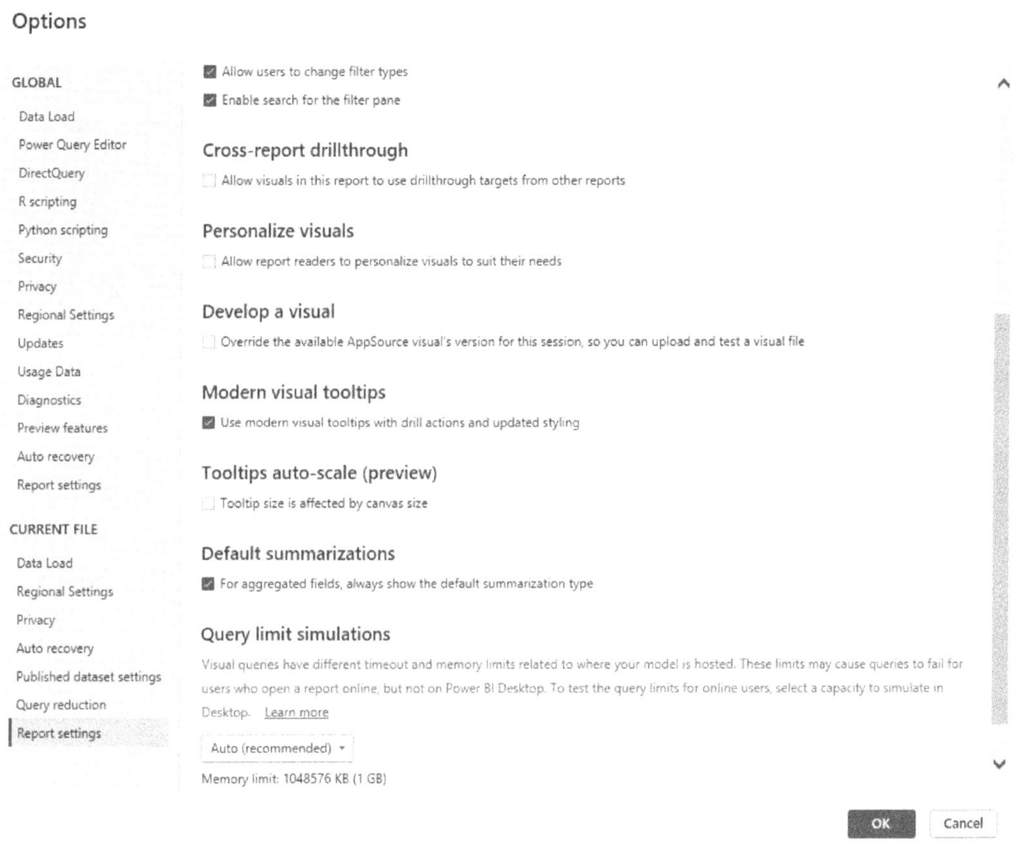

Options

GLOBAL

Data Load

Power Query Editor

DirectQuery

R scripting

Python scripting

Security

Privacy

Regional Settings

Updates

Usage Data

Diagnostics

Preview features

Auto recovery

Report settings

CURRENT FILE

Data Load

Regional Settings

Privacy

Auto recovery

Published dataset settings

Query reduction

Report settings

☑ Allow users to change filter types

☑ Enable search for the filter pane

Cross-report drillthrough

☐ Allow visuals in this report to use drillthrough targets from other reports

Personalize visuals

☐ Allow report readers to personalize visuals to suit their needs

Develop a visual

☐ Override the available AppSource visual's version for this session, so you can upload and test a visual file

Modern visual tooltips

☑ Use modern visual tooltips with drill actions and updated styling

Tooltips auto-scale (preview)

☐ Tooltip size is affected by canvas size

Default summarizations

☑ For aggregated fields, always show the default summarization type

Query limit simulations

Visual queries have different timeout and memory limits related to where your model is hosted. These limits may cause queries to fail for users who open a report online, but not on Power BI Desktop. To test the query limits for online users, select a capacity to simulate in Desktop.   Learn more

Auto (recommended) ▾

Memory limit: 1048576 KB (1 GB)

[OK]   [Cancel]

Figure 8.5: Power BI Desktop report setting (CURRENT FILE)

These are the initial settings that we are going to touch on for now. However, feel free to explore each of them and familiarize yourself with the process.

> **Note**
>
> The **GLOBAL** settings are permanent, while the settings for **CURRENT FILE** only apply to the currently open report.

Editing page dimensions

By default, Power BI creates pages with a ratio of **16:9**. If you click on any blank area of the page and go to the **Format** pane in the **Canvas settings** section, you can see the different ratios you can use, such as **4:3**, **Letter**, **Tooltip**, and **Custom**. Refer to *Figure 8.6*:

Figure 8.6: Power BI Desktop – Canvas settings menu

This default **16:9** ratio corresponds to a resolution of 1280 x 720 pixels. However, if you want your report to have a larger ratio, you can choose the **Custom** type and enter the dimensions you desire, such as 1920 x 1080, which is commonly used.

Keep in mind that the ratio you choose will greatly influence the size of the components you add to the report. In other words, some components will appear smaller with a higher resolution. Therefore, consider the audience who will be consuming the report and ensure that most devices where the report will be viewed match (or at least come close to) the ratio you choose.

In the same menu, you have another option: **Vertical alignment**. This allows you to adjust the vertical alignment of the report. As shown by the arrow in *Figure 8.7*, there is a larger space from the bottom of the report to the edge, indicating that the vertical alignment of the report is set to the top. The options available in this menu are **Top** and **Middle**. I prefer to set it to **Middle** to maintain symmetry and have more flexibility with background images.

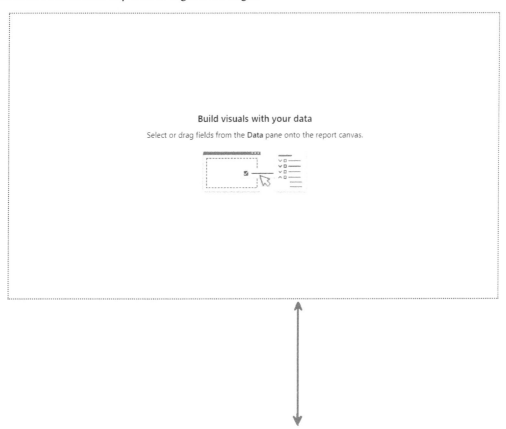

Figure 8.7: Power BI Desktop – wallpaper and background

The next options you should consider before adding your first measure to the report are **Wallpaper** and **Canvas background**. However, these may vary during the development of the report as elements are added or removed, which will affect the design.

Although they may seem similar, there is a difference between the wallpaper and the background. On one hand, the wallpaper is the larger area in *Figure 8.7*, while the background is the dotted rectangle in the center. Both settings allow you to change the color or, more commonly used, add an image.

As you can see in *Figure 8.8*, you can use a combination of wallpaper and background to enhance the design of your report. In both options, you can modify the image adjustment to **Normal**, **Fit**, or **Fill** and adjust the transparency.

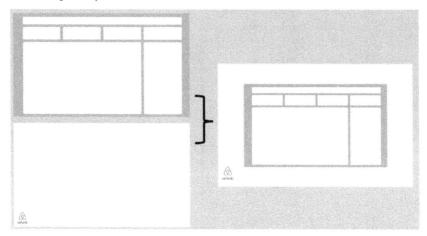

Figure 8.8: Background and wallpaper composition

- Another option that should be enabled at the beginning to avoid confusion and errors when starting to use DAX measures is marking your calendar table as a date table. Remember that **Time intelligence** functions require the existence of a calendar table and that it is marked as such. You can do this from the **Report View** or from the **Data View** by selecting the calendar table and going to the **Table Tools** menu that appears when you click on the table. Then, click **Mark as date table** and select the column containing the date, as shown in *Figure 8.9*:

Mark as a date table   ✕

To enable the creation of date-related visuals, tables and quick measures using this table's date data, mark it as a date table.

Keep in mind any built-in date tables that are already associated with this table will be removed. Visuals or DAX expressions referring to them may break. Learn more

Mark as a date table

🔘 On

Choose a date column

| Choose a column   ⌄ |
| Date |

Figure 8.9: Marking the calendar table as a date table

Now that you've learned some of the best practices to set up your report, it's time to add your first visual. In the next section, we will learn how to choose the most appropriate visual object based on the information you want to show.

Choosing the appropriate visual

As I mentioned in previous chapters, one of the skills every analyst should master is the ability to communicate through data. Within Power BI, we have a myriad of visual objects and charts that can help make storytelling much more effective. However, the success of effective communication will depend on the type of visual object you choose to display the results.

Firstly, Power BI provides a default list of visual objects that you can use in your report. However, you can also add elements from the **Get more visuals** option located in the highlighted area of *Figure 8.10*:

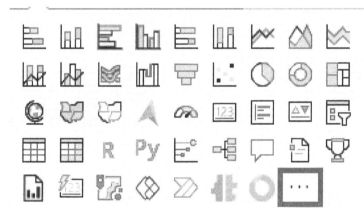

Figure 8.10: Power BI default visuals

A solid understanding of each chart and its usage is crucial for a data analyst. Many companies take this matter seriously, and questions about this topic may arise during the interview process. So, keep this in mind and be well-prepared.

Bar charts

Bar charts are the most effective way to visually represent comparisons of values between different categories. In Power BI, you have the following types of bar charts available:

- Stacked bar chart
- Stacked column chart

- Clustered bar chart

- Clustered column chart

- 100% stacked bar chart

- 100% stacked column chart

Figure 8.11 illustrates all the types of bar charts:

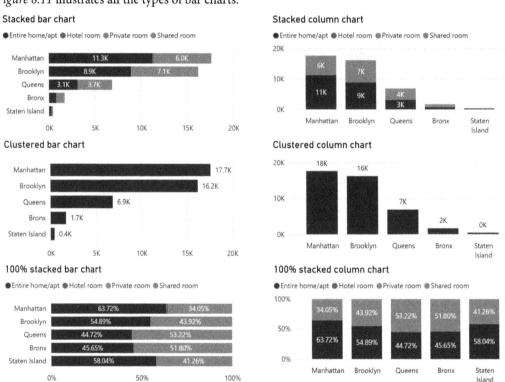

Figure 8.11: Power BI bar charts

These charts share similar properties:

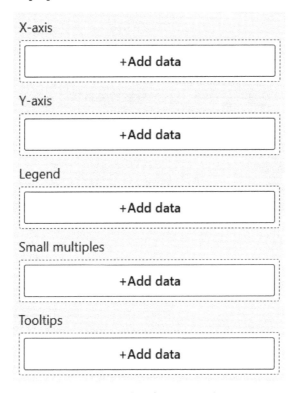

Figure 8.12: Bar chart properties

As shown in *Figure 8.12*, you can add data to the vertical axis, horizontal axis, and a legend.

Line and area charts

When it comes to comparing values over time, the best chart to choose is a **line chart**. It allows you to analyze trends and patterns over time. In Power BI, you have the following options for line charts:

- Line chart
- Area chart
- Stacked area chart

Figure 8.13 illustrates the types of line charts:

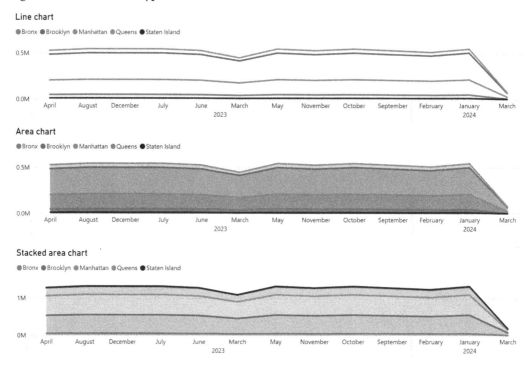

Figure 8.13: Power BI line and area charts

These charts share similar properties, with the only difference being that the line chart and area chart are the only ones that have a secondary *y* axis if you don't use legends.

Figure 8.14: Line chart properties

> **Note**
>
> The area chart is similar to the line chart, but the line chart has a shaded area.

Combo charts

Combo charts are a type of chart that combines bar charts with line charts. They are ideal when you want to compare trends and totals, contrast trends over time, and also display cumulative totals. A common example of this is the Pareto chart. In Power BI, you have the following options available for combo charts:

- Line and stacked column chart
- Line and clustered column chart

Figure 8.15 illustrates a combo chart:

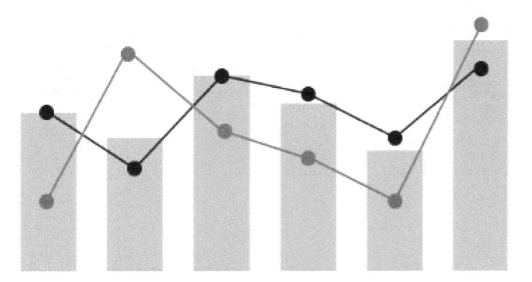

Figure 8.15: Power BI combo charts

Ribbon chart

Ribbon charts are a type of bar chart, but with connecting ribbons. Here is how they look:

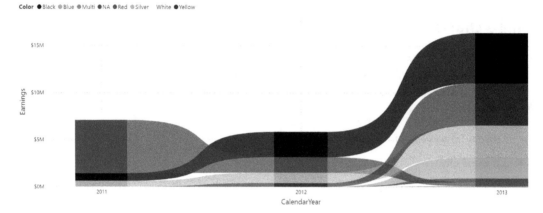

Figure 8.16: Power BI ribbon charts

They are commonly used to highlight the progressive ranking of categories, with the highest-ranked bar displayed at the beginning.

The properties of this chart are as follows:

Figure 8.17: Power BI ribbon chart properties

Waterfall chart

The **waterfall chart** is especially used when you want to view values in an accumulated manner and observe their increase or decrease over time. The name is due to its appearance resembling a waterfall:

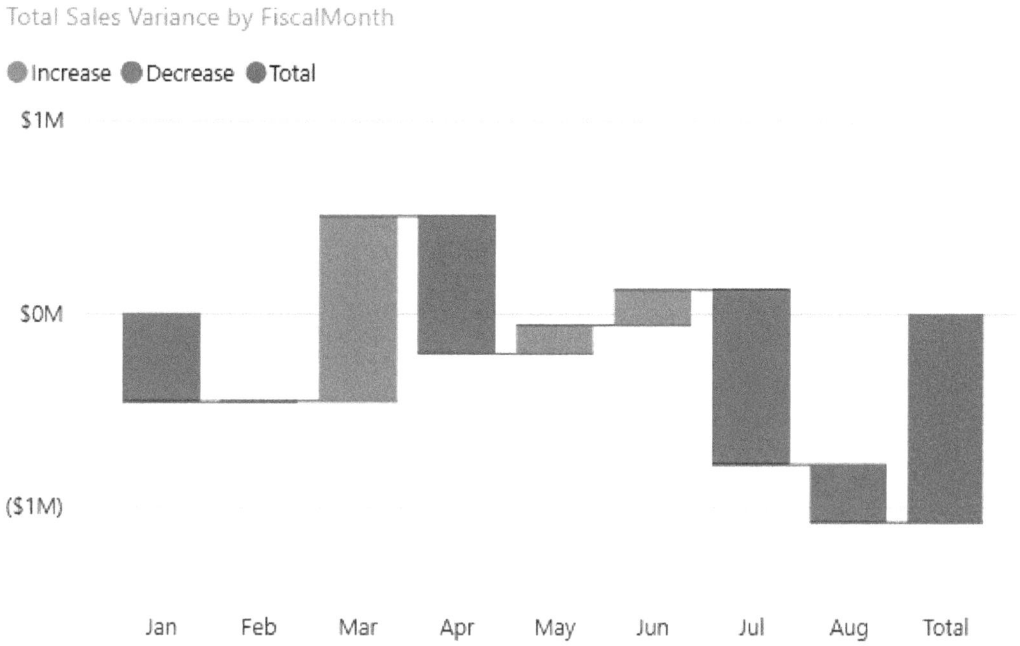

Total Sales Variance by FiscalMonth

● Increase ● Decrease ● Total

Figure 8.18: Power BI waterfall chart

These types of charts are usually used in fields such as finance or project management to analyze the variation of data over a series of stages.

This type of graph is also useful when we want to know the positive or negative impact on the total result – that is, how each stage influences the increase or decrease of the total value.

Funnel chart

The **funnel chart** is a type of chart where bars are centered and arranged in descending order. Each bar represents a percentage of the total.

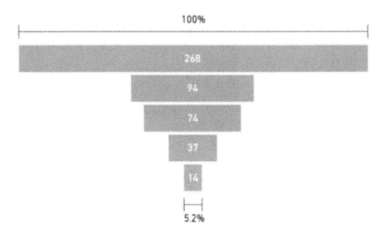

Figure 8.19: Power BI funnel chart

In addition to representing the percentage of categories, you can use this chart to identify bottlenecks when data must pass through multiple stages or when data is sequential and moves through different stages.

Pie and donut charts

The **pie and donut charts** are quite similar, with the only difference being that the donut chart has a hole in the center that allows you to add aesthetic details such as icons or a card with additional information.

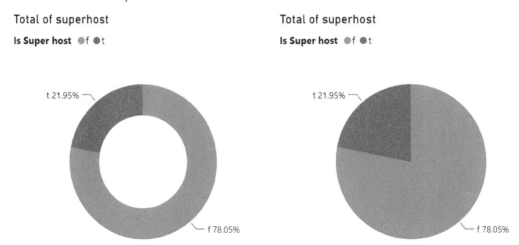

Figure 8.20: Power BI pie and donut charts

This chart is recommended when comparing two or more categories that are part of a whole. However, it is generally not recommended to exceed two categories in this chart.

Gauge

The **gauge** is a half-circle used to measure the progress of a value compared to a target value. This target value is represented by a line, and the progress is shown with a bar that follows the arc of the semi-circle.

Figure 8.21: Power BI gauge

This chart requires a minimum value, a maximum value, a value, and a target value to be passed to it.

> **Note**
> If you only add one measure or column to the value property, the minimum value will be zero and the maximum will be twice the property.

Cards and KPI

When you want to display a single value, **cards** are the right choice in Power BI. However, if you need to compare that value to another, the ideal chart for this is the **KPI**.

Figure 8.22: Power BI cards and KPI visuals

Starting from the June 2023 update, Microsoft introduced another type of card that allows you to have more formatting options, such as text justification, adding multiple measures to the same card, displaying images and icons, and an accent bar that you can customize to your liking.

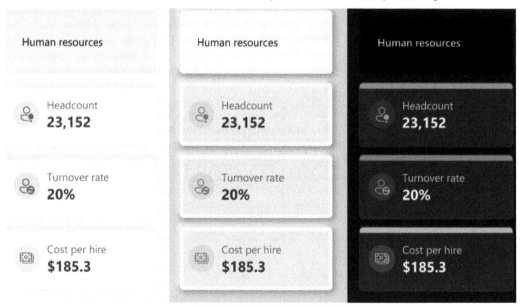

Figure 8.23: Power BI new cards

There are other visualizations that I will briefly mention, such as the **treemap**, which allows you to visualize categories as rectangles, and the size of these rectangles depends on the value assigned to the visual. This is a useful chart if you want to see the proportion that each category represents within the whole.

Other charts worth mentioning are **maps**, which essentially allow you to visualize data distributed geographically, similar to searching for addresses on platforms such as Google Maps.

As an analyst, it is important to know how to transform data into useful information, and visual objects support this process. Now that you know how to choose your visuals, it is time for you to discover some of the available AI-powered visuals that will help you further enrich your reports.

AI-powered visuals

In addition to the conventional charts you saw earlier, certain charts leverage **artificial intelligence** (**AI**) to display the data you want. Let's take a look at these one by one.

Key influencers

The **key influencers** chart is a visual object that allows you to identify variables that significantly impact a specific measure within your data. This chart also leverages machine learning techniques to determine which variables are correlated with the measure you want to evaluate.

Figure 8.24 illustrates a key influencers chart:

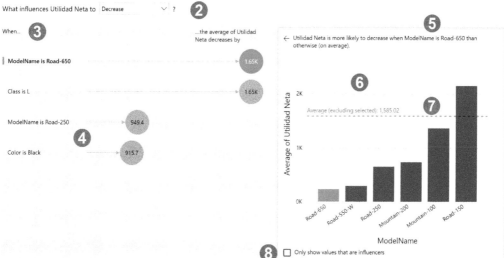

Figure 8.24: Power BI key influencers visual

Here's a list of components of key influencers charts, in the order of numbers placed on the preceding figure:

1. *Tabs*: Use the tabs to switch between different views. The **Key influencers** tab shows you the main factors that contribute to a specific metric. The **Top segments** tab shows you the important groups that affect the metric. A segment is a combination of values. For example, a segment could be customers who have been with us for at least 20 years and live in the Western region.

2. *Drop-down box*: This lets you choose the metric you want to investigate. In this example, we are looking at the metric called **Rating**. The selected value is **Low**, but this will depend on the value added, as sometimes it can say **Increase** or **Decrease**.

3. *Restatement*: This helps you understand the information in the left pane.

4. *Left pane*: The left pane has one visual. In this case, it shows a list of the top key influencers.

5. *Restatement*: This helps you understand the information in the right pane.

6. *Right pane*: The right pane has one visual. Here, it's a column chart that displays all the values for the selected key influencer called **Theme**, but this can be a scatter chart sometimes. The specific value for **usability** is shown in green, while the other values for **Theme** are shown in black.

7. *Average line*: The average is calculated for all the other values of **Theme** except **usability** (the selected influencer). So the calculation applies to the values shown in black. It tells you what percentage of the other themes had a **Low** rating. In this case, it's 11.35%, indicated by the dotted line. This line only applies when a bar chart is shown; when having a scatter chart, this will be a trend line.

8. *Checkbox*: This filters the visual in the right pane to only show values that are influencers for that field. In this example, it filters to display **usability**, **security**, and **navigation**. Again, this checkbox will only be shown when having a bar chart.

Decomposition tree

The **decomposition tree** is a chart that allows you to conduct a detailed analysis when it comes to finding the root cause of a particular situation. This visual adds data to each of the categories and creates a tree structure that you can expand.

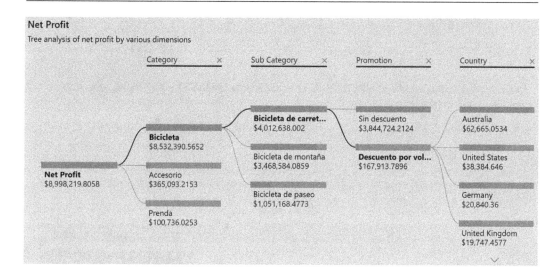

Figure 8.25: Power BI decomposition tree

This chart incorporates AI features such as AI splits, which help you select the next category to expand based on the influence of values within the categories.

Anomaly detection

Although this is not a chart that you can find in the list of visual objects, **anomaly detection** is one of the AI features that you can use in conjunction with the line chart. It uses an algorithm to detect anomalies in your data over time.

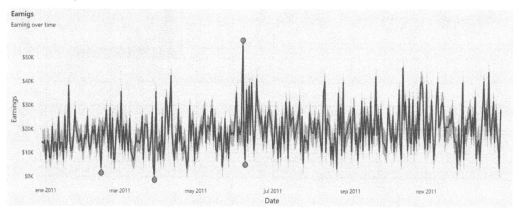

Figure 8.26: Power BI anomaly detection

In addition to detecting anomalies, this feature helps you find an explanation for these anomalies, as you can see on the left side of *Figure 8.26*.

You can find this option in the **Analytics** section inside the visualization pane as shown in *Figure 8.26*.

> **Note**
>
> One limitation you need to consider is that this visual is only available for line charts containing time series data in the axis field.

Smart narratives

Smart narratives are visual objects that allow you to create a summary of the information contained in the report. It provides a different perspective of the results in natural language.

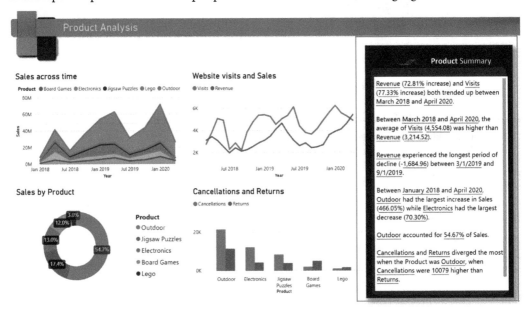

Figure 8.27: Power BI smart narrative

In addition to adding the visual object individually to the report, you can create one based on a specific visual by right-clicking and selecting **Summarize**.

It's important to note that while the text and indicators are generated by AI, they can be modified and enriched to add a personal touch to the result.

The Q&A visual

The **Q&A visual** is a powerful and user-friendly feature that allows users to interactively query and explore their data using natural language. Instead of just relying on traditional methods of creating charts and reports, users can simply type their questions or queries into the **Q&A** box and Power BI will generate visualizations based on the underlying data.

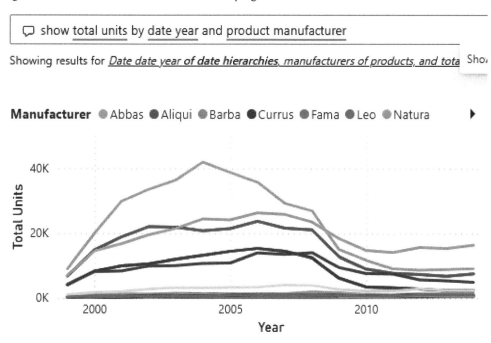

Figure 8.28: Power BI Q&A feature

This feature leverages natural language processing capabilities, enabling users to ask questions in a conversational manner, such as *Show me sales by region* or *What is the trend in revenue over the past quarter?*. The Q&A visual interprets the queries, understands the context, and dynamically generates visual representations of the requested information.

Undoubtedly, the most searched term on Google in recent years has been AI and related topics. Therefore, being knowledgeable about these types of visual objects will give your interviewer enough reasons to consider you as a strong candidate.

Conditional formatting

In Power BI, you can apply formatting to each visual object, which can be conditioned by a measure, a rule, or a field value that you pass to it. The formatting options will depend on the type of visual object you are using.

For example, consider the table shown in *Figure 8.29*. It displays a list of average ratings given by users to Airbnb apartments in different neighborhoods of New York City. You can apply conditional formatting to this table to highlight neighborhoods whose rating exceeds 4 . 6.

Neighbourhood ▲	AVG Review
Bronx	4.64
Brooklyn	4.67
Manhattan	4.59
Queens	4.64
Staten Island	4.71
Total	**4.64**

Figure 8.29: Power BI table with average ratings by neighborhood

To apply such formatting, you need to select the visual object and click on the **Format visual** pane located in the **Visualizations** section. Then, expand the **Cell elements** menu. Here, you will find a menu divided into two groups. The first group allows you to choose the indicators added in the columns to which you want to apply the formatting. Then, you have different conditional formats that you can apply to a column, as shown in *Figure 8.30*.

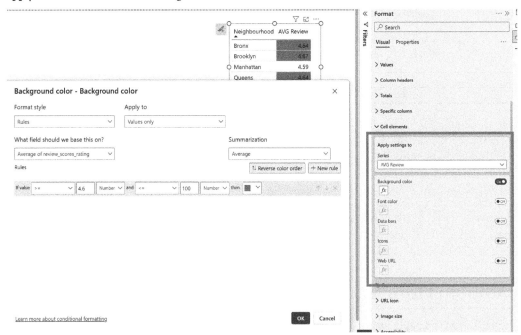

Figure 8.30: Power BI table conditional formatting

These conditional formats include the following:

- **Background color**: Allows you to change the background color of the cell
- **Font color**: Allows you to change the font color
- **Icons**: Allows you to add icons as conditional formats
- **Data bars**: Adds a bar to the column
- **Web URL**: Allows you to activate any link that you have as data in a column

In *Figure 8.30*, you can see how you can apply conditional formatting to the background of the **AVG Review** column. In this example, values exceeding 4.6 are highlighted in green.

When enabling any conditional formatting, a pop-up window will appear as shown in the center of *Figure 8.31*. In this window, you have several options, such as the formatting style, which can be **Gradient**, **Rules**, or **Field value**. You can also choose whether to apply the formatting only to values or include the total row of the table. Additionally, you can select the measure or column based on which you want to create the conditional format and the type of aggregation you want to use. In this case, we used the average since it matches the aggregation used in the table, and we created a single rule for this formatting.

Please note that this pop-up window may vary depending on your chosen data type and formatting style. For example, the following figure is a reference to how it would look if you chose a gradient formatting style.

> **Note**
>
> When using **Field value**, it gives you more flexibility since the value can be controlled from the DAX measure.

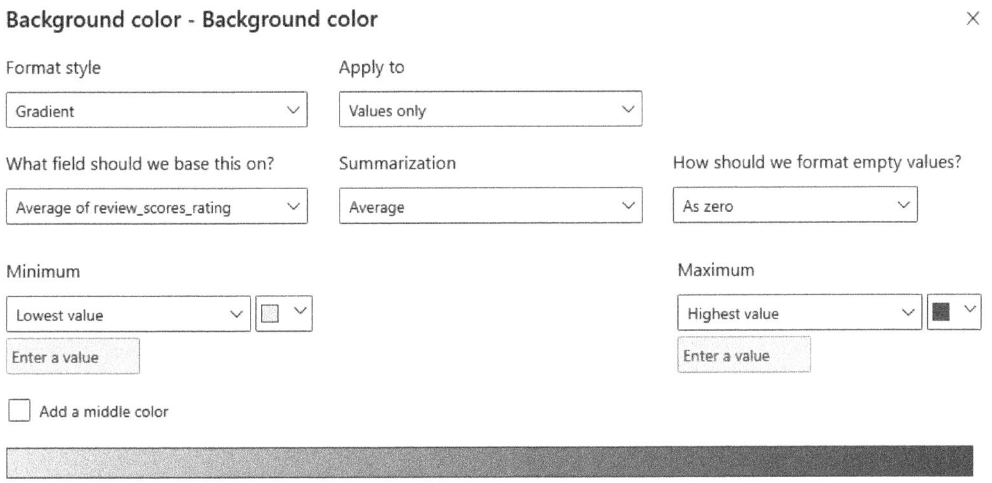

Figure 8.31: Power BI table gradient conditional formatting

In addition to applying conditional formats to individual columns in tables, there are properties of the visual object itself that can also be conditioned. An easy way to identify whether a property allows conditional formatting is by checking whether it contains the **fx** symbol next to it. In *Figure 8.32*, you can see that you can condition the color of the labels displayed at the end of each bar and the color of the bar itself.

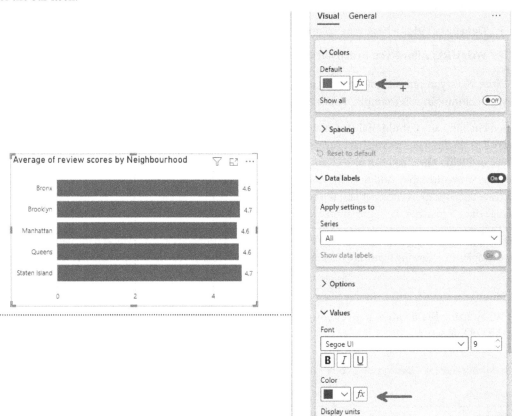

Figure 8.32: Power BI stacked bar chart conditional format

> **Note**
> Starting from the May 2023 update, you can even condition the labels based on any measure, allowing you to add valuable information directly to the labels.

Pinpointing data points with conditional formats is a plus, but mastering filters and slicers in Power BI is even more exciting. In the next section, you will learn a little more about filtering and slicing data.

Slicing and filtering

Having solid knowledge about the way Power BI slices and dices data points will raise your technical level, give you more weapons to master any interview, and enrich your professional profile as an analyst. This has relevance because, in many cases, the reports are simply a surface where users slice and dice the data until they get what they ask in the report.

One feature that has brought Power BI to its current level is the ability to dynamically apply filters and see the resulting cross-filtered information. In Power BI, you can apply filters in two ways: from the **Filter** pane or a slicer.

Power BI slicers

The slicer is one of the visual objects that Power BI includes by default. With it, you can apply filters to your report's visual objects. It can appear in various forms depending on the type of data it contains. For example, if you add a **Date** field, you can access a list of filtering styles, as shown on the right in *Figure 8.33*.

Each of these styles changes the graphical interface of the slicer to facilitate its use. In *Figure 8.33*, the **Between** style is selected, allowing you to choose a range of dates using a slider with selectors at both ends.

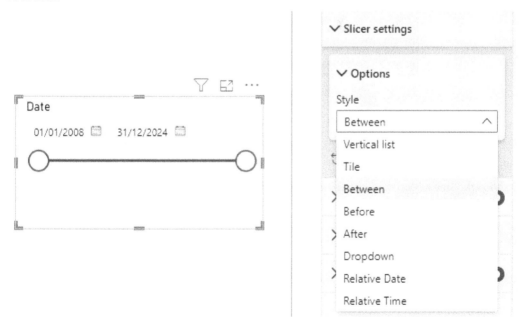

Figure 8.33: Power BI date filter styles

By default, filters will be applied to all visual objects in the report. The filter will depend directly on how the dimension you place in the filter is related to the data of other visual objects.

Although this interaction is the default behavior for slicers and any other visual, it can be changed if you want to apply filters only to a specific group of visual objects or simply exclude some charts. You can do this by selecting the slicer, going to the **Format** menu, and clicking on the **Edit interactions** option. By doing this, you will see two options at the top of the visual objects that allow you to exclude or include them in the specific filter.

In *Figure 8.34*, you can see that the bar chart on the right will not be affected by the date slicer, while the one on the left will be.

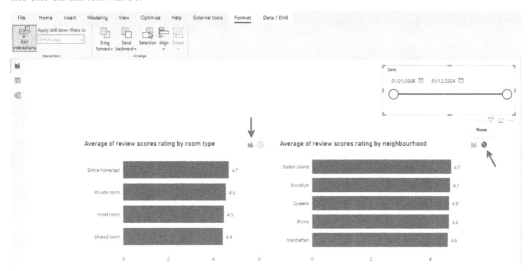

Figure 8.34: Power BI Edit interactions

> **Note**
> Although visual objects are affected by the slicer, remember that you can override that filter context with DAX.

If, in addition to filtering visual objects on a page, you want to filter the other pages from the same slicer, you can do so by enabling the **Sync slicers** pane from the **View** menu. In this pane, you have two options. The first allows you to choose which pages you want to filter, and the second allows you to choose whether you want the slicer to be visible on those pages.

Figure 8.35: Power BI Sync slicers menu

In *Figure 8.35*, you can see that the slicer will filter **Page 4** and **Page 5** and will be visible on the source page, as well as **Page 3** and **Page 4**.

Filters pane

The other method used to filter information in your visual objects is through the **Filters** pane. It has the advantage of being a collapsible pane, which takes up less space in the report. Unlike the slicer, in the **Filters** pane, you can add dimensions that are not necessarily included in any of the visual objects in your report. This means you can add product categories to the **Filters** pane without having a chart in your report with values grouped by product categories.

You can find the **Filters** pane on the right side of your report, but if you wish, you can hide it by selecting the eye icon located in the top-right corner of the pane, as shown in *Figure 8.36*.

Figure 8.36: Power BI filter pane expanded

In this pane, you will find three different groups where you can add your filters:

- **Filters on this visual**: This group will only appear when you select a visual. In *Figure 8.36*, you can see that this refers to the filter on the bar chart.

- **Filters on this page**: The filters you add here will be applied to all visuals on the current page.

- **Filters on all pages**: The filters you add here will be applied to all pages in the report.

The dimensions you add to any of these groups can be modified to be hidden from the end user or locked, preventing the user from modifying a specific filter. When choosing any of these options, the filter should appear as shown in *Figure 8.37*.

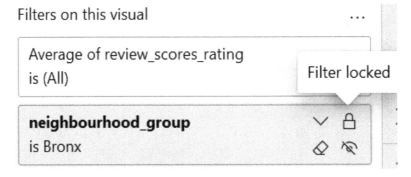

Figure 8.37: Power BI locked filter

To reset a filter, you can do so by clicking the *eraser* button in Power BI Desktop, as shown here:

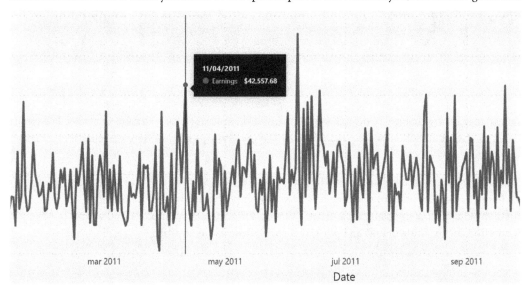

Figure 8.38: Power BI Clear filter in the Filters pane

Configuring visual tooltips

When space is limited in your report, a useful add-on is **tooltips**. Tooltips allow you to display additional information when you hover over a specific part of the visual object, as seen in *Figure 8.39*.

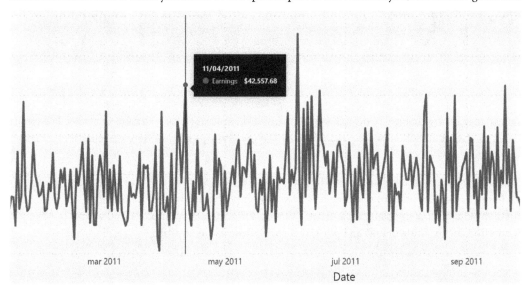

Figure 8.39: Power BI default tooltip

There are three types of tooltips available in Power BI:

- **Default tooltip**: When you add a visual object such as a bar chart, as shown in *Figure 8.39*, and hover over one of the bars, you will see a tooltip displaying information about that specific dimension.

- **Modern tooltip**: This is an enhanced version of the default tooltip. In this tooltip, you have more formatting options and access to **Drill-down** and **Drill-through** buttons.

- **Page tooltip**: This type of tooltip is versatile. With it, you can configure an entire page to be used as a tooltip for a visual object, as shown in the following figure:

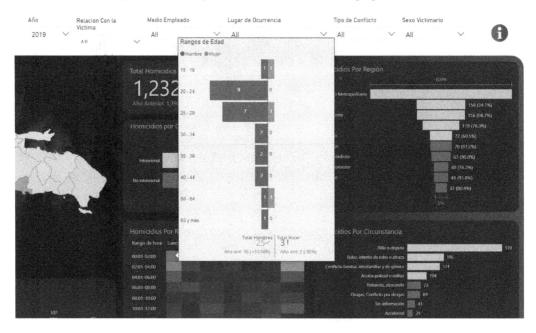

Figure 8.40: Power BI page tooltip

Although tooltips are enabled by default, you can disable them at any time by navigating to the **Format** pane. In the **General** section of the pane, you will find the **Tooltips** menu where you can simply turn off the option.

In the same menu, you can also choose the type of tooltip you want to use and select the page you want to use as a tooltip. Before selecting a page as a tooltip, you need to indicate that it will serve as a tooltip by clicking on any blank area on the page, accessing the **Format** pane, and within the **Page Information** menu, you will find an option that says **Allow use as tooltip**.

If you are not seeing the modern tooltips, it is likely because you need to enable them by going to the **File** menu, selecting **Options and Settings**, then **Options**. Within **Report settings** under the **CURRENT FILE** group, you will find an option to enable modern tooltips.

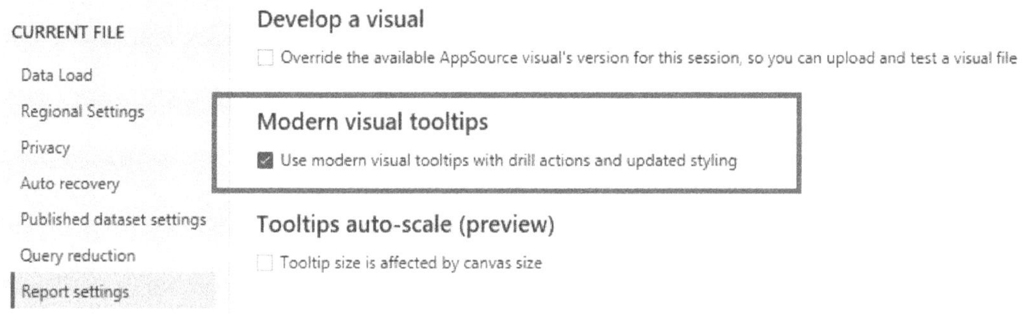

CURRENT FILE

Data Load

Regional Settings

Privacy

Auto recovery

Published dataset settings

Query reduction

Report settings

Develop a visual

☐ Override the available AppSource visual's version for this session, so you can upload and test a visual file

Modern visual tooltips

☑ Use modern visual tooltips with drill actions and updated styling

Tooltips auto-scale (preview)

☐ Tooltip size is affected by canvas size

Figure 8.41: Power BI enabling modern tooltips

> **Note**
>
> When you use a page as a tooltip, you are essentially filtering all the information on that page based on the dimension where the cursor is positioned. For this type of page, keep in mind that the size should be smaller than usual to fit within the tooltip area.

Knowing when to use tooltips is a skill that you develop over time, as using them excessively can lead to confusion for users and undermine the main objective of efficiently conveying information found in the model. Keep this in mind if you encounter any questions or scenarios during the interview process that require you to resolve them through tooltips.

Adding bookmarks

Esthetics is a crucial aspect that you always take care of in Power BI. A good combination of colors will make your report stand out. However, as data analysts, you aim to make your reports resemble and provide a similar experience to a web application. One of the elements that help us achieve this goal is bookmarks.

Bookmarks in Power BI store your page's state and its visual elements. This allows you to switch between these states using bookmarks. In other words, you can dynamically show or hide any element within your report, or even save the state of multiple filters and access them when needed.

To create a bookmark, you first need to have the **Bookmarks** pane visible. You can enable it from the **View** menu by selecting **Bookmarks**. Then, you can click on **Add** and automatically create a bookmark with the current status of the visual elements.

> **Note**
> Make sure you have the status of your charts as you want them before creating the bookmark.

Once you create a bookmark, you can rename it by double-clicking on the name or accessing the two dots to the right of the name and clicking on **Rename**. In this menu, you will also find some additional options, such as the following:

- **Update**: This option allows you to update the already created bookmark. For example, if you forgot to hide a visual or add a filter, you can position yourself on the bookmark, make the additional changes, and click on **Update**.

- **Delete**: With this option, you can delete the bookmark.

- **Group**: If you select multiple bookmarks, you can group them into a bookmark group. This can be useful later for creating a menu with bookmarks from a specific group.

- **Data**: By default, when creating a bookmark, this option is enabled. It determines whether filters are considered when creating or updating the bookmark. This option also includes the **Order** and **Drill-through** settings.

- **Display**: This option, also enabled by default, determines whether the visual state of the visuals will be included.

- **Current Page**: This is another option enabled by default and is used to define whether the current page should be included in the bookmark. For example, you can create bookmarks solely for navigating between pages, leaving only this option enabled.

- **All Visuals**: With this option, you can define whether the bookmark will store the state of all visuals in the report.

- **Selected Visuals**: With this option and by selecting multiple visuals from the selection pane while holding the *Ctrl* key, you can make the bookmark only save the states of the selected visuals.

> **Note**
> The **Data**, **Display**, and **Current Page** options are the ones you should master. For instance, you can create bookmarks that only save the state of certain filters by selecting only the **Data** option. On the other hand, you can create bookmarks that focus only on the visual aspect of your charts by enabling the **Display** option and disabling the **Data** option.

Once you create the bookmarks, there are several ways in which you can make the user interact with them, as we'll see next.

Buttons, shapes, and images

When you add one of these three elements to the report, you have the option to trigger a bookmark by going to the **Format** pane and then **Action** and selecting the **Bookmark** action type, as shown in *Figure 8.42*.

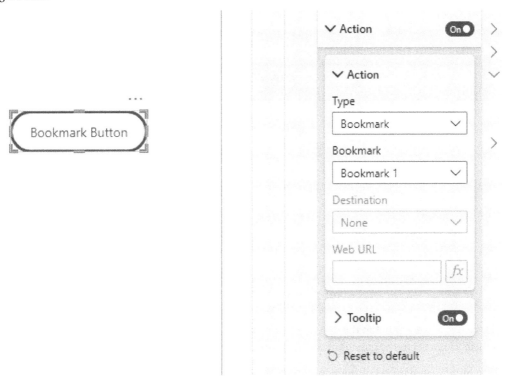

Figure 8.42: Power BI button actions

Clicking this button will trigger the saved states in the selected bookmark.

Bookmark menu

Another option for interacting with bookmarks is to create a bookmark menu. To do this, go to the Insert menu followed by Buttons | Navigator | Bookmark navigator. This creates a menu that contains the bookmarks you have created, as shown in the figure. This element has properties that you can modify, such as background colors, shape type, and styles such as vertical or horizontal layout.

Similarly, if you only want to display certain bookmarks in the menu, you can do so from the formatting pane of the visual object. In the Bookmarks section, you can choose the bookmark group you want to show.

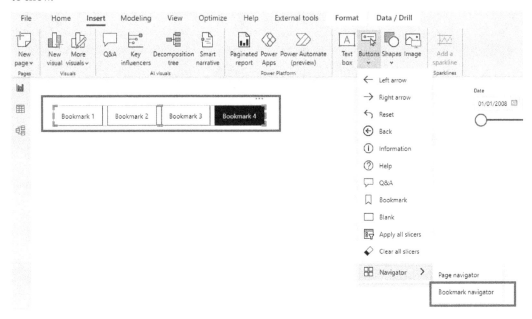

Figure 8.43: Power BI Bookmark navigator

Undoubtedly, at some point in the development of a report, you will have to create bookmarks. These are crucial elements in the pursuit of continuous improvement in user experience.

Keep in mind that many recruitment processes include Power BI scenarios and bookmark situations can also be present; for example, you can be asked to solve a situation where a report filters data when switching between bookmarks, which is a common real-life situation that companies need to determine whether you know how to solve.

Using Drill-through

Usually, the information displayed in Power BI reports is aggregated and summarized, often to show more information and provide a global context of what is being presented. However, some users may require a deeper level of detail within the report that allows them to delve further into the data.

To achieve that higher level of detail, you can use **Drill through** to get to another page where more detailed information is available. To do this, you need to configure the page you want to use. This can be done by going to the **Visualizations** pane and adding the columns that you want to use for filtering this detail page. When you add a column in the **Add drill-through fields here** field, you can choose to use the column as a category or as a summarized value.

In the example shown in *Figure 8.44*, I created a page with a bar chart displaying the average rating of Airbnb apartments by neighborhood in New York City. On the detail page, I have added the neighborhood column used in the bar chart and a map showing the locations of the apartments. Additionally, I have added a table with more information such as the number of beds and bathrooms. Notice that when you add this column to the detail page, a button with an arrow is added in the top-left corner, allowing you to navigate back to the page that led you there.

Figure 8.44: Power BI Drill through

In addition to accessing the **Drill through** menu by right-clicking, you can also do so from a tooltip. Keep in mind that to do this, you need to have modern tooltips enabled, which I discussed earlier in this chapter.

> **Note**
>
> Another method you can use for drill through is by using a button. In this case, the button will not be enabled until you select a category that is part of the **Drill through** fields on a page.

You can also perform a drill-through to another report by enabling the **Cross Report** option, but this is a topic that goes beyond the scope of this book. Demonstrating your knowledge of these types of functions and showcasing them in a portfolio of projects are advanced skills that can be positively considered by your interviewer.

Page navigation

In previous sections, I mentioned that one of the challenges of a data analyst when developing a report is to ensure that the user experience is as smooth, intuitive, and interactive as possible. This can be achieved by utilizing the various techniques that you have learned about so far. However, a significant part of achieving this experience is optimizing the way users navigate between pages.

As you know, in Power BI, you can create multiple pages that can be used in your reports, such as drill-through pages or tooltip pages, as seen in previous sections. The latter is a page that is usually hidden because the intention is not for the user to directly click on this page but to access it through tooltips. Similarly, drill-through pages are often hidden as the intention is to reach them through a visual object, as seen in the previous section.

In addition to navigating directly from the page tabs at the bottom of the report, there are various techniques you can use to create navigation menus directly within the report. Let's look at these in detail.

Bookmarks

As you saw in the previous *Adding bookmarks* section, when you create a bookmark, it stores the state of the current page. This means that if you access the bookmark from another page, it will navigate you to the page that is saved in the bookmark. In summary, if you create a bookmark with only the **Current Page** option enabled, you are essentially customizing the navigation to that specific page, and you can do so using any of the methods discussed in the *Adding bookmarks* section of this chapter.

Navigation menu

Another option that you have to customize navigation between pages (and the most recommended one specifically for navigation) is to add a navigation menu. You can do this by going to the **Insert** menu, selecting **Buttons**, then **Navigator**, and finally, **Page navigator**.

This will add a series of buttons to your report, representing each page in your report. You can apply various formatting options to this element, such as borders, backgrounds, and colors. Additionally, you can choose which pages you want to include in this menu.

As you can see in *Figure 8.45*, from the **Format** panel, you can determine whether to show hidden pages in the menu, tooltip pages, or all pages by default.

Furthermore, you can specifically choose which pages to show or hide using the **Show** option in the **Pages** section of the formatting panel for the visual object.

Figure 8.45: Power BI Page navigator

Button

Finally, another option you have available for navigating between pages is through a button. When you add a button to your report, you can choose the actions that the button will execute when clicked, and one of these options is **Page navigation**.

The difference with this option compared to the previous ones is that the page can be conditioned based on a measure. In other words, you can create a measure that returns the name of the page you want to navigate to based on some logic applied within the measure. The name returned by this measure must be the same as the name of the page you want to navigate to.

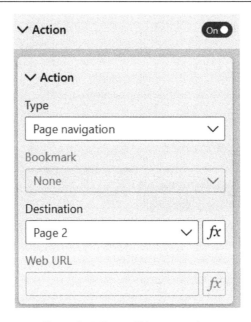

Figure 8.46: Power BI button action

For example, if you add the following measure as a condition in the **Destination** section of the **Action** settings when you click the button, it should take you to page 2 of your report; the value of the pageNumber variable can be any expression that returns the number of the page to which you want to navigate:

```
Navigation =
    VAR pageNumber = 2
    Var result =
        SWITCH (
            pageNumber,
            1, "Page 1",
            2, "Page 2"
        )
    Return
        Result
```

In this section, you learned about different methods that you can use to navigate between pages in a Power BI report: you can use traditional methods such as bookmarks or the navigation page, or you can condition your navigation based on a conditioned value using buttons.

Q&A

Within the data analysis process, the creation of the report materializes the analysis and provides us with something tangible and visual. For this reason, you should focus your efforts on mastering all the parts involved, basically all what you saw in this chapter. That's why many recruiters may ask you a series of questions related to this topic during the interview process.

Below, I show you some of those questions that may arise.

Question 1: A user reports that, after creating a bookmark menu (which shows and hides some charts in a report), when selecting one of the bookmarks, the filters that the user had previously selected, such as the date, are modified. What do you think could be happening in this situation?

Answer: Since it involves bookmarks, the situation may be related to the data option of the bookmark. Probably, when the bookmark was created, this option was left enabled, indicating that the bookmark considered the filters that were selected at that time.

Question 2: The sales department needs to see a comparison of the monthly fluctuations in sales for the current year 2024 vs. 2023. What chart would you recommend to show this information?

Answer: Line charts are the most suitable for showing variations or trends over time, so that's what I would use.

Question 3: The human resources department of a company has a Power BI dashboard where they can see indicators related to employees such as turnover, absenteeism rate, etc. However, several users have expressed that they would like to have more detail on the data they visualize in the charts. What solution do you propose to meet this request?

Answer: To add more detail to the dashboard, I would add an extra page to serve as a detail page, enabling the drill-through feature. This allows users to have more granularity and they can access this page from the same visual object from which they need more detail.

Question 4: After adding the detail page to the report, users complain that they get lost in lines when looking for employees with the highest absenteeism rate or the lowest night hours worked. To solve this, the department has defined some value ranges and they need only the records that fall within this range to be highlighted in the table. They have also provided you with the hexadecimal color codes they want for each range. What method would you use to highlight those records in a table?

Answer: To highlight records in a table, it is necessary to apply conditional formatting to the columns containing these indicators or to the columns to be highlighted. In this particular case, since they have created custom ranges and colors, the formatting style should be rule-based. Subsequently, these rules are created to ensure they meet the provided ranges, then the color is chosen from the palette, and the format is created.

Question 5: Nowadays, the trend is the use of artificial intelligence for almost everything. Knowing this, how can we leverage artificial intelligence in Power BI reports?

Answer: Within Power BI, there are a series of visual objects and features that use artificial intelligence behind them. These include the decomposition tree, key influencers, Smart narrative, anomaly detection & Q&A.

Summary

In this chapter, you learned about the key elements that are relevant to the development of a Power BI report. You started by exploring some tips to consider before adding the first chart to your report. Then, you discovered a list of commonly used charts and their appropriate uses, including those that leverage artificial intelligence.

You also learned about conditional formatting and how to identify whether a report property supports it. We covered different types of filters in Power BI and how tooltips and bookmarks can enhance the user experience. Lastly, you delved into creating detailed pages and the various ways to navigate between pages in your report.

Having knowledge of these topics and understanding their proper usage can instill confidence in your portfolio, which will be conveyed to the interviewer. In the next chapter, you will learn how to complement these technical skills with effective storytelling techniques.

Effective Data Storytelling

In today's data-driven world, the ability to communicate insights derived from data has become a crucial skill. **Data storytelling**, the art of presenting data in a compelling and meaningful way, has emerged as a powerful tool that enables organizations to not only understand complex information but also engage and inspire their audience. Humans have an innate tendency to connect with stories. By incorporating a narrative in data visualization, data storytelling makes the information presented in visuals more engaging, relatable, and actionable, thus enabling decision-makers to gain valuable insights and act upon them effectively.

In this chapter, we will cover the following main topics:

- Fundamentals of data storytelling
- Choosing the right visualization
- How to craft a compelling narrative
- Data storytelling using Power BI

Technical requirements

- Power BI Desktop

Fundamentals of data storytelling

At its core, data storytelling is about transforming raw data into a narrative that resonates with people. Traditionally, storytelling has always been there as a tool to communicate and even teach about sharing information. The human brain responds to stories much better than looking at numbers. A lot of research has been done about how storytelling affects the brain, as shown in *Figure 9.1*:

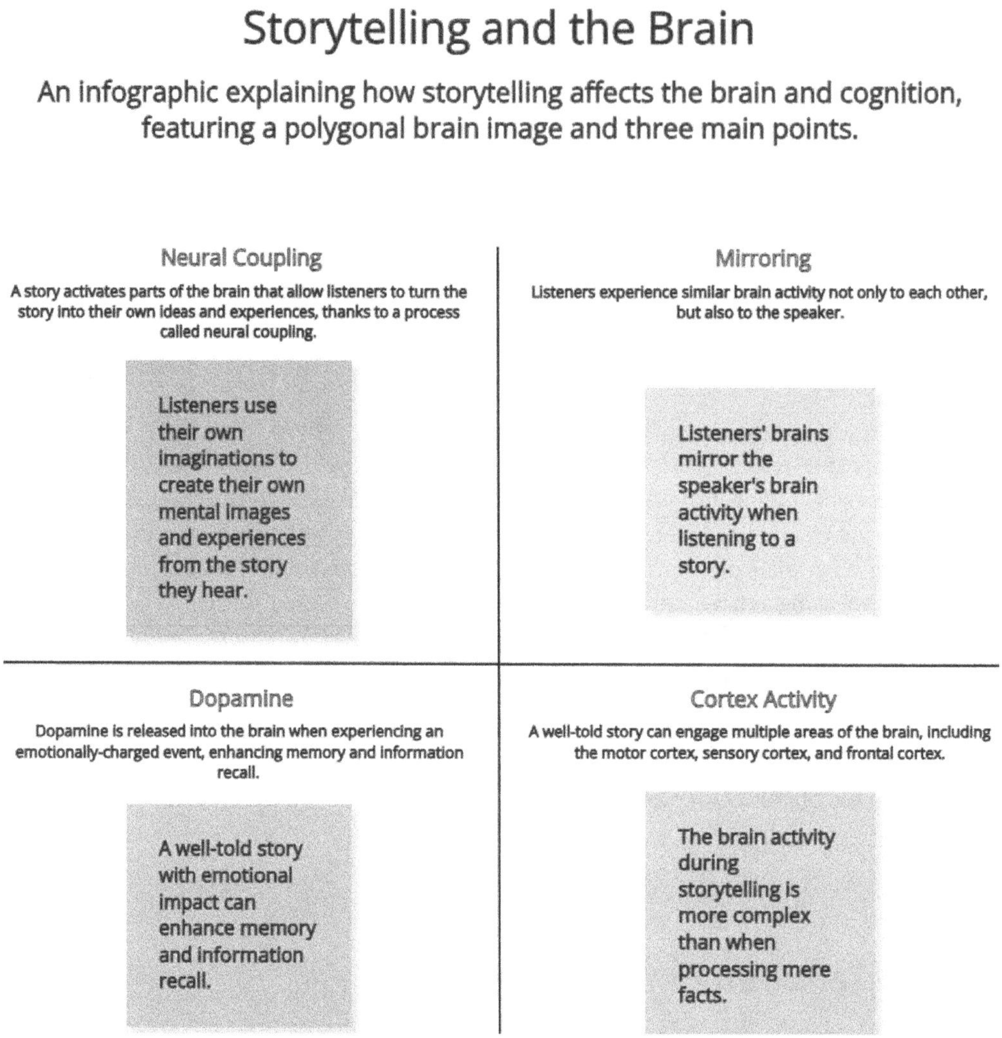

Storytelling and the Brain

An infographic explaining how storytelling affects the brain and cognition, featuring a polygonal brain image and three main points.

Neural Coupling

A story activates parts of the brain that allow listeners to turn the story into their own ideas and experiences, thanks to a process called neural coupling.

Listeners use their own imaginations to create their own mental images and experiences from the story they hear.

Mirroring

Listeners experience similar brain activity not only to each other, but also to the speaker.

Listeners' brains mirror the speaker's brain activity when listening to a story.

Dopamine

Dopamine is released into the brain when experiencing an emotionally-charged event, enhancing memory and information recall.

A well-told story with emotional impact can enhance memory and information recall.

Cortex Activity

A well-told story can engage multiple areas of the brain, including the motor cortex, sensory cortex, and frontal cortex.

The brain activity during storytelling is more complex than when processing mere facts.

Figure 9.1: How storytelling affects the brain

In terms of the data analytics ecosystem, the goal of analytics is to persuade, allow people to make decisions, and create change. So, data storytelling is at the heart of those decisions that, using just raw numbers, are very hard to take.

Let us look at some of the key fundamentals of data storytelling and why it is an essential skill for data analysts to learn.

The essence of data storytelling

Data storytelling, at its heart, is a fusion of two distinct disciplines: data analysis and storytelling. It is a process that transforms hard, impersonal raw numbers into a living narrative. Data storytelling is not about bombarding your audience with complex graphs and figures or dazzling them with high-tech visualizations. It is about communicating with the audience by thinking about how these graphs and visuals can be transformed into a compelling story. It is the art of translating data analyses into layman's terms and presenting it in an engaging, understandable way. Let's take a look at the three key elements of data storytelling:

- **Simplicity**: One of the key elements of data storytelling is simplicity. In our increasingly data-driven world, the volume, variety, and velocity of data can be overwhelming. Data storytelling is about distilling that complexity down into simple, understandable insights. Imagine you are looking at a table filled with rows and columns of numbers representing quarterly sales data. To a data analyst, these numbers may tell a clear story. However, to everyone else, they are just numbers. A data storyteller can take those numbers and transform them into a clear, simple narrative.

- **Relevance**: Another crucial aspect of data storytelling is relevance. The role of a data storyteller is to sift through the data and find only the data that is relevant and valuable to the audience. This involves understanding the needs, interests, and goals of the audience and tailoring your data story to fit those needs. For instance, if you are presenting to a group of marketing executives, they may be interested in data about customer behavior, market trends, or marketing campaign performance. Instead of showing multiple visuals covering the survey results and marketing campaign numbers, the data storyteller can highlight just a few **key performance indicators** (**KPIs**) and add the narrative, *"Our latest marketing campaign has resonated strongly with our target demographic, leading to a significant increase in brand engagement."*

- **Forging a human connection**: Perhaps the most defining characteristic of data storytelling is its ability to forge a human connection. Data is a collection of numbers, statistics, and facts. However, as humans we do not connect with impersonal data; we connect with stories. Data storytelling bridges the gap between impersonal data and the human audience. To illustrate, instead of saying, *"Our new product has reduced customer complaints by 20%,"* a data storyteller might say, *"Our new product has made a real difference in our customers' lives as we have seen a 20% reduction in customer complaints, meaning more customers are satisfied with our service."*

In conclusion, the essence of data storytelling lies in its simplicity, relevance, and human connection. It is about making data speak in a language that everyone can understand and connect. In an age of data overload, effective data storytelling is not just a nice-to-have skill; it is a necessity for anyone who wants to communicate data effectively.

The power of visuals in data storytelling

Once you have access to raw data, you perform **extract, transform, load** (ETL) operations, build a star schema data model, and perform computations using **Data Analysis Expressions** (DAX), then the next step is to visualize information. This process has already been explained in *Chapter 3*. The human brain processes visual information far quicker than it does numbers. Well-designed charts, graphs, and other visual aids can help your audience quickly grasp the key points of your data story. The power of visual elements in data storytelling cannot be overstated. *Figure 9.2* shows raw numbers in the form of an Excel spreadsheet:

	A	B	C	D	E	F
1	Address	Suburb	Dwelling Type	Number of Bedro	Sales Agent	Sale Price
2	317 Gina Trail	Fairfield	Apartment	1	Ruby Skelly	$ 296,232
3	7 Stuart Trail	Bayfront	House	3	Zoe Gunton	$ 491,486
4	2 Old Gate Lane	Winslow Junction	Duplex	4	Sergey Madorski	$ 998,466
5	62 Eastwood Avenue	Meadowbank	Apartment	3	Ruby Skelly	$ 403,559
6	2250 Surrey Trail	Winslow Junction	Apartment	4	Ruby Skelly	$ 556,267
7	28 Grim Terrace	Oak Flats	House	4	Zoe Gunton	$ 438,388
8	3 Northridge Street	North Winslow	Apartment	3	Melinda Lim	$ 918,504
9	90 Northwestern Place	Winslow Junction	Apartment	2	Chris Jones	$ 877,246
10	77 Briar Crest Way	Meadowbank	Duplex	4	Ashton Singh	$ 469,022
11	12986 Bartillon Circle	Chatswood	Duplex	3	Sergey Madorski	$ 535,232
12	64 Schmedeman Circle	North Winslow	House	3	Chad Turman	$ 1,218,681
13	81986 Helena Court	Sutton Forrest	Duplex	3	Ruby Skelly	$ 475,423
14	80284 Oakridge Pass	Chatswood	Duplex	3	Ruby Skelly	$ 1,063,663
15	206 Sunfield Park	Bayfront	House	3	Chad Turman	$ 598,565
16	27410 Sunfield Lane	Sutton Forrest	House	3	Zoe Gunton	$ 362,927
17	44907 Fremont Avenue	Fairfield	Duplex	3	Melinda Lim	$ 368,984
18	128 Nelson Way	Meadowbank	Apartment	1	Ruby Skelly	$ 234,088
19	8 Erie Road	Meadowbank	Duplex	2	Ashton Singh	$ 435,060
20	6068 East Street	Meadowbank	House	4	Chris Jones	$ 786,513
21	33905 American Ash Crossing	Chatswood	Duplex	2	Melinda Lim	$ 101,842
22	10 Elka Street	Fairfield	Apartment	2	Ruby Skelly	$ 523,445
23	0 Waubesa Drive	Chatswood	Duplex	1	Sergey Madorski	$ 367,817
24	830 Tony Terrace	Bayfront	House	5	Melinda Lim	$ 770,076
25	1 Twin Pines Point	Bayfront	House	5	Melinda Lim	$ 792,233
26	52552 Ridgeview Parkway	Bayfront	House	4	Chad Turman	$ 876,025
27	5 Meadow Valley Terrace	Bayfront	House	5	Chad Turman	$ 465,685
28	20780 Warner Hill	Fairfield	Apartment	2	Chad Turman	$ 362,637
29	98 Moland Alley	Fairfield	Apartment	4	Ruby Skelly	$ 513,220

Figure 9.2: Raw numbers in an Excel spreadsheet

In *Figure 9.3*, sales by dwelling type are presented as a bar chart:

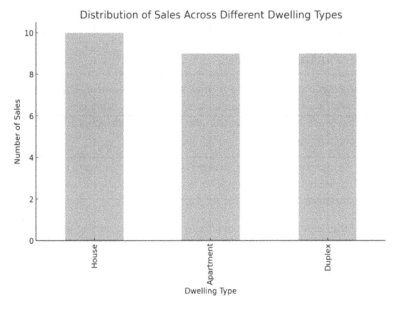

Figure 9.3: Number of sales by dwelling type

And in *Figure 9.4*, the sale price by the number of bedrooms and dwelling type is presented as a scatter plot:

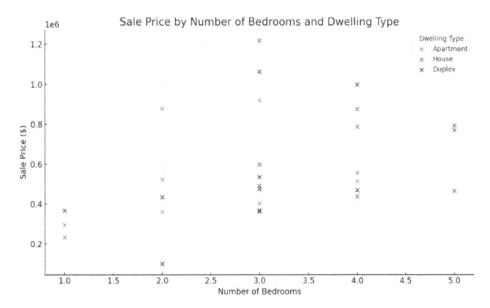

Figure 9.4: Sale price by number of bedrooms

Humans are inherently visual creatures as our brains process visual information rapidly and efficiently. As humans, we tend to understand and remember visual information better than textual or numerical information.

Turning numbers into narratives

The last step in data storytelling is to turn your raw data into a narrative. This means finding the "story" in your data. To do this, you need to understand the context. What is the background? What are the key events? What is the problem or opportunity? Understanding these factors allows you to frame your data in a way that resonates with your audience.

For instance, if you are presenting sales data, instead of saying, "*Sales increased by 15% in Q3,*" by adding effective data storytelling, you could say, "*Due to our new marketing strategy and the hard work of our marketing team, we saw a 15% increase in sales for Q3.*"

Once you understand the importance of a narrative and learn that having just numbers without context is not enough, the storytelling process starts. Next, you try to find the right visualization that supports this narrative.

Choosing the right visualization

The biggest problem with data storytelling is that it takes a tremendous amount of time to develop stories. Most Power BI developers spend time pulling data from data sources, cleaning and transforming the data, and developing complex calculations in DAX. That leaves little time for creative thinking and putting storytelling at the heart of their reports. Similarly, most data analysts think that they are not good designers or storytellers, so this area is neglected mainly for all these reasons.

However, the critical thing to remember is that the report or dashboard being created is what the audience sees. The audience does not see how much effort a report developer puts into doing data cleaning or transformation or how complex logic was built using DAX. A poorly designed chart, visual, or report can confuse your audience or even lead them to misinterpret the data. The best visuals and reports are those that enhance the story, not distract from it.

With a plethora of visualization types at our disposal — from simple bar charts and line graphs to complex heat maps and scatter plots — how do we choose the right one? To comprehend this aspect further, let us list some factors that are essential for selecting and building visuals for data storytelling:

- Understanding the underlying data
- Understanding the audience
- Matching visualization to data
- Reducing clutter and complexity
- Using preattentive attributes

Understanding the underlying data

The first step in the process of choosing the right visualization for data storytelling is understanding the underlying data. You need to know where the data is coming from. How many data sources are being used to generate this data? How much control do you have in terms of any transformation that can be performed on this data? Another important thing to consider is data quality. Are there any inherent errors or data formatting requirements that need to be addressed before it becomes part of any visualization? The format and quality of data greatly affects the choice of visualization and hence impacts the steps you need to perform in Power BI, before pulling the data into any visualization. Similarly, the volume and refresh rate of the data is another consideration that must be kept in mind. Pulling a few rows of data inside a visual is entirely different from pulling millions of rows of data as it can directly impact overall performance.

Understanding the audience

Once the process of understanding the underlying data has been completed, then comes the crucial steps of understanding your audience. It is the requirements of the audience, their knowledge, their concerns, and their goals that will fundamentally shape how you choose the right visuals and ultimately add the most suitable narrative to your data stories.

As a part of understanding the audience, you must first identify who your audience is. Your audience could be anyone from top-level executives requiring high-level overviews for strategic decisions to technical experts seeking detailed analyses. They could be colleagues within your department who have a working understanding of your subject matter, or they could be clients unfamiliar with the intricacies of your industry.

Understanding your audience's background knowledge is an integral part of choosing a visual. If your audience already has a deep understanding of the data, they may not need much background information. Instead, they might appreciate you diving straight into the insights and implications. This audience could be colleagues in your department or industry peers who already have a certain level of familiarity with the subject matter.

After identifying the audience and their background, the next crucial step is to assess their needs and goals. Are your audience members seeking to answer specific questions or explore broad trends? Are they seeking to make a decision, or do they simply want to understand a complex issue better? All of this is critical because this dictates what kind of information the end user needs to see in the report and will influence your choice of the right visual and the insights to highlight within that.

Lastly, another minor but very important consideration is knowing how the report will be consumed. Will the end users be using laptops or **personal computers** (**PCs**) or will they be using mobile or tablets to consume the report? The answer to this question can greatly affect the choice of picking up a particular visualization that works well on a certain device but might not be as effective on another device.

Matching visualization to data

The science of data visualization lies in its foundations in data and statistics. It is about understanding the nature of your data — whether it is categorical or numerical, whether it is time-series or cross-sectional, whether it is skewed or normally distributed. It is about choosing the right visual representation for your data that accurately reflects these characteristics. On the other hand, the art of data visualization is where creativity comes into play. It is about using colors, shapes, sizes, and layouts to enhance your visualization, making it not just informative but also visually appealing. The process of matching the visualization to the data type is a critical step in creating effective data stories.

Numerical data

Let us start with numerical data, which can be further classified into discrete and continuous data. Bar charts are used to represent discrete data, such as the number of sales transactions in a month or the count of users on a platform. This type of chart allows for clear comparisons between different categories or time periods:

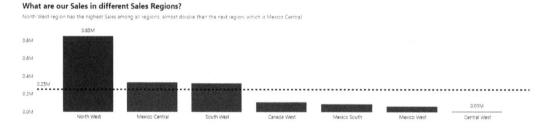

Figure 9.5: Example of a bar chart

Continuous data, on the other hand, is data that can take on any value within a certain range. Examples include temperature readings over time or a company's stock price. Line charts are often used for this type of data, especially when it is collected over time, as they can clearly show trends and patterns:

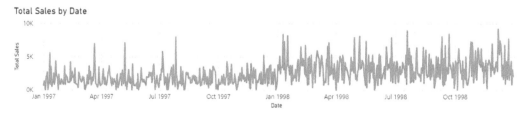

Figure 9.6: Example of a line chart

Categorical data

Next, we have categorical data, which is data that can be divided into groups or categories. If the categories have a natural order (such as "low," "medium," "high"), it is called ordinal data. Bar charts and line charts can work well here too, but it is also common to use stacked bar charts or area charts to highlight proportions within categories. For nominal data, where there is no inherent order (such as "apple," "banana," "orange"), donut charts can be used to represent proportions, while a simple bar chart can show frequency counts in the form of a histogram:

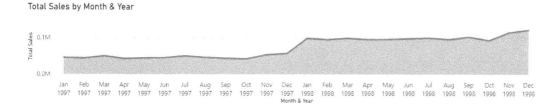

Figure 9.7: Example of an area chart

Relational data

When dealing with relational data, which shows how two or more variables interact with each other, scatter plots are a popular choice. They can reveal correlations, clusters, and outliers, providing a holistic view of the data. More advanced techniques such as heat maps or contour plots can show density and concentration within a scatter plot. For example, if you want to understand the relationship between profit and transactions across a superstore chain in different regions, correlation, clustering, and outliers will come into play:

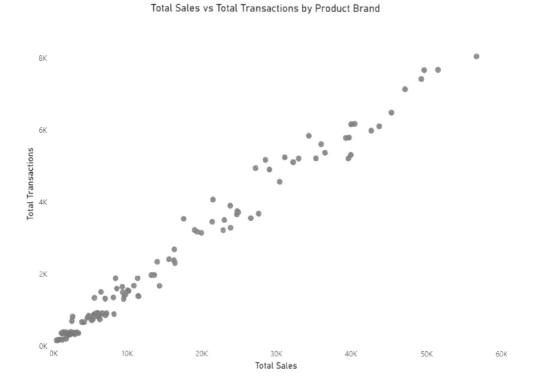

Figure 9.8: Example of a scatter plot

Geographical data

Geographical data, which relates to specific locations or areas, can be best represented using maps. Heat maps, choropleth maps, or even bubble maps can visualize data in a geographical context, making the data more relatable and understandable. Here's an example:

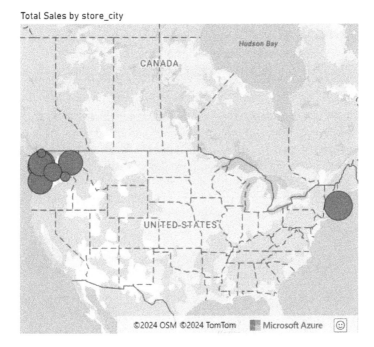

Figure 9.9: Example of a map visual

Hierarchical data

Lastly, when it comes to hierarchical data, which shows relationships of "above" and "below" or "contains" and "contained in," tree maps, sunburst charts, or dendrograms can visualize these complex relationships in an intuitive manner.

Matching visualization to the data type is both a science and an art. When done correctly, it can transform your data from a collection of numbers into a powerful visual narrative that informs, engages, and impacts your audience. There are multiple guidelines, documents, and books that talk about selecting the right visualization.

> **Read more**
>
> Here is a quick reference for selecting the right visualization: `https://experception.net/Franconeri_ExperCeptionDotNet_DataVisQuickRef.pdf`

Reducing clutter and complexity

Complexity is the enemy of execution. (Tony Robbins)

After the selection of the right visualization for data storytelling, it is important to remove clutter and reduce complexity from the visuals. Removing clutter involves multiple things such as removing or reducing data labels, chart borders, and gridlines. Some of the axes' names can also be cleared as that information will most likely be captured in the title or subtitle, which is where your narrative will be.

Similarly, reducing complexity means just keeping the required information by removing anything unnecessary. These days, organizations generate hundreds of GB of data every day. There are dozens of reports and dashboards generated or updated daily. The ability to reduce the complexity of the visuals while capturing everything in the data is a vital aspect of data storytelling. Here is an example showing a cluttered and an uncluttered plot:

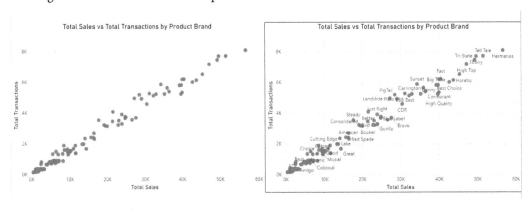

Figure 9.10: Example of a plot with clutter (right half) versus without clutter (left half)

Using preattentive attributes

The goal of any visualization is to highlight key insights and focus on the decision-making process. Several preattentive attributes such as text, color, size, and position can be used to grab the attention of the audience. We will explore the text part in the next section when we discuss the process of building a compelling narrative, but color, size, and position are directly linked to the visual. When highlighting key insights, your aim should be to focus on those aspects of your data that truly matter.

Adding a narrative to a visual is similar to selecting the title of a book. It captures everything that a visual is showing in terms of insights and action.

How to craft a compelling narrative

Creating a compelling narrative is the last significant and, perhaps, most important bit in data storytelling. As a report developer, your responsibility is to distill your data insights into a single, short, and compelling narrative that guides the audience to the desired conclusion. Without any narrative, most data visualizations are nothing but visual dumps.

Remember — the narrative is always present in the data. It is your job as a data analyst to find it, present it meaningfully, and engage the audience. Also, keep in mind that too much narrative can crash your data story and paralyze the minds of the audience.

In this section, we explore some important factors for constructing a powerful narrative. As part of crafting a narrative, we are looking to focus on the key message, influence decision-making, and drive user engagement through emotions. This process encompasses everything from start to finish in the report design process and defines the layout of your report, its flow, and meaningful engagement.

Let us list some of the factors that drive narrative building for a report or dashboard:

- Understanding the context
- Following a structure
- Influencing decision-making
- Driving engagement

Understanding the context

Contextualization is the process of giving data meaning by connecting it to the larger narrative, making it relevant to your audience, and creating impact. A good understanding of the context helps to understand which business questions are important and should be answered first. Context creates a connection between the problem, the expectations, and the solution. Adding context to your narrative amplifies the specified visuals by linking numbers with a purpose.

To understand the context, you must do some research on the business questions. You need to know about the metrics being shown in the visual and why these metrics are important. You must connect their importance to the decision-making process and the audience.

Following a structure

Every great story, whether it is an epic novel or a concise presentation, follows a structure. In data storytelling, the structure serves as the backbone of your narrative. The two most important parts of your narrative are the hook and the insights:

- **Hook**: This is a statement or question that grabs your audience's attention and makes them want to know more. The hook could be a surprising fact, a provocative question, or a bold statement.

- **Insights**: This is where you outline the structure of your narrative around key insights from the visual. Sometimes, there is more than one insight, so you need to decide on the order in which you present your data points and insights. Emphasize the key data points and insights that you want your audience to remember.

Remember — you are not writing an essay or a novel, but you are focusing on writing a 40-to-60-word short, compelling narrative that captures everything.

Influencing decision-making

The ultimate goal of data storytelling is not just to inform but also to influence decision-making. It is about turning data into action. By presenting the data in a compelling and persuasive narrative, data storytelling can drive strategic decisions, guide policy changes, and spur innovation. Data storytelling takes the guesswork out of decision-making and replaces it with data-driven insights.

A narrative that influences the decision-making process can have a profound impact on the organization. It can guide the organization toward better strategies, efficient processes, and effective solutions, thereby driving growth, innovation, and success.

Driving engagement

A compelling narrative is not just about enhancing comprehension; it is also about driving engagement. Together with the right choice of visual, a well-crafted narrative can draw the audience in, hold their attention, and make the data exploration process more enjoyable. Human beings have emotions, which makes them sensitive and creates feelings of joy, surprise, anger, anxiety, and satisfaction. Adding emotion to a narrative can humanize your data, bringing it to life and enabling it to connect with your audience on a deeper level.

We have seen the theoretical aspect of the fundamentals of data storytelling and how it is important to choose the right visualization and build a compelling narrative for effective storytelling. In the next section, it is time to put everything into action and see how we can do data storytelling using Power BI.

Data storytelling using Power BI

Have you heard the sentence, "My report doesn't look that nice, and I have no idea why or how to make it look better"? Power BI is an amazing visualization tool, but as with any visualization tool it does not know what report you are trying to build, the data you want to highlight, the problem you are trying to solve, or how you want to tell your story.

In this section, we explore the unique blend of art and science that is data storytelling using Power BI. We will put into practice what we explored in the previous sections of this chapter. Here, we explore how Power BI, one of the world's leading business analytics tools, can transform raw numbers into a narrative that drives decisions and inspires action.

In this section, we will explore the following topics:

- Process of data storytelling in Power BI
- Enriching your story with advanced Power BI features

Process of data storytelling in Power BI

The process of developing a data story in Power BI begins with business analysis or requirements gathering and concludes with building a report in Power BI. Here, we are going to elaborate on the report design part covered in *Chapter 8* and see how data storytelling elements can be added to a report in Power BI.

In this section, we will start with designing a report theme and selecting an appropriate color palette based on color theory. We will then discuss how to start wireframing a prototype and convert it into a final design using some external applications. We will then talk about designing a report navigation experience on the report page and choosing the right visuals on the canvas. Finally, we will see how a narrative can be added to different visuals using the available options inside Power BI Desktop.

Data storytelling in Power BI can be divided into the following steps:

- Creating a report theme
- Creating a report layout
- Adding report navigation
- Selecting and formatting visuals
- Adding a narrative to visuals and reports

Creating a report theme

Before you put anything on a blank canvas in the Power BI report view, the first step is to decide which colors you are going to use on the canvas. This includes deciding on colors for the background, visual elements, and text.

In this section, we look at the steps involved in creating a report theme in Power BI by first understanding the theory of choosing colors and their significance. We will then explore what options are available in Power BI to choose a particular theme for a report. Lastly, we will explore how we can create a custom color theme in Power BI and also look at some of the best available resources that facilitate this process.

Why are colors important?

Color stands as an important element in visual communication, enabling the ability to shape our emotions, moods, and actions. This underscores the necessity for report designers to choose their colors with great care and deliberation. Selecting colors should not be a random process or merely reflect personal preferences. Although there is some room for individual choice, it is crucial that these selections adhere to established principles of color theory.

Color theory is a collection of roles and guidelines that designers use to communicate with visual interfaces. These rules are followed by all kinds of **user interface (UI)** and **user experience (UX)** designers, whether they are designing web applications, mobile applications, or **business intelligence (BI)** reports. Color theory was established in the 1600s based on human perceptions of wavelengths. A color wheel, similar to the one shown in *Figure 9.11*, is used to select primary, secondary, and tertiary colors. The Primary colors are red, blue, and yellow. By mixing these primary colors we can have secondary colors such as green, orange, and purple. This process continues, and we generate more colors by mixing primary and secondary colors, which are called tertiary colors:

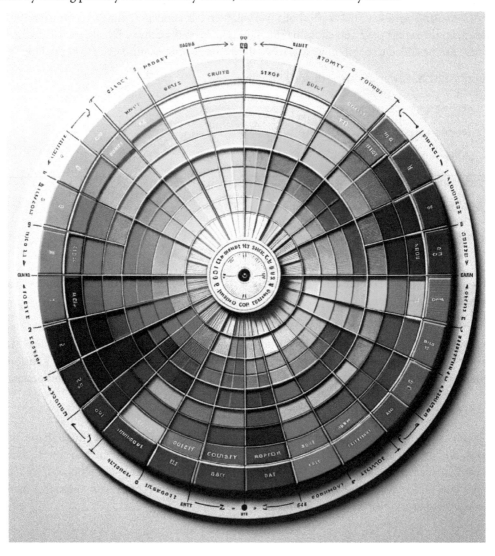

Figure 9.11: Color theory and color wheel

Based on this understanding, the RGB color mode was developed by designers, and some color schemes or combinations were developed that work well together. A combination of these colors is picked to create a color palette, which defines your color theme in Power BI. While choosing a color combination from the color wheel, keep in mind the following considerations:

- **Complementary colors**: These are opposite each other on the color wheel and can make each other stand out when used together. For example, yellow and blue are on the opposite sides of the wheel, and combining these will bring out the best in any visualization.

- **Analogous colors**: These are next to each other on the color wheel and usually match well and create serene and comfortable designs.

- **Triadic colors**: These are evenly spaced around the color wheel and tend to be quite vibrant, even if you use pale or unsaturated versions of your hues.

- **Complementary scheme**: Uses colors across from each other on the wheel. This provides high contrast and is great for highlighting important data points.

- **Consider color blindness**: Use patterns and color palettes that are color-blind friendly to ensure that your visualizations are accessible to a wider audience.

- **Keep it simple**: Do not use too many colors as it can overwhelm the viewer. Limit the number of main colors to three to five.

- **Use neutral colors for the background**: Use neutral colors for the background and gridlines to help the main colors stand out.

Choosing a built-in color theme

Power BI provides its users with some built-in color themes that can be easily used. These themes can also be modified, saved, reused, and shared with other users.

The option for selecting themes is available in the **View** | **Themes** menu of Power BI Desktop, as shown in *Figure 9.12*. The user can select any of the themes available (highlighted by a red border in *Figure 9.12*):

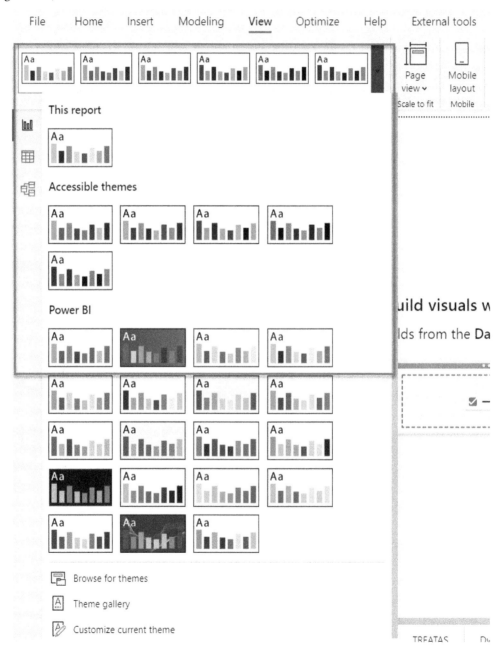

Figure 9.12: Color themes in Power BI Desktop

Here, we have selected the color theme named **Bloom**, as shown in *Figure 9.13*. By selecting this theme, we see that the background of the canvas has changed to purple based on the background of the selected theme:

Figure 9.13: Current theme (Bloom) selected from the Themes option

Once a particular theme has been selected by the user, the same theme appears in all other options inside the **Format page** option of the **Visualizations** pane in Power BI Desktop. For instance, as shown in *Figure 9.14*, the same color palette can be seen inside the **Canvas background** options. The user can select any color from within the color palette, and the same color will be applied. The same principle applies to all color-related options for any visual that is placed on the Power BI canvas:

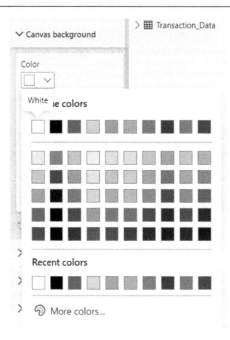

Figure 9.14: Color palette shows color options of the selected theme

The user still has the option to click on **More colors…** and select any color from the options available by using the mouse or putting the hex code of the selected color or the RGB color value combination, as shown in *Figure 9.15*:

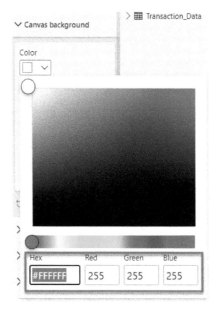

Figure 9.15: Option to select More colors… from the color palette

We will discuss how hex codes can be used to select color values in the next section.

Customizing a color theme

Power BI Desktop provides a lot of flexibility in selecting and modifying color themes for generating color palettes, but in certain situations, there is a requirement to create custom themes, save those themes, and then distribute them among the team members within the organization. Normally, custom color themes are generated using external websites too, where the logo for a company can be uploaded to get the most dominant colors from it, and then those colors are used to generate a color palette.

One very useful website for this purpose is `coolors.co`. It has the option to generate custom themes based on its own color generator, and it also shows the dominant colors from a picture or logo uploaded on the website, as shown in *Figure 9.16*. There are some other theme-generator resources such as **Power BI Theme Generator** by BIBB (`https://www.bibb.pro/post/power-bi-json-report-theme-generator-by-bibb`), **themes.pbix** by POINT (`https://themegenerator.point-gmbh.com/`), Enterprise DNA (`https://app.enterprisedna.co`), and **PowerBI.tips** (`https://powerbi.tips/`):

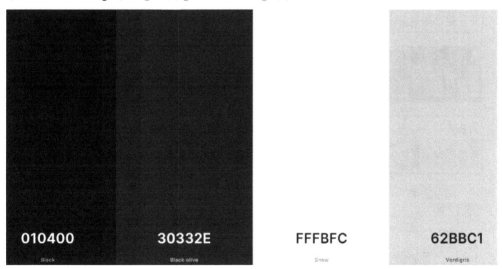

Figure 9.16: Color theme generator on coolors.co

The hex code for each color can be copied and pasted inside the color theme in Power BI. There are two ways to do that in Power BI Desktop. The first option is to use the **Customize current theme** option, as shown in *Figure 9.17*:

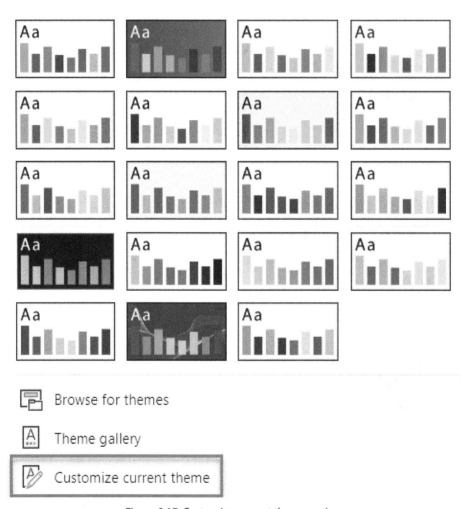

Figure 9.17: Customize current theme option

By clicking on this option, a **Customize theme** window opens, and any of the eight colors can be replaced by the hex codes copied from the `coolors.co` theme generator, as shown in *Figure 9.18*:

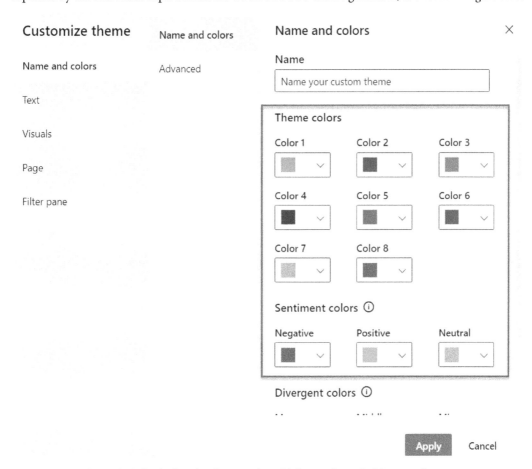

Figure 9.18: Replacing the theme color with hex code copied from coolors.co

The second option is to save the current theme file on your machine as a JSON file and replace the hex values inside the JSON file. You can save the current theme by using the **Save current theme** option, as shown in *Figure 9.19*:

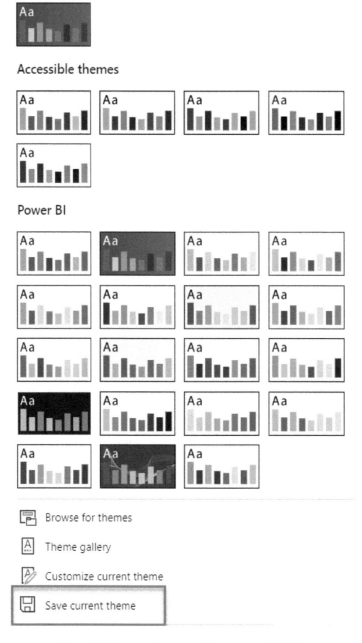

Figure 9.19: Saving the current theme as a JSON file

The current theme is saved as a JSON file on the computer, which can be opened in any text or JSON editor, as shown in *Figure 9.20*:

```
{
    "name":"Accessible City park",
    "dataColors":[
        "#59A33A",
        "#2D386D",
        "#AD8F21",
        "#7B1C25",
        "#5C97D2",
        "#661F89",
        "#E56E1D",
        "#14482C",
        "#3599B8",
        "#DFBFBF",
        "#4AC5BB",
        "#5F6B6D",
        "#FB8281",
        "#F4D25A",
        "#7F898A",
        "#A4DDEE",
        "#FDAB89",
        "#B687AC",
        "#28738A",
        "#A78F8F",
        "#168980",
        "#293537",
        "#BB4A4A",
        "#B59525",
        "#475052",
        "#6A9FB0",
        "#BD7150",
        "#7B4F71",
        "#1B4D5C",
        "#706060",
        "#0F5C55",
        "#1C2325"
    ],
    "foreground":"#111111",
    "background":"#FFFFFF",
    "foregroundNeutralSecondary":"#5D5C60",
    "backgroundLight":"#F0EEF8",
    "foregroundNeutralTertiary":"#8E8C93",
```

Figure 9.20: Theme saved as a JSON file

You can replace the hex code in the file directly after the # part, save the file, and then upload the theme using the **Browse for themes** option, as shown in *Figure 9.21*:

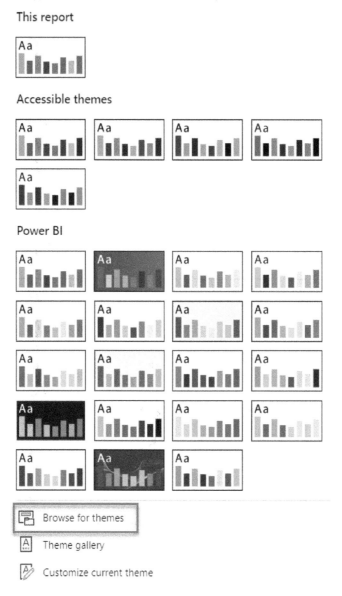

Figure 9.21: Browse for themes option

The saved theme is uploaded in Power BI and available for all the color options.

Creating a report layout

The next step for data storytelling in Power BI is creating a report layout. This layout needs to be designed for all pages in the report. The process starts by creating a wireframe or prototype using a pen or pencil and ends by designing a complete report layout in some external tool such as PowerPoint or Figma and saving the layout as an image file. The image file is then uploaded on each report page in Power BI Desktop as a background that serves as the layout for the page.

The process of creating a rough or low-fidelity prototype is called wireframing. A rough layout is shown in *Figure 9.22*:

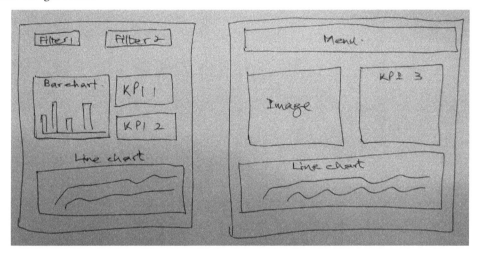

Figure 9.22: Wireframe report layout

It is important to design the report layout to include a report or dashboard title, which is the area where the title and sub-subtitle of the report or dashboard are mentioned. It must have report navigation, which is the area where text, icons, or buttons are placed for report navigation. KPIs or metrics associated with the business questions must also be placed. The most important part of the layout is a grid structure to place the report visuals. A company logo and report slicers are also an important part of the report layout.

Preparing the final design

Once the wireframe has been finalized after multiple iterations, then the final design is prepared using tools such as Microsoft PowerPoint, Figma, Adobe XD, Adobe Photoshop, or other UI/UX design tools. The objective is to create the complete design with any of these tools, including setting up the background, adding icons, texts, images, shapes, and so on. Different shapes can be selected to create the report layout. It is always better to work in the form of grids. Once the design has been completed, as per the wireframe, then it should be saved as an SVG, JPEG, or PNG file. SVG is the preferred option as it scales the best and does not get distorted. The SVG file can now be added in

Power BI Desktop on any report page as a background image inside the **Format** options for **Canvas background**, as shown in *Figure 9.23*. This allows interactive elements such as slicers, buttons, and visuals to be added in Power BI and makes the report design process simple to manage:

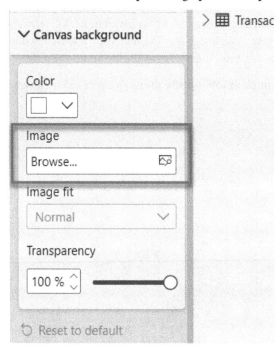

Figure 9.23: Import report layout design in Power BI Desktop

We have just looked at methods to do wireframing and the final design for a web-based report on a Windows desktop, which will be opened inside a web browser. The same principles apply to designing mobile reports, but with a few differences. Microsoft Power BI has provided an option to create a mobile-friendly layout so that you can pick and choose report elements that you want to go into this mobile report. Anytime someone is viewing the report on a mobile device inside the Power BI app for Android or iOS, then it is going to be much easier for them to view. You can take out any elements from your desktop design that just do not make sense when somebody is interacting with the report on a mobile device. This mobile layout can be created both inside Power BI Desktop and the Power BI Service, as shown in *Figure 9.24*:

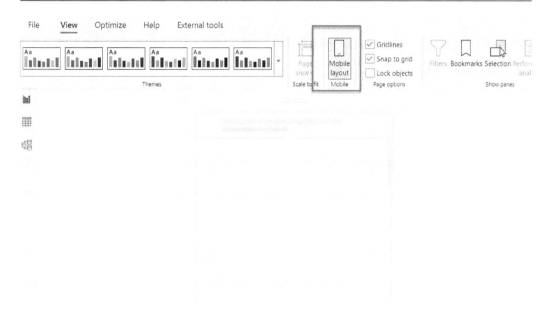

Figure 9.24: Mobile layout for report design in Power BI Desktop

In the mobile layout, you see a blank phone template set up where all report elements and objects can be placed. The idea is to place these elements in a way that the user scrolls up and down the mobile screen in a seamless way, and the information is shown in a sequence. Remember – a user is going to interact with the mobile report to get a quick overview of what is the most important information. Mobile layouts are not designed to show detailed analysis or provide features to drill up and down a particular hierarchy. So, important elements of the report, such as KPI cards and some carefully designed charts showing top N or bottom N values, should be shown in this view. All you need to do is drag these elements, resize them as per the mobile layout, and place them below each other. You can also save this theme in a template and store it in a common folder (such as in SharePoint) so that other users can use this template to develop the report.

Best practices for report design

There are infinite ways to develop a report design, but there are some best practices that must be followed in any report layout and design. So far, we have concentrated on the look and feel of our report, but every report design must have a structure. The way a report is structured can change the way data is interpreted and understood. The most important aspect of a report design is that it effectively communicates the data that meets our requirements. Here are some best practices to follow when designing a report:

- Good placement of report objects contributes to a very ordered and structured report design. Generally, the most important information is placed in the top-left corner, and then a Z-pattern is followed to arrange the rest of the information going from left to right and top to bottom. This is because of how our eyes are trained to read. If you are designing a report for people who are trained to read from right to left, then this pattern can be flipped.

- The report title, logo, and top-level KPIs should normally be placed near the top as these are the most important parts of a report. Similarly, report navigation also occupies either the top portion or the left portion of the report.

- The middle and bottom portions of the report should have other visuals such as bar charts and line charts that occupy more space and show trend-based and activity-based information.

- Slicers can be placed on the right side, or if some space is available on the top, then these can be placed there as well.

- All elements or objects on the report canvas must be properly aligned. It is important to leave a margin on all sides and put space in between objects so that there is symmetry and order, which is pleasing to the eye. A grid structure helps in achieving perfect symmetry and avoiding clutter on the canvas.

- Another aspect of symmetry on your report page is balance. Balance refers to the weight that is distributed across the whole page by your placement of objects. The recommended practice is to make the whole page look balanced with uniform symmetry in the placement of objects but with an element of asymmetry to highlight some important information that can catch the eye of the report user and serve the purpose. This can be done through annotations, shapes, changes of color, and so on.

- Another best practice in report design is to stay consistent with the design across all pages of the report. This includes having a similar layout, navigation experience, colors, fonts, and so on so that all pages of the report give the same UX.

- The last best practice in report design is to make sure that you are sticking to a single topic per page. Try to avoid combining subjects on a single page as this creates clutter and you have fewer visuals, cards, and slicers. The report page should have a good balance between ink and whitespace so that it is easier for the report user to focus on the information and not get lost in clutter.

After the report design process is completed and the image file has been imported in the background, now comes the part of placing interactive report elements on the canvas. *Figure 9.25* shows an example of the final report page design, which has been prepared in Figma, with all important sections highlighted:

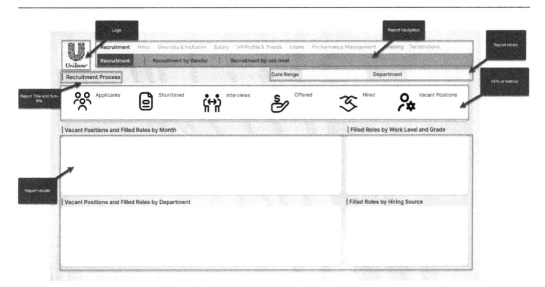

Figure 9.25: Final report page design in Figma

In the next section, we are going to first talk about the report navigation experience on the report canvas using images, buttons, and icons. This will be followed by placing the visuals and adding a narrative to each visual by using some of the options available inside Power BI Desktop.

Adding report navigation

After the report layout design process, your report page is ready for other elements to be placed on the report canvas. The first elements that can be placed relate to the report navigation. The report navigation portion is already a part of the report design, but now the interactivity and control elements need to be added. We use the same report design example we saw in *Figure 9.25* and learn how interactive elements can be added to build a report navigation experience.

Inside Power BI Desktop, the **View** menu option contains interactable elements that can be added to the report page, as shown in *Figure 9.26*:

Figure 9.26: Interactable report elements

Buttons, shapes, and images can be added to any report and allow different interactable actions. One of these actions is **report navigation**, which allows you to move to different pages in the report. Here, we are just going to discuss buttons and how these can be configured to enable report navigation. The same process can be followed for shapes and images as well. As we have already built the **Report Navigation** menu for our report in Figma, we just need to add buttons on top of the text and configure the settings of each button to navigate across different pages of the report. For this purpose, we are going to use and configure **Blank** buttons, as shown in *Figure 9.27*:

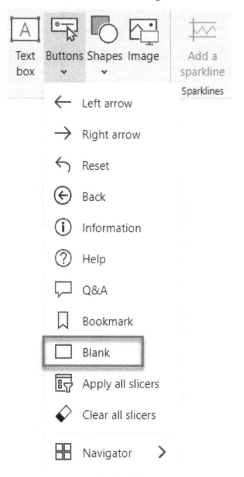

Figure 9.27: Accessing the Blank button

As soon as we click on the **Blank** option in the **Buttons** menu, a button appears on the canvas, just like any other visual element that can be moved around and resized. On clicking the button, a format option appears in the **Visualizations** pane area, as shown in *Figure 9.28*. These options can be used to change the shape and orientation and configure different styles such as adding or removing borders, changing colors, adding text, and so on:

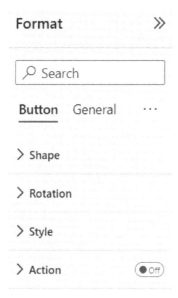

Figure 9.28: Format options for the Blank button

Now, we want to place this button on the text inside the report navigation area after resizing the button, as shown in *Figure 9.29*:

Figure 9.29: Placing the Blank button on text inside the report navigation area

The last step is to configure this button so that when a user brings the mouse onto this text and clicks it, the report navigates to the report page titled **Recruitment by Gender**. The same process then needs to be applied to all other text inside the navigation area. Button configuration can be done by turning **On** the **Action** toggle button and selecting **Page navigation** as the option for **Type** and selecting **Recruitment by Gender** as the option for **Destination**, as shown in *Figure 9.30*:

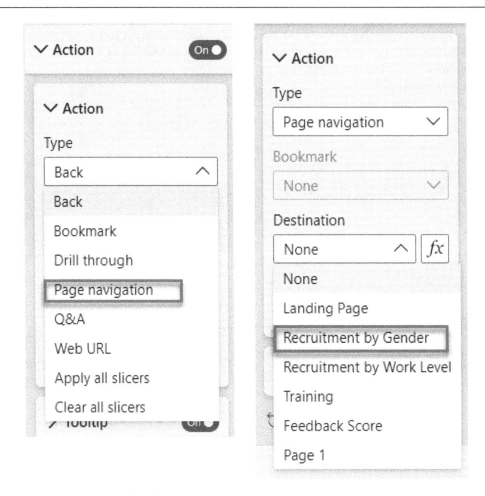

Figure 9.30: Configuring the Blank button for report navigation

Lastly, the button configuration needs to be tested. This can be done by hovering the mouse over the button to check if it allows interaction (the mouse icon changes to indicate that it has become interactive) and pressing *Ctrl + mouse left-click*. If the report navigation has been configured correctly, then it takes the user to the desired page in the report.

There are multiple ways to design report navigation, but it must be a part of the report layout and design and configured properly to make the UX easy and seamless.

Selecting and formatting visuals

Power BI offers dozens of native visuals and hundreds of options for custom visuals to choose from, making it one of the best BI tools to offer flexibility in choosing the right visual for your report.

Native visuals are always visible and available inside the **Visualizations** pane of Power BI Desktop, as shown in *Figure 9.31*. These visuals are an integral part of Power BI Desktop and offer the best performance:

Figure 9.31: Power BI native visuals

Custom visuals can be added to any Power BI report through AppSource. Users can access these visuals by clicking on the three dots and then selecting **Get more visuals**, as shown in *Figure 9.32*. You must have a Power BI account on app.powerbi.com to access this feature:

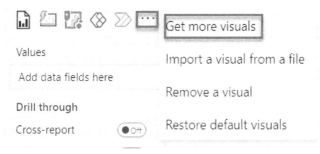

Figure 9.32: Accessing custom visuals in Power BI Desktop

This feature opens the window for Power BI custom visuals called the App Store, as shown in *Figure 9.33*:

Power BI visuals   ✕

ⓘ By clicking 'Add' and/or 'Download Sample' and downloading a visual, you agree to the provider's Terms and Conditions and Privacy Policy on the visual's page and agree Microsoft can share your account details to provider for their transactional purposes. Use of Microsoft's AppSource is subject to the Microsoft Commercial Marketplace Terms and Privacy Statement.

All visuals   Organizational visuals   AppSource visuals   🔍 Search

Explore all available visuals to magnify your business insights   Learn more

Filter by   All   Sort by: Popularity ⌄

Performance Flow -... ✿	Galigeo for PowerBI	Sparkline by OKViz ✿	Calendar by Datanau ✿	Text Filter ✿
xViz LLC	GALIGEO	OKVIZ Corp.	DATANAU - CONSULTORI...	Microsoft Corporation
★★★★★(13)	★★★★★(4)	★★★★★(22)	★★★★★(4)	★★★★★(179)

SuperTables	Chiclet Slicer ✿	Timeline Slicer ✿	Gantt ✿	Word Cloud ✿
Apps for Power BI	Microsoft Corporation	Microsoft Corporation	Microsoft Corporation	Microsoft Corporation
★★★★★(5)	★★★★★(247)	★★★★★(242)	★★★★★(164)	★★★★★(140)

Figure 9.33: Custom visuals in Power BI

The user can select any visual, and it appears in the **Visualizations** pane for use, just as with the native visuals, as shown in *Figure 9.34*:

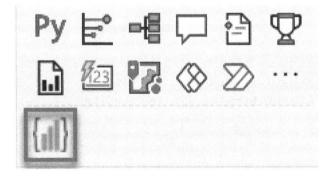

Figure 9.34: Deneb custom visual in Visualizations pane

Selecting a native or custom visual from the **Visualizations** pane and adding data fields to the visual is not data storytelling. Data storytelling requires using some of the formatting options available for each visual. This involves removing clutter from the visual, using formatting options to match color and text to the report design, and adding a narrative to the visual.

Formatting axes

Both bar charts and line charts have x and y axes, and the default setting in Power BI is to show the name of the variable on the axes. If the user is applying the best practices of data storytelling, then the axes' name is already covered in the title or subtitle. So, it is always recommended to remove variable names from the axes to reduce clutter in the visual.

Similarly, the names of labels should be clear and readable. Avoid showing names in a tilted position, especially on the x axis of a vertical bar chart (column chart). It is better to either convert the vertical bar chart (column chart) to a horizontal bar chart or increase the size of the chart so that labels are clearly visible and values are readable to the user.

Another important consideration is the range of the value axis. Power BI gives flexibility to define the range of the value axis. The scale can also be set to a logarithmic scale, which is not a recommended practice. Power BI automatically defines minimum and maximum values for the range of the axis, but the user can also adjust these values. In case the difference between the minimum and maximum values is too large, then a zoom slider can be provided so that the user can interact with the visual for better understanding. *Figure 9.35* shows how the axes labels have been removed and a zoom slider has been added on the value axis (y axis):

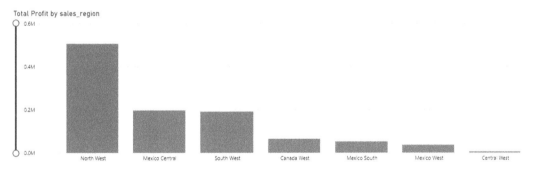

Figure 9.35: Bar chart with axes labels removed and a zoom slider added on the value axis

Formatting the chart area

The chart area represents the part of the visual that contains the data. These are bars in the case of a bar chart, lines in the case of a line chart, bubbles, circles, or other shapes in the case of a scatter chart, and similarly for other chart types. Color, size, text, and position are preattentive attributes that can be modified for any visual. This is normally achieved through conditional formatting options.

Conditional formatting, as the name implies, formats the data based on some condition. There are several areas in the formatting options of a visual where conditional formatting can be applied to the visual. If we talk about the chart area of a bar chart, then the data labels and color of the bar are two areas where conditional formatting can be applied. The same principle applies to other parts of the visual as well. Let us explore the conditional formatting options associated with changing the colors and data labels of a bar chart and how these are linked to showing insights and data storytelling.

First, let us look at the conditional formatting option related to the color of a bar chart. *Figure 9.36* shows the conditional formatting option for the bar chart visual in Power BI. The *fx* icon indicates that the conditional formatting option is available:

Figure 9.36: Conditional formatting for colors of bar chart

There are three formatting styles available inside the conditional formatting window: **Gradient**, **Rules**, and **Field value**. Let us look at each in detail:

- **Gradient**: In the **Gradient** option, the colors of the bar chart follow a gradient based on the minimum and maximum values of the selected field, as shown in *Figure 9.37*. This field could be any measure or expression in the dataset. In this case, the DAX measure [Total Sales] has been chosen as the field, and colors associated with the minimum and maximum values have been assigned:

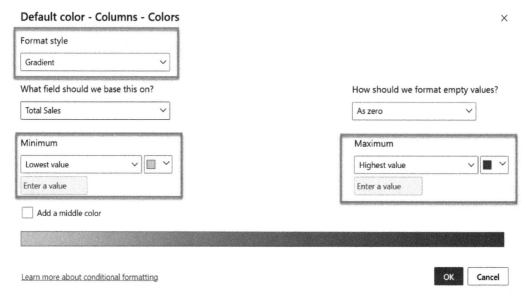

Figure 9.37: Configuring conditional formatting through the Gradient option

The colors associated with the minimum and maximum values are assigned to the respective bars in the visual, and a color gradient is associated with the rest of the values, as shown in *Figure 9.38*. A legend showing the color gradient can also be seen in the visual to guide the end user:

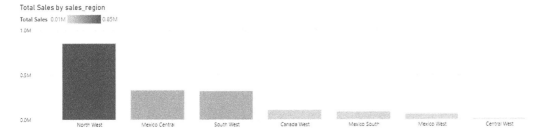

Figure 9.38: Conditional formatting on color applied to bar chart through the Gradient option

- **Rules**: The second option for conditional formatting is rule-based, whereby rules can be applied to change the color of the chart area, as shown in *Figure 9.39*. A simple rule to create three groups has been defined based on the value of the [Total Sales] measure, and each group has been assigned a different color:

Figure 9.39: Configuring conditional formatting through the Rules option

The color associated with each group is assigned to respective bars in the visual, as shown in *Figure 9.40*. A limitation of this approach is that it works for fixed numbers, but instead of fixed numbers, a rule can be created based on percentage values as well:

Figure 9.40: Conditional formatting on color applied to bar chart through the Rules option

- **Field value**: The last option to apply conditional formatting is based on the field value and relies on creating DAX measures to assign a color to the chart area. Here, we will look at an example where the color of the chart area has been changed to highlight minimum and maximum values only. This approach is fully dynamic and works with all kinds of filters and slicers applied to the visual. It will always highlight minimum and maximum values under all filtering conditions. The DAX code for the measure is shown here:

```
Max Region (chart) =
VAR __MaxValue =
MAXX(
    ALL(Regions[sales_region]),
    [Total Sales]
)
VAR __MinValue =
MINX(
    ALL(Regions[sales_region]),
    [Total Sales]
)
VAR __Result =
SWITCH(
    TRUE(),
    [Total Sales] = __MaxValue, "#104234",
    [Total Sales] = __MinValue, "#345dec",
    "#8D3452"
)
RETURN
__Result
```

This DAX measure will be added to the conditional formatting area, as shown in *Figure 9.41*:

Default color - Columns - Colors   ✕

Format style

| Field value | ⌄ |

What field should we base this on?

| Max Region (chart) | ⌄ |

Learn more about conditional formatting   **OK**   Cancel

Figure 9.41: Configuring conditional formatting through the Field value option

The color associated with minimum and maximum values is assigned to respective bars in the visual, as shown in *Figure 9.42*. DAX measures to use color as a preattentive attribute using conditional formatting through the **Field value** option can be developed for any scenario. This method is fully dynamic and offers complete flexibility over gradient and rule-based methods. The same principle for applying color formatting applies to all other visuals, such as line charts, scatter charts, table visuals, and so on:

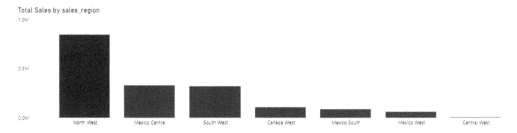

Total Sales by sales_region

Figure 9.42: Conditional formatting on color applied to bar chart through the Field value option

Another important aspect related to the formatting of the chart area is the data label. Data labels are text values that represent the number associated with the shape of the visual. Power BI allows adding data labels to charts. However, adding too many data labels can clutter the chart, so it is suggested to include data labels only for data points that show some insight. This can be achieved through conditional formatting. Here, we will modify the same DAX measure that we used for conditional formatting of the preceding color and use it inside the **Data labels** option. The DAX measure for conditional formatting of labels is shown here:

```
Max Region (label) =
VAR __MaxValue =
MAXX(
    ALL(Regions[sales_region]),
    [Total Sales]
)
VAR __MinValue =
MINX(
    ALL(Regions[sales_region]),
    [Total Sales]
)
// Labels for the bar chart
VAR __Result =
SWITCH(
    TRUE(),
    [Total Sales] = __MaxValue, __MaxValue,
    [Total Sales] = __MinValue, __MinValue
)
RETURN
__Result
```

To add this measure for applying conditional formatting, the **Data labels** option inside the **Format visual** menu first needs to be turned **On**, as shown in *Figure 9.43*:

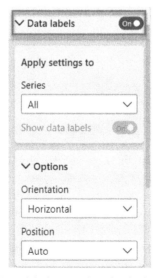

Figure 9.43: Data labels turned On for the bar chart visual

When this option is turned **On**, another option, **Custom label**, related to conditional formatting, is available and needs to be turned **On**. The DAX measure is added to this area, as shown in *Figure 9.44*:

Figure 9.44: DAX measure for conditional formatting added to Field area of Custom label

Figure 9.45 shows conditional formatting for both the color and data labels added to the original visual:

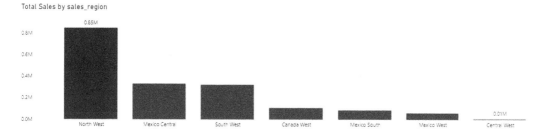

Figure 9.45: Conditional formatting on color and data labels applied to the bar chart

Formatting the background with analytics

Another area that can improve data storytelling is formatting the background of visuals. Normally, it is best practice to remove any clutter from the background and only include information that adds value or insights to data. In *Figure 9.45*, there are gridlines added to the background that do not add any value to the visual. These gridlines can be removed through the **Gridlines** option, as shown in *Figure 9.46*:

Figure 9.46: Gridlines settings for the bar chart visual

Inside the **Analytics** option of the **Visualizations** pane in Power BI Desktop, there are several ways to add insights to a visual, as shown in *Figure 9.47*:

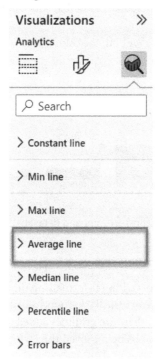

Figure 9.47: Option for adding analytics to a visual

Here, we will just focus on adding the **Average line** insights to the visual. The average line has been formatted as a dotted line, and only the value is being shown in the visual settings, as shown in *Figure 9.48*:

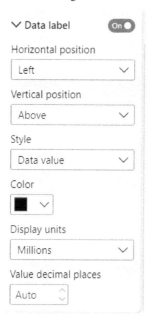

Figure 9.48: Settings for dotted line included as an average line

The final visual with the average value, formatted as a dotted line with a value, is shown in *Figure 9.49*. The gridlines have also been removed from the visual:

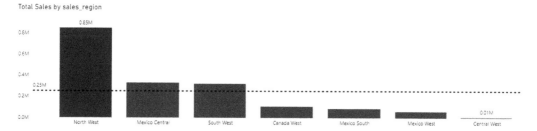

Figure 9.49: Dotted line with data label representing average value added through the Analytics option

Adding a narrative to visuals and reports

The final aspect of data storytelling is adding a narrative to visuals and reports. For each visual, this can be done using the **Title** and **Subtitle** options available in Power BI. We have already seen how a narrative is generated for storytelling in the previous section. Now, we will see how it can be added to any visual.

Adding a narrative to visuals

For every visual in Power BI, there is an option to add a title and subtitle. These can be combined to create a compelling narrative that adds insights to our data story along with elements of data storytelling that we have already seen in previous sections. The **Title** and **Subtitle** options are within the **Format the Visual** area of the visual, as shown in *Figure 9.50*:

Figure 9.50: Title and Subtitle settings

When both a title and subtitle are added to the visual, the storytelling aspect of the visual is complete. Both the title and subtitle can be made dynamic using the conditional formatting option that uses DAX, as we have seen in previous sections. The final result can be seen in *Figure 9.51*:

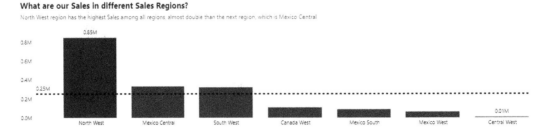

Figure 9.51: Title and subtitle added to the visual as a narrative of the data story

Adding a narrative to reports

Data storytelling involves putting a narrative not only in visuals but also in reports. Power BI has a visual called **Smart Narrative** that uses **artificial intelligence** (**AI**) capabilities and generates a narrative based on the visuals on a report page. A developer can also generate dynamic narratives using DAX, as we have already seen for the conditional formatting of color and data labels.

The **Smart Narrative** visual is a very simple visual and does not take any input from the user since it uses AI to generate a narrative itself. *Figure 9.52* shows the smart narrative generated by this AI visual:

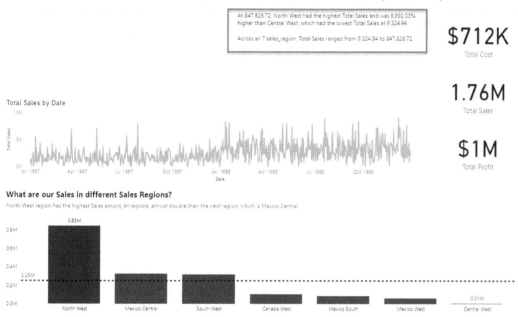

Figure 9.52: Narrative generated by the Smart Narrative visual (shown in red box) in Power BI

Adding narratives to visuals is very important for data storytelling. Now, we can have a look at some of the advanced features available within Power BI and how these can be used to enrich reports.

Enriching your reports with advanced Power BI features

Data storytelling can also be enhanced by using some advanced Power BI features that allow the user to use space on a report page more efficiently, provide an experience to filter on a summary, see a detailed view of any record, and complement the presentation of data using custom tooltips. These features are available in Power BI through **Drill through**, bookmarks, and custom tooltips.

Drill through

Drill through requires the Power BI report developer to develop an additional page that is more detailed than a single visual. It allows the report developer to give the report user an option to explore any data point in a visual in more detail on another page. The process works by adding a drill-through filter to the detailed report page, which normally is the column in your data on which detailed information needs to be presented. *Figure 9.53* shows the **Drill through** field on the detailed report page, where the sales region has been added as a drill-through filter:

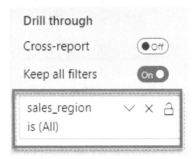

Figure 9.53: Drill-through filter added to the Drill through area on the detailed report page

The option can be enabled by right-clicking on the visual and clicking on the **Drill through** option, which takes the user to the detailed report page, or just hovering the mouse on any of the data points and clicking on the **Drill through** option, as shown in *Figure 9.54*:

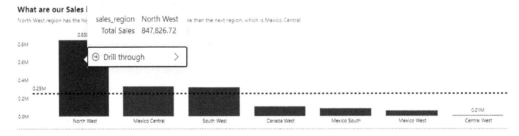

Figure 9.54: Drill through option for the visual

Power BI automatically generates a **Back** button to move from the detailed report page back to the original page. This button can be placed anywhere on the report page, but the button configuration is automatically been done by Power BI. *Figure 9.55* shows the view of the detailed report page, filtering the page on `sales_region = "North West"` and providing more details than the original visual. The **Back** button can be clicked to return to the original report page:

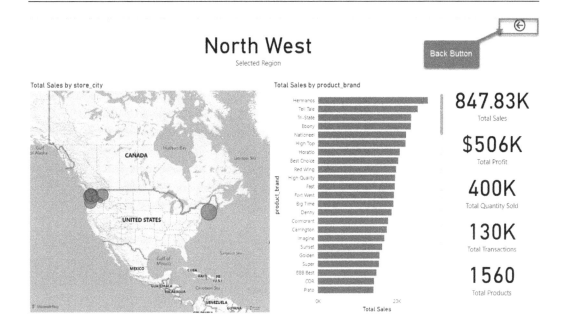

Figure 9.55: Drill-through page filtered for "North West" region with Back button

Bookmarks

Another very useful feature for data storytelling is bookmarks. Bookmarks capture the current state or configuration of a report page and can be used with the selection pane and buttons to show or hide visuals in a report. This allows the user to utilize the space on a report page efficiently and create an easier navigation experience within the same page.

Bookmarks save multiple elements on a report page, including filters, slicers, sort order, **Show as a Table**, visibility status, and focus or spotlight mode of any visible object. Each bookmark is linked with a button on the canvas, which when pressed shows that visual on the canvas. Bookmarks can be created using the **Bookmarks** option inside the **View** menu, as shown in *Figure 9.56*:

Figure 9.56: Bookmarks in Power BI Desktop

Custom tooltip

Another feature that helps the storytelling for any report is the custom tooltip. Custom tooltips add another report page to any visual of a report. In the case of a custom tooltip, the default tooltip is replaced with a custom design tooltip page, and that tooltip page is shown every time the report user hovers the mouse on any data point in the visual. *Figure 9.57* shows a custom tooltip that has been configured for a visual:

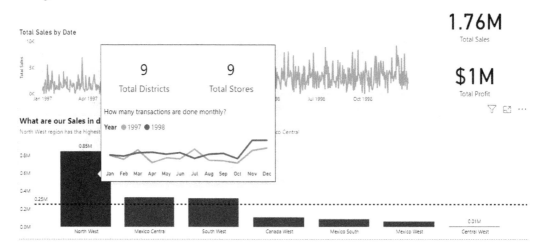

Figure 9.57: Report visual with a custom tooltip

Custom tooltips add a new dimension to visuals as more information is captured for a data point in the visual. The standard size of the tooltip page is 240 pixels (height) x 320 pixels (width), but this size is customizable and can be increased or decreased as per the choice of the report designer. A tooltip page is designed like a normal report page, where multiple visuals can be placed. There are three visuals in the custom tooltip: two card visuals and a line chart. When the tooltip is placed on one of the bars in the visual, the results for that data point are filtered and shown in the tooltip. The report designer can add more context and more information within the same visual.

Q&A

Data storytelling is a topic that is just not limited to Power BI but to all other BI tools. You may be asked generic questions in a job interview related to data storytelling. These questions are tool-agnostic and test your general ability to understand data visualization and how you will develop your reports and dashboards.

Here is a list of some sample questions and answers that you might encounter in a job interview:

Question 1: Can you describe a time when you used data storytelling to influence a business decision? What was the outcome?

Answer: I created a sales performance dashboard that highlighted emerging market trends, which convinced the leadership to reallocate resources, resulting in a 20% increase in sales.

Question 2: What are your go-to visuals in Power BI when you want to tell a story with data?

Answer: I frequently use line charts for trend analysis and stacked bar charts to show part-to-whole relationships, adding slicers for interactivity.

Question 3: How do you balance aesthetic appeal and functionality in your Power BI reports?

Answer: I follow design best practices, ensuring visuals are not only engaging but also provide clear insights, using consistent color schemes and uncluttered layouts.

Question 4: How do you create interactive reports in Power BI that allow end users to explore data and discover insights on their own?

Answer: I implement drill-downs, tooltips, and interactive filters to empower users to dig into the layers of data at their own pace.

Question 5: Can you walk us through your process for constructing a narrative around a set of data points?

Answer: I start with the key message or insight, then select data points that support it, and structure them logically to build up a narrative.

Question 6: How do you tailor your data stories to different audiences or stakeholders?

Answer: I adjust the complexity of visualizations and the granularity of data presented based on the technical proficiency and interests of the audience.

Question 7: Can you give an example of a DAX measure you created for a report that significantly contributed to the data story?

Answer: I created a year-over-year growth percentage measure that highlighted the success of a new product line, pivotal to the quarterly business review narrative.

Question 8: How do you maintain integrity and avoid misleading representations when telling a story with data?

Answer: I ensure all visualizations accurately represent the underlying numbers and provide context to avoid misinterpretations, upholding data integrity.

Summary

In this insightful chapter on data storytelling, we have journeyed through the transformative power of effectively communicating data. We began by understanding the essence of data storytelling – transforming complex data into compelling narratives that resonate with the audience. Key elements such as context, clarity, and relevance were emphasized as crucial for making data relatable and impactful.

We explored various techniques for visualizing data, emphasizing the importance of choosing the right charts and graphs to convey your message. Additionally, the chapter highlighted the role of narrative structure in data storytelling. The skills and concepts covered in this chapter are vital for anyone looking to convey data-driven insights persuasively. In an era where data is abundant, the ability to tell a compelling story with data stands out as a key differentiator in BI.

In the next chapter, we are going to go from Power BI Desktop to the Power BI Service, where we will learn how to create dashboards, ensure the security of our reports and semantic models, and explore the usage of apps to distribute content.

Further reading

There are hundreds of real-world examples of data storytelling where the choice of the right visuals, narrative, report layout, and navigation tell a compelling story to the report user. Here are links to five real-world case studies developed in Power BI so that report users can explore these links and learn how data storytelling works in practice:

- *Transport & Shipping* case study (Credits: Rachwen Misbehi)

  https://app.powerbi.com/view?r=eyJrIjoiZWU3YWM4ZjUtM2UyMS0
  0ZTdiLTkyOTYtODRjZWU0MDIxMzY0IiwidCI6IjJjNDQxN2EyLTZiZWEtNDgx
  My05NjJhLTdjYWRlNzUxMmY5ZSJ9

- *Living through Pandemic* case study (Credits: Alex Badiu)

  https://app.powerbi.com/view?r=eyJrIjoiNjNmNTIyYTMtN2RmNS00OWF
  hLWE5ZmUtMjYxZjMzNzljNWU4IiwidCI6IjliMjJlMTM0LWJlMmEtNGM0YS04
  MTZkLTk0NWJiNjgyYmFlYyJ9

- *Space Missions* case study (Credits: Federico Pastor)

- https://app.powerbi.com/view?r=eyJrIjoiODgzYWM0ZGEtNGYzZi00
  OGI3LTg2OWEtYWM0ZWJhOTk0ZWFjIiwidCI6IjAyYTU2OTVlLTk5NGYtND
  VlOC05MGFlLWEzZTI0NWY0MjVmMSIsImMiOjF9

  https://app.powerbi.com/view?r=eyJrIjoiNThjZTk0YjItMjYwZS00
  OWI1LThhMzMtODg1MTM4OGFkOWFhIiwidCI6IjJmODQ4YjNiLTRiMTIt
  NDkxNy1hZDQ3LTU5Y2I4N2JiZDdmYyJ9

- *Football Players Summer Transfer* case study (Credits: Sean Chandler)

  https://app.powerbi.com/view?r=eyJrIjoiMzNkNDRhMjgtMDM
  yOS00YTU1LTllYjktZjdiNjY0MjI0MjRmIiwidCI6ImRmODY3OWNkLWE
  4MGUtNDVkOC05OWFjLWM4M2VkN2ZmOTVhMCJ9

- *Resume Design* case study (Credits: Sean Chandler)

  https://app.powerbi.com/view?r=eyJrIjoiOTYxNjQzNzMtMDZ
  jZS00MGRkLThjNTUtZDY3ZjQ2N2JhNGI4IiwidCI6ImRmODY3OWNkLW
  E4MGUtNDVkOC05OWFjLWM4M2VkN2ZmOTVhMCJ9&page
  Name=ReportSection

10

Using Dashboards and Apps and Implementing Security

Believe it or not, there is life after Power BI Desktop. Although the utility of any good report largely depends on its development, your report will be incomplete or dysfunctional if you don't know how to manage, distribute, or apply some level of security to it. This is because many companies are strict about allowing users to only view or access authorized data. So, keeping this in mind will give you the tools to defend yourself if these topics are touched upon in any interview questions.

In this chapter, you will learn about Power BI dashboards, how to create them by adding pins from different reports, and understand the difference between dashboards and reports. Additionally, you will learn how to use Power BI apps to distribute your reports before we delve into implementing **row-level security (RLS)** within Power BI.

The topics we will cover in this chapter are as follows:

- Dashboards versus reports
- Creating a dashboard in Power BI
- Adding pins
- Sharing content through Power BI apps
- Implementing RLS

Technical requirements

- Power BI Free license

- Power BI Desktop installed on your PC:

    - From the web: `https://www.microsoft.com/en-us/download/details.aspx?id=58494`

    - From the Microsoft Store: `https://aka.ms/pbidesktopstore`

Dashboards versus reports

In the Power BI ecosystem, a dashboard is a page with visual objects in the form of tiles. These tiles aim to provide valuable insights. In general, the purpose of dashboards is to display information in one place. So, in Power BI, they are created on a single canvas or page, helping you view consolidated information from one or multiple reports.

Here are some key differences between the two:

- **Data consolidation**: So far, we have covered topics that are specific to creating Power BI reports connected to a dataset. However, sometimes, we may need to view information from different reports in one place. Power BI dashboards can assist with this since you can have visual objects from different reports integrated into a single location.

- **Cross filters**: An essential part of Power BI reports is applying cross filters through a slicer or the filter pane. This allows you to view filtered information in a single visual object. For instance, if you have a line chart displaying the monthly occupancy percentage of Airbnb apartments in New York City, you can apply filters such as sector, by customer, and apartment types to see only the occupancy that meets these criteria. This is something that you cannot do in a Power BI dashboard.

- **Tiles**: The flexibility of the tiles allows you to customize both their functionality and visual appearance. In addition to incorporating tiles derived from reports, designers have the freedom to include independent tiles such as text boxes, images, videos, live data feeds, and web content directly within the dashboard.

Figure 10.1 shows a table of differences between Power BI dashboards and reports:

Capability	Dashboards	Reports
Pages	One page.	One or more pages.
Data sources	One or more reports and one or more semantic models per dashboard.	A single semantic model per report.
Drilling down in visuals	Only if you pin an entire report page to a dashboard.	Yes.
Available in Power BI Desktop	No.	Yes. You can build and view reports in Power BI Desktop.
Filtering	No. You can't filter or slice a dashboard You can filter a dashboard tile in focus mode but can't save the filter.	Yes. There are many different ways to filter, highlight, and slice.
Feature content on colleagues' home pages	Yes.	Yes
Favorites	Yes. You can set multiple dashboards as favorites.	Yes. You can set multiple reports as favorites.
Natural language queries (Q&A)	Yes.	Yes, provided you have edit permissions for the report and underlying semantic model.
Set alerts	Yes. Available for dashboard tiles in certain circumstances.	No.
Subscribe	Yes. You can subscribe to a dashboard.	Yes. You can subscribe to a report page.
See underlying semantic model tables and fields	No. You can't see tables and fields in the dashboard itself, but you can export data.	Yes.

Figure 10.1: The differences between dashboards and reports

This section introduced the concept of Power BI dashboards, highlighting their role in consolidating visual insights. We explored data consolidation, cross-filter capabilities, and the flexibility of tiles.

Next, we'll dive into the practical steps of creating a dashboard in Power BI, where you'll learn how to transform data into dynamic, insightful visualizations.

Creating a dashboard in Power BI

To create a dashboard, you must log in with your Power BI account, go to the workspace where you want to create it, click on **New**, and then select **Dashboard**, as shown in *Figure 10.2*:

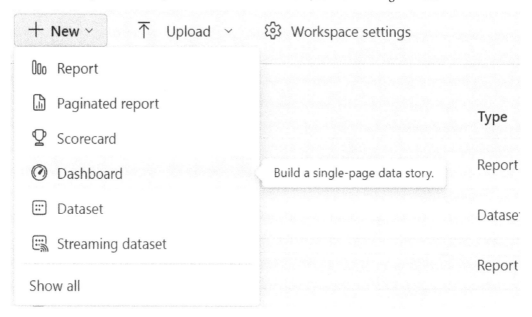

Figure 10.2: The Dashboard option in Power BI

Then, a pop-up window will appear, asking you to name the dashboard. Enter any name you desire and click **Create**.

Once you've done this, you will see a blank canvas where you can add the tiles that will form part of your dashboard. These tiles can come from a report, though you can add custom tiles such as web content, images, texts, or videos. Refer to *Figure 10.3* for reference:

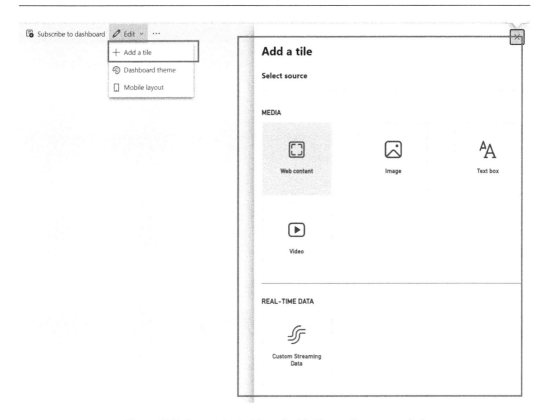

Figure 10.3: An empty dashboard with tiles options expanded

In addition to these options, you can also add real-time data from a streaming dataset, Azure Stream, or PUBNUB.

Adding pins

Dashboards are composed of tiles, and each tile represents a visual object. To add a tile that includes a report visual, you must go to the report that contains it. Each supported visual in the report will have an icon at the top that allows you to add it to the dashboard that you have already created. However, first, let's learn how to add tiles directly to the dashboard.

> **Note**
>
> Note that only visuals to show data points can be added as a tile in a Power BI dashboard. This means that buttons or shapes are not supported. As shown in *Figure 10.1*, filtering is not supported either.

Adding a text box

Figure 10.4 shows a demo dashboard to which we have added a tile with text that serves as a title. We achieved this by clicking on **Edit** | **Add a Tile** | **Text box**:

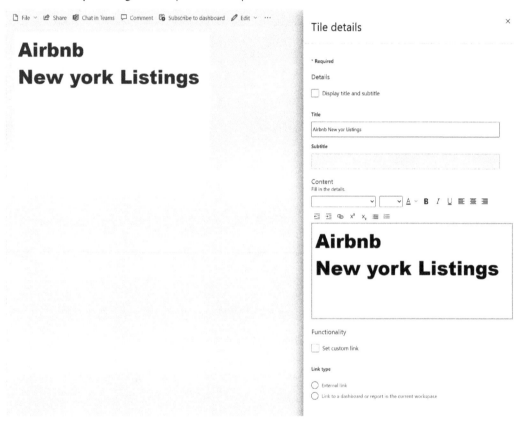

Figure 10.4: Adding text to a Power BI dashboard

Adding an image

In addition to text, you can also add images. As shown in *Figure 10.5*, we added the Airbnb logo to the dashboard. You can do this from the same **Add Tile** menu, but this time, select the **Image** option. In the window on the right, you can add the link to the image's location. Optionally, you can also add a title and subtitle to this tile:

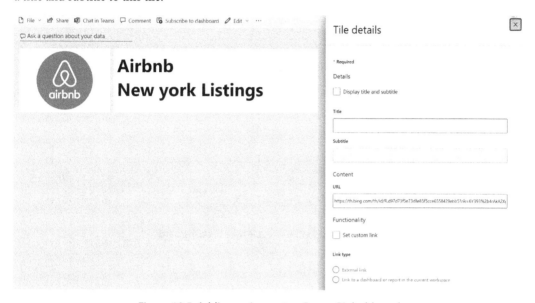

Figure 10.5: Adding an image to a Power BI dashboard

Adding a video

If you like, you can also add videos from YouTube or Vimeo. You can do this from the same **Add Tiles** menu, but this time, select the **Video** option. Search for the desired video and paste the video URL into the field. Almost instantly, you will see a tile with the video, which you can also resize as you wish and add a title or subtitle to:

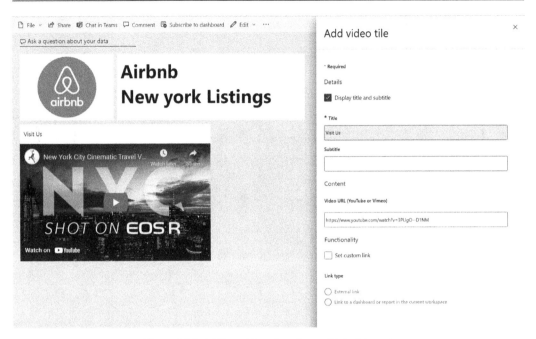

Figure 10.6: Adding videos to a Power BI dashboard

Pinning a visual object

After this, we will go to the report that contains the charts we want. In our case, we will use the report that contains the listings of Airbnb in New York City, which includes a table with the top 10 hosts with more properties in the city. We will add this table to the dashboard by clicking on the icon indicated in the header of the table on the right-hand side of *Figure 10.7*:

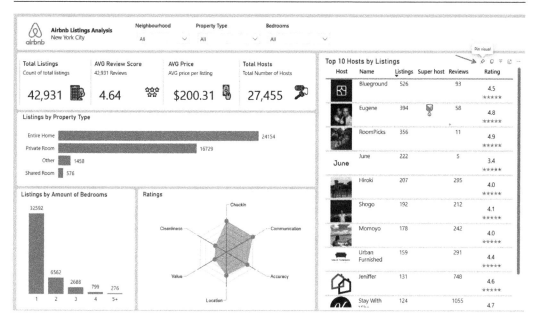

Figure 10.7: Airbnb listings report pin icon

This will open a pop-up window that will ask you which dashboard you want to send this table to. If you haven't created one, you can also create one from scratch here:

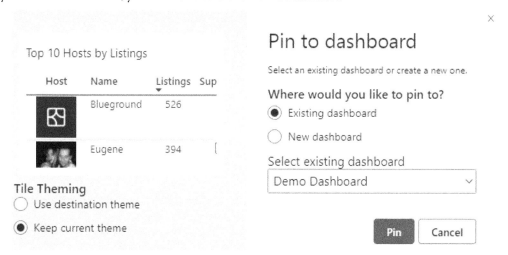

Figure 10.8: Adding a new pin to a dashboard

Note that you can also decide whether to use the dashboard theme by clicking on **Use destination theme** or use the report theme by selecting **Keep current theme**. To give you an idea, in *Figure 10.9*, we have added the same table twice with different theme options. In this case, we changed the dashboard theme to **Dark**, which only affected the table on the right. To change the theme, you can go to the dashboard and click on **Edit | Dashboard theme**:

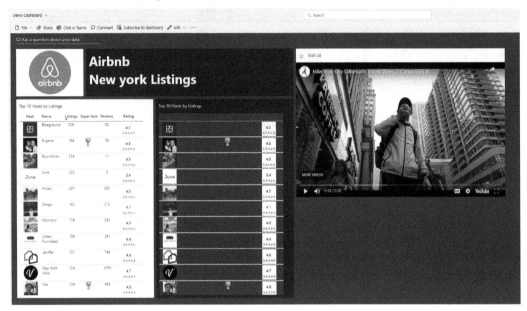

Figure 10.9: The dashboard with a dark theme with the same table added in a different format

Once you've decided on your desired visual objects, your dashboard will start taking shape. You can adjust the size of the tiles according to your preferences from the bottom-right corner of the tiles. However, if you click on any visual, don't expect it to have the same cross-filtering effect as in the reports. Instead, it will take you to the source report.

Each of the tiles on a dashboard has a menu of options you can access by clicking on **More Options** (the three dots in the top-right corner), as shown in *Figure 10.10*. From this menu, you can do the following:

- **Add a comment**: Add comments that will be visible to the collaborators who have access to the dashboard

- **Chat in Teams**: You can start a conversation in Teams about the tile

- **Copy visual as image**: Copy the tile as an image to send it by email or any other means

- **Go to report**: Go to the source report

- **Open in focus mode**: Open the tile so that it only shows the tile on a big screen

- **Export to csv**: Export the data behind the tile in CSV format

- **Edit details**: Edit the title and subtitle

- **View Insights**: You can use artificial intelligence to gain insights into the information displayed in the tile

- **Pin tile**: Pin the tile to another dashboard

- **Delete tile**: Delete the tile

Figure 10.10 shows the dashboard with a dark theme and the same table in a different format:

Figure 10.10: The dashboard with a dark theme with the same table added in a different format

Pinning a report page

In addition to adding charts from a report, you can also add an entire report to the dashboard. To do this, go to the report you want to include in the dashboard, then click on the three dots in the top menu, as shown in *Figure 10.11*. Finally, choose the **Pin to a dashboard** option:

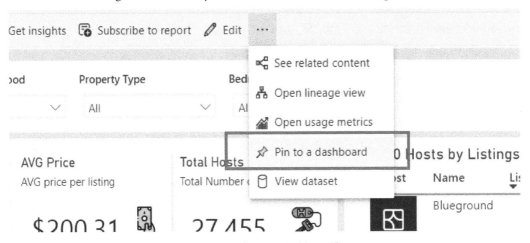

Figure 10.11: The "Pin to a dashboard" option

This will open the same pop-up window you saw in *Figure 10.8* but without the theme options. Click on **Pin live**; at this point, you're done. You will have the report page available on the dashboard, including the slicers. This is because any filters you apply will only affect the visual objects within this report tile.

> **Note**
> In the pop-up window, you will see the following message: **Pin live page enables changes to reports to appear in the dashboard tile when the page is refreshed.**

Pinning a table from Excel

In addition to charts and reports, you can add tables from an Excel document. To do this, you need to go to a workspace and click on the **Upload** button, as shown in *Figure 10.12*. You can upload the Excel document from your computer, SharePoint, or OneDrive.

Once uploaded, you will see a new file with the Excel icon:

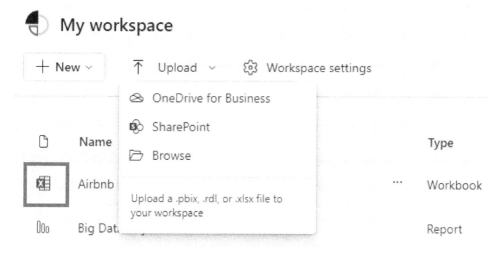

Figure 10.12: Pinning a report to a dashboard

Open the document and select the range of rows and columns that you want to add to the dashboard. Then, from the top left menu, click on **Pin**. Once again, the pop-up window will open, where you can choose whether to add it to a new dashboard or an existing one. Select the option you want and click on **Pin**:

Figure 10.13: Pinning an Excel table

This will add a new tile containing the portion of the table that we selected previously, as shown in *Figure 10.13*:

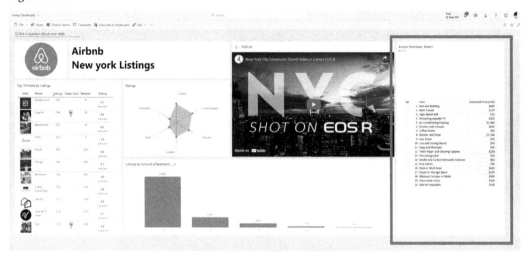

Figure 10.14: Power BI dashboard with an Excel table pinned

Dashboards can be very useful when people want to see easy access information without interacting with the base report. Many companies use them, and that is why you must know their purpose very well. Now, it's time for you to learn how to share those dashboards or reports. In the next section, we will talk a little more about how to share dashboards and reports in Power BI.

Sharing content through Power BI apps

Part of the magic of Power BI lies in sharing your dashboards and reports with your coworkers and collaborators. You can do this through workspaces or via Power BI apps. However, these two ways of sharing content have their differences. Let's explore them.

Apps versus workspaces

When discussing sharing content using workspaces or apps, you may have questions about the difference between the two.

Workspaces are the classic way of sharing reports in Power BI. A workspace is essentially a folder where you can add files; these can be reports, datasets, dashboards, datamarts, dataflows, and even Excel documents, as you saw in the previous section. Each user accessing this workspace can individually access the reports to perform their analysis. However, at some point, it becomes tedious for users to deal with multiple browser tabs or navigate between reports. This situation can be addressed with Power BI apps.

Unlike workspaces, a Power BI app is a kind of application composed of various elements, such as reports, dashboards, or paginated reports. These apps are created within workspaces and inherit all the corresponding permissions and restrictions.

Moreover, besides providing users with a more comfortable way to access all their reports in one place, apps have a more user-friendly interface that allows customization for more corporate branding.

Here are some of the key differences between the two:

	Workspaces	Power BI Apps
Organization	They are folders to store files	Easy to organize content in an app-like manner
Manage Content	Distributed content dealing with all report names	Centralized access to content just by accessing the app
Manage Updates	Updates to semantic models replaces previous changes	Can manage end user updates to semantic models
Customization	Lack of customization	Custom navigation and embedded content to make the reports more interactive
People Onboarding	Overwhelming for users the first time	New users just need to install the app and will have access to all reports needed

Figure 10.15: Key differences between workspaces and Power BI apps

In essence, workspaces serve as traditional folders for individual report access, while Power BI apps function as consolidated applications within workspaces. Apps offer a user-friendly interface, centralizing access to reports and dashboards and addressing the challenge of managing multiple browser tabs.

> **Learn more**
>
> Workspaces: https://learn.microsoft.com/en-us/power-bi/collaborate-share/service-create-the-new-workspaces
>
> Power BI apps: https://learn.microsoft.com/en-us/power-bi/collaborate-share/service-create-distribute-apps

Creating an app

Once you've decided to use apps, you need to have a clear definition of the content and the audiences that will be part of this app. In other words, even though you group multiple reports or dashboards within an app, you can add an extra layer of security by limiting the visibility of certain elements to up to 10 audience groups.

> **Note**
> Only one app can be created per workspace

To create an app, follow these steps:

1. Go to the workspace and click **Create app**:

Figure 10.16: Create app menu

2. This will open the **App configuration** window, where you will give your app a name, description, and logo. You can also choose a color for the theme:

① **Setup***   ② Content*   ③ Audience*

Build your app

App name *

PACKT App

Description *

Enter a summary

Describe your app.

App logo

⊼ Upload
🗑 Delete

App theme color

■ ⌄

Contact Information

◉ Show app publisher
○ Show items contacts from the workspace
○ Show specific individuals or groups

🔍 Enter a name or email address

Global App Settings

☐ Install this app automatically.

☐ Hide app navigation pane.

☐ Allow users to make a copy of the reports in this app.

Support site

Share where your users can find help

Next: Add content   Cancel

Figure 10.17: Create app form

3. Once done, click on **Add content** to include the app's content, and select the elements it will contain. In *Figure 10.17*, we have only one report selected as it is the only one available in that workspace:

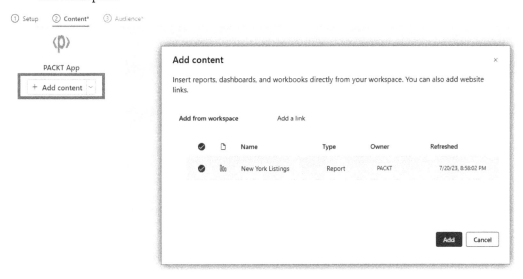

Figure 10.18: Choosing the content for the Power BI App

4. Click on **Add** when you've finished selecting your reports. From here, you can also rename the reports, delete them, or change the order in which they appear. Once you're finished, click **NEXT: Add audience**:

Figure 10.19: Options available on Apps elements

This will take you to the final stage in creating your app, where you can create audiences. By default, one audience with the same name as the app is created.

5.   To create a new audience, click on **New audience** and assign it a name by double-clicking on it:

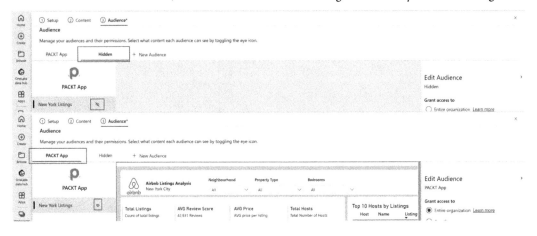

Figure 10.20: Adding a new audience

With this, an additional tab will be created. All the changes you make will only affect the tab that is currently in focus. For example, in *Figure 10.20*, you can see that in the **Hidden** audience, the report is hidden, but it is not in the default audience:

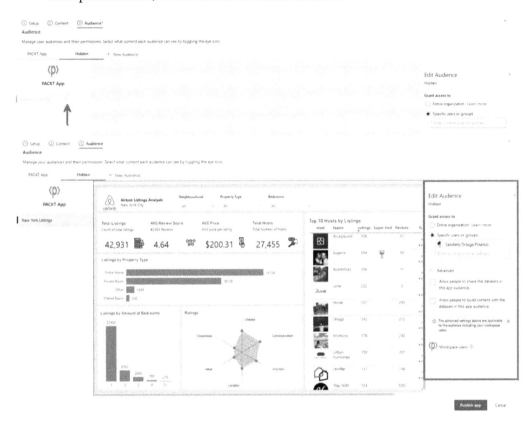

Figure 10.21: Comparing audiences' elements visibility

6. In each of these audiences, you can add the groups or individuals who will be part of them. You can do this from the **Edit Audience** section on the right in *Figure 10.21*. Once you've finished this last part, click **Publish app**.

> **Note**
>
> Hiding content from the audience makes it unavailable in the published app for that audience.
>
> Dashboard tiles pointing at reports that are hidden from the audience will no longer work. Instead, they will display an error: **The report shown in this tile doesn't exist, or you don't have permission to view it.**
>
> Paginated reports with subreports won't display the content of the subreport if it's hidden from the audience.
>
> Users of drill-through reports can't navigate to the destination reports if the destination reports are hidden.
>
> Also, keep in mind that If you want to modify the app to add or remove any report, you can do so by going to the workspace and clicking on the **Update app** button that appears in the top menu.

Upon completion, you will have a link that you can share with collaborators. However, users can also install these apps by going to **Apps | Get apps | Organizational apps**:

Figure 10.22: The Apps menu

In this section, we covered everything related to the creation of Power BI apps. Now, that you know how these are created, how about we explore how to use those created by others?

Using third-party apps

In addition to creating apps for organizational use, Power BI also offers third-party templates that you can add to your list of applications. These templates are public and are typically based on common data sources such as Google Analytics, YouTube, or Microsoft Dynamics.

To add a template app, go to the **Apps** menu, then **Get Apps**. This will open a window that shows three tabs: **All apps**, **Organizational apps**, and **Template apps**. If you know a specific app, you can search for it from the search panel on the right, as shown in *Figure 10.22*:

Figure 10.23: The Get Apps menu

Once the app you are looking for appears, click on it. In the next window, you will see more information about the application, such as its rating, developer, and several screenshots. In *Figure 10.23*, the **Microsoft Sample - Sales & Marketing** app is shown; it is an app with fictional data created by Microsoft for testing purposes. Click on **Get it Now**, then **Install**:

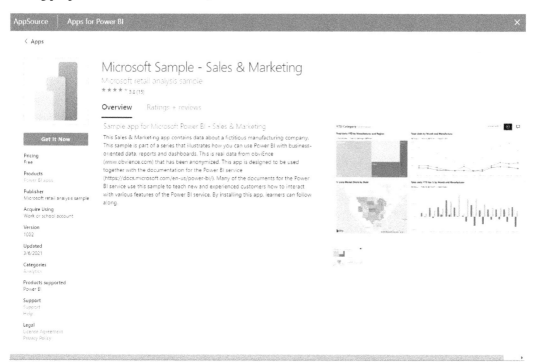

Figure 10.24: Third-party app details

The installation may take a few seconds, but once installed, it should appear in the list of apps. To use it, simply click on it.

When installing this type of app, a new workspace with the same name as the app is also added. Inside, you will find the dataset and the report or reports that feed the app:

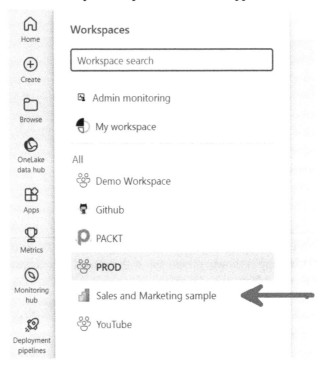

Figure 10.25: App name appearing in the workspace elements list

Power BI apps are now the most efficient way to share content with users. Keep in mind that content dissemination is a crucial phase within data analysis, where users engage and interact. Demonstrating your ability to use Power BI apps to distribute information can be a significant advantage and will make you stand out as a valuable and competent candidate.

Implementing RLS

Companies will always ensure that the right users have the right access. In the previous section, you saw the potential use of audiences as part of apps to restrict or allow the visibility of certain elements. However, even if you allow a user to view a particular report, there are situations where you need to limit the visibility of specific data within the model. In Power BI, this is called RLS.

RLS restricts data in the model based on certain defined rules. In other words, multiple users accessing the same report can see different data.

For example, let's consider a scenario where you want to analyze data from Airbnb properties in New York City. Your team is made up of four people, and the properties have been distributed among them based on neighborhoods. You have only one report, and you don't want to create separate reports for each group of properties. The goal is to use the same report and apply restrictions to each team member. This is because if you don't apply RLS, everyone can see each other's data, which is not the purpose of the analysis. By managing security in this way, each user can access the same report but only see the data they can view. See *Figure 10.25* for reference:

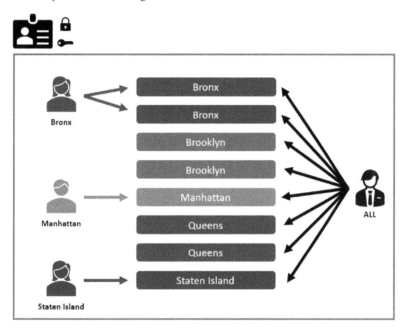

Figure 10.26: RLS diagram

Ensuring precise data access is vital, and Power BI's RLS is the key. With defined rules, RLS tailors data visibility, allowing users to access the same report while only seeing data relevant to them.

Now, let's move on to the next section, where you'll start creating roles to refine access control to users.

Creating a role

To apply RLS, you must first define the roles and then assign the users who will belong to them. These roles are defined in Power BI Desktop. Follow these steps:

1. Go to the **Modeling** menu and then click on **Manage roles**:

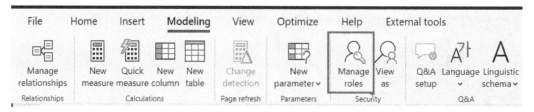

Figure 10.27: Manage roles

This will open a window with three sections – Roles, Select tables, and Filter data:

Figure 10.28: Roles, Select tables, and Filter data

2. In the first section, you create the role. Click on **New**; give it a name by clicking on the three dots and then **Rename**:

Figure 10.29: The Roles section

3. Once the role has been created, in the **Select Tables** section, all the tables available in your model will be displayed. Click on the table that contains the column that will be part of your condition and, in the **Filter data** section, create the rule, as shown in *Figure 10.29*:

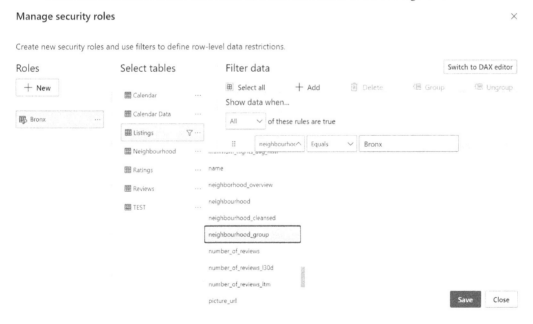

Figure 10.30: Creating a new role

As shown in *Figure 10.29*, we are creating a role called **Bronx**. The Listings table is selected because the **neighbourhood_group** column is being used as part of the rule. In the **Filter data** section, the rule is created, indicating that the value of the column must be equal to **Bronx**.

If you want to make this rule a bit more complex, you can click on **Switch to DAX editor** at the top-left corner. There, you can create your rules using DAX. Based on the previous example, if you click on that button, the formula that's created behind it would be as follows:

```
[neighbourhood_group] == "Bronx"
```

Once you have created your rules, click on **Save**. Then, from the **Modeling** menu, you can click on **View as** to test how users will see the report.

Adding users to a role

Now that you have defined your roles and verified that they are working as expected, it's time to assign the users who will be part of them. To do this, make sure you have published the changes to the workspace where the report is located:

1. Click on the **More Options** menu (the three dots on the right), then **Security**:

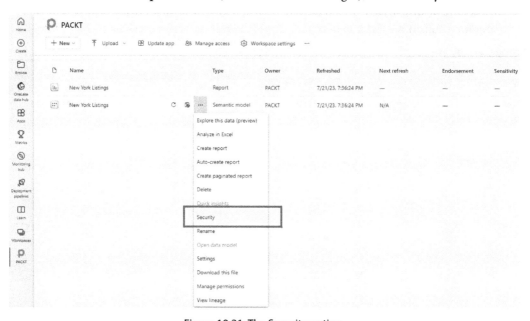

Figure 10.31: The Security option

2. This will open a window that contains the roles you created previously. Select the role and, in the right-hand field, add the users or user groups that will be part of the role:

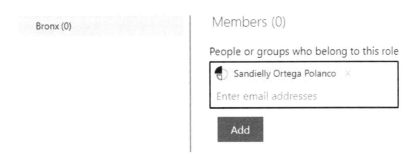

Figure 10.32: Members added to the RLS role

3. If you want to test the role from here, you can click on the **More Options** menu to the right of the role's name and select **Test As role**:

Figure 10.33: Test as role

4. Once you have confirmed that it is working correctly, click on **Save**. Now, users will be restricted based on the roles assigned to them.

In *Figure 10.31*, you can see that the **Neighbourhood** filter only allows you to filter for **Bronx**, and the data displayed in the report is only for that neighborhood:

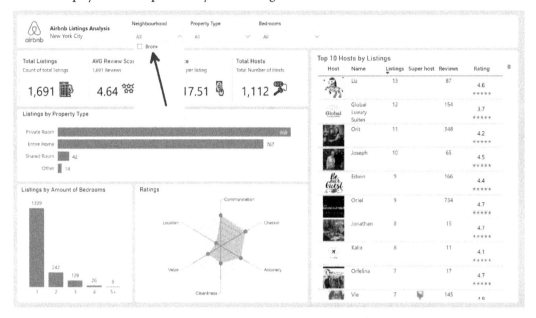

Figure 10.34: Power BI report viewed as a specific role

> **Note**
>
> RLS only restricts data access for users with Viewer permissions. It doesn't apply to Admins, Members, or Contributors.

The previous method we used for creating RLS is called static RLS as we have to manually input the neighborhood where the properties are located. However, there is another approach known as dynamic RLS, which provides a bit more flexibility. The following screenshot shows a straightforward example of how this type of security works:

host_id	Name	Email
501064484	Sandielly	sortega@dobletech.com
3223938	Demo	demo@dobletech.com

Figure 10.35: Sample table with two hosts

Figure 10.34 shows a sample table I have created called Users; this table has three columns: one for the host ID, another for the host's name, and the third for their email address. I imported this table into the model and established a relationship between the host_id column in the Users table and the host_id column in the table that stores the properties, which, in our case, is named listings:

Figure 10.36: The relationship between the Listings table and the Users table

Now, what I will do is create a measure that I will use as a label to identify which user is currently logged into the report. For this, I will use the USERPRINCIPALNAME function. This function takes no parameters, and the value it returns is the user who has logged into the report in the format of user@company.com. The measure that was created looks like this:

```
User Logged = "User Logged In: " & USERPRINCIPALNAME()
```

After creating the measure, I will place it in the top-right corner, as shown in *Figure 10.36*:

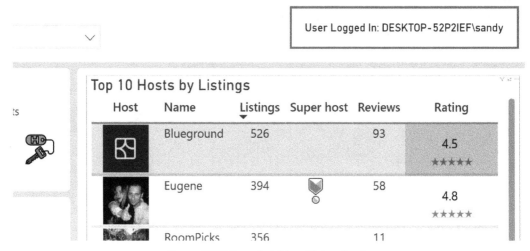

Figure 10.37: Sample table with two hosts

> **Note**
>
> Notice that the user that's returned by this measure is in the format of server\user. This is because the function is running locally on my computer, and that is the local user I am using. Once we publish the report to the Power BI service, the user should be in the correct format.

Now, what we will do is create the role in the same way we did when I showed you RLS. However, in this case, we will use the User table, and the condition will be that the email column is equal to the USERPRINCIPALNAME function, as shown in *Figure 10.37*:

Figure 10.38: Creating a role using USERPRINCIPALNAME

Once you've done this, save the changes and publish the report to a workspace. Remember that for RLS to function, you must follow the steps you saw in the *Adding user to a role* section. Additionally, ensure that members of the workspace where the report is located have "Viewer" permissions as RLS only applies to this type of permission. In other words, as the owner of the report or with "Admins," "Members," or "Contributors" permissions, I won't see any difference when opening the report in the Power BI service. However, if you log in with "Viewer" permissions, you will see the applied changes. In *Figure 10.38*, you can see that I logged in with demo@dobletech.com, and only the data related to that account is displayed:

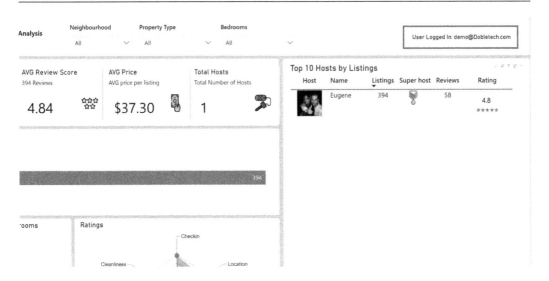

Figure 10.39: A report using dynamic RLS

Another thing to consider is that the email list you add to your user table must match the account the user uses to log into Power BI.

Security plays a crucial role in the process of distributing reports within companies. In this section, you gained insights into how to enhance the security of your reports by implementing RLS. Two main approaches to applying this security were explored. The first involves a static application, where you establish predefined and fixed security criteria. In contrast, the second method is more dynamic, allowing you to adjust security conditions based on the user viewing the report.

Q&A

The distribution of reports and dashboards is an important part of the data analyst role. Your report may be well-crafted, but if you don't know how to share it with your coworkers, or worse yet, if you share it with the wrong coworkers, the work is incomplete or simply poorly done. Therefore, it's important that you prepare to be bombarded with questions related to the security and distribution of reports and dashboards in Power BI.

Below are some of the possible questions surrounding these topics:

Question 1: If Power BI reports already exist, in what situations are Power BI Dashboards used?

Answer: Power BI reports allow for detailed analysis of information, enabling you to slice and dice data within the report itself. However, dashboards display aggregated metric information that needs constant monitoring for the business. These can contain data from one or multiple sources, making them ideal for visualizing metrics that change constantly, such as IoT sensors.

Question 2: A department requests that all its reports be in one place to facilitate analysis among reports and to make access for new employees more efficient. What solution do you propose for this situation?

Answer: The best option to meet this requirement is to create a Power BI app, as its capability to have all reports in one place, accessible from an intuitive side menu for the user, makes it ideal for this need.

Question 3: What does the USERPRINCIPALNAME function return?

Answer: This function is commonly used when applying dynamic row-level security. It returns the principal name of the user who logged into the report in the format user@domain.com.

Question 4: What is the difference between static and dynamic row-level security?

Answer: Basically, when using static row-level security, the condition or filter created within the role is hardcoded. For instance, it could be a fixed condition like "Country = 'Dominican Republic'", and users manually added to this role will be restricted to this fixed filter. On the other hand, with the dynamic approach, there's a list of users accessing the report, the users may come from an individual table or from a column in a table already part of the model. This allows for the use of functions like USERPRINCIPALNAME to validate who is viewing the report and create more complex conditions for each user. Security strictly depends on who has logged in, making it more secure.

Question 5: Recently, row-level security was implemented in a report showing salespeople of a company. One of them reported that he cannot see his sales information and that the report displays an error stating: "You can't see the content of this report because you don't have permissions to the underlying dataset. The underlying dataset uses row-level security (RLS). Contact the dataset owner." What do you think might be the possible causes of this situation?

Answer: One possible cause of this incident could be that after the report was published, the administrator did not add the specific user to the Azure AD group designated for this purpose, or directly in the security section of the semantic model. They should also ensure that if they are adding the user outside of an Azure AD group, they have the viewer role.

Summary

In this chapter, you learned about dashboards, how to create them, their purpose, and how to add content to them. You also gained a solid understanding of the differences between dashboards and reports in Power BI.

As dashboards are created of pins, you also learned about the different types of pins and how to add them to a dashboard.

Then, you saw the benefits of using Power BI apps to share your reports and highlighted some key differences between workspaces. Lastly, I showed you what RLS is and how to use it so that multiple users can see different filtered data in the same report based on roles.

In the next chapter, we will move away from the technical aspects and delve into the world of HR. Here, you will gain insights into how to prepare for the job interview process.

Part 3:
The Final Stretch – Preparing for the HR Round and Beyond

In the third and final part, we will explore the final stretch in the journey of an aspiring Power BI developer. This part of the book looks into the intricacies of the HR interview process, offering a comprehensive understanding of what to expect and how to prepare for success. Practical tips and strategies are shared to help applicants prepare for the HR interview process and clear it successfully. Then, we will discuss something often overlooked by job seekers: negotiating salary and benefits. Through real-life scenarios and expert advice, you will learn how to approach salary discussions with confidence and poise. Lastly, we will share tips and tricks on transitioning from receiving an offer to becoming a part of the organization. We will highlight the importance of evaluating job offers holistically, taking into account not just the financial aspects but also the cultural fit and long-term career growth opportunities. We will also touch upon the onboarding process and the key steps new hires can take to ensure a smooth and successful integration into their new roles.

This part has the following chapters:

- *Chapter 11, Understanding the HR Interview Process and Preparing for Success*
- *Chapter 12, Tips for Negotiating Salary and Benefits*
- *Chapter 13, Best Practices for Accepting and Rejecting Job Offers – Onboarding and Beyond*

11

Understanding the HR Interview Process and Preparing for Success

Most aspiring data analysts find their thoughts shrouded in anticipation and self-doubt when it comes to the enigmatic **human resources** (**HR**) rounds. By reading the preceding chapters, you have equipped yourself with the power of Power BI and have started to convert raw information into strategic insights. Now, it is time to claim your place in the arena. But how do you prepare for the unpredictable HR rounds? This is the question that haunts a lot of data analytics newcomers.

Understanding and preparing for the HR rounds is important for an aspiring Power BI data analyst and developer. It may seem daunting initially, yet beneath the perceived complexity lies a method and pattern that can be learned, understood, and mastered. This chapter will help you understand this process and help you start preparing – not just to partake but to excel in the HR rounds.

In this chapter, we will cover the following main topics:

- Overview of the HR rounds
- Key skills to highlight during the HR rounds
- Preparation strategies for success in the HR rounds

By the end of this chapter, you will have learned about the different components of the HR rounds, the questions posed during these rounds, and practical ways for effective preparation. You will have also understood how to showcase effective communication, professionalism, and confidence during the process. Finally, you will have learned how to acquire the knowledge and skills necessary to navigate the HR rounds with poise and efficiency and embark on a journey of learning and excellence in your dream job.

Overview of the HR rounds

The HR rounds are the final stage in the recruitment process and start with navigating the job searching process. Finally, after weeks and months of building networks, browsing hundreds of job postings, and sharing resumes and cover letters, you have been shortlisted for appearing in the HR rounds. This often evokes a lot of excitement, nervousness, and trepidation among candidates. In this decisive round, your skills, values, character, and cultural fit for the company are tested through various assessments. These days, the HR rounds are a multi-step process, which allows the organization to assess you thoroughly and understand who you are beyond your resume. It also allows you to assess your strengths and weaknesses and align your career aspirations with the organization's trajectory.

This section provides a comprehensive overview of the HR rounds, knowing their purpose and intricacies, and thus preparing you to navigate these confidently. Remember that the HR rounds are not a test, but a journey – a journey about you and your potential. Therefore, you must prepare well for this journey to become a perfect "fit" for the organization.

Decoding the purpose of the HR rounds

When we start to decode the purpose of the HR rounds, we encounter a multi-faceted process. At first glance, it seems to be the organization's way of assessing your suitability for a Power BI data analytics or developer role. However, upon closer examination, we find it is a process of evaluating the candidate, informing the candidate, and then making an offer to the candidate if he or she makes the cut.

These days, the process of evaluating a candidate is far more detailed and goes beyond the scrutiny of your technical skills or qualifications. It involves understanding your behavioral tendencies and values, and how these align with the company's culture. The HR rounds explore how you might react under stress, how you navigate challenges, and how you build relationships in a team. The process is designed to assess your "fit" for the organization. Most organizations divide this process into three parts: the initial aptitude test, the Power BI developer technical assessment, and the HR interview.

Initial aptitude test

These days, companies get thousands of applications for a certain opening. It is impossible to take technical assessments and interviews of such many applicants. So, aptitude tests are a common first stage in the hiring process that's used by employers to shortlist and assess candidates based on their ability to perform specific or general tasks related to a job role. These tests cover a range of competencies generally related to assessing a candidate's numerical, verbal, and logical reasoning abilities, which act as a precursor to any job role. The shortlisted candidates are then required to appear in the technical assessment and, subsequently, the HR interview.

These aptitude tests aim to assess a candidate's problem-solving skills, presence of mind, and speed of thought. These are usually multiple-choice tests that are administered under timed conditions, either paper-based or in some scenarios administered on a computer.

Types of questions asked in aptitude tests

Aptitude tests normally have three to five different types of questions in a multiple-choice format. Some of the most common types of questions belong to these categories:

- Numerical reasoning
- Verbal reasoning
- Logical or abstract reasoning
- Problem-solving
- Data interpretation

Let's take a look at each category in detail.

Numerical reasoning

These questions assess a candidate's ability to handle numerical data, make calculations, and interpret figures such as graphs and tables. A candidate might be asked to perform basic arithmetic operations, calculate percentages or ratios, or interpret data in graphs and charts.

Here is an example question related to numerical reasoning that a candidate can encounter on the aptitude test:

A store is offering a 20% discount on a shirt originally priced at $50. After the discount, a 10% sales tax is added to the price. What is the final price of the shirt?

A. $44

B. $48

C. $52

D. $56

Verbal reasoning

Verbal reasoning questions aim to evaluate the understanding and comprehension of the written information of a candidate. This could involve reading a passage of text and answering questions about it, identifying synonyms or antonyms, completing sentences, or spotting common spelling and grammatical errors.

Here is an example question on verbal reasoning that a candidate can encounter on the aptitude test:

Read the statement and choose the correct answer: "All elephants are mammals. Some mammals are carnivorous. Therefore, some elephants are carnivorous."

A. *The statement is logical and correct*

B. *The statement is logical but incorrect*

C. *The statement is illogical and incorrect*

D. *The statement is illogical but correct*

Logical/abstract reasoning

These questions test the ability of a candidate to identify patterns, logical rules, or sequences in sets of shapes or symbols. This information is then applied to solve a given problem. These questions might also require a candidate to think creatively and flexibly, outside the bounds of traditional numeric and verbal skills.

Here is an example question on logical/abstract reasoning that a candidate can encounter on the aptitude test:

Which number comes next in the sequence?

2, 3, 5, 8, 12, ____

A. *15*

B. *16*

C. *17*

D. *18*

Problem-solving

These questions are designed to assess the critical thinking and problem-solving skills of a candidate. These questions could include puzzles, scenarios, or situations where a candidate needs to apply logical thinking to arrive at a solution.

Here is an example of a problem-solving-related question that a candidate can encounter on the aptitude test:

If three ovens can bake three cakes in 3 hours, how many cakes can 10 ovens cook in 6 hours? What is the value of X here?

A. *10 cakes*

B. *20 cakes*

C. 30 cakes

D. 5 cakes

Data interpretation

These questions evaluate a candidate's ability to interpret, analyze, and draw conclusions from given data. This could involve interpreting data presented in tables, charts, or diagrams, and answering questions related to the data.

Let's look at a few examples of data interpretation-related questions that a candidate can encounter on the aptitude test.

Consider a bar graph showing the sales of a company in thousands from 2016 to 2020 with the following data: 2016 - 50, 2017 - 60, 2018 - 75, 2019 - 80, 2020 - 90:

- *In which year did the company see the highest increase in sales from the previous year?*

  A. 2017

  B. 2018

  C. 2019

  D. 2020

- *What was the total sales of the company from 2016 to 2020?*

  A. 250,000

  B. 275,000

  C. 360,000

  D. 500,000

For a Power BI developer or data analyst role, expect to solve this aptitude test in 60 minutes. There are normally 60 to 80 questions on the aptitude test, so the average time to solve a question is between 50 to 60 seconds. Some questions are very simple and can be solved in under 10 seconds, while others might take around 60 to 80 seconds to solve.

Power BI developer technical assessment

The technical assessment part is the core of the hiring process or the HR rounds. This technical assessment evaluates a candidate's technical proficiency with Power BI. In the previous chapters, we covered all the core concepts of Power BI development and some of the support skills, such as writing SQL, that a candidate needs to master to get a role in Power BI development. Now is the time to put all of that learning into practice and prepare for the most crucial part of the hiring process.

Normally, the assessment is designed as a two-step process, but different companies can tailor this process as per their procedures. The first step is to assess the candidate using a hands-on Power BI case study. The second step is the verbal round where common questions related to core areas of Power BI development are asked from the candidate. This part could also include a discussion about the case study, including some of the work you did in solving that.

In short, the exact pattern of the technical assessment can vary and differ between companies, but the underlying objective is to accurately gauge a candidate's hands-on skills and knowledge about the tool.

Hands-on case study-based assessment

It is essential to have practical expertise to work with Power BI as it is a business intelligence tool. Although theoretical knowledge of data analytics concepts is important, the focus these days is mastering hands-on development using that theoretical knowledge. Using the same logic, companies are increasingly leaning toward hands-on case study-based assessments to ascertain a candidate's technical skills realistically and practically.

Normally, these assessments are timed and involve providing the candidate with a dataset and a set of business questions. The candidate must then use Power BI to analyze the data using DAX, draw insights, and present these insights through a dashboard or a set of reports. A candidate can be given anything from 2 to 4 hours to develop a solution and present it to the technical team.

In some situations, a case study, along with the dataset, can also be emailed to the candidate and he or she is asked to develop a solution in Power BI using all the online resources, just like in real-life scenarios, and given 24 hours or more to report back. In short, the objective is to keep this assessment closer to the real-life development environment where Power BI developers consult online documentation and other resources to complete the assessment.

Power BI developers are normally expected to have some business or domain knowledge of the company they are applying to. For example, suppose the candidate is applying for a role in a financial company. In that case, he or she is expected to understand the core terminologies and business metrics associated with the working of a financial company. This applies to other sectors, such as **fast-moving consumer goods** (**FMCG**), retail, health care, logistics, and others. In most cases, the case study is directly related to a business problem related to that particular company, and a dataset is usually provided from a real-life business scenario, but this is not a mandatory requirement, and a generic case study can also be provided.

Let's look at examples from common sectors – retail, finance, FMCG, and logistics. The associated dataset has been provided in the online repository for this chapter.

Retail case study

A multinational retail chain is seeking to better understand its customers' shopping habits and optimize its store operations. They have tables for sales transaction data, customer demographic information, and inventory data for the past 2 years.

Here's a list of business questions:

- *What are the peak shopping hours and days across different store locations?*
- *Which products are frequently bought together? Can we use this information for cross-selling?*
- *How do sales trends vary by demographic factors such as age, gender, and location?*
- *Which stores have the highest and lowest sales performance? Can we identify the factors contributing to this variation?*
- *How does our inventory turnover rate compare across different categories of products?*
- *What is the impact of holidays and seasons on sales performance?*
- *How does the rate of return purchases vary across different customer segments and product categories?*

FMCG case study

An FMCG company wants to improve its supply chain efficiency and marketing strategy. They have data on production, sales, distribution, marketing campaigns, and customer feedback in tables.

Here's a list of business questions:

- *What is the correlation between marketing campaigns and sales for different product lines?*
- *Which distribution channels have the most efficient delivery times and why?*
- *How do production rates vary across different manufacturing facilities, and what factors influence these variations?*
- *Which products receive the most positive and negative customer feedback, and why?*
- *What is the effect of price changes on the sales of various products?*
- *How does consumer demand for our products change seasonally or during certain events?*
- *What are the most common reasons for product returns, and how can these be minimized?*

Finance case study

A multinational bank is looking to understand the behavior of their customers to tailor their products better and mitigate risks. They have shared tables with data on customer profiles, transaction history, loan applications, and risk assessments.

Here's a list of business questions:

- *What factors most significantly affect a customer's credit risk rating?*
- *What are the most common reasons for loan defaults?*

- *How does customer banking behavior (for example, frequency of transactions, types of transactions, and so on) vary across different demographic groups?*
- *What patterns can be identified in fraudulent transaction data?*
- *How do various economic indicators (for example, interest rates, inflation, and so on) affect the bank's lending activities?*
- *How effective are different marketing campaigns in acquiring new customers or cross-selling services?*
- *What customer behaviors or activities indicate an intention to close an account?*

Logistics case study

A global logistics company wants to enhance its delivery operations and customer satisfaction levels. They have shared tables with data on shipment details, tracking information, customer complaints, and feedback. There are issues with data consistency in the tracking information.

Here's a list of business questions:

- *What are the most common reasons for shipment delays, and how can these be mitigated?*
- *How does delivery efficiency vary across different transportation modes (air, sea, road, and so on)?*
- *Are there patterns in the locations that frequently experience delivery issues?*
- *How do customer satisfaction levels correlate with factors such as delivery speed, shipment safety, and communication quality?*
- *What impact do weather conditions or seasonal factors have on delivery timelines?*
- *How do fuel price changes affect the company's operational costs?*
- *What are the trends in the volume and type of goods being transported, and how can this information help in capacity planning?*

It is important to remember that the main purpose of this technical assessment is to gauge the hands-on Power BI skills of the candidate and how data-driven decisions are drawn from the dataset. In the next section, we will briefly discuss a strategy to develop an end-to-end analytics report that covers the best practices for all areas of development.

Verbal round

As part of the technical assessment, the hands-on development case study is usually followed by a shorter verbal round, which focuses on asking questions related to some of the development steps, important scenarios a developer can encounter during development, and best practices in Power BI development. Sometimes, this verbal round can also include questions on your work for the hands-on case study. These could include questions about steps performed for data cleaning and transformation in Power Query, DAX calculations, choice of visuals in the report, and data storytelling.

Breakdown of the HR interview

The last stage of the HR round is the HR interview, which is where the dream destination is in sight. However, this is often the stage in the hiring process since it's where the candidates enter with fear and anxiety. It is important to understand the common components of the HR interview to prepare yourself accordingly. The structure and theme of the HR interview are usually common and typical across most organizations, so this round has the least number of unknowns attached to it. Yet, most of the candidates find this round to be the biggest hurdle for many reasons. Let's take a look at the common components of this part one by one.

The introduction

If you successfully navigated the technical assessment part, you will be asked to appear for the HR interview. There could be one or more persons from the HR department who conduct this interview. The first question is normally the icebreaker, and you would often be asked, "Tell us about yourself" or "Kindly introduce yourself." This is not some kind of informal chit-chat, but an opportunity for the interviewers to gauge your communication skills and observe how you structure and present your narrative. The best way to respond is to provide a concise overview of your academic background, work experience, key skills, and career aspirations. Do not be too brief and do not take too much time narrating each and everything about yourself. There could be a brief discussion about a specific part of your introduction as the interviewer would have your CV or resume, so some of this discussion could be about your educational qualification, a particular work experience, a specific skill you mentioned on your resume or even something about your hobbies or interests. Your introduction will set the tone for the rest of the conversation, so remember to focus on elements most relevant to the role you are applying for, your experience, and skills that directly fit in with the job role you have applied for.

Behavioral assessment

Next comes the behavioral assessment part, where the interviewer will ask questions that are designed to understand your behavior in various situations. The goal is to assess your response in a challenging scenario or test your response under stress. You may be asked to share an experience where you made a mistake at work and how you handled it or how you have dealt with a difficult team member in the past. A typical question could be "*Tell me about a time when you had to handle a difficult team member.*" Your response should just focus on the situation that has been presented and you should highlight the action that you took and the result of those actions. Giving irrelevant details about any past event or explaining the team member's personality traits is viewed negatively by the interviewers. The answer should be crisp and focused on your problem-solving abilities, decision-making process, and the lessons you learned during this experience. The interviewer may ask specific questions about how to handle business communication, your views about senior leadership, your interaction with junior team members, and so on. The goal here is not just for you to tell your story but to help the interviewer understand your approach to handling day-to-day matters, your capacity to learn from your experiences, your interpersonal skills, and your approach to problem-solving. A hypothetical situation could be presented by the interviewer, such as "*You missed a very important project deadline and have been asked to clear your position about it – how will you respond in such a situation?"* Remember to just focus on the question being asked and give a response based on actions that you will take and the result of those actions. Interviewers give negative weightage to any irrelevant detail that you include in your answer, so including those serves no purpose at all.

Values alignment

The next set of questions is about values alignment, where your compatibility with the core values and culture of the company is assessed. You may be asked questions to explain what an ideal work environment looks like, how you define success at work, or what your views about work-life balance are. A very typical question is *"What values are most important to you in a work environment?"* Your answer should focus on the research that you did about the company before the interview. Try to incorporate words that resonate with the vision of the company as this provides you with the opportunity to demonstrate your alignment with the company's culture and values. You may be asked questions about certain preferences related to work timings, social life, your short-term and long-term career goals, and more. For example, you could be asked *"What are your thoughts on diversity and inclusion in the workplace?"* Again, this question is related to core values in the workplace. Your response should focus on the advantages of people coming together from different backgrounds and how it improves decision-making and increases innovation. You should sound respectful and open-minded in collaborating with people to create a positive work environment. Your responses help the interviewer evaluate your potential fit within the organization. The interviewer evaluates your responses to get an idea about your career aspirations and whether you are joining the company for a short ride or would be there for the long haul.

Role-specific questions

After the behavioral assessment, where the interviewer checks your alignment with the company's culture and values, they ask role-specific questions, where your understanding is gauged about the job role that you applied for. A typical question that you may be asked is, *"What makes you a good fit for this role?"* This question requires you to do some background research on the role that you are applying to. A good response should start with an emphasis on these core skills and your personal experience, understanding, and success using some of these skills. Next, you should highlight how you keep yourself up-to-date on the latest developments and then working as a team player how you are willing to go the extra mile to solve problems and become an asset for the team and company. Another typical question is, *"Where do you see yourself in 5 years?"* This question is designed to assess your career goals and ambitions while working in the job role that you have applied for. A good answer should start by focusing on the short-term goals of 1 to 2 years and then talk about long-term goals based on making significant contributions, learning new skills, taking more responsibility, and getting a promotion. Do not sound overly ambitious, confused, or pessimistic while you narrate your answer. This part can also come immediately after the introduction segment, but this is your opportunity to show how your skills and experiences align with the job requirements.

Compensation discussion

The last part of the interview is typically about the compensation discussion, where practical aspects of the job offer, such as salary, benefits, and start dates, are typically discussed. The interviewer gauges your seriousness about the role and your expectations and potentially negotiates terms. This may be preceded by an opportunity where you get to ask questions inquiring about the company's culture, team structure, or role expectations. If you get this chance, then ask these questions as this demonstrates your interest and preparedness.

The important point to remember about the HR interview is that each company and each interviewer may have their unique style and they might focus on different things. The general theme of the HR interview is the same as what has been explained here. Remember, the HR interview is a conversation that brings you closer to the organization and helps you understand its people, its culture, and its values.

Key skills to highlight during the HR rounds

As you are aspiring to become a Power BI developer or data analyst, most of your time is spent learning skills relevant to the world of data analysis. For a Power BI developer or analyst role, technical expertise is of the essence, but as we saw in the previous section, once you step into the HR rounds, it is the soft skills that cannot be undervalued and are equally important. Beyond the numbers, data, algorithms, and insights, you have to become part of a team, and interpersonal abilities that ensure harmony and efficiency play a pivotal role.

This section highlights those key skills you should showcase during the various steps of the HR rounds. It is not merely about knowing that you have them but about polishing and demonstrating these skills. This includes mastering the technical aspects of Power BI development, communication skills, problem-solving, adaptability, teamwork, and emotional intelligence. This also encompasses skills more specific to a data analyst role, such as attention to detail, critical thinking, and simplifying complex information.

Remember, the aim in the HR rounds is to successfully illustrate that you are not just capable of doing the job, but that you are someone who would be an asset to the team and will contribute positively to the workplace environment. So, let's unpack some of the essential skills to showcase in the various phases of the HR rounds.

Technical skills

In the preceding chapters, we talked about the core areas of Power BI development and explained various aspects that a developer needs to master. However, we need to focus on the important topics for the technical assessment part of the HR round. Not all aspects of Power BI development have the same complexity; at times, certain aspects require more time to master. Developers spend months and years excelling in some areas, while others can be mastered in a few days or weeks.

We can break down Power BI topics into beginner, intermediate, and advanced-level sections. Most entry-level Power BI positions require basic and intermediate-level knowledge, but some of the advanced-level questions could also be asked to understand the competence of a candidate:

- *Beginner*:

  - Connectivity with data sources

  - Import versus DirectQuery versus Live Connection modes

  - Import versus DirectQuery versus dual table storage modes

  - Common errors faced in Power Query

  - Data source credentials and privacy options

  - Resolving inconsistencies and data quality issues

  - Options for data profiling in Power Query

  - Important transformations, such as merge, append, split, extract, and so on, for columns and tables in Power Query

  - Configuration options for loading queries in Power BI

  - The difference between using Reference versus Duplicate in Power Query and their implication

  - OLTP versus OLAP

  - Star schema and dimension and fact tables

  - Relationships between tables and their types

  - Calculated columns and measures in DAX

  - The difference between implicit and explicit measures

  - The difference between aggregator and iterator functions in DAX

  - Filter context versus row context in DAX

  - Mathematical and statistical functions in DAX

  - The CALCULATE function in DAX and its usage

  - Calculated tables versus virtual tables

  - Configuring and formatting different native visuals in Power BI

  - Applying filters and slicers in Power BI

  - Configuring report pages in Power BI

  - Creating hierarchies for visuals in Power BI

- Using drill-up and drill-down for visuals
- Creating custom tooltips in Power BI
- Applying sorting and interaction between visuals in Power BI
- Power BI licensing options

- *Intermediate*:

  - Parameters in Power Query and their usage
  - Resolving errors in Power Query
  - Selecting appropriate data types for columns in Power Query
  - The difference between a shared dataset and a local dataset
  - Best practices for data transformation and loading
  - Pivot versus unpivot versus transpose in Power Query
  - Custom functions in Power Query
  - Important functions in M
  - Cardinality and cross-filter direction in Power BI
  - Role-playing dimensions
  - Implications of defining many-to-many relationships in Power BI
  - Best practices for data model design in Power BI
  - Implementation of **row-level security** (**RLS**) in Power BI
  - Context transition in DAX
  - Active versus inactive relationships and how to resolve these using DAX functions
  - Relationship functions in DAX
  - Table functions in DAX
  - Time intelligence functions in DAX
  - Semi-additive measures
  - Best practices for DAX programming in Power BI
  - Configuring themes in Power BI
  - Conditional formatting in Power BI
  - Configuring drill-through in Power BI

- Grouping, binning, clustering, and layering options in Power BI
- Configuring buttons, images, and other canvas elements in Power BI
- Report navigation options in Power BI
- Configuring and using bookmarks in Power BI
- Using custom visuals in Power BI
- Using AI visuals in Power BI
- Detecting outliers and anomalies in Power BI
- Using error bars, reference lines, and forecasting options in Power BI
- Publishing reports in Power BI Service
- Different types of data refreshes available in Power BI
- Configuring Power BI workspaces and workspace roles
- Setting up a Power BI data gateway
- Reports versus dashboards versus workspace apps
- Distribution methods in Power BI Service
- Applying sensitivity labels to workspace content
- Promote or certify Power BI content
- Configuring subscriptions and data alerts in Power BI Service

- *Advanced*:

  - Understanding query folding and its implications
  - Composite models
  - Hybrid tables
  - Managing aggregations
  - Calculation groups
  - Using the Analyze in Excel feature in Power BI
  - Configuring and developing paginated reports in Power BI
  - Create and share scorecards and metrics
  - Accessibility options in Power BI
  - Configuring scheduled refresh in Power BI Service
  - Implementing incremental refresh in Power BI reports

- Setting up and configuring a deployment pipeline in Power BI Service

- Dataflows versus datamarts in Power BI Service

- Power BI external tools such as DAX Studio and Editor and their usage

With the knowledge of technical skills under our belt, let's move on to critical thinking and problem-solving skills.

Critical thinking and problem-solving skills

Beyond the raw technical skills, a data analyst needs to possess strong critical thinking abilities and problem-solving skills. Critical thinking involves looking at data objectively, questioning assumptions, making logical connections, and identifying patterns or trends. Problem-solving involves identifying challenges and opportunities and determining the best course of action using data.

You will be required to showcase both critical thinking and problem-solving at various stages of the HR rounds. Demonstrating these abilities shows that you do not just process data but also understand and interpret it, providing valuable inputs for strategic decision-making and developing solutions that have an impact on the way business works.

Communication skills and emotional intelligence

The last of the HR rounds is all about communication skills. Effective communication is the cornerstone of any successful interaction and the HR interview is no exception. In this context, it involves expressing your thoughts clearly, listening actively, and responding appropriately.

Having emotional intelligence is critical for workplace success. This skill involves understanding and managing our own emotions, as well as recognizing and influencing the emotions of others. In an HR interview, demonstrating emotional intelligence can set you apart, showing that you are not just proficient in your work, but also adept at managing relationships and contributing to a positive workplace culture.

Emotional intelligence covers the following aspects, all of which are important during an HR interview:

- *Self-awareness*: Self-awareness is the ability to recognize your emotions, understand their origin, and see their impact on your work and relationships. Demonstrating self-awareness in an HR interview can involve talking about your strengths and weaknesses, discussing how you handle stress or frustration, or explaining how you have worked to improve areas of weakness.

- *Motivation*: Motivated individuals display a strong drive to achieve optimism despite failure and commitment to their work and company. During an HR interview, discuss your goals, what drives you in your work, and how you have persevered through challenges to achieve a desired outcome.

- *Empathy*: The ability to understand and share the feelings of others, empathy is critical to building and managing effective work relationships. Demonstrate empathy in an HR interview by discussing times when you have helped a struggling colleague, adapted your communication style to accommodate other team members, and considered their perspectives when making decisions.

- *Social skills*: These encompass a wide range of skills, from clear communication and conflict management to leadership and teamwork. In an HR interview, you can demonstrate your social skills by sharing instances where you have worked in a team, led a project, resolved a conflict, or influenced a positive change in your previous work environment.

Now that we are aware of the key skills that we can highlight during the HR rounds, let's explore some preparation strategies to ensure success in the HR rounds.

Preparation strategies for success in the HR rounds

Conquering the HR rounds demands more than just a summary of your skills and experiences – it calls for strategic preparation to showcase your best version. Whether you are a seasoned professional or stepping into the HR rounds for the very first time, you need to prepare for the HR rounds thoroughly to approach them with confidence.

In this section, we aim to equip you with a comprehensive toolkit to navigate the crucial stages of the HR rounds. We've already discussed the major components of HR rounds and what skills you need to highlight in each. Now is the time to discuss preparation strategies for each of these components.

The aptitude test and the technical assessment part in the HR rounds are all about technical jargon. You don't need to worry much about soft skills here, but you need to be on top of your technical knowledge to clear these rounds. We've talked about the format and content of the aptitude test, case study-based technical assessment, and the verbal round. Now, let's talk about preparation strategies for all of these.

Preparation strategies for the aptitude test

Aptitude tests are not meant to measure a candidate's technical ability or knowledge as the focus is primarily to assess analytical, problem-solving, and decision-making capabilities. Most of the questions require knowledge of elementary school algebra and geometry concepts and focus on the ability to pick the key part of the question and solve it correctly in the minimum possible time. The biggest concern for most candidates is to keep their minds sharp, focused, and ready before such a test.

Aptitude tests are mainly designed for screening and shortlisting candidates, so make sure you are well-prepared for such tests. A callous attitude or overlooking the importance of these tests can result in a candidate being rusty and not performing to the desired standard. Therefore, every candidate must have a preparation strategy for such tests to perform well.

Some of the common strategies to achieve this objective include the following:

- Understanding the format
- Regular practice
- Reviewing basic concepts
- Time management
- Staying calm and focused

Let's look at each strategy in detail.

Understanding the format

Before a candidate starts preparing for the aptitude test, it is important to understand the format of the test, including the types of questions, the time limit, and whether negative marking applies. This helps devise an effective preparation strategy and manage time during the test.

Regular practice

Practicing regularly is the most important strategy to stay focused, sharp, and prepared for such tests. Regular practice is the key to succeeding in aptitude tests. A candidate can start by taking a few practice tests to identify strengths and weaknesses and then focus their preparation on improving the weaker areas. Another important aspect is to simulate the conditions of the actual test as closely as possible. This could include the mode of delivery (paper-based or computer-based), keeping the same duration and a similar pattern as per the actual test.

Reviewing basic concepts

A candidate must ensure they have a solid understanding of the basic concepts required for the test. For numerical questions, brushing up on your elementary school arithmetic, percentages, ratios, and data interpretation skills helps a lot. For verbal questions, a candidate can work on grammar, commonly used vocabulary, and reading comprehension skills. For logical reasoning questions, a candidate can practice identifying patterns and applying logical rules to solve given questions.

Time management

Aptitude tests are not only timed but also require a lot of time management. It is essential to develop a strategy to manage the time effectively. This could involve answering easier questions first, allocating a certain amount of time to each question, or skipping questions that a candidate is unsure about and returning to these later if the time allows. Another aspect of time management is to check if negative marking applies or not, as discussed earlier. If for some reason a candidate is unable to finish the test, the last couple of minutes can be used to answer the remaining questions through smart guesswork.

Staying calm and focused

It is very important to stay calm and focused during the test. A candidate needs to practice relaxation techniques such as deep breathing to maintain a positive mindset until the very last second. If a candidate comes across a difficult question, then it should not rattle their nerves and the best strategy should be to skip that question and move on to the next one. If a candidate stays calm and focused and their concentration levels are high until the end, then there is every chance that difficult questions on the exam can be handled very well.

Preparation strategies for the technical assessment

The technical assessment comprises the hands-on case study and the verbal round. This is the core part of the technical stuff and probably the most important portion of the HR rounds. This is the opportunity to show technical and creative processes in Power BI, which you have mastered over time. However, without a clear strategy and focus on the key elements of Power BI report development, you can easily get distracted and cannot produce your best performance.

The best strategy to prepare for the technical assessment is practice, practice, and practice. For the case study, try downloading free datasets from Kaggle, Maven Analytics Data Playground, and other similar websites. Use the strategies we highlight to build a compelling report for answering business questions. We have also compiled close to 100 questions for the verbal round in this section. Make sure you know the answers to all these questions and the important topics highlighted in the previous section.

Let's look at the preparation strategy for the case study part of the technical assessment.

Case study

The business question on the case study is your roadmap to success on the case study part. Based on the introduction and the business questions, understand all the requirements and constraints related to the given dataset. A deep comprehension of these will prevent you from wasting time on irrelevant aspects and help you align your analysis with the expectations. Before diving into the dataset, take a moment to define the core objective of your analysis for each business question. What problem are you trying to solve? What insights do you hope to uncover?

Try and stick to the core practices of data cleaning, transformation, and star schema data modeling. This is very important as this part shows that you are always following the best practices and your data model is most suitable for generating answers to business questions. If the data modeling part has been done right, then DAX programming is relatively simple. Make sure that the DAX code is formatted and well-commented so that the reader can easily understand the logic that you have tried to implement.

When it comes to data visualization, less is more. Focus on creating a select few high-impact visualizations that effectively convey your key findings. Choose the most appropriate chart types for the data and ensure each visualization has a clear purpose and supports your overall narrative. Remember, a clutter-free presentation allows absorb the insights effortlessly. Humans are natural storytellers, and your data visualizations should be no different. Craft a compelling narrative that ties your insights together coherently.

Verbal round

The verbal round is mostly a question-and-answer session on some of the core concepts of Power BI development. It is important that answers to the most common concepts in Power BI development are known and you can explain those precisely and concisely.

In this section, we'll share questions and their most suitable answers to help you prepare for the verbal round. We have divided these into beginner, intermediate, and advanced level categories, just like the important topics we highlighted in the previous section.

Beginner

Here are some questions and their most suitable answers for the beginner category.

Question 1: What is the difference between M and DAX?

Answer: M stands for Mash-up data, the scripting language used in Power Query for various data cleaning and transformation operations, whereas DAX stands for Data Analysis Expression. It is a library of functions and operators used to build formulas for data analysis purposes.

Question 2: What is the use of the Column Quality option in Power Query Editor?

Answer: Column Quality focuses on valid values, errors, and empty rows for a query's columns.

Question 3: What is the use of the Column Distribution option in Power Query Editor?

Answer: Column Distribution focuses on distinct values and unique values (which appear only once) for all the columns of a query.

Question 4: What is the use of the Column Profile option in Power Query Editor?

Answer: Column Profile returns the minimum, maximum, average, standard deviation, count, null count, and distinct count of a column.

Question 5: What are dimension tables?

Answer: In simple terms, dimension tables are master tables and include product master, supplier master, customer master, date table, and others. Dimension tables in Power BI serve as reference tables that provide descriptive attributes and context to the data model. These contain the key values that are used to establish relationships with fact tables in a data model. These also provide filtering and grouping capabilities, enabling users to slice and dice the data based on various dimensions.

Question 6: What is the purpose of the funnel chart visualization?

Answer: Funnel charts are used to show sequential flow between different stages of a process or workflow. These must not be used as a replacement for bar charts to show categorical data.

Question 7: What is the best use of ribbon charts?

Answer: Ribbon charts are useful in showing the change in ranking between categories over time. These, however, should not be used to show a large number of categories as the visual becomes difficult to understand.

Question 8: What is the purpose of a waterfall chart visual in Power BI?

Answer: Waterfall charts are excellent in visualizing changes over time or across different categories. Positive or negative change is best captured in these charts.

Question 9: What are the available options for configuring interaction between visuals in Power BI?

Answer: Filter, highlight, and no interaction are the options that are available while configuring interactions between visuals.

Question 10: What is the use of the Sort by Column option in Power BI?

Answer: Custom sorting can be done by creating a calculated column and then using the Sort By Column option. We can sort column A based on column B, but it must have a unique combination.

Question 11: How do the drill-up and drill-down features work in Power BI?

Answer: The drill-up and drill-down features require a hierarchy in the visual to work. The "disconnected double arrows" icon takes down the visual to the next level of hierarchy. The "connected double arrow" icons add an additional level of hierarchy to the current view.

Question 12: What is the difference between an aggregator function and an iterator function in DAX?

Answer: DAX functions such as SUM, MIN, MAX, and others operate on a single column and perform aggregations. Aggregator functions are just sugar syntax for iterator functions. Understanding the difference in syntax and operation between these functions and iterator functions such as SUMX, MINX, MAXX, and others is very important. Iterator functions work on tables and execute the expression on a row-by-row basis.

Question 13: Why is CALCULATE the most important function in DAX? What is the purpose of CALCULATE?

Answer: CALCULATE is important as it can replace filter context, not simply modify it. Modification can be done by combining functions such as ALL and FILTER. If used within a calculated column, it can convert the row context into an equivalent filter context.

Question 14: What are the benefits of self-service BI platforms such as Power BI?

Answer: Self-service BI platforms such as Power BI enable users to access, analyze, and visualize data to promote data-driven decision-making, without relying much on technical people.

Question 15: How does Power BI compare to Tableau?

Answer: Power BI generally offers deeper integration with other Microsoft products and tends to be more cost-effective, while Tableau is often praised for its advanced visualization capabilities and flexibility. Both tools are leaders in the BI space but may suit different organizational needs and preferences.

Question 16: What are some of the disadvantages or risks that we should look out for as we use Power BI?

Answer: Some disadvantages or risks with Power BI include performance issues with large datasets for certain data sources, limited customization in certain visualizations, and dependencies on Microsoft's ecosystem that might not suit all organizational needs.

Question 17: What is Power Query Editor, and what is it used for in Power BI?

Answer: Power Query Editor is a tool embedded inside Power BI Desktop that is used to connect to different data sources and then clean or transform the data before it can be used in Power BI Desktop.

Question 18: What are the different types of filters in Power BI reports?

Answer: In Power BI reports, there are visual-level, page-level, and report-level filters.

Question 19: What's the difference between a report and a dashboard in Power BI?

Answer: A report can have multiple pages; anything created in Power BI Desktop and published to Power BI Service is a report. A dashboard in Power BI Service can have visuals from multiple reports in the workspace. By clicking any visual on the dashboard, users are taken to the report from which that visual was pinned on the dashboard.

Question 20: What's a star schema and how it is used in data modeling?

Answer: A star schema is a table structure where a central fact table contains the transactional data, and it's connected to one or more dimension tables via keys. This design simplifies queries and improves performance by reducing the number of joins needed, making it suitable for handling large datasets in BI tools such as Power BI.

Question 21: What are fact tables in data modeling?

Answer: Fact tables in data modeling contain quantitative transactional data such as sales, revenue, or quantities. They are typically surrounded by dimension tables in a star or snowflake schema.

Question 22: What's the difference between a star schema and a snowflake schema?

Answer: A star schema has a central fact table connected to denormalized dimension tables, resulting in a simple design with fewer joins. A snowflake schema normalizes the dimension tables into multiple related tables, reducing redundancy but increasing complexity with more joins.

Question 23: Explain the difference between single and bi-directional relationships.

Answer: In Power BI, a single-directional relationship allows filters to flow from one table to another in one direction, while a bi-directional relationship allows filters to flow in both directions between the tables.

Question 24: Describe a common issue with using many-to-many cardinality in a relationship.

Answer: Using many-to-many cardinality in a relationship can lead to ambiguity and incorrect aggregations if not managed properly.

Intermediate

Here are some questions and their most suitable answers for the intermediate category.

Question 1: Can you create a custom connector in Power Query for connecting to a data source?

Answer: If a connector is not available for a data source, Power Query SDK can be used to create a custom connector.

Question 2: What are the various authentication methods available for Power Query while connecting to a data source? Can you name a few of them?

Answer: The various authentication methods available for data sources include Basic, Windows, Database, Microsoft Account, Outh2, API key, and Anonymous.

Question 3: What is the Data Privacy Firewall in Power Query and what is its purpose?

Answer: There is a Data Privacy Firewall in Power Query that prevents unintentional leakage of data between different data sources during the merge or append operations.

Question 4: What are the various privacy levels that can be defined for a data source and what is their purpose?

Answer: Privacy levels (public, organizational, private) in Power Query are used to control how data from different sources can be combined (merged or appended), preventing potential leaks or unwanted exposure.

Question 5: What are the various connectivity modes in Power Query?

Answer: Connectivity modes include Import, DirectQuery, and Live Connection. Data sources such as Excel, CSV, text files, and some others only support Import mode. Live Connection is only available for Power BI datasets and Analysis Services data sources.

Question 6: What is the difference between pivoting and un-pivoting in Power Query?

Answer: Pivoting is the process of turning distinct rows into columns while un-pivoting is the opposite operation of turning columns into rows.

Question 7: What are the benefits of using the Import table storage mode?

Answer: Import storage mode supports all data source types, supports all Power Query (M) and DAX functionality, including creating calculating tables, and gives the best query performance due to caching as data is part of the Power BI file.

Question 8: What are some of the limitations of the Import table storage mode?

Answer: It supports a model size of up to 1 GB for the Pro license and 10 GB for the Premium license. However, datasets can grow beyond 10 GB through incremental refresh. Also, enabling large-format semantic models can greatly increase model sizes beyond this. The data refresh is a maximum of 8 times/day for Pro and 48 times/day for Premium and cannot work in an environment with data sovereignty concerns.

Question 9: What are the benefits of using DirectQuery table storage mode?

Answer: In DirectQuery table storage mode, the model size limitation of the Import mode does not apply and data models do not require scheduled data refresh as data is available in real time. In near-real time, it will refresh the data when the user interacts with any visual or refresh the page.

Question 10: What are some of the limitations of the DirectQuery table storage mode?

Answer: For DirectQuery (as well as dual) storage mode, M code statements must support query folding. Complex M and DAX transformations are also not supported. Query performance depends on the performance of the underlying data source.

Question 11: What is dual table storage mode?

Answer: Dual storage mode uses both Import and DirectQuery capabilities. At query time, Power BI determines the most efficient mode to use. Whenever possible, Power BI attempts to satisfy analytic queries by using cached data (Import mode).

Question 12: What is a shared dataset in Power BI?

Answer: A shared dataset is a dataset that is shared between multiple reports. You can connect to a shared dataset from within Power BI Desktop via Live Connection, which can be changed to DirectQuery in Composite Models.

Question 13: What are parameters in Power Query and what is their usage?

Answer: Parameters in Power Query can be used to change the data source dynamically (for example, database name, the Excel file path, the address of the data source, table names, and Excel sheets). Parameters are also used for passing values to custom functions in Power Query. You can pass any value or list query (a query whose output is a list) to the parameter.

Question 14: What is the purpose of the `Table.Trim()` *function in M for Power Query?*

Answer: It removes all the leading and trailing whitespaces from the text.

Question 15: What is the purpose of the `Table.Clean()` *function in M for Power Query?*

Answer: It removes all the control characters from the text.

Question 16: If you see an error in a cell inside Power Query Editor, what are the available options to handle that cell-level error?

Answer: You have the option to keep errors, remove errors, or replace errors. Removing errors will drop the entire row from the query. You can also analyze and solve the error.

Question 17: What is a step-level error in Power Query? Can you name a few common step-level errors that are often encountered while working in Power Query Editor?

Answer: A step-level error prevents the query from loading and displays the error components in a yellow pane. Some of the common step-level errors include "Query timeout," "Could not find file," "Data Source," and "Formula Firewall."

Question 18: What is the difference between using Reference and Duplicate in Power Query? Are there any implications of using each option?

Answer: Reference is used when you want to create a new query based on existing transformations while preserving the original query. Changes to the original query impact the referenced queries. Duplicate is used when you want a copy of the original query to modify it independently. Duplicate creates an entirely separate instance of data with all the "applied steps" of the original query.

Question 19: What is the difference between merging and appending queries?

Answer: Merging and appending are two options to combine tables or queries in Power Query Editor. For appending queries, table structures (the number of columns and data types) should be identical. The resulting table sees no changes in the number of columns and only sees an increase in the number of records. For merging queries, there must be at least one common column between the two queries and it must be comparable. Different join types (inner, left, right, full) can be used to correctly combine data based on shared values. Merging queries see an increase in both the number of columns and the number of rows in the resulting table.

Question 20: What are the various "Action" options associated with a button in Power BI?

Answer: A button can be set up for page navigation, bookmark action, drill-through action, back action, and conditional page navigation. Q&A, web URL, apply all slicers, and clear all slicers are the other options.

Question 21: What is the difference between grouping and binning in Power BI?

Answer: Grouping is done for categorical columns and binning is done for numerical columns by specifying either the bin size or number of bins. Binning helps to highlight trends and distribution patterns.

Question 22: What is the visibility of data sources for which the privacy level has been set to "Private" in Power Query?

Answer: Private data sources are completely isolated from other data sources, including other private data sources. Visibility can be restricted to authorized users.

Question 23: What are the isolation level data sources for which the privacy level has been set to "Organizational" in Power Query?

Answer: Organizational data sources are isolated from all public data sources but are visible to other private and organizational data sources.

Question 24: Is any isolation level specified for data sources on which the privacy level has been set to "Public?"

Answer: Public data sources are not isolated at all. Data can fold into other data sources and visibility is available to everyone.

Question 25: Can the table storage mode be changed from DirectQuery to Import? If yes, what is the impact?

Answer: Yes, the table storage mode can be changed from DirectQuery to Import. Changing the storage mode of a table to Import is an irreversible operation and cannot be reverted.

Question 26: What is query folding?

Answer: The ability of Power Query to create a single SQL statement for all M code transformations is called query folding. Query folding is mainly supported by relational databases. Other systems support query folding, not just SQL Server and not just SQL statements. For example, OData supports query folding but does not create a SQL statement. Broadly, query folding creates a native query that is executed by the source system.

Question 27: What is the impact of choosing the right data type for a column?

Answer: Choosing the appropriate column data type can have an impact on performance and storage, particularly with large datasets. The VertiPaq engine offers the best compression for numeric data types, so whenever possible, try and choose numeric data types with reasonable precision.

Question 28: What is the purpose of the Mark as Date Table option in Power BI?

Answer: The Mark as Date Table option will remove the autogenerated hierarchies. However, other autogenerated date hierarchies for date columns in other tables are not removed by doing this.

Question 29: What is the purpose of using the CALENDAR() *and* CALENDARAUTO() *functions in DAX?*

Answer: CALENDARAUTO() or CALENDAR() can also be used to build a common date table.

Question 30: What is cardinality in the context of data modeling?

Answer: Cardinality defines the nature of the relationship between tables (one-to-one, one-to-many/many-to-one, and many-to-many). For star schema models, ideally, all relationships should be one-to-many.

Question 31: What should be the cross-filter direction for data modeling in Power BI?

Answer: For all one-to-many relationships in a star schema model, the cross-filter direction should be from the one side of the relationship to the many side, indicating that "dimension tables filter the fact tables."

Question 32: What is the drawback of using bi-directional cross-filtering in Power BI?

Answer: Bi-directional cross-filtering can introduce multiple filtering paths through the data, which can create ambiguous results. It can adversely impact performance if the data volume is in millions.

Question 33: To set up RLS in Power BI Desktop, what steps should be followed?

Answer: To set up RLS, do the following:

Manage roles by creating static or dynamic rules and choosing Add Table Filter DAX expressions for the roles, then Enable bi-directional cross-filtering (if required). Static roles allow you to define filtered views for audiences such as TerritoryManagers. Dynamic roles allow you to define filtered views for a list of users with the USERNAME() or USERPRINCIPALNAME() functions.

Validate the roles and check their functionality.

Question 34: What is the benefit of splitting columns with the datetime data type into date and time columns?

Answer: Datetime columns have a lot of unique values, and it is better to split the datetime column into a date and a time column. Due to a lot of unique values, it will increase the file size. By splitting, you get better compression and a smaller overall semantic model (previously called dataset).

Question 35: How can the size of the semantic model in Power BI be reduced?

Answer: Some of the techniques that can reduce the size of the semantic model are as follows

Columns that are not used for either reporting or building relationships should be removed from the data model

Similarly, only bring in the rows in the data model, especially for fact tables, which are necessary for data analysis

Try to aggregate or summarize the fact table by reducing the level of detail

Question 36: What is the ideal table storage mode for composite models in Power BI?

Answer: For composite models, set the dimension tables storage mode to dual, fact tables to Direct Query, and aggregated tables in Import mode.

Question 37: What is the use of Performance Analyzer in Power BI?

Answer: Performance Analyzer is used to determine the total time spent in executing a query for any visual in the Power BI report page.

Question 38: What is the benefit of using VAR variables in DAX?

Answer: A measure calculation can be split into multiple steps using VAR as it not only improves performance but also the readability of a measure. We can reuse the value within the measure.

Question 39: What are table functions in DAX?

Answer: Table functions are used to create calculated tables and are also used as virtual tables in all DAX functions that return a table. Some of the most common table functions in DAX are `FILTER`, `VALUES`, `DISTINCT`, `ALL`, `SUMMARIZE`, `SUMMARIZECOLUMNS`, `ADDCOLUMNS`, `SELECTCOLUMNS`, `TOPN`, `CROSSJOIN`, and `TREATAS`.

Question 40: What are time intelligence patterns in DAX?

Answer: Time intelligence DAX patterns compute the results for a period; any measure can be used inside these patterns. Some of the most important time intelligence DAX patterns are running total, performance to date, and previous period calculations. However, time intelligence functions generally only support standard calendar tables and not fiscal calendars.

Question 41: What roles are created for a workspace in Power BI Service?

Answer: Viewer, Contributor, Member, and Admin are the roles that can be assigned for any shared workspace. Viewer has the lowest permissions, while Admin has the highest.

Question 42: How are data alerts configured in Power BI dashboards?

Answer: Data alerts can be set on dashboard tiles pinned from report visuals. Only gauges, KPIs, and card visuals support this functionality. Power BI sends an alert to the notification center and, depending on the configuration of the data alert, an email is also sent. Each alert contains a direct link to the data.

Question 43: What is a data gateway in Power BI and why it is needed?

Answer: A gateway is needed when a connection to an on-premises data source is required. Virtual machines running in the cloud also require a data gateway. It is also necessary to perform a scheduled data refresh for on-premises data sources. DirectQuery or Live Connection to on-premises databases also needs a gateway connection.

Question 44: How is a scheduled refresh configured in Power BI Service?

Answer: To configure a scheduled dataset refresh in Power BI, a Pro or a Premium license is required. A Pro license allows you to refresh up to 8 times per 24 hours (refresh frequency), while a Premium license allows you to refresh up to 48 times per 24 hours.

Question 45: What is the difference between the USERNAME() and USERPRINCIPALNAME() functions in DAX?

Answer: USERNAME() returns the domain name and username of the currently logged-in user in the `domain-name\user-name` format. USERPRINCIPALNAME() returns the user's email address – for example, `johndoe@dataanalytics.com`.

Question 46: What is the difference between DAX functions and expressions?

Answer: DAX functions are predefined formulas that are used for calculations and expressions that combine functions, operators, and constants to return a single value for a DAX measure.

Question 47: What are circular dependencies in DAX expressions?

Answer: Circular dependencies occur when a calculation relies on itself, either directly or through a series of other calculations.

Advanced

Here are some questions and their most suitable answers for the advanced category.

Question 1: What are Power BI Data Source (PBIDS) files?

Answer: PBIDS files ease the process of passing credentials to a data source. When opened, these prompt the user for credentials to authenticate and connect to the data source.

Question 2: What are Power BI Template (PBIT) files?

Answer: PBIT files contain information about queries, query parameters, and data models, including their schema, relationships, measures, report pages, visuals, and other visual elements.

Question 3: What are hierarchical slicers?

Answer: Multiple categorical values can be added to a slicer visual to make hierarchical slicers. Visual level filters do not affect the slicers on the report canvas.

Question 4: What is the purpose of the Analyze in Excel option in Power Service?

Answer: The Analyze in Excel feature allows you to analyze data in Excel, either with Excel PivotTables or Excel tables from within Power BI Service. You must have at least the Contributor role in the workspace for this option to work.

Question 5: Which data sources are not supported by the Analyze in Excel option?

Answer: Power BI datasets using Live Connection with Analysis Service (both Azure Analysis Service and SQL Server Analysis Service) do not support the Analyze in Excel option.

Question 6: What are paginated reports in Power BI?

Answer: Paginated reports are used to create pixel-perfect artifacts involving sales invoices, receipts, purchase orders, and tabular data for high-resolution rendering requirements.

Question 7: What are color classes in the color theme JSON file?

Answer: In the custom JSON theme file, color classes are used to set the structural colors for elements in the report, such as axis gridlines, highlight colors, and background colors for visual elements.

Question 8: What is the purpose of the `colorAccent` *color class in the JSON file for color themes?*

Answer: In the custom JSON theme file, table and matrix grid outline color can be specified using the `tableAccent` color class.

Question 9: How does conditional navigation work in Power BI?

Answer: Conditional navigation uses a disconnected table that specifies the name of each report page as a row. A slicer can be used with this table to enable the conditional navigation feature.

Question 10: What are the available options for exporting report contents in Power BI?

Answer: PDF, PowerPoint, and Excel are the main options for exporting report content in Power BI. When sharing externally, data privacy and security aspects must be kept in mind. Some additional export options are available for paginated reports.

Question 11: Which visual is normally used to showcase outliers in data?

Answer: Outliers are best visualized through scatter plots. Use DAX functions to calculate measures that can help identify outliers and anomalies.

Question 12: How does the clustering option work in Power BI?

Answer: Clustering uses machine learning to reveal patterns and insights that may not be immediately apparent. It is best visualized in a scatter plot.

Question 13: What fields should be placed in the Analyze by and Expand by panes of the Key Influencers AI visual?

Answer: In the Key Influencers AI visual, fields that are considered as influencers for Analyze are placed in Explain by. Fields placed in Expand by are never considered influencers for Analyze. Expand by fields specify the level of detail for Analyze when a measure or summarized column is placed.

Question 14: What is the purpose of reference lines inside the Analytics pane of a visual?

Answer: Reference lines can be used to highlight specific values or ranges in visuals to help in comparison and trend identification.

Question 15: What is the purpose of error bars inside the Analytics pane of a visual?

Answer: Error bars provide a visual representation of variability in data, which can be important in a statistical context.

Question 16: What is the purpose of forecasting features in the Analytics pane for line chart visuals?

Answer: The forecasting features that are available in line charts can predict future trends based on historical date and time data.

Question 17: How can a scorecard visual be created in Power BI?

Answer: When creating scorecards, the most relevant metrics that align with the business goals are included. Both hard-coded values and measures in the reports can be used to track progress.

Question 18: What is a role-playing dimension?

Answer: A role-playing dimension is a dimension that can filter related facts differently. Multiple date tables are created, where each date table acts as a dimension and allows simultaneous filtering by different date roles.

Question 19: What are semi-additive measures?

Answer: Semi-additive measures are unlike normal summation measures as these deal with inventory balances and closing balances. The `LASTDATE` function can be used inside of `CALCULATE` for this purpose.

Question 20: How can the Quick Measure option be used in Power BI?

Answer: For creating measures using the Quick Measure option, "Base value" is the value on which the measure must be created, and "Field" refers to the category for which it has to be created.

Question 21: What is the best way to create and manage workspaces in Power BI Service?

Answer: A shared workspace is created and configured based on the organizational hierarchy and is project-based or job function-based. Permissions must be set up for secure and controlled access

Question 22: What is the difference between promoted versus certified content in a Power BI workspace?

Answer: Any content owner, as well as any member with write permissions, can promote the content in the workspace. A Power BI admin can specify content reviewers and set up a method to certify content in the workspace.

Question 23: What are the suggested ways to distribute content in Power BI Service?

Answer: For distribution, Power BI reports are normally for individual users, dashboards are for teams, and apps are for organization-wide users. Reports must be shared via Active Directory groups to avoid maintenance if someone joins/transfers/leaves the company.

Question 24: What is the purpose of DAX Studio in Power BI development?

Answer: DAX Studio is a free external tool that can be used to optimize a data model's performance and also to debug DAX functions and their working.

Along with these questions, you'll be asked about your project experience as well as some real-time scenario-based queries. Make sure you are also prepared regarding the concepts of SQL and data warehousing as some of the questions might also be asked from these areas.

Things to do before the HR interview

The last stop on your journey in the HR rounds is the HR interview. The HR interview has more known associated with it than actual unknowns, so the types of questions you can expect in the HR interview are more predictable than the other rounds. However, there is a need and requirement to prepare well for this final round as this is the round where you get the opportunity to showcase yourself as a person and get to know your prospective employers.

In this section, we will highlight some homework that you need to do while preparing for the HR interview and master everything related to these points.

Research and understand the company's culture

As part of the preparation for the HR interview, you need to spend some time researching the company and its culture, vision, and values. The company's website and social media accounts (LinkedIn, Facebook, Twitter, Instagram, and so on) are valuable resources to know about the company. Companies often use social media to showcase their work environment, corporate events, social initiatives, and achievements. You can also use websites such as Glassdoor, Indeed, and LinkedIn to read reviews from former and current employees to learn more about the company, its work culture, and its management.

Prepare an elevator pitch

The **elevator pitch** is a concise and well-practiced description of some of the most asked questions in the HR interview. We've talked about these questions in the previous sections. You need to write down answers to some of these questions and then practice your response using clear and simple language. Practice your pitch until you can deliver it naturally and confidently. Pay attention to your tone, pace, and body language as these contribute to your overall impression. Try to sound as authentic as possible and be flexible to leave room for the unexpected during the interview. You can practice these questions with friends, family, or your mentors to get feedback and adjust your responses accordingly.

Dress appropriately for the occasion

Lastly, it is very important to dress professionally and appropriately for the HR interview. This means wearing decent, clean, and well-fitting clothes. It is also important to avoid wearing dresses that are either too casual or too revealing. You need to be the best version of yourself, and this is an important aspect of the HR interview preparation.

Summary

After all your hard work mastering Power BI, the HR rounds are the final hurdle you need to cross to get the job. In this chapter, we've covered everything you need to do to prepare for the HR rounds, from tips and tricks on technical assessments to practicing common interview questions. Now, it is time to prepare for the final call, which will likely involve salary and benefits negotiations and discussing your start date. We will cover all of this in detail in the next chapter.

Further reading

A lot of college standard exams, such as the **Graduate Record Examination** (**GRE**) and **Graduate Management Admission Test** (**GMAT**), have a lot of questions similar to what a candidate will see on the aptitude test. A lot of free and subscription-based material is available that you can use to prepare and practice:

- **Practice Aptitude Test** (https://www.practiceaptitudetests.com) is a website that offers a library of free practice tests from a range of providers. It also offers tailored packages for specific job roles.

- **Assessment Day** (https://www.assessmentday.co.uk) is another website that offers various free and paid practice tests with solutions. It also provides detailed advice on how to tackle each type of question.

- Another useful website for aptitude test preparation is **Jobtestprep** (https://www.jobtestprep.com). This website provides comprehensive preparation packages tailored to specific job roles. Each package includes practice tests, study guides, and detailed explanations of the answers to all questions.

12

Tips for Negotiating Salary and Benefits

Whether you are entering the job market for the first time or navigating a career shift into the realm of data analysis, waiting for a job offer is the culmination of a long and hard struggle. After clearing the HR rounds, you have a feeling of satisfaction and gratitude that the company has recognized your worth and has offered you a job. However, before you cross the finish line, the home straight in your journey has one little hurdle of negotiating salary and benefits that needs to be cleared. The ability to effectively negotiate your salary and benefits package can significantly impact your income and your job satisfaction, career growth, and work-life balance.

Negotiating salary and benefits often tends to be a source of discomfort for many aspiring Power BI developers and data analysts. This is understandable for multiple reasons, as it is perhaps an annoying step at the end of a long journey and demands us to venture beyond our technical comfort zone. It requires you to evaluate your worth and assertively communicate it. Accepting or rejecting a job offer is a significant decision that can shape your career trajectory and personal life for years to come. Hence, it is crucial to evaluate the offer from all aspects. We will discuss the best practices for accepting and rejecting a job offer in the next chapter. For the moment, we will focus on the salary and benefits negotiations process.

In this chapter, you will understand more about effective strategies for negotiating salary and benefits during the job offer stage. Negotiating compensation is a critical component of the job search process and requires careful consideration of factors such as relevant experience, industry standards, job responsibilities, and individual qualifications. The chapter explores key negotiation techniques, including researching market salary ranges, preparing a persuasive argument, and leveraging competing offers.

In this chapter, we'll cover the following main topics:

- Importance of negotiating salary and benefits
- Tips and strategies for successful negotiations
- Common questions and best ways to answer

By the end of the chapter, you will be better equipped to negotiate a salary and benefits package that reflects your value and supports your professional and personal growth.

Importance of negotiating salary and benefits

In the final step of becoming a proficient data analyst comes a pivotal juncture: negotiating your salary and benefits. Let's be honest – this negotiation is more than just a dialogue about numbers; it can be daunting and uncomfortable for most people. Most people would rather get it over and finish before it even starts. But remember this conversation reflects your self-worth, your understanding of the market, your value of non-monetary benefits, and your perception of equality, diversity, and inclusion. You simply cannot allow the employer to determine this value without agreeing.

The most common reason job seekers hesitate to negotiate their salary is because they believe they do not have the ability to bargain. A fresh graduate might think, "*This is my first job – I have no experience and no bargaining power.*" Even experienced professionals might think the same way. But you must understand that the recruitment process is also stressful and costly for the other party. Employers need to sift through hundreds of resumes, spend countless time analyzing and selecting applicants, and finally decide to hire a few. At this point, the employer is investing in these candidates. So, both experienced and fresh graduates have some bargaining power, and it is important to use it. If you choose not to actively negotiate your salary after receiving a job offer, then the onus of not doing it is on you.

This section looks into the importance of these negotiations, especially in the context of a high-demand field such as Power BI development and analytics. We focus on crucial aspects, such as recognizing the value of your technical skills and the impact they can have on a data-centric organization. As the world is totally connected these days, the influence of market trends, industry standards, and global best practices has a direct impact on your negotiation strategy. We will highlight the importance of these factors and look at some of the non-monetary benefits that can enhance job satisfaction.

Lastly, factors such as equality, diversity, inclusion, and cultural differences also help to shape a successful negotiation, and we will highlight their importance as well. Each of these aspects contributes to a comprehensive negotiation strategy that ensures fair compensation and adds value, respect, and fulfillment in your role as a Power BI data analyst.

Recognizing the value of your skills and experience

In an increasingly data-driven world, the skills and experience of a Power BI data analyst are highly valued. Organizations have started to realize that "data is the new oil" and have revamped the way they work. As a result, most companies are willing to pay a premium for professionals who can navigate complex data, extract meaningful insights, and drive business strategies using Power BI. If you have some years of experience working with this tool, then the worth is even more. But before you negotiate this worth, you need to understand and recognize it.

Assessing your skill set relative to the Power BI role is a crucial step. Understand your core skills such as data cleaning and transformation, data modeling, ability to develop complex calculations using DAX, developing reports and dashboards, and so on, and rate your proficiency in these areas. Prior work experience has a lot of value as you are familiar with the day-to-day Power BI development and deployment issues and best practices. As a data analyst, you also possess important soft skills such as problem-solving, communication, and teamwork, which are equally important for any job environment.

Negotiation begins with the belief that all these skills have value and that this value should be reflected in your remuneration. So, recognizing the worth of your skills and experience is the first and most crucial step in the negotiation process.

Market trends and global best practices

With a good grasp of your skills' importance and value, it is time to align them with market trends. Several factors, such as location, industry, company size, and experience level play a part in determining a Power BI data analyst's salary.

It is very important that you research the average salaries for similar roles in your area and industry. This can be done in a variety of ways, especially through websites such as **Glassdoor**, **Indeed**, and **LinkedIn**, which offer valuable insights into current job market trends and salaries. Another useful website is `payscale.com`, which will give you the average salary being paid across all the major companies. Also, keep in mind factors such as the state of the economy and inflation. In an economic downturn, companies might be tightening their belts, which could influence the salary they are willing to offer. Similarly, with high inflation, cost of living, transport, and other essential items seeing a rise in prices, you need to factor all of these in the salary and benefits negotiation.

Another important practice these days is that a lot of work from Western countries is being outsourced to digital nomads, start-ups, and freelancers who work remotely at relatively cheaper rates than their Western counterparts. This has opened up new opportunities for remote work and also opened up this particular segment of Power BI development. Working in different time zones is the new norm, which brings challenges to setting up home offices, high-speed internet, or going to offshore offices in the middle of the night. Make sure you also consider all these factors as you prepare for the negotiation process.

Remember – being informed about market rates and global best practices gives you a solid foundation for your negotiation. It equips you with real, on-ground information you can refer to during the negotiation process, strengthening your case.

Significance of non-monetary benefits

If you are applying for work in a company, salary is just one compensation component. Non-monetary benefits often make up a significant portion of an employee's total compensation and can dramatically affect job satisfaction.

While understanding the importance of salary negotiation, do not forget the significance of non-monetary benefits. You must consider aspects such as flexible working hours, professional development opportunities, health benefits, retirement plans, and stock options. There might be a particular company that is offering a very high salary but nothing in terms of work-life balance compared to a company that is offering an average salary but offers continuous learning opportunities or has a great employee mentorship program. Similarly, a lot of employees these days champion a full or partial work-from-home policy that avoids the hassle of daily travel and provides a better work-life balance.

In the negotiation process, these non-monetary benefits can often be the differentiating factor, offering value that goes beyond numbers on the paycheck.

Cultural, equality, diversity, and inclusion factors

In the global job market today, the importance of negotiating salary and benefits cannot be separated from considerations around culture, equality, diversity, and inclusion.

Cultural norms and expectations not only influence negotiation practices but also impact your decision to choose one company over another. For example, in some cultures, aggressive negotiation may be seen as off-putting, while in others, it might be the norm. Similarly, in some cultures, the process of salary and benefits negotiation is more direct, while in other cultures, it is more indirect. By understanding cultural differences, you can be more effective in negotiating a salary that is fair and equitable.

The importance of equality in salary and benefits negotiation cannot be overstated. Equality ensures that everyone is treated fairly, regardless of race, gender, and other personal characteristics. Unfortunately, pay gaps still exist across gender and racial lines in most countries of the world. When prospective employees are not treated well in the negotiation process, it can lead to pay disparities and other forms of discrimination. As a prospective employee, being aware of these discrepancies and advocating for equal pay is an integral part of negotiation.

Lastly, it is important to include the important aspects of diversity and inclusion that a company offers in negotiations for salary and benefits. Companies that value diversity and inclusion often create an enriching work environment that respects and appreciates different perspectives. Such companies are also more likely to negotiate in good faith and value your skills.

Remember – when you negotiate your salary and benefits, you are not just taking up your own case; you are contributing to a broader culture of fairness and respect for the work that all Power BI data analysts do. You are acting as an ambassador for the entire community and putting across a point of view that represents the thoughts and aspirations of a broader group. Negotiation, therefore, is a vital process that helps ensure you are adequately compensated for the skills and expertise you bring to any organization.

Tips and strategies for successful negotiations

Now that we have explored the importance of negotiating salary and benefits, it is time to share important tips and concrete strategies to succeed in this process. We have already talked about this aspect – that most people feel nuanced about this process and are willing to just get done with everything, so remember that if you belong to this group of people, then you need to read the next few pages of this chapter carefully.

We will discuss the critical aspects of negotiation, explaining step by step how to be both prepared and effective in conveying the value you bring to the organization. We will emphasize the fundamental role of research and preparation in setting the stage for successful negotiations. Remember – it is your preparation that will determine the outcome.

An important part of the negotiation process is how to frame your narrative that reflects your research and preparation. From understanding industry standards to evaluating your own worth, we will discuss how focusing on assertiveness and confidence can shape the conversation in your favor.

Finally, we will discuss that an important aspect of navigating difficult conversations is active listening and maintaining silence. Strategic responses to handle counteroffers, managing emotions, and ensuring the discussion stays on track are perhaps the most important strategies for a successful negotiation.

The salary negotiation process

The process of negotiating a salary starts with the HR interview, as there is a good chance that the HR team member will ask you about your salary expectations during the interview. It is a good strategy to politely say "*I will get back to you on this*" or give a salary range based on the research and preparation you have done for the role. Remember – any range that you provide at this point will act as the benchmark for further negotiations once you are offered a job. So, make sure that you have done proper research and preparation to give a concrete answer to this question.

The salary negotiation process can take place in the following three ways:

- Face to face
- On the phone/live call
- Email

Regardless of the mode of communication, the process of preparation remains almost the same. If the HR team is communicating through email, then the process becomes a bit different as you need to frame the right text in the email correspondence and you are unable to understand the body language of the resource on the other end, and vice versa. So, make sure you have all ends covered and know how to prepare for the process depending on the mode of communication to be used. We will be sharing a template at the end of this section for an email that can be used for salary negotiation.

Research and preparation

While the thought of negotiating salary and benefits may fill you with dread, it is important to understand that preparation is the bedrock of a successful negotiation. It begins with understanding the importance of this process, which we explored in the previous section. Once you have understood the importance of this process, it is important to prepare accordingly by doing research and knowing information about the company, industry standards for compensation, and current market trends. This includes researching the company's size, the industry it operates in, its financial health, and its compensation philosophy. All of this is needed to build a case that determines your own worth and value that you will advocate in the negotiation process. Failing to conduct proper research or rushing the process can lead to missed opportunities and a lack of appreciation of your true value and worth.

Having a well-planned negotiation strategy can present a strong case for why you deserve a better salary and associated benefits. Preparing for a negotiation involves researching the market rate for your position, understanding your company's financial situation, and clearly understanding your own skills and contributions to the organization. By gathering this information, you can make a compelling argument in the negotiation process.

Tips for research and preparation

The preparation begins by evaluating your confidence in the whole exercise. Remember – it is okay to feel nervous about this process as most people feel the same way. Before you even start preparing for this process, select from one of these four options how you feel about the process:

- Extremely confident
- Somewhat confident
- Unsure
- Not confident

If you belong to the bottom three categories in the preceding list, read the following tips carefully.

Capture everything!

As part of the preparation process, you must capture everything about yourself. You need to contemplate the key elements you can incorporate into the negotiation process to optimize your chances of success. Try to capture all the points highlighted next in a notebook or document. We will discuss all these points in this section:

- **Skills**: Identify your most relevant and valuable skills. List any specialized certifications or training. Consider skills that set you apart from others in your field.

- **Experience**: List past roles and relevant accomplishments. Include any relevant internships or volunteer experience. Note the number of years you have worked in your industry.

- **Past achievements**: Detail your most significant accomplishments in your current and past roles. Quantify your achievements where possible (for example, increased sales by 30%). Highlight awards, recognitions, or promotions you have received.

- **Market research**: Gather information on the market value for professionals with similar skills and experience. Use resources such as salary surveys, job boards, and professional networking sites.

- **Salary range**: Decide on an "ideal number" and a "willing-to-settle number" to allow room for negotiation.

Determine your market value

It is very important to have a realistic picture of data related to the range of salaries with similar roles. This includes data on geographies, job roles (office, remote, hybrid), job timings (day job, night shift), and work experience.

Headhunters and recruiters are the best people to get this kind of information, and they have the most up-to-date information. You can talk to connections on LinkedIn who have a similar kind of job role, job description, and level of experience. It is also very important to do proper due diligence while collecting and collating this information and not to rely on a single source for this information. This is a very important exercise and will help you determine an average salary number for yourself, which you can reasonably expect to get based not only on your own expectations but is also something that is supported with data. As highlighted in this chapter's previous section, consider the larger economic context. If the economy is strong and the demand for Power BI data analysts is high, you may have more leverage in your negotiation. On the contrary, companies may be more conservative during an economic downturn with their compensation packages.

Establish your salary range

Once you have a general idea of what the average salary for your position is, you can think about your own work history and experience to determine a fair salary expectation. This is important because when you negotiate your salary, you will require this data to back up your claims. This could include examples of times when you went beyond expectations in your previous roles, saved the company time or money, successfully completed projects, or contributed to revenue growth. Be as specific as possible and use numbers whenever possible. Focus on your accomplishments and the value you can bring to the company rather than focusing on your personal financial needs.

By the end of this process, you should have two numbers in mind. One is your **dream salary**, which is the number that would make you ecstatic because it's slightly above what you expect to get and may even be more than you think you're worth (at least right now). The other number is your **walk-away salary** or **willing-to-settle salary**, which is the lowest amount you are willing to accept. This is the number that you know you truly deserve and that you are worth. Don't agree to work for less than this amount.

Figure 12.1 shows a template that you can use as a preparation strategy for the negotiation process:

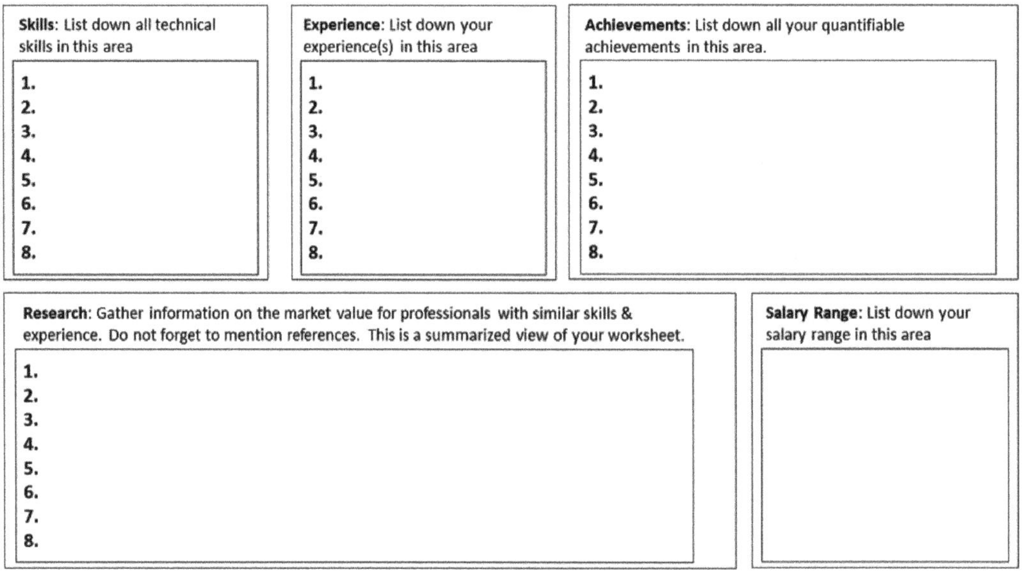

Figure 12.1: Template for preparation of the salary negotiation process

The preceding sheet lists down all the points we have covered in this section. This template can act as a cheat sheet for the negotiation process, as you will build your entire narrative based on this document.

Framing your narrative

After you have conducted thorough research and prepared the necessary data, it is then time to frame your narrative for the negotiation process. This determines how you will approach the conversation when it happens. The most important aspect of the conversation is to keep a balance between assertiveness and confidence without appearing arrogant or entitled.

The process of framing your narrative begins with communicating your value effectively. For a Power BI data analyst, this could mean highlighting how your data interpretation skills have led to business growth or cost savings in the past. It is important to keep achievements quantifiable and relevant to the role you are negotiating for. During the conversation, your body language plays an essential role in conveying confidence. Maintaining eye contact, using open body language, and speaking clearly can signal confidence to your negotiation counterpart.

Lastly, being clear about your expectations without sounding rude or rigid is important. Always remember that every successful negotiation's goal is to reach an amicable compromise, but this does not mean that you should undervalue yourself. If you have done your homework right, you know your bottom line and stand firm during the negotiation process.

Tips for framing your narrative

Remember that negotiation is a skill. The more you practice, the better you will be. Develop your negotiation skills by practicing and role-playing how you would articulate your performance and the reasons why you deserve a higher salary. Role-play with a friend or mentor and be prepared for different outcomes. Aim to quantify your achievements as much as possible to strengthen your argument.

If the negotiation process is email-based, then it cuts down some of the work we have explained in this section, but the narrative has to be carefully built and communicated in a professional way. Here is a template that can be used in email as part of the salary negotiation process. With a ton of free **generative AI (GenAI)** tools available in the market now, you can use these to draft an email by providing the relevant context and prompts:

Dear Sir/Madam

Thank you so much for the offer and for considering me for the job role.

I am excited about the role, and I'll be happy to accept an offer with an adjusted total annual (or monthly) compensation that equates to approximately a 20% total increase. This accounts for an increase of base from $XK to $XK, an increase in stocks from $XK to $XK over 4 years (if applicable), and an adjusted bonus year 1 from $XK to $XK.

I've conducted extensive research on salary ranges for (X roles) at some of the companies in the region, and I feel that the current offer is lower than my expectations given the role scope (and job description, if applicable).

The adjusted salary expectation accounts for four things, including:

- *The fact that I'm a perfect fit for this role with (X) years of experience doing Y*

- *A competing company is offering me a role (if you have one)*

- *I have technical skills in X and Y areas, and I know these skills will be very valuable in the coming months and years, considering a lot of companies are moving toward Power BI as their tool of choice for all data analytics requirements.*

- *I have achieved XX in my previous role at YY (mention all quantifiable achievements from the template)*

If we can reach an agreement on the adjusted expectations, then I could join as soon as (X date).

Thank you for your consideration, and I look forward to your response.

Stay calm and focused

Breathing deeply before and during the negotiation will help you maintain a clear and relaxed mindset. This will allow you to better articulate your points and make a stronger case for your desired salary. Keep in mind that the entire process is a professional discussion. Try to keep it amicable and open-ended. This conversation is about finding the right value, not winning a battle of arguments.

Remember – salary negotiation is all about communicating your value to a potential employer. It is not about being aggressive or greedy, but rather approaching it with a positive attitude. This will increase your chances of getting a good outcome.

Communicate your worth

Once you have done your research and determined your value, the most important part of the negotiation process is communicating it effectively. Remember to base the conversation on facts and not be driven by feelings. You should present all the evidence that supports your value and why you are asking for it. If you have experience, then share examples of times you have helped past employers increase profits, reduce costs, or save time. You must highlight any recognition you have received for being a top performer. While communicating, try to be assertive and tactful while staying calm and confident. When you communicate in a relaxed and confident way, people are more likely to listen to what you have to say.

Time your responses

In a negotiation, timing is everything. The biggest mistake that most people make in the negotiation process is to mention things at the wrong time. If you are negotiating salary and benefits, just keep your responses to what is being asked or discussed. The only time that you want to mention what your salary expectations are is when the employer asks you. Never bring it up on your own. This also includes the conversation that takes place during the HR interview as well. Never bring this point up on your own because it makes you look desperate, and this is not the impression that you want to set.

When the employer brings up this question "*What is your salary expectation?*" this is the time that you have been preparing for. If you have prepared well, then you have an **ideal number** and a **willing-to-settle number**." You start the negotiation by giving your "ideal number" only. Do not give any range, and stick to the "ideal number" only. You should also never disclose your "willing-to-settle number" during the negotiations. If you have done your homework well, your "ideal number" is not over the mark of your "willing-to-settle number." You want to give that "ideal number" because the employer will likely look at it and think you want this much and feel you are worth it. The employer will know that they really cannot go too far from your "ideal number," which means that you are most likely to negotiate something between your ideal number and your "willing-to-settle number."

Embrace the power of silence

Silence can be an effective tool in negotiations. Don't feel pressured to fill every pause or respond immediately to every statement. Take your time to think through your responses, and let silence work in your favor. By becoming comfortable with silence, you can gain a strategic advantage and create space for thoughtful reflection during the negotiation process.

What "not" to say

Understanding the right things to say in a salary negotiation is crucial. Equally important is recognizing what you should avoid saying during these discussions. It's important to be mindful of your language. Try to choose your words carefully, and avoid phrases that may come across as demanding or confrontational. Here are some things you must "not" say during the negotiation process:

"*I accept the offer.*" Refrain from immediately accepting the initial offer without negotiation, as this could mean missing out on a better deal. Companies often don't present their best offers upfront.

"*I need extra money to pay my rent and bills.*" Keep the negotiation focused on your professional qualifications, accomplishments, and the value you bring to the company. Avoid discussing your personal financial situation or needs, as these factors are not relevant to the negotiation process.

"*I know that Mr. X is drawing a $$$ salary, so why are you offering me $$?*" Comparing your salary or job offer to that of colleagues or others in your field can create an uncomfortable dynamic. Instead, base your salary request on objective market data, your skills, and accomplishments.

"*You must be kidding.*" Maintain professionalism, even if you feel the offer is inadequate. Counter with a proposal based on your market value and performance record, or explore alternative options such as a higher budget, a title change, or additional vacation time.

What should be your response to a lower offer?

There may be instances during a salary negotiation where the overall experience has been quite positive. You have showcased your skills and experience, and the employer seems genuinely interested in hiring you. Internally, you feel confident that they will make you a good offer, and you eagerly await the next step. However, when the offer finally arrives, it is significantly lower than your "willing-to-settle number."

This situation can sound very depressing, but you have to remain confident and resolute and respond in a professional manner. Some of the steps that you need to take to handle a situation where you have been given a lower offer than what you anticipated are set out here:

- Maintain composure and avoid reacting emotionally to the low offer. You must express appreciation for the offer by saying, "*Thank you for the offer.*"

- Politely and confidently mention that the current offer is below the market value for someone with your skills and experience by saying, "*I have researched the industry standards, and the current offer is lower than the market value for professionals with my background, skills, and experience.*"

- Share what you believe is fair compensation for a high-performing individual in the position, anchoring the range higher than your "willing-to-settle number." Giving a number higher than this is important because you still want to have some leverage in negotiation. You can say, "*Based on my research and accomplishments, I believe a competitive salary for this role would fall between $X and $Y.*"

    Note that both X and Y should be higher than your "willing-to-settle number."

- If the employer is unable to meet your salary expectations, consider discussing other benefits or perks that could make up for the difference. This could include a signing bonus, additional vacation days, or professional development opportunities. You can say, "*Thank you for considering my request for a higher salary. I understand there may be budget constraints, so I would like to explore alternative benefits or perks to balance the compensation package. We could discuss options such as a signing bonus, extra vacation days, or professional development opportunities. I am open to discussing any other creative solution for a fair agreement.*"

- Ask for some time to think over the proposal, giving yourself a chance to weigh your options and decide whether the offer aligns with your career goals and financial needs. You can simply say, "*Thank you again for extending the offer. I appreciate this opportunity and would like to take some time to carefully consider the proposal and evaluate how it aligns with my career goals and financial needs. Could you please provide me with a deadline for my decision? I want to make the most informed decision possible and will get back to you as soon as possible.*"

- If the employer is unwilling to negotiate a more acceptable offer, be prepared to politely decline and continue your job search elsewhere. It is crucial to know your worth and seek opportunities that align with your value. You can conclude the discussion by simply saying, "*I appreciate the time and effort you have invested in discussing this opportunity with me. After carefully considering the package, I have decided that the current offer doesn't align with my career goals and expectations. While I am grateful for the opportunity, I must respectfully decline the offer. It is important to me to find a role that matches my skills, experience, and value. Thank you once again for your time.*"

Sticking to morals and ethics

There should always be a moral code in salary negotiations. In the case of successful negotiation, you should only negotiate with an employer you intend to accept a job opportunity from. Even if your expected conditions are met, you should not negotiate with an employer you have no intention of accepting a job opportunity from, which is unethical.

In simple words, if you reach an acceptable salary level, it is assumed that you will accept the position. Once you accept the job opportunity, you should not continue to interview with other employers. If you are interviewing with other companies, you should tell them directly that you have accepted a job opportunity and you want to exit the application process. At this point, do not burn your bridges as you might have business cooperation with these companies in the future, or you might contact them again for job hunting.

Navigating difficult conversations

Salary negotiation is a process most people would like to avoid nine times out of ten. Sometimes, the conversation can get lengthy when neither party can come to an amicable solution. This can lead to arguments and counterarguments. As human beings, we cannot have a dialog until at least one of the parties gets the opportunity to say everything without judgment. So, when we have a lengthy conversation and one person stops talking, the other person tends to defend or litigate against the arguments of the other. The worst may happen, and the other person starts to interrupt the conversation and point out flaws in logic, which is very frustrating as pointing out flaws tends to take the conversation in another direction, and people end up choosing the wrong words at various times, leading to deadlock or even conflict.

Challenging or difficult conversations can take place during the salary negotiation process. These conversations are unavoidable sometimes and equally stressful. In such a situation, it is important to take the emotion out of the conversation and use a very important trait of communication – active listening. Listening is as crucial in negotiation as speaking. Actively listening to the other party's perspective allows you to respond strategically. It is about being present in the conversation, understanding the other person's point of view, and then responding thoughtfully.

When the other party makes a point or proposes an offer, take your time to respond. Consider the implications of what's being said, and do not be afraid to ask for clarification if something is unclear. Your responses should be well thought out, aligning with your negotiation strategy. If the proposed offer is lower than expected, counter the offer by referring to research you have conducted. If the salary is non-negotiable, shift the focus to non-monetary benefits.

In such situations, it is essential to remain composed and maintain a problem-solving attitude. Look for win-win solutions that satisfy both parties. If the conversation becomes heated, take a step back, and suggest continuing the conversation after a break. This allows both parties to cool down and approach the conversation with a fresh mindset. Remember – you are not just negotiating for a fair compensation package; you are also setting the tone for your future relationship with the employer. By handling these difficult conversations gracefully, you are demonstrating your ability to manage stress and conflict: a trait that is valuable in any role.

Common questions and best ways to answer

Doing a successful salary negotiation is totally different from your technical expertise in Power BI as a developer or data analyst. So, if you feel that you are not fully prepared for this conversation, then getting prepared for it is the best choice. Preparation means you need to understand what the possible outcomes of this conversation are so that you approach it with confidence and know what can or might happen. As we explore the world of salary negotiations, it is crucial to prepare for the most common questions you might face. These questions can range from your salary expectations to your future financial aspirations. How you answer can significantly influence the negotiation's direction and outcome, emphasizing the importance of thoughtful and strategic responses.

In this section, we will discuss questions and answers through a mock conversation between a candidate and a recruiter. We will share three possible scenarios of a salary negotiation conversation, where each conversation leads to a different outcome. Make sure that you read the questions and answers for each of these mock conversations, and prepare yourself to handle each situation with confidence and presence of mind.

The three different scenarios that we will discuss here are the following:

- An ideal and successful salary negotiation
- A conversation with an initial stand-off but a successful conclusion
- A difficult conversation that ends in a stalemate

Let's look at each of these in detail.

An ideal and successful salary negotiation

The first situation or scenario that we are going to discuss is an ideal, textbook, and successful salary negotiation where everything follows the perfect pattern. Keep in mind that this might be rare, but if you have done your homework well, then you can control the flow of the conversation and follow it as per the template shared next.

Remember that nine times out of ten, the HR team will ask you about your salary expectations during the HR interview, so we will start the conversation with that question during the HR interview and then take it from there to the salary negotiations.

Here's an example of an ideal and successful salary negotiation:

Recruiter: Hey, XYZ.

Candidate: Hi, ABC.

Recruiter: We really enjoyed meeting with you and would like to offer you the position. However, before we do that, there is a slight problem. The salary that you asked for during the HR interview is a little higher than average. Can you please review this number and what makes you feel worthy of this number?

Candidate: First of all, thank you for your positive response. I really appreciate the offer. To answer your question, I have been working in Power BI for the last year. You can have a look at the projects on my data portfolio, my certifications, and some of the reviews that I have got on my work from people on LinkedIn. It shows the amount of hard work and effort I have put into learning this tool. Also, I have done a lot of research on the local industry and some of the other companies, where developers with similar skill sets are getting a salary in the same range that I have given. So, I feel that the number I have shared with you is totally as per the industry standards.

(Here, you can share all the factors you put down on the worksheet, such as specific experience, specific skills, and other factors for the market value you have given. Try to be brief and to the point, and do not spend too much time explaining irrelevant things.)

Recruiter: OK, XYZ. I take your points and appreciate you sharing these with us, but we still believe that this number is still too high. We are one of the leading companies with one of the best work environments in the industry today. You get to work 3 days a week from home and also get a very good non-monetary package as well. So, I would like you to give a revised number of $110,000. What are your thoughts on that?

Candidate: Thanks for this offer, XYZ, but as you mentioned some of the non-monetary benefits, you have some very good monetary benefits as well, such as salary bonuses. So, let me just give you a counteroffer. I know you might be looking at a reduced annual salary figure, but you can consider a starting bonus or a bonus at the end of the probation period to go with this number. I have to feel comfortable in the job, and a salary of $110,000 is too low based on what I believe I am worth to your company. If you are unable to consider this counteroffer, then it is fine; otherwise, I would say consider $120,000 as the starting salary offer from my side.

Recruiter: Are you open to discussing some of the non-monetary benefits?

Candidate: Sure – it would be great if you could share the details. That would be great.

Recruiter: In addition to a good annual leave package and flexibility in working from home, we also offer comprehensive health benefits.

Candidate: Thanks for sharing this information. You can consider adjusting the additional remuneration in my annual paid leave or give me the premium package in health care benefits. If you are able to do that, then I can come down to $115,000 in salary.

(Here, the recruiter might take some time to analyze some of the options that were discussed. You need to just stay silent and answer only if some question is asked.)

Recruiter: Looks like I have some leverage in adjusting some of the monetary and non-monetary benefits to go with a starting salary of $115,000. I have noted down the requirements, and I will get back to you with a formal offer. What is your timeline for making a final decision?

Candidate: I would like to make a decision within 2 weeks and inform you accordingly. Thank you so much.

This is a perfect textbook salary negotiation that should not take more than 15 minutes to complete. Remember to always be prepared and respectful, with a positive tone and body language.

A conversation with an initial stand-off but a successful end

The second situation or scenario that we are going to discuss is a conversation that starts with an initial stand-off but ultimately ends in a successful win-win situation for both parties. Keep in mind that this will be the most likely conversation that you will have in a salary negotiation meeting. It is important to stay persistent on core values but also show some form of flexibility to avoid making the conversation a difficult one.

Remember that HR spends a lot of time and energy in the recruitment process. Often, there is pressure on them from higher management to complete the recruitment process as soon as possible, as they understand time is of the essence for everyone involved in the process and they need to onboard a resource in the shortest possible time to compete with other businesses, especially in the field of data analytics.

So, if the HR team is willing to compromise, then you should also show some flexibility during the negotiations while keeping in mind all the points that we discussed in the previous section of this chapter.

Here's an example:

Recruiter: Hey, XYZ.

Candidate: Hi, ABC.

Recruiter: We really enjoyed meeting with you and would like to offer you the position. However, before we do that, there is a slight problem. The salary that you asked for during the HR interview is a little higher than average. Can you please review this number and what makes you feel worthy of this number? We can only offer a salary of $90,000.

Candidate: First of all, thanks for the offer. I appreciate it, but I have already shared my salary range with you, and this number is much lower than that range.

Recruiter: We are not able to go that high, unfortunately.

Candidate: I am a little disappointed to hear that, but my skills and experience in Power BI are worth at least $110,000. I have not shared this number randomly, but I have done a lot of research about this job role and existing trends in the local industry. You must have taken a good look at my portfolio, the projects I have completed, and the positive feedback that you have seen on my LinkedIn profile. Based on all this, I would like you to consider the revised number that I have shared.

(Now, this is a very important stage in the conversation. The candidate has presented a good case based on the last conversation, and now, the important sign to look for is the level of flexibility or compromise that the recruiter is willing to show. If the recruiter shows some flexibility, then the candidate should also show some flexibility as this number is still higher than the "willing to work number.")

Recruiter: I understand your concerns, but we are operating on a tight budget, and it is almost impossible to offer you a salary higher than $90,000 right now. But we can discuss some other monetary and non-monetary benefits.

Candidate: I appreciate your flexibility on this, and it would be great if you could share some of the monetary and non-monetary benefits. I am willing to compromise on this number as well once I have a look at these benefits.

(Here, the recruiter will share details about the monetary and non-monetary benefits. It is important to stay calm and let them share everything. The candidate knows that the bottom line is $100,000 and there is still time to reach a compromise.)

Recruiter: So, this is what we have to offer to you in terms of the monetary and non-monetary benefits. What are your thoughts?

Candidate: Thank you so much for sharing these points. I believe that it will be difficult for you to offer something substantial in terms of these benefits, so I would like to reach a compromise with you on the starting salary number. I think we can come to a middle number. I am willing to come down to $100,000, which is a very fair and reasonable number based on all the factors that I have shared.

Recruiter: Let me talk to my manager and see if anything can be done about it.

(Here, the recruiter will discuss a few things with their manager, but again, this is a good sign that some sort of agreement will be possible because of the negotiation process. Here, the candidate has given their "willing-to-go number," and settling on anything below that would be considered as accepting something that is below the market value, so hopefully, a compromise can be reached on this number.)

Recruiter: We can do $100,000. What is your timeline for making a final decision?

Candidate: Thank you so much for this offer. I will communicate my decision in 2 weeks.

This is the most likely flow of a salary negotiation process where there will be a few twists and turns, but in the end, a compromise will be reached between the recruiter and the candidate. Remember to always be prepared, respectful, and persistent on the numbers that you have worked out as part of research work. Never accept an offer below the "willing-to-work number" as that would mean you have undervalued yourself, and that can set the tone for the rest of your professional career.

It is important to show flexibility and have an attitude where you are willing to compromise, but remember – the underlying principles must never be compromised. It is better to walk away with dignity and look for other options than accept an offer that goes against your principles and you feel bad about in your heart.

A difficult conversation that ends in a stalemate

The last situation or scenario that we are going to discuss is a conversation that starts with an initial stand-off and neither of the parties is willing to make enough compromise, and the conversation ends in a stalemate. Keep in mind that this situation will again be rare, as with the first scenario, as both parties always try to reach a compromise and come to a mutually agreed position. Difficult conversations are a reality not only for salary negotiations but in most real-world job roles, so it is very important to stay respectful and never lose control of your emotions or get angry. The best policy is to walk away from the table with respect and dignity.

Remember – this outcome is the least desirable for both parties. The HR team has its own set of constraints, and they work with a fixed budget for these roles and also have limited flexibility in negotiating other benefits. But it is the candidate who is joining the company and bringing all the value to the workplace. Some of that value can never be monetized or compensated through any kind of benefit. So, keep in mind that you must be persistent with the number that you have worked out for yourself in terms of your value, and try to never compromise on the worth that you bring to the company.

Here's an example:

Candidate: Hi, ABC.

Recruiter: We really enjoyed meeting with you and would like to offer you the position. However, before we do that, there is a slight problem. We believe you would be an excellent fit for our Power BI role. We would like to offer you a starting salary of $90,000 annually, along with our standard benefits package, which includes health insurance, retirement contributions, and annual bonuses based on performance. The number we have offered aligns with our internal grades, especially for newcomers to the company. Moreover, the benefits package includes a generous leave policy and other professional development opportunities, which are some of the best in the industry. The salary that you asked for during the HR interview is a little higher than average. Can you please review this number and explain what makes you feel worthy of this number?

Candidate: Thank you for the offer. I really appreciate it, and I am excited about the potential of joining your team. However, based on my research and the market value for Power BI specialists with my level of expertise and experience, the average salary seems to be around the mark that I have already shared with your team. You must have taken a good look at my portfolio, the projects I have completed, and the positive feedback that you have seen on my LinkedIn profile. Considering my proven track record and the value I can bring, I was hoping for something within that range.

Recruiter: I understand where you are coming from. Our offer was based on our current salary scales and budget, but also on the average pay for this role within our company and in our location. But I value the research you have done. Would you be open to a salary of $95,000 with a potential for a performance-based bonus that could take your compensation closer to the $100,000 mark in your first year?

(Here, the recruiter has shown some flexibility and given a counteroffer that is closer to the "willing-to-work offer" but has linked another $5,000 to a potential performance-based bonus, which might or might not come. So, technically, the offer is still at $95,000 as strings are attached to the "willing-to-work offer" that the candidate wants. Also, the recruiter has spent more time emphasizing other factors such as professional development and leave policy, which is a sign that they are not willing to move from this counteroffer.)

Candidate: I appreciate your flexibility. While the performance bonus is tempting, my primary concern is the base salary because it sets the tone for future increments and benefits. Considering the unique skills I bring, especially with some of the advanced Power BI functionalities and the cost savings my optimizations can bring, I firmly believe a base of $100,000 would be fair.

Recruiter: I totally value your expertise and the value you bring to the table. Let me discuss this with our finance team and see if there's any room for change. Let me get back to you in a day or two.

(Here, the long delay is an indicator that the HR team will not change its stance. Normally, these negotiations are over in half an hour, so a longer delay is not a positive signal.)

Recruiter: Hi, ABC. After discussing it internally, the highest we can go at this moment is $97,500 as a base. We truly value your talent, but we have certain budget constraints we need to adhere to.

Candidate: I truly appreciate your offer and the fact that you are willing to meet halfway. While the role and the company are very attractive to me, the salary is a significant factor in my decision. I am expecting some other opportunities aligning more closely with my salary expectations in the near future, so I would have to respectfully decline this offer. I truly appreciate the time that you have spent during the recruitment process, and it was a pleasure talking to you and the team.

Recruiter: I completely understand. It is crucial for both parties to feel content with the terms for a productive working relationship. While I am disappointed that we could not come to an agreement, I respect your decision. I hope our paths might cross again in the future under different circumstances. All the best in your future endeavors!

This is the most likely outcome of a difficult salary negotiation process, but it is important to walk away respectfully from the table and not burn your bridges completely with the company for any future role that comes along. Remember to always be prepared for the worst, yet stay respectful and persistent on the numbers that you have worked out and shared with the HR team.

Remember – engaging in a salary negotiation can be challenging, and a candidate must be prepared to handle these discussions with professionalism. It is very natural to feel emotions during a negotiation, especially if the stakes are high. However, it is important to remain calm and not let your emotions dictate responses. Your homework, especially the worksheet that you developed, is always the reference for everything that you share with the HR team.

While you communicate points from your research, by demonstrating the return on investment (ROI) to the HR team, do not view the conversation as a battle that you have to win at all costs. Try to negotiate a solution that is beneficial for both parties. Show your flexibility by negotiating everything that the HR team brings to the table. If a higher base salary (within your willing-to-work range) is off the table, then try to get the best out of the other monetary and non-monetary benefits. Regardless of the outcome, always remain respectful and professional, even if you decide to walk away from an offer that is below your baseline number.

Lastly, always leave the door open for future collaborations by ending the conversation on good terms and walking away with a positive mindset and a lasting impression.

Summary

In this chapter, we discussed the art of successful job negotiation, equipping you with key strategies and insights to navigate this crucial stage of your career journey. We started by understanding the importance of preparation, emphasizing the need to research industry standards and know your worth. We then explored the art of effective communication, highlighting how active listening and clear articulation of your needs can lead to mutually beneficial outcomes. The chapter also addressed the significance of flexibility, demonstrating how to find a balance between your aspirations and the employer's limitations.

These lessons and skills are invaluable not only for securing a job offer that meets your expectations but also for laying the groundwork for a positive, long-term relationship with your employer. Mastering negotiation techniques ensures that you start your new role with confidence and satisfaction, setting a precedent for future growth and opportunities.

In the next chapter, we will talk about the onboarding process and how to plan the learning journey to become an expert Power BI developer.

13

Best Practices for Accepting and Rejecting Job Offers – Onboarding and Beyond

Congratulations on making it to the final milestone on your journey to becoming a Power BI data analyst! You have cleared all the hurdles, from learning the skills to applying to jobs to negotiating your salary. Now comes the tricky part: accepting or rejecting the job offer. Like any major life decision, this one should be made carefully. There are pros and cons to each option, and you want to be sure you're making the best choice for yourself.

Accepting a job offer is a big step. It means opening a new chapter in your life, full of new challenges and opportunities. It is also a bit daunting, especially if you have multiple offers. You don't want to burn any bridges, but you also don't want to miss out on the perfect opportunity. This is where the **dos and don'ts** of accepting and rejecting job offers come in. Knowing the right way to go about it can help you make a confident decision and start your new role on the right foot. Once you accept a job offer, the next step is to join the company and understand the onboarding process.

Onboarding is your first real chance to get to know your new team and company. It is a time to learn about your role, the company culture, and all the new things you will be doing. It is important to be prepared for this process so that you can make the most of it and have a smooth transition to your new job. One of the most important things you can do during onboarding is to get to know your new team members. This means introducing yourself, learning about their roles, and understanding how you all work together. You need to ask questions and be proactive in seeking out information. The more you know about your team and the company, the better prepared you will be to succeed.

Another aspect of onboarding is understanding your role and responsibilities. This includes knowing what you are expected to do, who you report to, and who your customers or stakeholders are. You need to fully understand the company's goals and objectives so that you can align your work accordingly.

Finally, remember that onboarding is just the beginning of your journey. As you settle into your new role, you will need to continue to learn and develop. The world of Power BI data analysis is constantly changing, so staying up-to-date on the latest trends and technologies is a must. You can do this by attending conferences, reading industry publications, and taking online courses.

In this chapter, you will gain an understanding of the best practices for accepting and rejecting job offers. Accepting or rejecting a job offer can have a significant impact on a candidate's career path and professional reputation, making it crucial to handle the process with care and professionalism. The chapter expands on our knowledge from the previous chapters and provides strategies for accepting and rejecting job offers in a polite and professional manner as well as some email-based templates to communicate your decision in an effective manner. By the end of the chapter, you will be equipped with the knowledge and skills necessary to decide in the best possible manner.

Similarly, in this chapter, you will understand what to expect during the onboarding process and beyond. Onboarding is a critical step in the employee lifecycle, as it sets the tone for the employee's experience in their new role and the organization. The chapter explores the typical components of an onboarding program, including orientation, training, and introduction to the team members and company culture. Additionally, the chapter provides insights into what to expect beyond onboarding, such as ongoing learning and development opportunities and some points about performance management.

In this chapter, we'll cover the following main topics:

- Accepting a job offer – the dos and don'ts
- Rejecting a job offer – how to do it professionally
- Onboarding process – what to expect
- Setting expectations with the team
- Beyond onboarding – continual learning and development

By the end of the chapter, you will have a clear roadmap for your Power BI developer career and how to make the most of your new job that reflects your value and supports your professional and personal growth.

Accepting a job offer – the dos and don'ts

Receiving a job offer as a Power BI developer is a major milestone in anyone's career. You look back at the time when you opened Power BI for the very first time, started learning about data analytics, and went through the recruitment process with flying colors, and find that it has been a long, hard journey, so well done on your consistency, perseverance, and hard work. Before you accept the offer, it is important to take some time to consider all your options and make sure you are making the best decision for yourself. There are a few simple things that you need to consider before making a final decision and communicating it professionally and effectively.

Recognizing the value of your skills and experience

In an increasingly data-driven world, the **skills and experience** of a Power BI data analyst are highly valued. Organizations have started to realize the importance of data; a very commonly used phrase attributed to many people in the technology world sums this up: "Data is the new oil." Based on this, they have revamped the way they work. As a result, most companies are willing to pay a premium for professionals who can navigate complex data, extract meaningful insights, and drive business strategies using Power BI. If you have some years of experience under your belt working with this tool, then the worth is even more. Before you negotiate this worth, you need to understand and recognize it.

Assessing your skillset relative to the Power BI role is a crucial step. You need to understand your core skills, such as data cleaning and transformation, data modeling, ability to develop complex calculations using DAX, developing reports and dashboards, etc., and rate your proficiency in these areas. Prior work experience has a lot of value as you are familiar with the day-to-day Power BI development, data governance, deployment issues, and best practices. As a data analyst, you also possess important soft skills, such as problem-solving, communication, and teamwork, which are equally important in any job environment.

Negotiation begins with the belief that all these skills have value and that this value should be reflected in your remuneration. Recognizing the worth of your skills and experience is the first and most crucial step in the negotiation process. We covered this process in a lot of detail in *Chapter 12*.

Carefully reviewing the offer

Once you receive the job offer, as per the salary negotiation process, you need to review all aspects of the offer before you accept. You need to be sure that the offer meets your expectations and that you understand the terms and conditions laid out in the offer. You need to go through each section and ask the hiring manager for clarification about any discrepancies.

Here are some of the important sections to look for in a job offer:

- **Job title and description** – Make sure that the job title and description match what you were expecting.

- **Salary and benefits** – Review the salary and benefits package to make sure that it meets your expectations from the salary negotiation phase.

- **Start date and end date** – Carefully review the start date (and end date if the position is contractual) and look at any probation period and clauses associated with it.

- **Non-compete clause** – Some job offers include a non-compete clause, which prevents you from working for a competing company for a certain period after you leave your job. If the offer includes a non-compete clause, be sure to review it carefully and understand its implications.

- **Other terms and conditions** – Be sure to review all the other terms and conditions of the offer, such as vacation policy, sick leave policy, medical benefits, etc.

In addition to reviewing the job offer on your own, it is also a good idea to have someone else review it for you, such as a trusted friend, family member, mentor, or career counselor. It is always helpful to get a second opinion as this is an important milestone in your professional life.

Your final response

After you have reached a decision, the next step is to determine your response method. If the employer has extended an official offer via email, it is appropriate to convey your acceptance through an email response. In cases where you have received a hard copy of the offer letter, it is advisable to respond in kind with a physical letter. However, if choosing to mail your response, it is also recommended to send your acceptance message in an email to ensure that it reaches the employer.

You need to draft a reply to the employer after carefully reading the offer letter. The tone of your reply should reflect the tone of the communication from the employer. You should start by thanking the employer for this opportunity and restating the final offer details to show that you have carefully read and understood them. Then, clearly state that you officially accept the company's offer of employment. Try to not mention irrelevant details and conclude with well-wishes for the company. Clearly restate the start date to avoid any confusion on their end. Make sure that the subject line of the email or letter is clear and easy to understand, for example, *Job Offer Acceptance – [your job role and name here]*. The last thing before you send your response is to proofread it. Proofreading helps to avoid any mistakes, so make sure to engage a friend or mentor in the process. Remember, you want a second opinion, and another person's view is helpful when drafting a response.

If you are accepting your job offer over a phone call or an online call, make sure you practice what you have to say as part of the acceptance and prepare for any questions. Just make sure you repeat the stuff that is part of the offer letter so that the communication is clear and there is no ambiguity or confusion.

Rejecting a job offer – how to do it professionally

Receiving a job offer is a great feeling, but it is not always easy to know what to do if you cannot accept the position. There can be multiple reasons for **rejecting a job offer**, such as getting a better offer from another company, not feeling that the offer meets your expectations, etc. However, it is important to reject the offer professionally and respectfully, just as you would do to accept a position. There are a few simple things to consider to communicate your response in a professional manner.

Reasons for rejecting a job offer

We have talked about the sections in the offer letter and how to evaluate them carefully in the previous section. If some of these sections do not align with your thinking or expectations, then you need to discuss these factors with the hiring manager or, if they have not been addressed after a discussion, you can decline the job offer.

Some of the other factors at play in declining a job offer can be your realizing that the job or company is not the right fit for you or receiving multiple offers or offers much better than this one. You might even be in a position where you want to give yourself more time to evaluate other offers or you could have simply realized that now is not the best time to make a move.

Whatever the reason, just remember that when you decline the job offer, you want to do so in a way that does not burn any bridges. Remember that taking too much time to respond to a job offer or not responding at all is considered bad manners, as the company might have lined up a few other candidates as a backup and they would like to approach them instead.

Communicating a job rejection

Just as we discussed the process of accepting a job offer in the previous section, it is equally important to communicate a job rejection in a professional manner. The medium of communication can be an email, letter, or call, just like we discussed for accepting a job offer. However, the content of the communication is very different from the acceptance process.

If you have made up your mind to reject a job offer, then make sure that you respond to the offer as soon as possible. This shows the hiring manager that you respect their time and that you have given them time to consider another option. You should thank the hiring manager for the offer and express your gratitude for their consideration. Simply explain that you are not interested in the position, but be sure to do so in a polite and professional manner.

If possible, be specific about why you are rejecting the offer. This will help the hiring manager to understand your decision and to improve their hiring process in the future. Even though you are rejecting the offer, you still want to leave a positive impression on the hiring manager. In the end, wish them luck in their search for the qualified candidate most suitable for the position.

Onboarding process – what to expect

As soon as you accept the job offer, the job onboarding process starts. The purpose of **job onboarding** is to integrate the new employee into the company and its culture. The process can last from a few days to even a few weeks depending on the size of the company. There are specialized teams in the HR department who manage the onboarding process. Their goal is to slowly complete the paperwork and make sure that the new employee integrates seamlessly into the work environment through orientation sessions, training, and provision of the right resources.

Onboarding is important for both new employees and employers. By providing a comprehensive onboarding experience, employers can help new hires get up to speed quickly and become productive members of the team. New hires can make the most of their onboarding experience by being proactive, asking questions, and seeking out feedback. A well-executed onboarding process is the first step toward achieving higher job satisfaction and ensuring better job performance and reduced turnover, all of which contribute to the overall success of the organization.

What is job onboarding?

Onboarding is a crucial phase where newcomers acquire the knowledge and skills they need to become productive members of the organization. An effective onboarding strategy can significantly impact a new hire's long-term performance and increase the likelihood of their staying in the company.

HR teams have a neatly organized **onboarding plan**, which is more like a schedule and serves to make new employees more familiar with the company. The main benefits of a successful onboarding plan include sharing information about the company, setting tasks, reviewing the relationships between tasks and their assigned experts, and sharing tools to help employees optimize their daily duties.

What to expect during the onboarding process

The onboarding process for a new hire can vary between companies and positions, but there are some standard things that can be expected during this process:

- **Welcome orientation** – This is the basic introduction to the company and its history, mission, values, culture, and organizational structure. The new hire can expect a tour of the office and a detailed introduction to the team. This can go a long way to making the new employee feel welcomed and valued.

  For larger companies, this orientation can last a few days, where the new employee is taken to various areas of the organization. For a Power BI developer role, you should not expect this process to be too long, as data-driven companies value every minute of their employee's time and want to get their employee to start delivering from day one.

- **Completion of paperwork** – The new hire is required to complete the necessary paperwork, which can include signing off on a few documents. These documents can be related to account creation in the IT system, opening a bank account, HR documentation related to your job contract, and perks. Make sure you provide the right credentials and read everything carefully to avoid any confusion at a later stage.

- **Introductions** – The new hire is introduced to the manager, team members, and other key stakeholders. This is a great opportunity to get to know your new colleagues and learn more about the role in the team. As a Power BI developer, you will be introduced to other developers working in the same role. You might also meet fellow data engineers, data warehouse developers, UI/UX designers, and solution architects. These are the people with whom you will be working and communicating on a daily basis for various projects. The new hire is given time to socialize with their team members and get comfortable with the work environment.

- **Access to resources** – The new hire is given access to the company's resources, such as the employee handbook, intranet, and IT systems. This includes setting up the workstation, providing access to necessary software, and ensuring that office supplies are provided.

As a Power BI developer, you will spend a good amount of time with the IT team to understand IT policies, data governance and management, licensing, on-premises and cloud infrastructure, system roles and privileges, etc. As a Power BI developer, you might feel a bit overwhelmed at first, so make sure that you note down and understand everything, as this will be your day-to-day work.

Most companies have their own data governance and security policies, and IT teams are generally very strict about their implementation. It is therefore important that these policies, processes, and procedures are understood very well. In the event of any confusion, you should feel free to ask questions and seek advice at the outset, as subsequently, IT teams will require you to raise a ticket for any assistance. The sooner you understand the processes, the easier it will be for you to integrate into and succeed in your new role.

- **Training** – Some companies have mandatory training for all new employees related to the various systems and processes in place. This could include using different applications, utilities, and tools for performing specific tasks and responsibilities.

    Training on IT-related matters usually leads to the formal onboarding process, which is mainly handled by the HR team.

Tips for making the most out of the onboarding process

As part of the job onboarding process, you must understand the importance of first impressions. At the start of a new job, a positive **first impression** will go a long way toward impressing your manager and establishing a good relationship and connection with your colleagues.

Here are some tips that will help you make a strong first impression and get off to a positive start as a confident, productive, and supportive employee in your new job:

- **Understand the importance of the first day** – The first day is perhaps the most important day of a job because everyone at the workplace will be watching you. They will form an opinion of you within the first few hours of your starting work there. You will be like a magnet on your first day; people will be intrigued as to who you are, what you look like, how you dress, how you communicate, and how you are going to fit into their team.

- **Dress properly** – Make sure you come in formal dress that fits in well with the social and cultural norms of the workplace. It is best to wear a smart and professional outfit to show your manager and work colleagues that you have a good dress sense.

    People have a habit of judging others based on what they wear; a smart and presentable outfit will show you to be a confident person who is serious about work. Casual clothes and shoes should be avoided as these don't convey the right message to your manager or colleagues.

    Most people in the IT industry are not very particular about clothes, as Power BI developers tend to sit for long hours in their office chairs and prefer casual clothing, but the onboarding period is all about making impressions and the right clothes have a very important role to play in that. Similarly, make sure you take proper care of personal hygiene as well.

- **Follow the office timings** – It is important to follow the office timings not only during the onboarding period but also on all normal days, too. Whatever you do, do not be late during the onboarding period as punctuality is crucial in all jobs. The best thing to do is to turn up at least 15 minutes before the scheduled start time and leave 10 to 15 minutes after closing time.

- **Avoid gossip** – While interacting with your new team, avoid gossip or talking disrespectfully about anyone, even your former employer. If you have heard anything negative about your new employer, do not ask your co-workers about it, even if it is true. Instead, show yourself to be a positive and professional person who has integrity. Remember: you do not know your team members yet or who you can trust.

- **Talk less and listen more** – Talking too much is one way to make your new co-workers wary of you. People who talk too much or show off tend to be insecure and need the admiration of others to boost their confidence. If you are great at something, wait until someone asks you about it or it comes up in conversation; this way, people will have more respect for you. Your focus should be on listening to what people have to say and only talking if they ask a question or expect you to say something.

- **Look positive and confident** – Try to greet everyone you meet with a smile, a firm handshake, or whatever the local custom is for greeting another person, and do so while looking them in the eye. If you do not introduce yourself to your team members, they might think you are rude. A confident greeting with a smile always does wonders for a first impression.

- **Take notes** – You will have so much information to absorb during the onboarding period that you simply cannot rely on your memory to remember everything. So, it is better to take notes on information about your role, what your team members do, their names, where the facilities are, how the business operates, etc. Taking notes on the important things so that you can refer to them later on helps you avoid asking the same questions over and over again.

- **Organize your work area** – Be sure to organize your desk or working environment. It is important to keep your working space tidy and organized, as team members observe the tidiness and organization of the working area. If your working space is organized and free of rubbish and clutter, people will respect you for being a good professional.

- **Thoroughly read the company policies and procedures** – A company's policies and procedures are important to learn because these are the rules employees must follow. If you do not know what the rules are, you are more likely to make mistakes. This area is often neglected by newcomers during the onboarding period. It is always better to ask your manager or supervisor about these policies and procedures and thoroughly understand them.

- **Be open to feedback** – Be sure to listen to feedback from your manager, team members, and other stakeholders. Use this feedback to learn new things and improve yourself.

- **Networking** – Networking can help you learn more about the company and make connections that can benefit your career in the long run. Try to participate in team meetings and social events. This is a great way to get to know your new colleagues and learn more about the company culture.

The onboarding process is all about the HR department and the next step is to meet your team, the people whom you would be working in your role as a Power BI developer.

Setting expectations with the team

As a new hire, you may still be learning about the company, your team, and your job role, but the most important thing is to set clear expectations with the team from the start. This is very important for your new role so that you can work toward a clear goal and objective. There is often a massive gap between the employees and the managers when it comes to expectations, so this can be a very challenging thing for a new hire in the team.

If you set your expectations too high, then you are always living with the fear of underperforming and putting yourself under extra pressure. If you set your expectations too low, then your manager and team members might start to think about your worth and importance in the team. So, it is important that your expectations are realistic and that they balance your role as per your skillset, qualifications, experience, and the task at hand.

How to set expectations

Setting expectations with the team, including your supervisor or manager, is arguably one of the hardest things to do because it is so hard to ensure that the expectations we are communicating have been understood. As a Power BI developer, you would know that the bulk of your time will be spent using Power BI Desktop, but there might be some expectations from team managers and members that go beyond Power BI.

For example, your team members might expect you to know or learn other BI tools, such as Tableau or Qlik, or your manager might expect you to work in Azure Synapse Analytics, too. It is very important to understand that these expectations are real and there are multiple factors due to which team leaders and members have expectations from their new hires. Maybe a person working previously in the team knew these tools and utilities based on their experience or interests and was able to contribute their knowledge and expertise in something that went beyond the job description or their role within the team. Now, you have come into the team primarily as a Power BI developer, but you are expected to know this stuff as well.

Therefore, it is critical that as soon as you make yourself comfortable in the working environment and as the onboarding process is coming to an end, you engage with your manager and team members proactively to learn more about their expectations and tell them how you can best support them in terms of the immediate, short-term, and long-term goals of the team. This will set the tone for your goals, objectives, and workload within the team.

Remember, as a Power BI developer you will be required to learn new stuff all the time, so make sure that you spare some time during the week to learn new stuff, whether related directly to Power BI or another similar tool or utility that supports your day-to-day work. The mindset of feeling satisfied with what you know now and simply surviving on that knowledge for the foreseeable future is unrealistic and can be damaging to your growth in the job and within the data analytics industry.

When setting expectations, be clear and specific about what you want to achieve. Avoid using vague or ambiguous language. For example, instead of saying "*I want to improve my DAX programming skills,*" say "*I want to increase my DAX programming skills by learning and working on 10 new functions that have been rolled out recently.*" Another example is to complete five new learning modules on the Microsoft learning portal or to clear the Microsoft Power BI certification within the next quarter.

> **Read more**
>
> These learning modules are available on the Microsoft Learn website at `http//learn.microsoft.com`.
>
> For Power BI certification, simply search for "PL-300" and you will get all the links relevant to the certification.

Another important aspect is to remain realistic. When setting expectations, be realistic about your capabilities and the team's overall workload. Do not set yourself up for failure by setting unrealistic goals that cannot be achieved or will require huge effort on your part. Most new hires can get carried away and commit to something similar to create an impression and then end up giving excuses or new timelines for completion.

You need to make yourself fully aware of your capabilities and workload and only then commit to something. At the same time, be sure to ask the manager and team members for feedback on your expectations. This will help you to ensure that your expectations are aligned with the team's goals and objectives.

Beyond onboarding – continual learning and development

In today's modern workplace, it is more important than ever for a Power BI developer to continue learning and developing throughout their career. Power BI emerged as a business intelligence tool in 2015 and has since evolved to become one of the most important members of the Microsoft Power Platform family. At the same time, the organic support for Power BI within the Azure cloud ecosystem is phenomenal, so expecting to limit your learning to the areas we have explained in the previous sections of the book is not sufficient these days. Within the Power BI development role alone, there is a whole new area of Azure Synapse Analytics and Microsoft Fabric that can be learned, and you can move from being a Power BI developer to being an Enterprise level Data Analyst or an Analytics Engineer.

There are many reasons why continual **learning and development** as a Power BI developer is crucial. First, it helps developers stay ahead of the curve in their field. New features and trends are emerging every month, with some major updates coming out almost every six months. All developers need to be able to adapt and learn new things in order to remain competitive.

Second, continual learning and development helps Power BI developers become a prime resource for the company. Learning new features about the field and the data analytics industry not only makes them more valuable to their employers but also opens up new opportunities for career advancement.

Third, continual learning and development can help Power BI developers stay motivated and engaged in their work. When developers are constantly learning and growing, they are more likely to be excited about their work and produce high-quality results. This can lead to benefits such as hefty bonuses, early promotions, and much more. This results in an overall sense of well-being and can boost self-confidence and self-esteem. A happy and satisfied worker is the biggest asset of an organization.

A continual learning plan for a Power BI developer

For a Power BI developer who has just entered the job market as a data analyst, there must be a continual learning plan for both the short term and the long term. The good thing in this field is that the goals and objectives are well defined to a large extent in terms of learning areas, certifications, and skills. There are many ways to continue learning and developing. You can take formal courses, read books and articles, attend workshops and conferences, or simply learn from your colleagues and manager. It is important to choose learning activities that are relevant to your goals and that fit into your schedule.

Here are a few tips for developing a **continual learning and development plan**:

- **Set specific and measurable goals** – What do you want to achieve by the end of your plan? How will you measure your progress?

- **Identify the resources you need** – What courses, books, or other resources will you need to achieve your goals?

- **Create a timeline** – When will you complete each learning activity?

- **Be flexible** – Keeping in mind that things change, how will you adjust your plan as needed?

In this section, we are going to share a two-year continual learning plan based on our experience, the emerging features inside Power BI and its ecosystem, and the demand it will generate in the analytics market. This plan assumes a monthly learning dedication of 20–25 hours for a full-time working professional. This is almost an average of four to five hours of weekly commitment in total either during weekdays or on weekends.

Let us take a look at the tasks by month.

Month 1

Strengthen the foundation first. The pillars of Power BI are Power Query, DAX, data modeling, visualization and reporting, data storytelling, and online distribution. All these pillars need to be strengthened to close any gaps you find in your learning and understanding of the core concepts.

Month 2

Start preparation for the **PL-300 certification**. Microsoft Power BI has two certifications that are globally recognized. If you have not cleared these, make sure that they are at the top of your list of goals. For a beginner- or intermediate-level Power BI developer, PL-300 is the exam that needs to be cleared to earn the certification of *Power BI Data Analyst*.

A certification validates your learning and being a globally recognized credential, it is very important for somebody working in Power BI. You can put this as a recognition on your CV/resume as well as your LinkedIn profile. A beginner-level resource requires two to three months to clear the PL-300 exam based on the 20-25 hours of monthly commitment we have assumed for this plan.

Months 3–4

Keep preparing for the PL-300 certification as per the official course syllabus shared by Microsoft. We will list all the resources in the next section.

Month 5

Appear in the PL-300 certification exam to clear it. If you have used the right resources to prepare and spent enough time doing it, this should not be a problem. If you cannot clear the exam, you can re-attempt it based on the report shared by Microsoft, which highlights the areas in which you might not score well on the exam. Go back and revise the topics and re-appear within a few weeks.

Month 6

One of the tools you should feel comfortable with as a Power BI developer is ChatGPT. ChatGPT is one of the most popular generative AI tools in the market that can boost your analysis quality, creativity, and robustness, and speed up your productivity immensely. Make sure you understand how it works and try to use it in your day-to-day work.

An important consideration with generative AI tools is security and privacy. Make sure you strictly adhere to your company's policy on using ChatGPT at work. Otherwise, you can use dummy or mockup data from open datasets to understand the features and capabilities it offers.

Month 7

Start using Power BI templates to learn from the past and boost your productivity using pre-made solutions. You should focus on reducing the development time by using templates and on developing reports and dashboards quickly by cutting down on the things that are repeatable. You should also prepare your own library of commonly used DAX measures, background templates, themes, and other artifacts to make your development process fast and increase your productivity.

Months 8–9

The most neglected bit of the Power BI tool suite is Power Query. If you know it well, it can be your secret weapon. Power Query is important, as this is where the end-to-end analytics journey starts. If you invest your time in mastering Power Query, it streamlines the entire process and makes things such as Data Modeling and DAX simpler. Make sure you spend time getting to know some of the things such as query folding, custom functions, parameters, and how you can re-use some of the M-code to create an impact in your daily work.

Months 10–12

Most Power BI developers think about DAX as the thing that is the most difficult to master. Writing DAX is one thing; optimizing it for performance along with your data model is another. If you want to create reports and dashboards that can work for billions of row tables and datasets, this is the area where you want to spend a lot of time.

DAX and data model optimization require you to learn about a few external tools such as DAX Studio and Tabular Editor. If you can understand this bit, you are well on your way to becoming a Power BI expert because very few people can handle the complexities of optimizing this area. As the size of the data increases, this bit impacts report performance, and this is where your expertise can make a huge difference.

Months 13–15

Power BI is a business intelligence tool, and there are certain scenarios in day-to-day analysis work that require an understanding of advanced analytical concepts. This is where higher-level programming languages such as **Python** or **R** come to the rescue. It is a good investment to spend time learning R or Python. You do not need to learn both, as either one is good enough to help you understand advanced analytical concepts within the Power BI environment.

Months 16–20

After working for almost 15–16 months and using Power BI daily, now is the time to take your learning to the next level by preparing for the **DP-500 exam** and becoming an *Azure Enterprise Data Analyst*. Enterprise-level data analysis expertise requires much more than being a master of Power BI. It requires you to understand how the complete ecosystem works for an enterprise where hundreds or even thousands of users are utilizing data for analysis. This data architecture also needs to have proper governance in place.

Governance comes with security, privacy, data discovery, data classification, and end-to-end data lineage. All these aspects are covered under the DP-500 exam, which is the advanced-level certification involving Power BI as one of its components.

You will need to understand the Azure cloud data infrastructure for data and how utilities like Azure Synapse Analytics, Microsoft Purview, and Azure Data Factory are used for different data transformation and governance functions. This is a major milestone in your Power BI development journey; clearing the DP-500 exam can open new opportunities for your career.

You also have the option to explore a brand-new learning path based on the DP-600 exam called the "*Fabric Analytics Engineer.*" Fabric is a new **Software as a Service** (**SaaS**) offering from Microsoft, which is an end-to-end analytics environment but less complex than Azure Synapse Analytics, as Microsoft takes care of all the configuration required for Azure Synapse. With Fabric, it is easy to simply build an analytics solution inside one tool and leverage the flexibility without having to go to any other service or tool. Just like Azure Synapse, Power BI is a critical item inside Fabric and part of the end-to-end analytics ecosystem.

Months 21–24

In terms of learning and continual development, this is the time when you should have a look at the gaps you see in your Power BI portfolio. You must have learned a lot of things at work and fine-tuned some of the aspects related to advanced DAX calculations, performance tuning, and complex data transformations. You should fully understand what areas you need to improve and where the gaps are.

Now you can start to deep dive into books, workshops, and community data challenges, start posting in forums, attend Power BI user group meetups and conferences, and build a strong network of professionals in the BI field. Remember: the learning is never going to stop and you will always feel that there is an area you need to work on or improve.

Keep in mind that you cannot be an expert on everything. You should know enough stuff to grow your career and focus on improving every day. You need to be aware of the major updates and look out for material that is useful in your day-to-day work.

Throughout this roadmap, regular practice by working on projects and reflecting on your experiences during the learning journey is the most important thing. Remain flexible and be ready to adapt your plan as new features and updates to Power BI are released. Remember: the key to success in any tech field is lifelong learning and staying curious.

For further learning, advanced concepts in SQL, Python programming, and data warehousing concepts must be pursued. All of these skills are necessary for working with Microsoft Fabric.

Resources for continual learning and development

In this section, you will find a wealth of resources that can be used to take your skills from basic-level to advanced-level knowledge and expertise in Power BI development. This is not an exhaustive list, as we have proposed these resources based on our own expertise. Do check for updates, as the field is always evolving and new content is frequently shared.

Websites, blogs, courses, and tutorials

- *Microsoft Learn official website*: For official Power BI learning paths and modules (www. learn.microsoft.com)
- *Udemy*: A variety of Power BI courses for all levels (www.udemy.com)

- *Datacamp*: Power BI Data Analytics learning track with almost 50+ hours of content for beginners and intermediate-level developers (`www.datacamp.com`)

- *SQLBI*: In-depth training and resources related to Power BI, particularly for DAX, by Alberto Ferrari and Marco Russo. The website also offers the most comprehensive guide on DAX functions and links to YouTube videos (`www.sqlbi.com`)

- *LinkedIn Learning*: A variety of Power BI courses from beginner to advanced levels (`www.linkedin.com/learning`)

- *Maven Analytics*: A variety of courses on learning Power BI from basic to advanced level and also a preparation course for clearing the PL-300 exam (`www.mavenanalytics.io`)

- *Enterprise DNA*: A variety of courses on learning Power BI, including learning some of the AI tools and utilities such as ChatGPT. It also has detailed courses on clearing the PL-300 and DP-500 exams (`www.enterprisedna.co`)

- *Goodly*: A blog, multiple videos, and courses for learning Power Query and DAX (`www.goodly.co.in`)

- *Havens Consulting*: Multiple articles, videos, and tutorials on DAX, reporting and visualization, and other aspects of Power BI learning (`www.havensconsulting.net`)

- *Data Mozart*: A blog and multiple courses related to data model optimization and performance improvement in Power BI. It also offers video-based courses on these topics and on clearing the DP-500 exam (`https://data-mozart.com`)

- *Storytelling with data*: A blog and multiple courses on storytelling with data and visualization (`www.storytellingwithdata.com`)

- *Power BI Blog*: The official Microsoft blog with the latest updates, features, and resources (`https://powerbi.microsoft.com/en-us/blog`)

- *RADACAD Blog*: Articles and resources from Power BI experts, mainly Reza Rad and Leila Etati (`https://radacad.com/blog`)

- *Data Goblins*: Detailed articles about everything related to Power BI by Kurt Bohler (`https://data-goblins.com/power-bi`)

- *Chris Webb's BI blog*: Detailed articles on DAX, data modeling, M, and Power Query by Chris Webb (`https://blog.crossjoin.co.uk/`)

- *Datahai*: Detailed articles on Azure Synapse Analytics and its integration with Power BI (`https://www.datahai.co.uk/blog`)

- *Coates Data Strategies*: Detailed articles on Power BI adoption and data governance by Susan Coates (`https://www.coatesdatastrategies.com`)

- *Power BI Tips*: Detailed articles, podcasts, and training sessions on everything related to Power BI (`https://powerbi.tips`)

Books

- *Supercharge Power BI: Power BI Is Better When You Learn to Write DAX*, by Matt Allington

- *The Definitive Guide to DAX*, by Alberto Ferrari and Marco Russo

- *DAX Patterns – The most comprehensive collection of ready-to-use solutions in DAX for Power BI, Analysis Services, and Power Pivot*, by Alberto Ferrari and Marco Russo

- *Storytelling with Data: A Data Visualization Guide for Business Professionals*, by Cole Nussbaumer Knaflic

- *Storytelling with Data: Let's Practice!*, by Cole Nussbaumer Knaflic

- *Storytelling with You*, by Cole Nussbaumer Knaflic

- *Effective Data*, by Brent Dykes

- *Expert Data Modeling with Power BI: Enrich and optimize your data models to get the best out of Power BI for reporting and business needs*, by Soheil Bakhshi

YouTube channels

- *Guy in a Cube*: Run by Adam Saxton and Patrick LeBlanc from Microsoft; provides tips, tricks, and tutorials (`https://www.youtube.com/@guyinacube`)

- *SQLBI*: Offers excellent content on DAX and data modeling (`https://www.youtube.com/@sqlbi`)

- *BI Elite*: Covers Power BI tutorials and advanced visualization techniques (`https://www.youtube.com/@bielite`)

- *Curbal*: Focuses on Power BI tutorials, including DAX and data analysis examples (`https://www.youtube.com/@curbalEN`)

- *Goodly*: Focuses on Power Query, M, and DAX (`https://www.youtube.com/@goodlychandeep`)

- *PowerBI.Tips*: Focuses on a lot of different topics related to Power BI (`https://www.youtube.com/@powerbitips`)

- *Enterprise DNA*: Focuses on most topics within Power BI but also covers some topics of Power Platform; focuses on the use of Generative AI within Power BI development (`https://www.youtube.com/@enterprisedna`)

- *How to Power BI*: Gives tips and tricks on reporting and visualization related to Power BI (`https://www.youtube.com/@howtopowerbi`)

- *Havens Consulting*: Gives tips and tricks on reporting and visualization in Power BI (`https://www.youtube.com/@havensconsulting`)

- *Pragmatic Works*: Covers Power BI tutorials and other tools in Power Platform (`https://www.youtube.com/@pragmaticworks`)

- *Taik 18 – Mohammed Adnan*: Covers Microsoft Fabric, Power BI, Power Query, Paginated Report (SSRS), Azure Purview, Power Automate, Power Apps, Power Virtual Agent, SQL Server, MS PowerPoint, MS Excel, MS Teams, and MS Dataverse (`https://www.youtube.com/@taik18`)

Final words

As we approach the end of this incredible journey with our book, *The Complete Power BI Interview Guide*, I would like to take a moment to extend my heartfelt gratitude to you, the readers. Taking you on this experience of learning Power BI and getting to know everything about the process of becoming a Power BI developer has been a fulfilling experience.

This book was conceived with a vision to empower aspiring Power BI professionals like you with the knowledge, insight, and confidence required to excel in job interviews and advance in your careers. We have explored the technicalities of Power BI as a tool and uncovered the secrets to successful interviews. It is my sincere hope that these pages have helped you develop a robust understanding of Power BI and have illuminated the path toward achieving your professional goals.

Remember – the journey to mastering Power BI and acing interviews is continual and ever-evolving. The landscapes of data analytics and business intelligence are dynamic and changing with new advancements such as Generative AI and cloud technologies, so staying abreast of the latest trends and updates is crucial. I encourage you to keep learning, practicing, and growing. Let the knowledge you have gained from this guide be the foundation upon which you build your expertise and make your mark in the world of Power BI.

As we close this book, I hope you carry forward not just the technical skills, but also the confidence and enthusiasm to face your interviews head-on. Thank you for choosing this guide as your companion on this journey. I wish you all the best in your future endeavors and look forward to hearing about your successes in the world of Power BI.

Until our paths cross again in the realm of data and analytics, farewell, and best of luck!

Index

Packtpub.com

Subscribe to our online digital library for full access to over 7,000 books and videos, as well as industry leading tools to help you plan your personal development and advance your career. For more information, please visit our website.

Why subscribe?

- Spend less time learning and more time coding with practical eBooks and Videos from over 4,000 industry professionals

- Improve your learning with Skill Plans built especially for you

- Get a free eBook or video every month

- Fully searchable for easy access to vital information

- Copy and paste, print, and bookmark content

Did you know that Packt offers eBook versions of every book published, with PDF and ePub files available? You can upgrade to the eBook version at packtpub.com and as a print book customer, you are entitled to a discount on the eBook copy. Get in touch with us at customercare@packtpub.com for more details.

At www.packtpub.com, you can also read a collection of free technical articles, sign up for a range of free newsletters, and receive exclusive discounts and offers on Packt books and eBooks.

Other Books You May Enjoy

If you enjoyed this book, you may be interested in these other books by Packt:

Learn Power BI

Greg Deckler

ISBN: 978-1-80181-195-8

- Get up and running quickly with Power BI
- Understand and plan your business intelligence projects.
- Connect to and transform data using Power Query
- Create data models optimized for analysis and reporting.
- Perform simple and complex DAX calculations to enhance analysis.
- Discover business insights and create professional reports.
- Collaborate via Power BI dashboards, apps, goals, and scorecards.
- Deploy and govern Power BI, including using deployment pipelines.

Microsoft Power BI Data Analyst Certification Guide

Orrin Edenfield | Edward Corcoran

ISBN: 978-1-80323-856-2

- Connect to and prepare data from a variety of sources.
- Clean, transform, and shape your data for analysis.
- Create data models that enable insight creation.
- Analyze data using Microsoft Power BI s capabilities.
- Create visualizations to make analysis easier.
- Discover how to deploy and manage Microsoft Power BI assets.

Packt is searching for authors like you

If you're interested in becoming an author for Packt, please visit authors.packtpub.com and apply today. We have worked with thousands of developers and tech professionals, just like you, to help them share their insight with the global tech community. You can make a general application, apply for a specific hot topic that we are recruiting an author for, or submit your own idea.

Share Your Thoughts

Now you've finished *The Complete Power BI Interview Guide*, we'd love to hear your thoughts! Scan the QR code below to go straight to the Amazon review page for this book and share your feedback or leave a review on the site that you purchased it from.

https://packt.link/r/1-805-12067-0

Your review is important to us and the tech community and will help us make sure we're delivering excellent quality content.

Download a free PDF copy of this book

Thanks for purchasing this book!

Do you like to read on the go but are unable to carry your print books everywhere?

Is your eBook purchase not compatible with the device of your choice?

Don't worry, now with every Packt book you get a DRM-free PDF version of that book at no cost.

Read anywhere, any place, on any device. Search, copy, and paste code from your favorite technical books directly into your application.

The perks don't stop there, you can get exclusive access to discounts, newsletters, and great free content in your inbox daily

Follow these simple steps to get the benefits:

1. Scan the QR code or visit the link below

https://packt.link/free-ebook/9781805120674

2. Submit your proof of purchase

3. That's it! We'll send your free PDF and other benefits to your email directly

Printed in the USA
CPSIA information can be obtained
at www.ICGtesting.com
CBHW050212220524
8909CB00011B/84